REFORMATION AN
THEOLOGIES OF

MW01199578

Presenting a comprehensive survey of the historical underpinnings of baptismal liturgies and theologies, Bryan Spinks presents an ecumenically and geographically wide-ranging survey and discussion of contemporary baptismal rites, practice and reflection, and sacramental theology.

Writing within a clear chronological framework, Bryan Spinks presents two simultaneous volumes on Baptismal Liturgy and Theology. *Early and Medieval Rituals and Theologies of Baptism* summarizes the understandings of baptism in the New Testament and the development of baptismal reflection and liturgical rites throughout Syrian, Egyptian, Roman and African regions.

In this second volume, *Reformation and Modern Rituals and Theologies of Baptism*, Spinks traces developments through the Reformation, liturgies in the eighteenth and nineteenth centuries, and explores important new ecumenical perspectives on developments of twentieth-century sacramental discussion. Present practices of Baptists, Amish, as well as Methodist, Roman Catholic, Lutheran, Reformed and Anglican denominations are also examined.

LITURGY, WORSHIP AND SOCIETY

SERIES EDITORS

Dave Leal, Brasenose College, Oxford, UK
Bryan Spinks, Yale Divinity School, USA
Paul Bradshaw, University of Notre Dame, UK and USA
Gregory Woolfenden, St Mary's Orthodox Church, USA
Phillip Tovey, Ripon College, Cuddesdon, UK

The Ashgate Liturgy, Worship and Society series forms an important new 'library' on liturgical theory at a time of great change in the liturgy and much debate concerning traditional and new forms of worship, suitability and use of places of worship, and wider issues concerning interaction of liturgy, worship and contemporary society. Offering a thorough grounding in the historical and theological foundations of liturgy, this series explores and challenges many key issues of worship and liturgical theology, currently in hot debate within academe and within Christian churches worldwide – issues central to the future of the liturgy, to public and private worship, and set to make a significant impact on changing patterns of worship and the place of the church in contemporary society.

Other titles in the series include

Daily Liturgical Prayer
Origins and Theology
Gregory W. Woolfenden

West Syrian Liturgical Theology
Baby Varghese

Inculturation of Christian Worship
Exploring the Eucharist
Phillip Tovey

Reformation and Modern Rituals and Theologies of Baptism

From Luther to Contemporary Practices

BRYAN D. SPINKS
Yale University, USA

ASHGATE

Published by
Ashgate Publishing Limited
Gower House
Croft Road
Aldershot
Hants GU11 3HR
England

Ashgate Publishing Company
Suite 420
101 Cherry Street
Burlington, VT 05401-4405
USA

Ashgate website: http://www.ashgate.com

British Library Cataloguing in Publication Data
Spinks, Bryan D.
Reformation and Modern Rituals and Theologies of Baptism (Liturgy, worship and society) From Luther to Contemporary Practices
   1.Baptism–History–To 1500–
   I.Title
   265.1'0902

Library of Congress Cataloging-in-Publication Data
Spinks, Bryan D.
   Reformation and modern rituals and theologies of baptism: from Luther to contemporary practices / Bryan D. Spinks.
      p. cm. – (Liturgy, worship, and society series)
   Includes bibliographical references and index.
   ISBN 0-7546-5696-9 (hardcover: alk. paper) – ISBN 0-7546-5697-7 (pbk: alk. paper)
   1. Baptism.   I. Title. II. Series: Liturgy, worship, and society.
   BV811.3.S65 2006
   265'.10903–dc22

2006012515

ISBN-13: 978-0-7546-5696-8 (Hbk); ISBN-10: 0-7546-5696-9 (Hbk)
ISBN-13: 978-0-7546-5697-5 (Pbk); ISBN-10: 0-7546-5697-7 (Pbk)

Typeset by Manton Typesetters, Louth, Lincolnshire, UK.
Printed and bound in Great Britain by TJ International Ltd, Padstow, Cornwall.

Contents

List of Figures		vii
Acknowledgements		ix
Introduction		xi

Part I   Divergent Rivers

1	Luther and the Lutheran Tradition	3
2	The Reformed Tradition: From Ulrich Zwingli to Eugène Bersier	31
3	The Anglican Tradition: From Thomas Cranmer to F.D. Maurice	65
4	The Radical Reformation Tradition: Anabaptists, English Separatists, Baptists and Quakers	83
5	Some New Churches of the Eighteenth and Nineteenth Centuries	101

Part II   Converging Streams

6	Cross-currents: Some Baptismal Theologies of the Twentieth Century	137
7	Tidal Marks: Some Contemporary Baptismal Rites	164
8	Some Reflections on the Waters	200

Appendices	213
Bibliography	221
Index	249

List of Figures

8.1   Baptism of Caroline Goodman in Niteroi, Brazil, 2 January 2000   207
8.2   The Revd Dr Bryan Spinks baptizing Alexander Irving at St Mary's
      Church, Eaton Socon, Cambridgeshire, 20 June 1993   210

Acknowledgements

This work forms a sequel, though separate work, to *Early and Medieval Rituals and Theologies of Baptism. From the New Testament to the Council of Trent*, and shares a common bibliography. I am grateful for assistance from Professor Bruno Bürki who kindly supplied me with texts from Geneva for the eighteenth century. The Revd Norman Ryder gave helpful information on the background to the New Church liturgies, and Swedenborg House in London kindly made available photocopies of the early liturgies of the New Church. My thanks also to the librarians at the Yale Divinity School, Cambridge University Library, and the Bodleian Library, Oxford. Marylou Shoemaker of Epiphany Church, Durham, Connecticut kindly tidied up my rough translation of the 1743 Genevan baptismal rite. As for the previous book, I wish to record my thanks to my research assistants, the Revd Kate Heichler and Ms Melanie Ross, who helped check footnotes and quotations.

Bryan D. Spinks

Yale Institute of Sacred Music and Yale Divinity School,
New Haven, Connecticut
Epiphany 2005

Introduction

In the Introduction to *Early and Medieval Rituals and Theologies of Baptism. From the New Testament to the Council of Trent*, I drew attention to Larry Hoffman's important strictures that liturgy and ritual have many layers of meaning beyond the public meaning of the text, including the impact and reflection on the mind, heart and body of the recipients and those witnessing the rituals.[1] Ritual studies as a discipline is helpful in seeing the ritual as a whole, and appreciating its many layers of understanding, but does not equip the theological historian and interpreter with a vocabulary to express this multi-level event. In her stimulating study, *Beyond Ritual*, Siobhán Garrigan points out the shortcomings of current methods in ritual studies for writing a liturgical theology, and suggests that the communicative action theory of Jürgen Habermas supplies some useful tools to do this. She stresses, however, that field study – witnessing real, live ritual events (in her case, the eucharists of mainline and marginal communities) – is essential for this task.[2] Likewise the extremely perceptive work of James Steven, *Worship in the Spirit*, stresses the social character of ritual; his brilliant reflection on Trinitarian theology in charismatic worship is based on field study, as is Christian Scharen's study of congregational worship and commitment.[3]

Although I am an ordained pastor, and have presided over the ritual of baptism in parish and college settings on both sides of the Atlantic, this study does not purport to be a liturgical theology of that genre, and it is not based on field study. Indeed, while this method has potential for assessing contemporary worship in specific congregations, it is impossible for any historical study and wider denominational discussion. The focus of this study, therefore, is the first levels of meaning identified by Hoffman – the texts, or forms and structures; or the memory and imagination of the churches as articulated in their public rites of baptism. It is also concerned with some of the more influential secondary-level theology – the reflection by theologians and commentators on the theological meaning of those rites which have emanated from the Churches of the Reformation in the sixteenth century, some of the 'New Churches' of the eighteenth and nineteenth centuries, and modern contemporary theology and practices.

In many ways, this undertaking is simply impossible to fulfil. To begin with, the liturgical traditions presented here could each form the subject of a whole book in

---

[1] L.A. Hoffman, *Beyond the Text: A Holistic Approach to Liturgy*, Indiana University Press, Indianapolis, 1987.

[2] Siobhán Garrigan, *Beyond Ritual*, Ashgate Publishing, Aldershot, 2004.

[3] James H.S. Steven, *Worship in the Spirit. Charismatic Worship in the Church of England*, Carlisle, Paternoster Press, 2002; Christian Scharen, *Public Worship and Public Work. Character and Commitment in Local Congregational Life*, Pueblo Liturgical Press, Collegeville, MN, 2004.

their own right, and many have. Second, though I have tried to make this study as wide as possible, I am aware that it is impossible to cover all liturgies and all traditions. There are many of which I am totally unaware, and their omission here is one of ignorance, rather than one based on the importance or not of a particular rite or tradition. Another factor is that, because of my Church of England background and the areas of my previous research, some traditions are presented here in more depth than others. My denominational background, together with my training in the older comparative liturgy methodology mean that I may not always use the most appropriate hermeneutic to evaluate a particular tradition. As Christopher Ellis has recently pointed out with reference to the Baptist tradition, the worship and celebration of the sacraments of that tradition are more about values and response to scriptural mandate than about liturgical history.[4] There is thus an obvious unevenness in the depth of treatment of some rites and some traditions, for which I apologize.

In spite of these weaknesses and limitations, I hope that this work, like *Early and Medieval Rituals and Theologies of Baptism*, breaks some new ground. It includes three liturgical texts of the eighteenth century which are not easily accessible to scholars and students. Although not a liturgical theology, it is hoped that the theologies of baptismal liturgies are sufficiently addressed to map something of the different developments and understandings that have emerged beyond that one crucial and all-significant baptism of Jesus in the River Jordan.

The point of departure for the Churches of the Reformation was, liturgically, the medieval Western baptismal rites and practices. The 'national' rites such as the Gallican and Spanish usages had all but disappeared, and the rite used throughout the Northern European Churches was basically the hybrid forms of the Roman-Germanic ritual, with local diocesan variations. The theological point of departure was the prevailing scholastic understanding of sacraments. These were discussed in detail in Chapter 7 of *Early and Medieval Rituals and Theologies of Baptism*, including the Magdeburg Agenda known to Luther, and the Sarum rite known to Thomas Cranmer. For the details, readers are directed to my previous book.

---

[4] Christopher J. Ellis, *Gathering. A Theology and Spirituality of Worship in Free Church Tradition*, SCM Press, London, 2004.

PART I
DIVERGENT RIVERS

CHAPTER 1

Luther and the Lutheran Tradition

Martin Luther's Theology and Rites of Baptism

The more or less universal baptismal rite with local variants throughout the West, together with the scholastic methods of theology, were brought to an abrupt end in the sixteenth century with the Reformation. The Reformers challenged much in the inherited ritual, and some of the prevailing theology on baptism, though of course the Reformers differed amongst themselves as to the nature and extent of change needed in both. In Germany the Reformation was sparked by the Wittenberg professor, Martin Luther. Many of the more recent Luther studies have been concerned with a developmental approach, and have tended to trace the growth and change in his theology from his early works through to his more mature writings. Three phases are helpful in considering his baptismal theology: the Young (pre-1519) Luther, the Reformation or anti-Roman Luther, and the Mature or anti-Enthusiasts Luther.

The Young Luther

Among Luther's early writings, those most relevant to baptism are the lectures on the Psalms, Romans, Galatians and Hebrews. What is remarkable is the paucity of references and discussions on baptism in these works, given Luther's later emphasis on baptism as the central event in the Christian life. For example, in the *Dictata Super Psalterium* (1513–15), there are occasional references to the Jordan as mystically denoting baptism, but otherwise very little. Similarly the *Lectures on Romans* have references to baptism, but no detailed discussion. Commenting on 6:3, the Reformer noted in the Glosses:

> 3. Do you not know, brethren, as if to say, you ought not to be ignorant, that all of us who have been baptized, because the threefold dipping of Baptism signifies the three-day death period and the burial of Christ, into Christ Jesus, that is, by faith in Christ Jesus, were baptized into his death, that is, through the merit and power of his death? Hence 'Baptism' (*baptismus*), 'dipping (*mersio*), 'to baptize' (*baptiso*), and 'to dip' (*mergo*) all mean that 4. We were buried therefore together ...[1]

In the corresponding *Scholium* the discussion is about sin, not baptism. Werner Jetter has attempted to examine the various background influences on the young Luther

---

[1] *Luther's Works, American Edition*, 55 vols, Jaroslav Pelikan and Helmut T. Lehman (eds), Concordia and Fortress Press, St Louis, MO and Philadelphia, PA, 1955ff, 25:50 (hereafter cited as *LW*); *Luthers Werke, Kritische Gesamtausgabe*, 57 vols, J.F.K. Knaake et al. (eds), Bühlau, Weimer, 1883–2003ff, 56:57 (hereafter cited as *WA*).

which would explain this neglect, though without any convincing conclusion.[2] However, we can discern one important shift that was crucial, although it does not immediately deal with baptism. In the *Lectures on the Psalms*, Luther was still using and thinking in scholastic categories, and he examined Scripture under the headings of historical, allegorical, tropological and anagogical. In this work he also still drew on the medieval *via moderna* and its *pactum* (covenant) theology and the *humilitas fidei*.[3] Humanity was understood to be active in the process of justification.

However, in the *Lectures on Romans*, Luther had moved towards a new understanding of justification. In justification it is God who turns humanity to himself. Justification is *propter Christum*, not *propter fidem*, and even less *propter pactum* or our cooperation with God. Thus in 1520 Luther could write, 'Baptism, then, signifies two things – death and resurrection, that is, full and complete justification.'[4] The bond between justification and baptism will imply that the latter too must become from start to finish the gracious work of God to humankind. Ideas of cooperative grace will have no place.

The 'Reformation' Luther

With the 'Reformation' Luther we turn to two important writings which were directed against the prevailing Roman interpretation of baptism: *The Holy and Blessed Sacrament of Baptism* (1519), and *The Babylonian Captivity of the Church* (1520). Both writings were polemical.

In the 1519 work we find a concern for generous use of water in baptism:

> Baptism [*Die Taufe*] is *baptismos* in Greek, and *mersio* in Latin, and means to plunge something completely into the water, so that the water covers it. Although in many places it is no longer customary to thrust and dip infants into the font, but only with the hand to pour the baptismal water upon them out of the font, nevertheless the former is what should be done. It would be proper, according to the meaning of the word *Taufe*, that the infant, or whoever is to be baptized, should be put in and sunk completely into the water and then drawn out again. For even in the German tongue the word *Taufe* comes undoubtedly from the word *tief* [deep] and means that what is baptized is sunk deeply into the water. This usage is also demanded by the significance of baptism itself. For baptism, as we shall hear, signifies that the old man and the sinful birth of flesh and blood are to be wholly drowned by the grace of God. We should do justice to its meaning and make baptism a true and complete sign of the thing it signifies.[5]

We also find the idea of death/resurrection and regeneration linked together:

> The significance of baptism is a blessed dying unto sin and a resurrection in the grace of God, so that the old man, conceived and born in sin, is there drowned,

---

[2] Werner Jetter, *Die Taufe beim jungen Luther*, Mohr, Tübingen, 1954.

[3] Alister E. McGrath, *Iustitia Dei. A History of the Christian Doctrine of Justification*, Vol. 2. *From 1500 to the Present Day*, Cambridge University Press, Cambridge, 1986, pp. 10–20.

[4] *The Babylonian Captivity*, 1520, *LW* 36:67; *WA* 6:534.

[5] *LW* 35:29; *WA* 2:727.

and a new man, born in grace, comes forth and rises … Through this spiritual birth he is a child of grace and a justified person. Therefore sins are drowned in baptism, and in place of sin, righteousness comes forth.[6]

Luther also introduces an eschatological element; because man is *simul iustus et peccator*, baptism's significance is not fulfilled completely in this life. It is something which is ongoing. More important still is the emphasis in 1519 and in 1520 on the importance of the Word, as God's promise, and of faith. Reacting against the extreme forms of *ex opere operato* scholastic teaching on sacraments, Luther first insisted that the most important thing is the divine promise (*divina promissio*) which says he who believes and is baptized will be saved. Luther wrote:

A great majority has supposed that there is some hidden spiritual power in the word and water, which works the grace of God in the soul of the recipient. Others deny this and hold that there is no power in the sacraments, but that grace is given by God alone, who according to his covenant (*ex pacto*) is present in the sacraments which he has instituted.[7]

However, he argues, both of these views, which drive a wedge between the signs of the old covenant and those of the new, are to be shunned; signs have attached to them a word of promise, requiring faith (*verbum promissionis, quod fidem exigat*):[8] 'The sign, the assurance of my salvation, will not lie to me or deceive me. God has said this: God cannot lie.'[9] What is important is not the blessing of the water, but the fact that God has instituted baptism. Word and water go together, not a priestly blessing of water. Thus it is not man's baptism, but Christ's and God's baptism which is received:

Hence we ought to receive baptism at human hands just as if Christ himself, indeed, God himself, were baptizing us with his own hands[10] … The Doer and the minister are different persons, but the work of both is the same work, or rather, it is the work of the Doer alone, through my ministry. For I hold that 'in the name of' refers to the person of the Doer …[11]

However, in these two works Luther is also at pains to stress the importance of faith in what he calls the signs or sacraments of justification: 'Thus it is not baptism that justifies or benefits anyone, but it is faith in that word of promise to which baptism is added. This faith justifies, and fulfils that which baptism signifies.'[12]

The importance of faith in the sacraments was stressed in Luther's *Lectures on Hebrews*, where he asserted that it is not the sacrament which justifies but faith in the sacrament; the sacrament justifies not because it is performed but because it is believed.[13] In *The Babylonian Captivity* he could say:

---

[6] *LW* 35:30; *WA* 2:727–8.

[7] *LW* 36:64; *WA* 6:527.

[8] *LW* 36:65; *WA* 6:532.

[9] *LW* 42:109; *WA* 2:693.

[10] *LW* 36:62; *WA* 6:530.

[11] *LW* 36:63; *WA* 6:530–31.

[12] *LW* 36:66; *WA* 6.532–3.

[13] *LW* 29:172; *WA* 57(3):170.

> For unless faith is present and is conferred in baptism, baptism will profit us
> nothing; indeed, it will become a hindrance to us, not only at the moment that it
> is received, but throughout the rest of our lives. That kind of unbelief accuses
> God's promises of being a lie, and this is the greatest of all sins.[14]

Faith is such a necessary part of the sacrament, said Luther, that it can save even
without the sacrament.[15] However, it seems that Luther meant by 'faith' simply
accepting that in the sacrament God will do what he promises. Thus he wrote:

> We must humbly admit, 'I know full well that I cannot do a single thing that is
> pure. But I am baptized, and through my baptism God, who cannot lie, has bound
> himself in a covenant (*sich vorpunden hatt*) with me. He will not count my sin
> against me, but will slay it and blot it out.'[16]

And again,

> For no sin can condemn him save unbelief alone. All other sins, so long as the
> faith in God's promise made in Baptism returns or remains, are immediately
> blotted out through that same faith, or rather through the truth of God, because he
> cannot deny himself if you confess him and faithfully cling to him in his
> promise.[17]

It would seem that by 'faith' Luther here means acceptance that God will grant
justification and salvation through this strange ritual with water which is performed
in his name.

Luther also used the word 'covenant' (*bund; vorpindung*). In the 1519 work on
baptism Luther notes that you must give yourself up to what baptism is and what it
signifies, that is, that God accepts your desire for baptism and what it signifies. You
must pledge yourself (*vorpindest du dich*) to continue in this desire and to slay sin
until your dying day. So long as you keep your pledge to God (*Die weyl nu solch deyn
vorpinden mit got steet*) he in turn gives his grace, and pledges not to impute to you
the sins which remain in your nature after baptism.[18] Admittedly this sounds like the
pactum theology, but in fact the pledge is to be understood within the concept of the
faithfulness of God, and the eschatological nature of continually returning to baptism.
In the early commentary on Galatians, Luther argued that *pactum*, *testamentum* and
promissiones were all the same in meaning, and refer to the death of Christ and its
benefits.[19] In *Treatise on New Testament* he made it quite clear that a testament is a
gift:

> For a testament is not *beneficium acceptum, sed datum*; it does not take benefit
> from us, but brings benefit to us ... Just as in baptism, in which there is also a
> divine testament and sacrament, no one gives God anything or does him a service,

---

[14] *LW* 36:59; *WA* 6:533–4.

[15] *LW* 36:67; *WA* 6:533–4.

[16] *LW* 35:36; *WA* 2:732.

[17] *LW* 36:60; *WA* 6:529.

[18] *LW* 35:33ff; *WA* 2:730–31.

[19] *LW* 27:263; *WA* 57(2):82.

but instead takes something, so it is in all other sacraments and in the sermon as well.[20]

Thus for Luther 'covenant' is explained as God's promise in the sacraments which are signs of justification. The human response is to trust that the covenant is indeed unilateral – that it is God's work from start to finish. Finally, we may note that in *The Babylonian Captivity* infant baptism is defended on the grounds of *fides aliena*, but with the reminder that the Word of God is powerful enough when uttered to change even a godless heart, which is no less unresponsive and helpless than any infant.[21]

What we have in summary in these two works is a refutation of the *opus operatum* theology, and of the idea that grace resides in the water. Luther holds that grace comes from the promise of God, and that promise is unilateral. The Word of promise and the water make the sacrament. Faith is important, but our lack of faith cannot undermine God's promise.

The Mature Luther

From the mature Luther we have much more material which deals specifically with baptism, such as *Concerning Rebaptism* (1528), the two *Catechisms*, the *Ten Sermons on the Catechism*, and the much later *Sermon at the Baptism of Bernhard von Anhalt* (1540). Furthermore, P.D. Pahl and Jonathan Trigg have both drawn attention to the importance of the *Lectures on Genesis*; when allowance has been made for editorial additions to these, the work still has Luther's insights.[22]

Lorenz Grönvik compared Luther's treatment of baptism in *The Babylonian Captivity* in 1520 with that in the *Catechisms* of 1529, and found an essential continuity.[23] While this is true, nevertheless there are also different emphases and new issues which result from Luther's new perspective. Roman teaching is still on the agenda, but once the 'Schwärmer' and Anabaptists had entered the fray, Luther had to adjust his focus. Where, against Rome, Luther had had to stress Word and faith, against his new opponents he had to stress the importance of the sign. Andreas Karlstadt, for example, insisted that water without faith is the same as bath water, and can have no effect on the soul. C.A. Pater has traced how Karlstadt began with a baptismal theology dependent upon Aquinas and Augustine, but severed the link between *res* and *signum* and moved to believe in Spirit baptism.[24] From Luther's point of view, the same was true of the teaching of the Zurich Reformer, Ulrich Zwingli.

---

[20] *LW* 35:93; *WA* 6:364.

[21] *LW* 36:73; *WA* 6:538.

[22] P.D. Pahl, 'Baptism in Luther's Lectures on Genesis', *Lutheran Theological Journal* 1 (1967), 26–35; Jonathan Trigg, *Baptism in the Theology of Martin Luther*, E.J. Brill, Leiden, 1994.

[23] Lorenz Grönvik, *Die Taufe in der Theologie Martin Luthers*, Åbo Akademi, Åbo, 1967.

[24] C.A. Pater, *Karlstadt as the Father of the Baptist Movement: The Emergence of Lay Protestantism*, University of Toronto Press, Toronto, 1984, pp. 92–114.

In the *Large Catechism*, Luther discussed baptism in terms of Word and water, what is accomplished in baptism, the relationship of faith, its signification, and infant baptism. It is useful to follow this outline. First Luther grounded baptism in the Word. Quoting Matthew 28:19 and Mark 16:16, he writes:

> Observe, first, that these words contain God's commandments and ordinance (*Gottes gebot und einsetzung*). You should not doubt, then, that baptism is of divine origin, and not something devised and invented by men.[25]

Similarly, in *Concerning Rebaptism* in 1528, Luther insisted that baptism is commanded by God – a shift from a promise to a command. The force of this shift is brought out in the *Lectures on Genesis*, where Luther notes that in each of the encounters with God in the Old Testament it is God who takes the initiative. God has promised to reveal himself in the sacraments. In the *Large Catechism* Luther wrote:

> Note the distinction, then: Baptism is a very different thing from all other water, not by virtue of the natural substance but because here something nobler is added. God himself stakes his honor, his power, and his might on it. Therefore it is not simply a natural water, but a divine, heavenly, holy, and blessed water – praise it in any other terms you can – all by virtue of the Word, which is a heavenly holy Word which no one can sufficiently extol, for it contains and conveys all the fullness of God. From the Word it derives its nature as a sacrament, as St Augustine taught, '*Accedat verbum ad elementum et fit sacramentum.*' This means that when the Word is added to the element or the natural substance, it becomes a sacrament, that is, a holy, divine thing and sign.[26]

In his *Sermons on the Gospel of St John 1–4* (1537) Luther stressed that the glorious company of the three persons is present in baptism. In his sermon of 1540 he stressed that the person who is baptized is washed in the blood of Christ. Faith was still important, but should not become a substitute for the gift which comes from God. Ultimately, Luther always falls back to the need to trust in the promise of God.

In defending infant baptism, Luther appealed to the fact that everything depends on God's Word and command. He cited the concept of *fides infantium*, and *fides aliena*. And preaching on St John 1:32–4, Luther said:

> Since Baptism is a divine act in which God Himself participates and since it is attended by the three exalted Persons of the Godhead, it must be prized and honored. One must agree that Baptism was not invented by any man but was instituted by God. It is not plain water but has God's Word in it and with it; and this transforms such water into a soul bath and into a bath of rejuvenation. Furthermore, we must maintain that a Baptism is a proper and valid Baptism even if the person baptized is unbelieving and ungodly. For is it conceivable that God would be faithless because of my faithlessness (Rom. 3:3)? Those impious knaves surely don't know themselves whether the people whom they rebaptize really believe. We do know that our little children believe; for regarding them we have

---

[25] *Large Catechism*, 4, 6; *The Book of Concord*, T.G. Tappert (ed.), Augsburg Fortress, Philadelphia, PA, 1959, p. 437.

[26] *Book of Concord*, p. 438.

a trustworthy declaration of Christ: 'Let the children come to Me, do not hinder them; for to such belongs the Kingdom of God' (Mark 10:14). They cannot adduce such a statement for those whom they rebaptize. Furthermore, they have no more inside information than we have about the heart; they cannot peer into anyone's heart either.[27]

Luther's baptismal rites

In the light of his developing theology, then, what did Luther do with the baptismal rite which he inherited? Luther made no liturgical reforms until 1523, and when he did, it was in reaction not primarily to his Roman opponents, but to those he regarded as fanatics, who had rushed ahead dangerously. In addition to Karlstadt there was Thomas Müntzer of Allstedt. Müntzer, when pastor of Allstedt, issued an outline for a baptismal rite. Luther was furious – mainly because, like Karlstadt, Müntzer appealed to the Spirit, but also because his apocalypticism called for radical social changes, which he expressed through his German liturgical forms. Luther's *Taufbüchlein* of 1523 is itself a fairly conservative rite. It has the following structure:

1 *Exsufflation (3 times)*
2 'Come out unclean Spirit'
3 *Signing with cross and formula*
4 'Almighty and eternal God'
5 'Immortal God'
6 *Reception of the salt with formula*
7 *Flood Prayer (sindflutgebet)*
8 *Exorcisms*: 'Therefore accursed devil', 'Hearken, accursed Satan', ' I exorcize thee'
9 'O Lord, holy Father'
10 *Gospel: Mark 10*
11 *Laying-on of hands and Lord's Prayer*
12 Effeta *with spittle*
13 *Entrance into the Church*
14 *Renunciations*
15 *Credal interrogations*
16 *Anointing with oil and formula*
17 *Question of desire of baptism*
18 *Baptism in threefold name*
19 *Anointing with formula*
20 *Giving of white robe and formula*
21 *Giving of candle with formula*

---

[27] *LW* 22:174; *WA* 46:687.

As has been demonstrated by Gustav Kawerau, F.K. Nümann and, most recently, Kent Burreson, Luther seems to have used and followed closely the *Magdeburg Agenda* of 1492 and the *Agenda Communis (AC)* of 1505–20.[28] Luther made no reference to making a catechumen, but the first action, as in the two agendas, is the exsufflation, and here his German was a word-for-word translation of *AC*. This was followed by the signing of the cross, and the prayer 'Almighty and eternal God'. He retained the giving of salt (though not its exorcism), and the exorcisms, as well as the ritual entrance into the church. Yet, although this rite was structurally conservative, there are some changes which should not be underestimated. In the Epilogue to this rite Luther wrote:

> For the time being I did not want to make any marked changes in the order of baptism. But I would not mind if it could be improved. Its framers were careless men who did not sufficiently appreciate the glory of baptism. However, in order to spare the weak consciences, I am leaving it unchanged, lest they complain that I want to institute a new baptism and criticize those baptized in the past as though they had not been properly baptized. For as I said, the human additions do not matter very much, as long as baptism itself is administered with God's Word, true faith, and serious prayer.[29]

It would seem that any changes he made were in order to show 'the glory of baptism'. In fact, his rite can be considered under three headings.

Those features which added nothing to baptism but were adiaphora — In the Epilogue Luther carefully listed those ceremonies which, though retained, were of no importance to baptism:

> Now remember also that in baptism the least importance attaches to these external things, namely, breathing under the eyes, signing with the cross, placing salt in the mouth, putting spittle and clay on the ears and nose, anointing with oil the breast and shoulders, and signing the top of the head with chrism, vesting in the christening robe, and giving a burning candle into the hand, and whatever else there is that men have added to embellish baptism. For certainly without all such things baptism may take place, and they are not the kind of devices that the devil shuns or avoids. He despises much greater things than these. Here is earnestness required.[30]

Luther kept these elements since they were traditional, and did not undermine the sacrament.

---

[28] Gustav Kawerau, 'Liturgische Studien zu Luthers Taufbüchlein von 1523', *Zeitschrift für kirchliche Wissenschaft und kirchliches Leben* 10 (1898), 407–31, 466–77, 519–47, 578–99, 625–43. F.K. Nümann, 'Zur Entstehung des lutherischen Taufbüchleins von Jahre 1523', *Monatschrift für Gottesdienst und kirchliche Kunst* 33 (1928), 214–19; Kent Burreson, 'The Saving Flood: The Medieval Origins, Historical Development, and Theological Import of the Sixteenth Century Lutheran Baptismal Rites', Ph.D. dissertation, University of Notre Dame, 2002.

[29] *LW* 53:103; *WA* 12:48.

[30] *LW* 53:102; *WA* 12:47.

Those features retained which were the core of the rite — These include first of all the exorcisms. For Luther the devil was very real, and baptism was about being saved from sin and evil. Hence he regarded the exorcisms as appropriate to the rite. Next, the Gospel reading and Lord's Prayer. Luther's rite was for infants, and the Gospel reading from Mark 10 is the Word effecting grace. Christ took the children in his arms and blessed them; Luther had the priest lay his hand on the head of the child and repeat the prayer given by Jesus to all the children of the heavenly Father – the Lord's Prayer. He retained the *effeta*, and the command for the devil to flee, as fitting ceremonies after the reading of the Gospel.

Crucial too were the vows. Luther in fact argued that all other vows should be abolished so that all could be recalled to the vows of their baptism: 'For we have vowed enough in baptism, more than we can ever fulfil; if we give ourselves to the keeping of this one vow, we shall have all we can do.'[31]

The vow in Luther's rite takes the form of the Creed because, according to Luther, the Creed teaches what we have received from God.[32] Luther also retained dipping or immersion in the font. We have already noted the importance Luther gave to the meaning of the word *baptismos*. It was crucial to the sign of baptism:

> The sign consists in this, that we are thrust into the water in the name of the Father and of the Son and of the Holy Spirit; however, we are not left there but are drawn out again … The sign must thus have both parts, the putting in and the drawing out.[33]

Dipping/immersion fully symbolized the dying to sin and the rising in Christ – that is, justification.

Also crucial was the triune formula. As noted above, for Luther 'The Doer and the minister are different persons, but the work is the same work, or rather it is the work of the Doer alone, through my ministry.' What the 'Doer' was doing was offering the recipient forgiveness of sins.

Omissions and alterations to make clearer the glory of baptism — Luther removed the exorcism of salt, and the traditional blessing of the font. In some rites both of these were completed at some time previously, and that may be a contributing factor. However, in *The Babylonian Captivity* Luther was critical of blessing objects because such actions could obscure the true meaning of sacraments. Such things as salt and vessels could be consecrated by the Word and prayer as in 1 Tim. 4:4–5, but this should not be confused with a divinely instituted sacrament. In the *Sermon at the Baptism of Bernard von Anhalt* in 1540, Luther dismissed the idea that to add the Word to the water implied a blessing of the water:

> For example, the magicians, witches and weather prophets also employ a sign or creature, such as a root or herb, and speak over it the Lord's Prayer or some other

---

[31] *Babylonian Captivity, LW* 36:74–5; *WA* 6:539.

[32] *Sermons on the Catechism*, 1528. The Creed, *LW* 51:162ff. *WA* 52:162ff.

[33] *The Holy and Blessed Sacrament of Baptism*, 1519. *LW* 35:30; *WA* 2:727.

holy word and name of God. This they say is not an evil thing but rather both: a creation of God and precious words and holy names; therefore it should possess power and accomplish what it is used for; just as the Pope also juggles and conjures with his chrism, holy water, and salt … Do you too have a word and command of God which says you should consecrate salt or water and speak such words over them?[34]

For Luther, the Word must be added to the water, but this was not the same as blessing the water. It certainly meant following the command in Matthew 28, where, with natural water, there was:

God's word beside and with the water, which is not something we have invented or dreamed up, but is rather the Word of Christ, who said 'Go into all the world and baptize them in the name of the Father and of the Son and of the Holy Spirit'. When these words are added to the water, then it is no longer simple water like other water, but a holy, divine, blessed water. For when the word of God, by which he created heaven and earth and all things, is present, there God himself is present with his power and might.[35]

Also important in this theology is Luther's *sindflutgebet*, or flood prayer. This seems to have been an original composition, though it echoes themes found in many ancient writers on baptism, and he draws on the traditional prayers 'God of our Fathers' and 'God of Abraham'.[36] This prayer replaces the blessing of the font. It contains no specific petition for blessing the water, since, like some of the Eastern prayers, it says that God 'through the baptism of thy dear child, our Lord Jesus Christ, hast consecrated and set apart the Jordan and all water as a salutary flood and a rich and full washing away of sins'. In other words, Christ the Word has already sanctified all water by his baptism in the Jordan.

There are references in Luther's sermons on St John which suggest that he also recognized the presence of the Holy Spirit in connection with the water without any special petition or blessing. Thus on St John 3:4, he writes:

Here Christ also speaks of the Holy Spirit and teaches us to regard Baptism as a spiritual, yes, a Spirit-filled water in which the Holy Spirit is present and active; in fact, the entire Holy Trinity is there … But after the Holy Spirit is added to it, we have more than mere water. It becomes a veritable bath of rejuvenation, a living bath which washes and purges man of sin and death, which cleanses him of all sin.[37]

However, since baptism is an event at which the Trinity is present, and since God the Word was baptized in the water for all, Luther saw no absolute need to articulate a reference to the Spirit in the prayer.

In this flood prayer, Luther makes reference to both Noah and the crossing of the Red Sea. These are both patristic 'types' of baptism, but apparently for Luther they

---

[34] *LW* 51:321;*WA* 49:128–9.

[35] *LW* 51:320; *WA* 49:128.

[36] For a full discussion, see Burreson, 'The Saving Flood', pp. 173–253.

[37] *LW* 22:283; *WA* 47:11.12–25.

were types of Justification. Thus in his lectures on Genesis 9, with reference to Romans 6:3 he said:

> In accordance with the meaning, the Red Sea is truly a baptism, that is, death and the wrath of God, as is manifest in the case of Pharaoh. Nevertheless, Israel, which is baptized with such a baptism, passes through unharmed. Similarly, the Flood is truly death and the wrath of God. Nevertheless, the believers are saved in the midst of the Flood. Thus death engulfs and swallows up the entire human race; for without distinction the wrath of God goes over the good, and the evil, over the godly and the ungodly. The Flood that Noah experienced was not different from the one which the world experienced. The Red Sea, which both Pharaoh and Israel entered, was not different. Later on, however, the difference became apparent in this: those who believe are preserved in the very death to which they are subjected together with the ungodly, and the ungodly perish. Noah, accordingly, is preserved because he has the ark, that is, God's promise and Word, in which he is living; but the ungodly, who do not believe the word, are left to their fate.[38]

Thus his prayer asked that candidates be drowned in Christ and engulfed, and be preserved and secure in the holy ark of Christendom.

Although we have noted that Luther retained the exorcisms, he removed any distinction between males and females. Already this distinction was blurred in some rites, such as those of Constance. But again, this seems to accord with Luther's theology. Although Luther did not believe that women were equal in glory and prestige to the male, he did affirm that they were joint heirs of redemption. Commenting on Genesis 1:27 he wrote:

> However, here Moses puts the two sexes together and says that God created male and female in order to indicate that Eve, too, was made by God as a partaker of the divine image and of the divine similitude, likewise the ruler over everything. Thus even today the woman is the partaker of the future life, just as Peter says that they are joint heirs of the same grace (1 Peter 3:7).[39]

In the matter of redemption there is for Luther no distinction between male and female. Thus in his *Commentary on Galatians* (1519), with regard to 3:27–8, Luther appealed to Augustine that, although distinctions remain in the body, they are removed in the Spirit through the unity of faith. Commenting on the same verses in the 1535 commentary he wrote:

> For in Christ Jesus all social stations, even those that were divinely ordained, are nothing. Male, female, slave, free, Jew, Gentile, King, subject – these are, of course, good creatures of God. But in Christ, that is, in the matter of Salvation, they amount to nothing, for all their wisdom, righteousness and devotion and authority.[40]

Since baptism was very much the focus of salvation, it would seem that Luther was of the opinion that separate exorcisms for each sex were inappropriate. Thus, although

---

[38] Genesis Lectures, *LW* 2:153; *WA* 42:369.
[39] Genesis Lectures, *LW* 1:69; *WA* 42:52.
[40] *LW* 26:354; *WA* 40(1):542.

conservative and retaining many elements from the medieval Western rites, Luther nevertheless set his own theological seal on the rite.

In 1526 a second order appeared. Here Luther removed many of those ceremonies deemed *adiaphora* but which might distract from the 'glory of baptism'. The exorcisms are reduced, but an exorcism is certainly retained. The giving of salt and the anointings before and after baptism were removed. The white robe remained, but the giving of a lighted candle was removed.

Lutheran Reformers and Lutheran Orders

Luther and his writings were central to the development of Lutheranism, but he did not work alone. Other key figures such as Philip Melanchthon, Johannes Bugenhagen, Justus Jonas, Andreas Osiander and Johannes Brenz worked for the Lutheran Reformation, though in their theology they sometimes expressed nuanced differences with Luther. Luther also had a *laissez-faire* attitude to liturgy, with his own orders being an example that others might follow if they wished. Each city and duchy was left to make its own provisions, guided by other Lutheran Reformers. In Germany at least three distinct families of baptismal rites can be delineated.

Saxony

Philip Melanchthon and Justus Jonas were heavily involved in the development of rites in Saxony such as those of Herzog Heinrich (1539), Prussia (1544), and Mecklenburg (1552), and Johannes Bugenhagen in North Saxony on rites such as that of Braunschweig (1528) and Pomerania (1535).

Melanchthon was a close friend of Luther, and his *Loci Communes* of 1521 were regarded as a first systematic statement of Lutheran theology. However, the *Loci* continued to be modified and, as Harold Lentz noted, became less polemical toward scholastic theology, and more respectful of the Church Fathers, evincing a deeper respect for philosophical method in theology: 'there became ever more evident an independent spirit which held a varying viewpoint from Luther'.[41]

In the 1521 *Loci*, Melanchthon stated that there were two sacraments, baptism and the Table of the Lord, and referred to Luther's work, *The Babylonian Captivity*. On baptism, he argued that the immersion was a sign of the divine will, and a pledge of divine grace.[42] The triune words indicate that the Father, Son and Holy Spirit mutually baptize. This was adumbrated by the Israelites when they passed through the Arabian

---

[41] Harold H. Lentz, *Reformation Crossroads*, Augsburg Publishing House, Minneapolis, MI, 1958, p. 5.

[42] C.L. Hill, *The Loci Communes of Philip Melanchthon*, Meador Publishing House, Boston, MA, 1944, p. 244; see also Mark David Tranvik, 'The Other Sacrament: The doctrine of baptism in the late Lutheran Reformation', Th.D. thesis, Luther North Western Seminary, 1992, pp. 48ff.

Sea.[43] Melanchthon seems to have interpreted the 'sign' as Luther did in 1521, as witness or seal of the divine promise. Against Lombard's view that John's baptism was merely a washing in water, whereas that of Christ gives grace, Melanchthon argued that John's baptism was a sign of grace to come, and Christ's a pledge and seal (*kai sphragis*) of grace already conferred.

In his 1540 commentary on Romans, Melanchthon has practically nothing to say on baptism with reference to Romans 6:3, though he interprets it as a 'comparison of our conversion with the death, burial, and resurrection of Christ'.[44] However, he was also the main architect of the Augsburg Confession, and there we find but a brief reference to baptism:

> It is taught amongst us that Baptism is necessary and that grace is offered through it. Children, too, should be baptized, for in Baptism they are committed to God and become acceptable to him. On this account the Anabaptists who teach that infant Baptism is not right are rejected.[45]

On the whole, the rites for Saxony took Luther's rite of 1526 as their model. The 1539 Herzog Heinrich rite, prepared by Jonas and Caspar Cruciger, was prefaced by an admonition which defends infant baptism on the grounds of freedom from original sin. The 1540 edition has an admonition following the Gospel reading, which includes the statement that 'he [God] now provides for you only with great grace and receives you in a most friendly way'.[46] A further admonition was provided for the godparents, outlining the expectations and duties of godparents. Kent Burreson observes:

> However, the admonition texts were intended to communicate more than facts and information. As the admonition to the godfathers shows, they were intended to shape the church into believing and living in a certain way. They were intended to mold and form a holy people, holy because of what God had done for them in Christ as that work came upon them and was done to them in holy baptism.[47]

Commenting on Bugenhagen's instructions on baptism in the 1528 Church Order for Braunschweig, Burreson observes:

> It would appear that Bugenhagen's comments in 1528 pointed towards the priority of prayer, exorcism, renunciation of Satan, creedal confession, and the baptismal name and water as the central elements conveying confidence in God's action in baptism.[48]

All this reflected Luther's rite of 1526, and thus in his 1535 rite for Pomerania he stated that 'baptism shall be done in German, as it stands in the German baptismal book'.[49]

---

[43] Hill, *Loci Communes*, p. 245.

[44] *Commentary on Romans*, translated by Fred Kramer, Concordia Publishing House, St Louis, MO, 1992, p. 146.

[45] Tappert, *The Book of Concord*, p. 33.

[46] For full discussion, see Burreson, 'The Saving Flood', p. 310.

[47] Ibid., pp. 312–13.

[48] Ibid., p. 317.

[49] Cited in ibid., p. 317.

One rite derived from the 1528 Braunschweig rite was the 1530 rite for the city of Minden, prepared by Nicolaus Krage, the pastor. Burreson notes that this rite provided a commentary on the use of the water consecration prayer, teaching that it was not necessary:

> Christ in his command spoke no separate words over the water, or gave a special command to consecrate the water, except that one should baptize with water. In baptism the Holy Spirit works and we are baptized and incorporated into Christ, which is accomplished not by the nature of the water, but especially by the command of Christ. [A consecration] of the baptismal water would emphasize the element above the benefit of baptism. This is similar to what the re-baptizers and *Schwärmerei* do. They despise the command of Christ.[50]

Brandenburg and East and Central Germany

In this particular family, Luther's rite of 1523 and local diocesan custom were influential. For example, in the city of Nürnberg, the pastor in change of reforming the rite was Andreas Osiander (1496–1552). Osiander's teaching was set forth in the Nürnberg Catechetical sermons 1533.[51] In these Osiander taught that baptism is a second birth 'whereby our inward humanity and mind is renewed by the Holy Spirit, so that our hearts and minds receive new desires which they did not have in their first birth or nativity'.[52] In this bath of regeneration, our sins are forgiven, and the Holy Spirit is poured upon us 'so that by the power and working of the Holy Spirit, we are born again spiritually, and made new creatures'.[53] Osiander still held Luther's original numbering of three sacraments to include absolution, and he described the sacrament of baptism as 'the foundation and pillar of the truth'.[54] It is a putting-on of Jesus Christ, and an assurance that we are Christians: 'When we are born again by baptism, then our sins are forgiven, and the Holy Spirit is given to us, who makes us holy and moves us to all goodness.'[55] Interestingly, Osiander seems to regard baptism as a *pactum*, since he listed what God gave to the baptized, but then said of the baptizand:

> And for his [the baptizand's] part he promises to God again, and solemnly vows, that he will fight against sin with all his strength and power, and that he will gladly bear the cross, and all such afflictions, as it pleases God to lay upon him, and that also he will be content to die, that he may be perfectly healed and delivered from sin.[56]

---

[50] Ibid., p. 318, quoting from A.L. Richter, *Die evangelischen Kirchenordnungen des sechzehnten Jahrhunderts*, 2 vols, B. Degraaf, Nieuwkoop, 1967, Vol. 1, p. 139.

[51] Translated into Latin by Justus Jonas in 1539, and into English by Thomas Cranmer in 1548.

[52] *A Catechism set forth by Thomas Cranmer*, D.G. Selwyn (ed.), Sutton Courtenay Press, Appleford, 1978, p. 181. I have modernized the text.

[53] Ibid., p. 182.

[54] Ibid., p. 183.

[55] Ibid., p. 185.

[56] Ibid.

Baptism is the water of God, and works in us all the things that God has ordained it to work. In baptism not only are sins forgiven and the Holy Spirit given, but also 'the whole righteousness of Christ is given to us, that we may claim the same as our own'.[57] In baptism, righteousness is imputed to us.[58] This gives rise to new affections and spiritual motions in our souls.[59] In answer to the question, 'How can water do this?', Osiander explained that these things are done because of the Word and faith: 'When the word of the living God is added and joined to the water, then it is the bath of regeneration, and baptism water, and the lively spring of eternal salvation, and a bath that washes our souls by the Holy Spirit'[60] and 'Baptism is not water alone, but it is water inclosed and joined to the word of God, and to the covenant of God's promise.'[61]

Osiander drew up a rite for Nürnberg in 1524, and based it on the rite of the diocese of Bamberg (1491).[62] He included three elements from Luther's 1523 rite – the second catechumenal prayer, the *sindflugebet*, and the Gospel reading from Mark 10. It had a double renunciation, separate exorcism prayers for males and females, and anointing and the giving of a robe, though it omitted the giving of a candle. But perhaps in line with his idea of *pactum* expressed in the catechism, Osiander included an admonition immediately after the Gospel, instructing godparents on their duties. He drew up a new rite in 1533 with the aid of Johannes Brenz, following Luther's 1526 rite, and the admonition was removed until after baptism. A note in the Preface explained that the blessing of the font, oil, salt and spittle all darken the ceremony of baptism.[63]

The rite of Brandenburg 1540 represents a more conservative strain, akin to that of Nürnberg 1524. In fact it had been drafted by Jacob Stratner, George Buchholzer and George Witzel – the latter had returned to the Roman Catholic Church in 1533.[64] It was shown to and given approval by Luther, Melanchthon and Jonas, but apparently they were less than enthusiastic about its retention of so many Catholic ceremonies.[65] Burreson noted:

> Its most characteristic facet was the retention of a preponderance of ceremonies and texts that had appeared in the medieval rituals, but did not appear in either of the aforementioned reformed rites: both catechetical prayers; the reception of salt;

---

[57] Ibid., p. 187.

[58] Ibid., p. 189. In his treatise on the Power of the Keys Osiander says that in baptism we are made one flesh with Christ, and he views salvation as the actual infusion of Christ's nature in the believer. My thanks to my colleague Ronald Rittgers for drawing my attention to this, R. Rittgers, *The Reformation of the Keys. Confession, Conscience, and Authority in Sixteenth-Century Germany*, Harvard University Press, Cambridge, MA, 2004.

[59] Ibid., p. 189.

[60] Ibid., p. 190.

[61] Ibid., p. 191.

[62] Text in J.C.D. Fisher, *Christian Initiation: The Reformation Period*, SPCK, London, 1970, pp. 17ff.

[63] Text in ibid., pp. 26ff.

[64] For Witzel's contribution see John Patrick Dolan, *The Influence of Erasmus, Witzel, and Cassander in the Church Ordinances and Reform Proposals of the United Duchy of Cleve During the Middle Decades of the Sixteenth Century*, Aschendorff, Münster, 1957, pp. 30ff.

[65] Ibid., p. 32.

the prayers *Deus patrum nostorum* instead of the Flood Prayer; the complete set of exorcism texts; the signing of the candidate at the announcement of the Gospel; the delivery of the Creed (omitted from most evangelical rites) in addition to the Lord's Prayer; the inclusion of the final exorcism, *Nec te latet*; the pre-baptismal, catechumenal anointing; the naming of the child in addition to the question of desire; the post-baptismal, presbyteral anointing, *but with chrism*; the giving of a candle to the neophyte, and the final dismissal and peace prior to the blessing.[66]

The text of the giving of the candle was:

Receive this burning torch, which here signifies the light of the Christian faith, which you in your baptism have now received and vowed, and keep your baptism blameless, so that, when our Lord will come to the wedding, you may run to meet him with all the saints in the court of heaven, since you have in Christ Jesus eternal life. Amen.[67]

South Germany

If the Nürnberg/Brandenburg rites represent a conservative revision looking towards the pre-Reformation liturgies, those of South Germany look towards the Reformed rites. The initial German-speaking Reformers in the south were in the Swiss cantons – Leo Jud, Ulrich Zwingli and Oecolampadius. Though at first they seemed to be all part of the same movement, distinct differences and disagreements with Luther quickly emerged. Johannes Brenz, who was involved in many of the Lutheran reforms in South Germany, had been taught by Oecolampadius, and still moved in the orbit of the Swiss German Reformed theology. Burreson explains:

While Brenz, an independent theologian, remained very close to the Lutheran position, the Lutheran reformers throughout southern and south-central Germany, including Augsburg, interacted with and were influenced much more readily by the Swiss Reformed. Thus, the church orders and baptismal rites of these territories mediate the characteristics of those interactions and exchanges.[68]

Brenz published one catechism in 1527, and another, better known, in 1535.[69] In the latter baptism is explained as

… a sacrament and divine word-sign by which God the Father through his Son Jesus Christ together with the Holy Spirit promises that he will be a gracious God to the one being baptized and will forgive him all his sin. Through adoption by God the baptizand is promised an inheritance of all heavenly goods.[70]

Brenz explained that faith alone justifies, but that baptism was administered because of Christ's example and command, and the need for a public witness to God's prior election. He likened baptism to the Old Testament anointing of kings, and also to a

---

[66] 'The Saving Flood', pp. 345–6.

[67] Cited ibid., p. 347.

[68] Ibid., p. 363.

[69] See Tranvik, 'The Other Sacrament', pp. 79ff.

[70] Ibid., p. 81.

wedding – a public confirmation of a heavenly marriage. He urged that undue attention not be given to externals – font, water, or godparents – but bid his readers remember that the Holy Trinity with all their gifts are present at baptism. Brenz insisted on the importance of faith at baptism, and so had to defend infant baptism. While he did not rule out *fides infantium*, he stressed *fides alienum*, the faith of the community. But in the final analysis, unlike the mature Luther, Brenz separated faith and baptism, and contended that only the former is necessary:

> Indeed, baptism is useful and necessary. However, it receives its usefulness from faith … thereby, whoever does not believe in Christ, even if he has all the sacraments, all treasures and earthly and spiritual gifts, all wisdom and all power of the world, nevertheless he will be damned.[71]

In 1526 Brenz had issued a Church Order for Schwäbisch Hall that included guidelines for baptism, though not a liturgy, and he helped to prepare the 1533 Brandenburg-Nürnberg rite. In 1535 he accepted an invitation to help with the Church Order for Württemberg. Other compilers were Ambrosius Blarer from Constance, who was a disciple of Zwingli, and the Lutheran Erhard Schnedf. The 1536 Württemberg rite included admonitions to the congregation and godfathers from the 1533 Brandenburg-Nürnberg rite. However, in comparison with 1533, it omitted the initial naming of the child, the exorcism, the sign of the cross and formula, the *sindflutgebet*, the longer exorcism and text, the laying-on of hands, the formula for the movement to the font, the renunciations, the credal interrogatories, the peace, and the robing – all in line with Swiss German Reformed rites. The idea of baptismal regeneration was played down, and a distinction made between external sign and spiritual baptism. Sprinkling was the mode of administration.

Brenz went on to prepare an order for Schwäbisch Hall in 1543, which seems to have combined elements from the 1533 and 1536 rites in which he had previously been involved. In comparison to 1536, it did restore the renunciation and credal questions. However, it also contained lengthy admonitions which gave a summary of the purpose and benefits of baptism. In addition to including as options the old Western 'Almighty everlasting God', and the *sindflutgebet*, Brenz provided as a third option the following, which may have been his own composition:

> Almighty eternal God, you have given all authority in heaven and on earth to your only-begotten Son our Lord Jesus Christ, and he has commanded that his gospel be preached to all people, and that they be baptized in the name of the Father and of the Son and of the Holy Spirit, and has also promised that whoever believes and is baptized, shall be saved. We entreat you with all confidence that you would graciously permit to flourish in this child, N., through baptism, the saving bath and renewal of the Holy Spirit, which he desires, not for the sake of the work of righteousness which he does, but on account of your grace; through Jesus Christ our Lord. Amen.[72]

---

[71] Ibid., p. 86.
[72] Cited in Burreson, 'The Saving Flood', pp. 374–5.

Hermann's Consultation for Cologne, 1543

One further rite may be mentioned, which was compiled by Philip Melanchthon and Martin Bucer for Archbishop Hermann von Weid of Cologne.[73] Although never used, it provided a source for Archbishop Thomas Cranmer of England. In so far as Bucer has come to be regarded as Reformed rather than Lutheran, it represents something of an sixteenth-century ecumenical liturgy, compiled by a Lutheran and Reformed for a Reformation-minded Catholic archbishop.

The rite was prefaced with a doctrinal statement on baptism, which may have been the work of Bucer. It stated that baptism is a sacrament of regeneration 'whereby we are planted and incorporated into Christ the Lord'. It expressed concern that the parents and godparents should be worthy people.

An opening exhortation to the godfathers was reminiscent of both the Strasbourg developments of Bucer, as well as the 1533 Brandenburg-Nürnberg rite, and part of the latter was incorporated. It rehearsed the fall of Adam, the need to be delivered from the tyranny of Satan. It noted that 'through baptism we determine certainly that we are acceptable unto God and joined unto him with an everlasting covenant of grace so that nothing can separate us from him, or condemn us', which seems to reflect Bucer's covenant theology. The rite provided a preparation for the day prior to the baptism, with credal interrogatories combined with the renunciation, and with a question outlining the duties of godfathers. It included a short exorcism, the signing of the cross with formula, prayer, the *sindflutgebet*, Mark 10, Lord's Prayer and Creed, and psalmody. A prayer and blessing concluded this preparatory rite.

The actual rite began with another exhortation, readings from Titus and Matthew, a prayer from the Strasbourg rite of 1537, the baptism, a prayer and the peace. Unction, robe and candle were all abolished in this Lutheran-Bucerian rite.

Martin Chemnitz

Martin Chemnitz (1522–86) was the chief author of the *Formula of Concord* in 1570, which sought to define Lutheranism over against those thought to be 'crypto-Calvinist'. He is a precursor of what later would be regarded as Lutheran Orthodoxy. His own theological views on the sacraments were set forth in *An Enchiridion*. The first edition appeared in 1569, and various editions continued well after Chemnitz's death. In this work Chemnitz affirms with Luther that baptism is concerned with remission of original sin:

> Paul points out that the effect of Baptism is twofold, namely regeneration and renewal. Tts 3:5. For, first, sins are washed away in remission through Baptism by the Word, so that they are not imputed, if they who are baptized remain in Christ through faith; and thus guilt is taken away. Acts 2:38; 22:16; Ps 32:1–2; Ro 7:24–25; 8:2. And this remission is not half or partial, but full, perfect, and

---

[73] Text. Fisher, *Christian Initiation: The Reformation Period*, pp. 54ff.

complete. Second, in place of lost original righteousness, the Holy Ghost begins to crucify and mortify original depravity with its actions.[74]

The benefit, though, is not completed in this life. Baptism – citing Luther and Melanchthon – is the element of water and the Word of God, particularly the command in Matthew 28:19, though a subject for baptism is also necessary.[75] The words of administration of the rite, the threefold formula, signify that baptism is administered in the name or at the command of God who is Father, Son and Spirit, and into the name of God as Father, Son and Holy Spirit, and that God Himself – Father, Son and Spirit – is present.[76] Its benefits are forgiveness of sins, deliverance from the devil and death, and eternal salvation. But Chemnitz also describes baptism as a covenant of grace – though with the emphasis on grace, in the context of those who fall from baptism, and their return – and he refers to the words of the renunciation.[77] To the question of whether the effects of baptism are immediate, Chemnitz explained:

> Regeneration indeed, that is, adoption and the forgiveness of sins is complete and finished in believers immediately after Baptism, and yet it nevertheless extends through the whole life of a man. But renewal is indeed begun in Baptism and grows daily, but is finally completed in the life to come.[78]

Chemnitz felt obliged to defend infant baptism, noting Christ's reception of the children, but he also noted that Christ wants all to be saved, that infants are conceived and born in sin and need saving, that baptism has taken the place of circumcision, and that the prophecies spoken of in Acts are 'to you and your children'. He also attacked the 'sacramentarians' who suggest that, because of election, baptism is unnecessary.[79]

Some Later Theological and Liturgical Issues

The tendency noted in the South German rites – the shortening or omission of the exorcisms – would become a point of controversy amongst Lutheran pastors, and between the Lutheran and the Reformed churches. Bodo Nischan noted that the first controversy seems to have been between two Lutheran pastors from Thuringia, in 1549.[80] George Merula of St Margaret's Church in Gotha began to omit the second or longer exorcism, insisting that it was a useless relic. Justus Menius, who was the

---

[74] Martin Chemnitz, *Ministry, Word, and Sacraments. An Enchiridion*, edited, translated and briefly annotated by Luther Poellot. Concordia, St Louis, MO, 1981, p. 63.

[75] Ibid., p. 112.

[76] Ibid., p. 113.

[77] Ibid., pp. 115–16.

[78] Ibid., p. 116.

[79] Ibid., pp. 118–19.

[80] Bodo Nischan, 'The Exorcism Controversy and Baptism in the Late Reformation', *The Sixteenth Century Journal* 18 (1987), 31–50 for the information summarized here.

senior pastor, disagreed, and the controversy resulted in Merula being dismissed and banished in 1551.

In Prussia, John Aurifaber of Breslau had managed to delete the exorcisms from the 1558 rite, but they were restored in 1567. The controversy in the 1580s and '90s was seen as a wrestle between true (or even Gnesio) Lutherans and the 'crypto-Calvinists' or 'Phillipists' (a reference to Melanchthon by those who felt he departed from Luther's views). In Saxony the staunchly Lutheran elector August was succeeded by Christian, who tolerated those clergy who opposed the baptismal exorcisms, and although he promised to allow exorcism to continue, in July 1591 he issued a mandate prohibiting the rite. Christian died in September, and the new elector restored the old order and removed ministers who would not use the exorcisms.

In Anhalt the ruler Joachim Ernst and his son John George abolished the rites in 1589, despite the defence by Johann Arndt in his *Wahres Christentum*. John George remained adamant that the rites should remain abolished, and instructed Wolfgang Amling to produce a new baptismal rite (1590) with an explanation of why exorcisms were to be abolished. However, since Calvinists objected to exorcisms, those Lutherans who for whatever reason objected to them were deemed to be Calvinists in disguise. The dispute flared up in 1613 in Brandenburg when the elector John Sigismund took communion in the Reformed manner.[81] In Königsberg, one of the 'Reformed' court chaplains appointed by the elector baptized a child without the exorcisms, and was severely criticized by the Lutheran consistory, insisting that such action was contrary to the Prussian Church Order and the country's constitution.[82] It remained an issue well into the late seventeenth century, when many Lutherans began to omit it.

The seventeenth century also saw the rise of both Lutheran Orthodoxy (a codification of Gnesio-Lutheranism) and of Pietism. Martin Chemnitz of the sixteenth century is often seen as a precursor to theologians such as Mattheus Hafenreffer, Johann Konig and Johann Quenstedt, who freely used scholastic methods to codify Luther's theology. According to Quenstedt, the basic nature of all sacraments is the complete external action round about the earthly and the heavenly matter of any sacrament; the earthly matter of baptism is only water, even if used in a very small quantity.[83] Unlike Luther, however, Orthodoxy preferred aspersion to immersion, and defended that mode of baptism. According to Johann Gerhard, the word βαπτίζειν signifies any kind of ablution.[84] For Gerhard, the three essential parts of baptism are water, Word and act. The use of exorcisms became a burning question for Orthodoxy,

---

[81] See also Bodo Nischan, *Prince, People and Confession. The Second Reformation in Brandenburg*, University of Pennsylvania Press, Philadelphia, 1994.

[82] See Bodo Nischan, 'The Exorcism Controversy', p. 45.

[83] Friedrich Kalb, *Theology of Worship in 17th Century Lutheranism*, English translation Concordia Publishing House, St Louis, MO, 1965, pp. 92ff. J. Quenstedt, *Theologia Didactio-Polemica sive Systema Theologicum*, 1685, IV, pp. 75, 109.

[84] Cited by Kalb, *Theology of Worship*, p. 93.

and whereas they were essential for Luther, for Orthodoxy they became adiaphora. Quenstedt argued that:

> Exorcism is retained in our churches as an *adiaphoran* or an indifferent ceremony, useful to adumbrate the spiritual captivity of infants in the realm of Satan and the saving efficacy of Baptism, whereby they are set free from it.[85]

He also added:

> Granted that exorcism is an adiaphoristic rite and its nature such that it may be observed or omitted without hurt or conscience; nevertheless, it should not be abolished in those churches in which it has hitherto been in use.[86]

However, the Orthodox codification of baptism was also challenged by the rise of pietism. Johann Arndt (1555–1621) in his *True Christianity* (1605) challenged what he regarded as the shortcomings and sterility of Orthodoxy. Following Osiander, Arndt stressed the union of the Christian with God. Baptism is a glorious affirmation of the union, with a spiritual promise and vow which, like marriage, makes the two become one flesh.[87] It is a new birth. Breathing a very different air to that of Lutheran Orthodoxy, Arndt noted:

> This is the true new birth and the new creature that appears before God's face, pure and holy, cleaned and purified through the blood of Christ and the Holy Spirit without any blemish. So perfect is this washing in the blood of Christ that the Bridegroom says: *You are most beautiful my friend.* (Song 1:15).[88]

In a passage which is a prayer Arndt wrote:

> Dear Lord Jesus Christ, you who have … instituted the holy sacrament of baptism … I thank you from the heart that You have through this sacrament led me into the holy Christian Church and thereby made me a partner of all your heavenly and eternal benefits … through baptism you have clothed me with your holy obedience, merit, righteousness, holiness, and innocence. Through the waters of baptism the Holy Spirit has created new life and changed a sinner into one who has been justified … You have received me because of your eternal grace and promise and bound me unto yourself through this means of grace.[89]

In 1675, Philipp Jacob Spener published a book entitled *Pia Desideria*, in which he outlined a way of making religion more practical rather than merely theoretical. He also emphasized 'heart faith', religious feeling and moral worthiness. He argued that faith is *fiducia* rather than assent, and he stressed the role of sanctification. On baptism Spener urged:

> Your God has indeed given you Baptism, and you may be baptized only once. But he has made a covenant with you – from his side a covenant of grace and from

---

[85] Quenstedt, *Theologia*, IV, p. 169, cited by Kalb, ibid., p. 118.

[86] Ibid., p. 171, in Kalb, ibid.

[87] Johann Arndt, *True Christianity*, trans. Peter Erb, Paulist Press, New York, 1979, p. 264.

[88] Ibid., p. 265.

[89] Johann Arndt, *Paradislustgard*, F. and G. Bekjers Forlag, Stockholm, 1975, pp. 117–18.

your side a covenant of faith and a good conscience. This covenant must last through your whole life. It will be in vain that you comfort yourself in your Baptism and in its promise of grace and salvation if for your part you do not also remain in the covenant of faith and a good conscience or, having departed therefrom, return to it with sincere repentance. Accordingly if your Baptism is to benefit you, it must remain in constant use throughout your life.[90]

This did have resonances with Luther – but the early Luther. The use of covenant echoed the Reformed theologians, and was viewed by Lutheran Orthodoxy as pelagian and synagestic – that we cooperate in grace. Pietists accepted infant baptism, but argued that faith must be accompanied by personal faith as proof of regeneration in order to remain in grace – something which is hinted at in Spener's concern with doing 'your part'.

Another influential pietist was Johann Freidrich Stark (Starck) whose *Gebet-Buch* was published in 1728. According to Luke Wolfgramm, Stark departed from the typical Pietist doctrine by ascribing divine power to baptism.[91] Stark asserted that 'we have obtained in holy baptism: 1. The adoption by God; … 2. The righteousness of Jesus Christ; … 3. The indwelling of the Holy Spirit; … 4. also everlasting salvation'.[92] Stark also argued for baptism's permanent power and value. In a vivid prayer he says:

O what glory you have imparted to me in holy baptism, that you have adopted me as your child! People greatly extol the good fortune that is theirs by virtue of noble birth: possession of high posts of honour, great riches, considerable estates. Behold, I esteem my good fortune much higher, namely, that I am your child; we are your children, because if we are children, we are also heirs, namely, God's heirs and joint heirs with Christ.[93]

If Pietism was concerned with heartfelt personal religion, the Enlightenment brought with it rationalism, and the need to make preaching and liturgical rites sound 'modern'. This had direct liturgical consequences, since a number of private and then official liturgical revisions were authored.[94] *Evangelische Kirchen-Agende fuer Prediger welche an keine Landesliturgie ausschliesslich gebunden sind* was authored in 1834 and contained a baptismal rite for the baptism of a child 'of well-to-do, cultured and highly respected parents'![95] The exhortation is all about the importance of the new

---

90 Philip Spener, *Pia Desideria*, ed. and trans. Theodore G. Tappert, Fortress Press, Philadelphia, PA, 1964, p. 66.

91 Luke Wolfgramm, 'An Examination of the Pietistic Content of Johann Friedrich Stark's *Tägliches Hand-Buch, in guten und bösen Tagen,* Stark's *Gebet-Buch*', published at <http://www.wls.wels.net/library/Essays/Authors/w/WolfgrammPiet>.

92 Johann F. Starck, *Tägliches Hand-Buch in guten und bösen Tagen*, Verlag von Georg Brumder, Milwaukee, WI, p. 59.

93 Ibid., p. 60.

94 For a general discussion, Nicholas Hope, *German and Scandinavian Protestantism 1700–1918*, Clarendon Press, Oxford, 1995, Chapter 13.

95 Text in Lutheran Liturgical Association, 'The Liturgical Deterioration of the Seventeenth and Eighteenth Centuries', *Memoirs of the Lutheran Liturgical Association IV*, Philadelphia, PA, 1906–7, pp. 67–78.

arrival, and the hope for temporal blessings. The parents and 'esteemed sponsors' are bringing 'the dear child to this holy act of Christian consecration, and permit it, by means of the symbolic sprinkling of water, to be solemnly received into the congregation of those who as the confessors of Jesus should be cleansed of their sins'. The baptismal formula baptizes the child 'to the glory' of God the Father, of His Son Jesus Christ, and of the Holy Ghost – the child now glorifies God rather than God saving the child! The rite refers to the 'religion of Jesus', and after the baptism contains the following *exordium* addressed to the child:

> Water, an element required by the whole nature, has thus been the emblem of thy Christian consecration, dear child. May the religion of Jesus become the element of thy entire moral life!
>
> Water is the common property of the rich and the poor, the high and the low. Thus also the religion of Jesus is intended for all: and to thee, dear child, as we hope to God, it will come of purer quality and in larger measure than to countless others.
>
> Water, the best means for cleansing the body, is the most fitting emblem of soul-purity. May thy heart remain pure and thy life unspotted, thou still innocent angel!
>
> Water contains great and refreshing potencies for our bodies. Still greater healing-powers for the soul are contained in the genuine Christian belief. May the religion of Jesus prove to thee, dear child, a never-failing source of moral health!
>
> Water is related to heaven and earth, rises from the latter to the former, and falls down from the former upon the latter. May thy whole life, dear child, be directed toward the higher, heavenly things! Mayest thou often life thy heart toward heaven and bring down for thyself the heavenly into the earthly!
>
> Water, so often scorned by those in health, is generally the last physical refreshment of the dying. May the religion of Jesus be and remain throughout thy entire life thy daily refreshment! May it be to thee and to us all a quickening draught in life's sufferings, until we reach that better land, where we shall hunger and thirst no more! Amen.[96]

Nothing could be much further from Luther's theology and rite. However, other nineteenth-century rites were more traditional. The Prussian rite of 1829 began with the invocation of the Trinity, a brief exhortation, and prayer, Mark 10, and Lord's Prayer, Creed, baptism and prayer, with no exorcisms and renunciations.[97] The Dresden Liturgical Commission, having representatives from Bavaria, Hannover, Würtemberg and both Mecklenburgs, opted in 1854 to use Luther's 1523 baptismal rite as the model for its new Agenda, and the Prussian Church, though composed of Lutheran and Reformed, also took the 1523 rite as its first form.[98] And a widely representative expression of nineteenth-century Lutheran German theology was that

---

[96] Ibid., pp. 74–5.

[97] *Agende für die Evangelische kirche in den königlich Preußischen Landen*, Berlin, 1829, Part 2, pp. 3–7.

[98] H.S. Gilbert, 'The Liturgical History of Baptism', *Memoirs of the Lutheran Liturgical Association*, Philadelphia, PA, 1906–07, pp. 113–23.

of Heinrich Schmid of the University of Erlangen. Drawing on Luther and the tradition of Lutheran Orthodox authorities, Schmid taught that baptism is enjoined by the Lord, and is accompanied by a promise. It consists of water and Word, and it must be performed 'precisely according to the instructions of the Lord'. Its design is to work saving grace in humanity. Its efficacy is not limited to a certain period of time.[99]

Scandinavia

The Reformation in Scandinavia was closely linked with the political fortunes of Denmark, Norway, Sweden and Finland – the latter being regarded as part of Sweden. The union of the Kingdoms in 1397, in which Denmark dominated, unravelled at the beginning of the sixteenth century, with Gustav Vasa becoming King of Sweden/ Finland by 1521, and Duke Frederik of Schleswig and Holstein being king of Denmark/Norway. Both rulers were inclined towards the new evangelical (Lutheran) ideas.[100] Since Bugenhagen had been actively involved in the reforms of Schleswig and Holstein, it is no accident that in 1537 he presided at the coronation service of Frederik, and ordained seven superintendents for the Lutheran Church in Denmark. He also drew up the *Kirkeordinansen* in 1537 and 1539. The Norwegian Church was left to follow the principles of the Danish Church Ordinance until 1607, when it finally received its own. Supervision of the Norwegian superintendents was given over to Peder Palladius, superintendent of Zealand.

Prior to Bugenhagen's Church Order, Hans Tausen, a former member of the Order of St John of Jerusalem, issued a baptismal formula in Danish, based largely upon Luther's rite.[101] An Ordinance of 1536 does not give the actual rite, but stated that it was to begin with the words 'Depart, unclean Spirit.' Peder Palladius gave a translation of Luther's 1523 rite in his 1538 *Enchiridion*, though with slight variation in the longer exorcism. In the 1539 Order, the rite begins with questions as to whose child was being presented, and whether he or she had already been baptized. The minister was to give a few words of explanation of the sacrament. Then came the exorcism, followed by the Gospel and Lord's Prayer. The minister calls the sponsor to the font and says, 'The Lord preserve your coming in and going out', followed by the renunciation, the credal interrogatories, baptism, peace and admonition to the godparents.

No change was made in this rite until 1783, when the exorcism was removed. Exorcisms had been questioned by Niels Hemmingsen, who was one of the leading Danish leaders of the Reformation. In 1567 the minister of Stege, Iver Bertelsen,

---

[99] See further, Heinrich Schmid, *The Doctrinal Theology of the Evangelical Lutheran Church*, English translation Lutheran Bookstore, Philadelphia, PA, 1876, pp. 553–70.

[100] See Ole Peter Grell (ed.), *The Scandinavian Reformation,* Cambridge University Press, Cambridge, 1995; Martin Schwarz Lausten, *A Church History of Denmark*, Ashgate, Aldershot, 2002.

[101] Lutheran Liturgical Association, 'The Liturgy in Denmark', *Memoirs of the Lutheran Liturgical Association II*, Philadelphia, PA, 1906–07, pp. 63–73.

stopped using the exorcisms, and was dismissed. In 1606 Christian IV ordered the professors of divinity and bishops to submit their views on the baptismal exorcisms, and a month later he ordered the bishop of Lund to omit the exorcism at the baptism of his daughter. Lutheran Orthodoxy was asserted by two professors of theology, Jørgen Dybvad and Hans Poulsen Resen. The exorcism was omitted from the 1607 draft version of the Norwegian liturgy, but pressure from Resen resulted in its reinstatement. Bishops continued to urge pastors to use it, though the royal family continued to have its offspring baptized without exorcism.[102] The rite of 1895 had an address to the godparer*s ⸱i⸱ning with the cross, prayer, Gospel, Lord's Prayer, praise to God who will now ⸱⸱⸱⸱⸱⸱ the child, 'The Lord preserve your going out … ', renunciation and Cre⸱ ⸱⸱⸱⸱ ⸱⸱m is desired, baptism, the child commended to God, peace, adm⸱ ⸱inal collect.

Baptism feature⸱ ⸱ theology of the Danish theologian, hymn writer and ⸱ (1783–1872). Against the prevailing rationalism, Gru⸱ ⸱y of Scripture and the Apostles' Creed. So he asserted ⸱ altar/ Do we hear God's word to us.'[103] Grundtvig had⸱ ⸱parish according to the new rite of 1873, without the e⸱⸱⸱⸱ ⸱ling block that he had been the first child in that parish to be ⸱o ⸱⸱ ⸱d that the exorcism with the words of the signing of the cross were in⸱⸱

> Make a cross with the Lord's voi⸱⸱
> Before your face and your breast
> So that we can perceive
> That our Jesus is he
> Who despite the cross's death and shame
> Has the word of the Father.[104]

In a hymn he commented on the prayer which mentioned 'Ask and you will receive':

> Up to God's house we go
> And boldly knock.
> Open to us our prayer
> We seek the Son of God.
>
> As quick as lightning
> The door is opened for us,
> In baptism by the Spirit and word
> Here stands our Saviour.[105]

---

[102] Grell, *The Scandinavian Reformation*, pp. 130–31.

[103] Here I am indebted to Christian Thodberg, "The Importance of Baptism in Grundtvig's View of Christianity", in A.M. Allchin et al. (eds), *Heritage and Prophecy. Grundtvig and the English-Speaking World*, Aarhus University Press, Aarhus, 1993, pp. 133–52.

[104] *Grundtvigs Sang-Værk til den danske kirke*, Vols I–V, reprinted Copenhagen, 1982, Vol. I, No. 92, stanza 16, cited Thodberg, ibid., p. 135.

[105] 'Op til Guds hus vi ga', *Den Danske Salmebog* no. 376, stanzas 1–2, cited Thodberg, ibid., p. 137.

In Grundtvig's day some preferred to renounce 'evil' and turn to lead a moral life, rather than renounce the 'devil', which was regarded as superstitious. Grundtvig argued that the renunciation of the devil originates with Jesus himself:

> Certainly it is ludicrous from our point of view if people maintain that according to the bible our Lord Jesus Christ does not make forsaking the devil an essential part of his baptismal covenant, for even if the story of the temptation contained the Bible's only information about the personal relationship between the Saviour and the Tempter, even so the Lord's 'Begone, Satan' would be a guarantee enough that when he founded his kingdom on earth he would not forget to do something, which could keep his vicious enemy out of it, and that when he would take an oath of loyalty from his subjects he would also take their word of it, that they would not be like traitors and side with his enemy ... so this is obviously a foundation condition which must belong to the very basis of Christianity.[106]

He argued that 'the baptismal covenant' was not a human commandment, but Jesus Christ's testimony about what we must believe. The result of baptism was:

> The water-bath in the Word
> As the Lord, our hope,
> Girded with omnipotence
> Gives us a name in his baptism,
> Destroys our sins, renews God's image
> As surely as Jesus
> Is the Word of God on earth.[107]

On the final prayer of assurance Grundtvig commented:

> It ought to be noticed that we have made some arbitrary changes in this necessary Assurance of the saving efficacy of baptism (naturally under the conditions of the covenant), and this error, however small it may seem, should certainly be rectified. First we say 'By means of' water and the Holy Ghost, but the Church says 'By' water and the Holy Ghost, and the bible upholds the rightness of this when it says 'Unless a man is born again by water and the Holy Spirit he cannot enter into the Kingdom of God', John 3:5. Next we say, 'Has forgiven thee all thy sins' but the Church says 'Has given thee the forgiveness of all thy sins', which especially at infant baptism sounds much better. Finally we only say, 'strengthen thee with his grace', but the Church says, 'Anoint thee with oil of salvation in the same our Lord Jesus Christ' for eternal life, and this alteration was so unreasonable that it probably happened because the Church's expression seemed to refer to actual anointing at baptism which the reformers had abolished.[108]

Thodberg notes that Grundtvig would gladly have kept the concrete expression 'anoint', even if only as a sign. In sum, Grundtvig defended Luther's dualism in the rite, of God/devil, life/death, and he also emphasized the word in baptism as a word personally addressed to the baptized. He thus wrote:

---

[106] *Væker i Udvalg*, vol. VI, Copenhagen, 1944, p. 234, cited Thodberg, ibid., p. 143.

[107] *Grundtvigs Sang-Værk*, Vol. I, no. 399, stanza 3, cited Thodberg, ibid., p. 144.

[108] *Udvalgte Skrifter*, vol VIII, pp. 423–4, cited Thodberg, ibid., p. 145.

Now in this Church of Christ we must all know that baptism in the name of the Father, the Son and the Holy Ghost is the only way of gaining admission, with the witness that this baptism takes place not only with water but with 'water and spirit' and is therefore not merely a so-called Church practice (a ceremony) but a heavenly rebirth in water, through which the Holy Ghost in the name of Our Lord Jesus Christ grants forgiveness of sins and the child's right to a Father in heaven together with the hope of eternal life.[109]

In Sweden the Reformation was a gradual process, and although Olavus Petri studied in Wittenberg, the Reformation was tied up with Swedish nationalism, and it is perhaps not surprising that certain rites and ceremonies which were dear to Sweden were retained. In his *Manual* published as a proposal in 1529, he presented a rite which included his own material, material from the *Manuale Lincopense*, and Luther's 1526 rite. This rite began with an enquiry as to the child's name, and a short exorcism from the *Manuale Lincopense*. Then came a signing and formula, and the laying-on of hands with 'Almighty Everlasting God' and 'O God the immortal defence of all'. A rubric noted that exorcism of salt was not necessary, but salt was given with a formula. The *sindflutgebet* followed, with an exorcism and prayer, and then Mark 10. The laying-on of hands with the Lord's Prayer of Luther's rite followed, and then the child was led to the font for the renunciation, anointing and credal questions, a question of whether baptism is requested, and the baptism. This was followed by anointing with chrism and formula, a putting-on of the white robe, and the giving of a candle.

A similar suspicion of exorcisms was found in Sweden as in Germany and Denmark. The 1917 rite for infant baptism began with the invocation of the divine trinity, and a brief exhortation.[110] This was followed by a Gospel reading from Matthew 28:19 and then Mark 10:13–16, with the laying-on of hands on the child's head while the Lord's Prayer was recited. After a short prayer came the Creed, baptism, prayer, blessing from Numbers 6:24, and then an admonition to the godparents. The rite ended with the brief doxology and dismissal to go in peace. The exorcisms and renunciations had been removed.

Concluding Remarks

Luther questioned the received understanding of sacraments, and using Scripture rather than scholastic doctrine as the touchstone for truth, redefined the medieval understanding of sacraments. This led to a new articulation of baptism, which in turn led to some reforms of the received ritual. Such things as salt, oil and the lighted candle, while technically *adiaphora* – indifferent things – were removed because they

---

[109] 'Elementary Christian Teachings', in N.L. Jensen (ed.), *A Grundtvig Anthology*, James Clarke & Co, Cambridge, 1984, p. 130.

[110] See Eric E. Yelverton, *The Swedish Rite, a translation of 'Handbook for svenska kyrkan'* (1917), SPCK, London, 1921, pp. 88–91.

obscured the glory of baptism, which was centred around the dipping in the water with the triune formula. Nevertheless, Luther's latitude in matters liturgical allowed a broad spectrum of rites and theologies, though the growing suspicion towards exorcism and renunciations, found already in the sixteenth century, had impacted most Lutheran rites by the nineteenth century. The main emphasis of the Lutheran rites was salvation from sin (justification). Pietism required personal faith, and this became an element of importance amongst the Pietist groups. The more extreme Rationalism raised the question of why such a rite was necessary at all, and interpreted it as a birth rite about the glory of the child rather than a washing of sin. On the whole, however, the Lutheran rites remained truncated versions of the medieval German and Scandinavian medieval rites.

CHAPTER 2

The Reformed Tradition:
From Ulrich Zwingli to Eugène Bersier

The Reformed tradition embraces a wide variety of churches that derive their theologies from certain prominent Swiss, French and German theologians of the sixteenth century, whose ideas were conserved and developed in the Swiss cantons, Huguenot France, the German Palatinate, Hungary, the Netherlands and Scotland. The tradition is often dubbed 'Calvinist', but John Calvin, though perhaps the most outstanding theologian of this tradition, was not its only seminal thinker. In fact, the early formative rites and theological developments centred in Zurich, Berne and Strasbourg as much as Calvin's Geneva.

Zurich: Leo Jud and Ulrich Zwingli

Martin Luther, in Wittenberg, found himself suddenly fighting on two fronts. On the one hand, he was battling the Roman Catholic teachings; on the other, he was countering all those who he identified as 'Schwärmer', or enthusiasts, whose views he regarded as dangerous. Among these were the Zurichers. In the Swiss cantons a parallel but independent reformation movement had developed. Though in touch with the Wittenbergers, the Swiss reformers were inspired by the humanism of the age, and had a different approach to Scripture than did Luther.

Already in 1523 the pastor of St Peter's Church in Zurich, Leo Jud, who was a close associate of Ulrich Zwingli, and who took a leading part in the translation of the Zurich Bible, published a rite of baptism. It was basically Luther's rite, with the German language altered to fit Swiss German. Jud also made some changes, some suggested by the local medieval rite of the diocese of Constance, and some for doctrinal reasons.[1] He retained the exsufflation, the signing, prayer of reception (old catechumenate) and salt. He recast Luther's *sindflutgebet*, shortening it by omitting, for example, the reference to Christ's sanctifying and setting apart the Jordan and all waters for a saving flood, and adding the exorcism of the devil. He retained the *effeta* and the renunciations, but gave a précis of the creed. There is a pre-baptismal anointing, the baptism with formula, signing of the cross with chrism, and vesting.

Jud's rite remained in use until it was replaced in 1525 with a rite apparently authored by Ulrich Zwingli, which followed considerable controversy in Zurich over

---

[1] For fuller discussion, H.O. Old, *The Shaping of the Reformed Baptismal Rite in the Sixteenth Century*, Eerdmans, Grand Rapids, MI, 1992; text, Fisher, *Christian Initiation: The Reformation Period*, pp. 126ff.

baptism, and the emergence of an Anabaptist group. Zwingli had been educated in the Universities of Vienna and Basel, and in 1519 was called to be a pastor in Zurich. By 1522 he had openly adopted reformation principles, and called for the abolition of indulgences, fasting, veneration of saints, clerical celibacy and pilgrimage. At some time between 1523 and 1524, Zwingli appears to have either reached the conclusion that baptism of infants was wrong, or had given the impression that he had. The 'Taufer' who advocated rebaptism of adults argued that Zwingli had expressed agreement with them – so Balthasar Hubmaier was later to accuse him: 'Then and there you said I was right in saying that children should not be baptized before they were instructed in the faith.' Zwingli recoiled from this, and expounded a defence of infant baptism alongside a Neoplatonist approach to sacraments.

Zwingli's understanding of baptism rested on several fundamental theological convictions.[2] First, that nothing which is not warranted by Scripture is necessary; indeed, it is to add to the Gospel. Thus in baptism, breathing, giving of salt and anointing were regarded as 'magic' and were human additions. Second, he believed in the immediacy of grace through faith in Christ, which is mediated by the Holy Spirit and is spiritual. It cannot be mediated by a physical rite or ceremony. This latter belief was a result of his Neoplatonism; he drove a sharp wedge between the physical and fleshly, and the spiritual. Third, Zwingli rejected the traditional understanding of original sin. For Zwingli, original sin was to be understood as a disease or condition by which humans are prone to sin, but do not inherit original guilt.

Zwingli defined the word 'sacrament' according to the old Latin meaning, as an oath taken by soldiers. So he saw the sacraments like tokens or badges which we wear, just as a monk might wear a habit, or a soldier wear the emblem of his Swiss canton. Sacraments become ecclesial events or signs, not signs mediating something from God. Zwingli wrote:

> If a man sews on a white cross, he proclaims that he wishes to be a confederate. And if he makes the pilgrimage to Nähenfels and gives God praise and thanksgiving for the victory vouchsafed to our forefathers, he testifies that he is a confederate indeed. Similarly the man who receives the mark of baptism is the one who is resolved to hear what God says to him, to learn the divine precepts and to live his life in accordance with them.[3]

Thus baptism is something the Church does to show who its members are, and Christians do it to show they are Christians. It requires faith, which is imparted in the soul and mind by the Spirit. So what about infant baptism? Since for Zwingli original

---

[2] See Peter Stephens, 'Zwingli's Sacramental Views', in E.J. Furcha and H. Wayne Pipkin (eds), *Prophet, Pastor, Protestant*, Pickwick Publications, Allison Park, PA, 1984, pp. 155–69 and *The Theology of Huldrych Zwingli*, Clarendon Press, Oxford, 1986; Timothy George, 'The Presuppositions of Zwingli's Baptismal Theology', in Furcha and Pipkin, *Prophet, Pastor, Protestant*, pp. 71–87. Adolf Fugel, *Tauflehre und Taufliturgie bei Huldrych Zwingli*, Peter Lang, Berne, 1989.

[3] Zwingli's Works in *Corpus Reformatorum*, IV.217, cited in Stephens, 'Zwingli's Sacramental Views', p. 159.

sin was caught rather than passed on, baptism was not needed to remove original sin; he saw no need for some regeneration through a water ritual. Instead, Zwingli appealed to circumcision in the Old Testament, and for infant baptism as the Christian counterpart. The basis of both was covenant. Just as in the Old Testament, children (males) were circumcised as a sign that they were in the covenant, even though they could not keep the law until they were older, so also children of Christians could be baptized by virtue of the fact that their parents were in the covenant.[4] Baptism comes as part of a family ticket! It does not confer or replace election by grace.

Zwingli thus placed great store in the personal faith of the parents who offered the child for baptism. Only parents who were in the covenant – conscious participants in the covenanted community – should present their infants for baptism. 'We do not,' wrote Zwingli, 'allow children to be brought to baptism unless their parents have first been taught.'[5] The parents made a confession of faith on behalf of the child, by proxy as it were, and the Church accepted the confession of faith, presuming until proven wrong that the child was amongst the elect. Zwingli thus gives emphasis to the ecclesial dimension of baptism over against a soteriological dimension.

The May 1525 rite began with the following rubric/statement: 'Now follows the form of baptism which is now used in Zurich, and all the additions, which have no foundation in the word of God, have been removed.' It opens with a *votum* found in some medieval rites: 'Our help is in the name of the Lord.'[6] Immediately the minister asks if the godparents wish the candidate to be baptized 'with the baptism of our Lord Jesus Christ', and the child's name is asked. The retention of godparents was through force of tradition and social expectations, but in reality, covenant theology made them superfluous. A version of the *sindflutgebet* is retained, though the second half is much altered. It includes the petition to God to 'kindle the light of faith in his heart whereby he may be incorporate into your Son' – leaving open the possibility that this incorporation may not be according to God's election. The Gospel reading from Mark 10 follows, then a second request is made of the child's name. The baptismal formula actually reads '*N*, I baptize you **into** the name of the Father and of the Son and of the Holy Spirit' – Zwingli himself was quite insistent on the correct meaning of the Greek εἰς, which fitted with his concept of a sacrament as a pledging.[7] He retained the white garment, and ended the rite with a dismissal in peace.

Zwingli died on the battle field in 1531. His successor at Zurich was Heinrich Bullinger, who felt duty bound to maintain Zwingli's teaching. He was in dialogue with John Calvin of Geneva, since there were fundamental differences between the Zurich-Basel-Berne theologians and Geneva on the question of sacramental teaching. Bullinger

---

4 Jack Warren Cottrell, 'Covenant and Baptism in the Theology of Huldreich Zwingli', Th.D. dissertation, Princeton Theological Seminary, 1971; J.Wayne Baker, *Heinrich Bullinger and the Covenant: The Other Reformed Tradition*, Ohio State University Press, Athens, OH, 1980.

5 Z IV.238, cited by George, 'Presuppositions', p. 82.

6 Text in Fisher, *Christian Initiation: The Reformation Period*, pp. 129ff.

7 Stephens, *The Theology of Huldrych Zwingli*, p. 198, and note 11.

modified the Zurich position slightly. Bullinger's views were set forth in his *Absoluta de Christi Domini et Catholicae eius Ecclesiae Sacramentis* (1545), and in the *Decades*. He also expressed his views in the *Second Helvetic Confession* (1566). Both Bucer at Strasbourg and Calvin in Geneva spoke of sacraments as instruments which exhibit. Bullinger had difficulty with such language. Writing to Calvin, he said:

> If by 'instrument' you mean 'sign', fine. But if it is something more than sign, you seem to ascribe too much to the sacraments … It is God who saves and receives us in grace. But this you ascribe to an instrument through which it is worked, some implement or flow-sluice or canal, the very sacraments, though which grace is infused into us … But we do not believe this … God alone works our salvation … God, and no created thing, confers and indeed confers through the Spirit and faith … The sacraments neither offer (*exhibent*) nor confer, nor are they instruments (*instrumenta*) of offering and conferring, but they signify, testify, and seal.[8]

For Bullinger, baptism has as its sign water, and it is a badge or cognisance of the people of God, and an assured token of our purification by Christ. It is a sign, a testimony and sealing of our cleansing, and of ingrafting into the Church. Infant baptism was defended on analogy with circumcision and covenant theology, and Bullinger taught that salvation comes through the covenant, of which baptism is simply the outward sign. He could write:

> The baptizer giveth visibly the sacrament of regeneration, and a testimony of the remission of sins; but the Lord by his Spirit doth invisibly regenerate, and forgiveth sins, and sealeth the regeneration.[9]

Here the outward sign and inner grace do not coincide. In the second *Helevtic Confession*, the chapter on baptism taught that

> … to be baptized in the name of Christ is to be enrolled, entered, and received into the covenant and family, and so into the inheritance of the sons of God; yes, and in this life to be called after the name of God; that is to say, to be called a son of God; to be cleansed also from the filthiness of sins, and to be granted the manifold grace of God, in order to lead a new and innocent life. Baptism, therefore, calls to mind and renews the great favor God has shown to the race of mortal men.
>
> For we are all born in the pollution of sin and are the children of wrath. But God, who is rich in mercy, freely cleanses us from our sin by the blood of his Son, and in him adopts us to be his sons, and by a holy covenant joins us to himself, and enriches us with various gifts that we might live a new life. All these things are assured by baptism. For inwardly we are regenerated, purified, and renewed by God through the Holy Spirit and outwardly receive the assurance of the greatest gifts in the water, by which also those great benefits are represented, and, as it were, set before our eyes to be beheld.

---

[8] *Corpus Reformatorum* 35:695, quoted from Paul Rorem, *Calvin and Bullinger on the Lord's Supper*, Alcuin/GROW Liturgical Study 12, Grove Books, Bramcote, 1989, p. 34.

[9] Heinrich Bullinger, *Decades*, Parker Society edn, Cambridge University Press, Cambridge, 1850, vol. 5, pp. 367–8.

And therefore we are baptized, that is, washed or sprinkled with visible water. For the water washes dirt away, and cools and refreshes hot and tired bodies. And the grace of God performs these things for souls, and does so invisibly or spiritually.[10]

This dualism, where the inward and outward grace do not necessarily coincide, has aptly been termed 'symbolic parallelism' by Brian Gerrish; the two may happen, but not at the same time.[11]

Strasbourg: Diobald Schwartz, Wolfgang Capito and Martin Bucer

In January 1524, Martin Zell, preacher at the cathedral in Strasbourg, began baptizing using the German language throughout the rite. The first published rite dates from June 1524, and was the work of Zell's assistant, Diobald Schwartz. It followed the medieval rite as used in Strasbourg, but drew on Luther's 1523 rite. It retained the initial exorcism, the signing of the cross, the giving of salt and further exorcisms, the Markan Gospel, and the giving of the Lord's Prayer, *Ave* and the Creed, and the *effeta*. After the renunciations came the pre-baptismal anointing, the naming, the traditional formula of baptism, the post-baptismal anointing and the giving of the white robe.[12] It was a conservative rite, departing very little from its Latin counterpart.

According to H.O. Old, it is with Wolfgang Capito, in his October 1524 work, *Was man halten unnd antworten soll, von der Spaltung zwischen Martin Luther und Andres Carolstadtt*, that we first find suggestions for liturgical reform. Capito wrote:

> To baptism belongs only water and this word, I baptize thee in the name of the Father and of the Son ... etc. All the rest is supplementary which from ancient times was used for decoration. We leave out the chrism and the oil, when people come who will allow us to leave it out, because those things have been considered far too highly and for us they darken the grace of baptism. One gives more respect to the chrism and the oil which the suffragan bishop has bewitched with his consecration formulas than to simple water which God has blessed with his Word. It is from this that has arisen that other misuse, that so many ignorant people have their sickly children baptized once again in the Church, who without chrism and oil had been baptized at home by midwives. When occasion and time present themselves, which we hope will be soon, we want to bring this into greater conformity with the Word and to improve the entire procedure in a Christian manner.[13]

---

[10] Chapter 20. Text (Latin) in Philip Schaff, *The Creeds of Christendom*, Vol. 3, Baker Books edn, Grand Rapids, MI, 1998. English translation <http://www.ccel.org/creeds/helvetic.htm>.

[11] Brian Gerrish, 'The Lord's Supper in the Reformed Confessions', in Donald K. McKim (ed.), *Major Themes in the Reformed Tradition*, Eerdmans, Grand Rapids, MI, 1992, pp. 245–58.

[12] Fisher, *Christian Initiation: The Reformation Period*, pp. 30–33; German text, F. Hubert, *Die Strassburger Liturgischen Ordnungen in Zeitalter der Reformation*, Vandenhoek und Ruprecht, Göttingen, 1900, pp. 25ff.

[13] Cited in Old, *The Shaping of the Reformed Baptismal Rite*, pp. 52–3.

In December 1524 a work entitled *Grund und Ursach*, mainly written by Martin Bucer, explained a number of reforms which were taking place. Bucer himself had at first aligned himself with Luther, but by 1524 his views on sacraments were closer to Zwingli, and made a similar distinction between the inner working of the Holy Spirit, and exterior rites. Thus in *Grund und Ursach*, Bucer denied that God binds grace to water in baptism. What is important is inner cleansing, new birth and renewal of spirit: 'The outward water of baptism is nothing other than a sign of that inner, spiritual baptism which is the cleansing from all sins, which we must accept by faith and which the Spirit of God works within us as long as we live.'[14] He argued for the removal of all human traditions in baptism, such as exorcisms, salt and anointings with oil. The rite, shorn of such things, is described thus:

> Therefore after a short exhortation on what baptism is and what it means, we offer prayer together that Christ would baptize the child through his Spirit and purify him from all sin. Quite simply then, the children are baptized. The sponsors, together with the other brethren, are admonished to love these children as fellow members of the body of Christ and, as soon as possible, they should be brought to Christ through sound teaching. For such a service we have a basis in Scripture, but for these other things we do not.[15]

The result was a liturgy set forth in 1525, which went through four editions with minor changes until 1530.[16] The opening statement forbade the use of oil and blessing the water, and warned people not to rush with sick children to be baptized; on the other hand, it argued, baptism must not be neglected. After asking if the child is to be baptized, and its name, the minister then gives a short exhortation which carefully distinguished between the gift of faith 'which is bound neither by time nor place, youth nor age', and the temporal rite about to take place:

> Let us pray, therefore, that the Lord will baptize him with water and the Holy Spirit, so that the outward washing which he will perform through me may inwardly be fulfilled in deed and in truth by the Holy Spirit.[17]

The same teaching was put forward by Capito in the Catechism of 1527:

> Outward baptism signifies the baptism of Christ. Inward baptism is given in the Spirit and in fire, to purify consciences of their sins. It confers true righteousness. It concerns the soul and is spiritual. But Scripture generally uses images to describe that which it signifies; so, baptism of water signifies baptism of the Spirit.[18]

Rather like Bullinger's view, this seems to be 'symbolic parallelism'.

---

[14] Cited in ibid., p. 55.

[15] Cited in ibid., p. 56.

[16] Fisher, *Christian Initiation: The Reformation Period*, pp. 34–7; Hubert, *Die Strassburger Liturgischen*, pp. 37–43.

[17] Fisher, ibid., p. 36.

[18] Cited in René Bornert, *Le Reforme Protestante du Culte à Strasbourg au XVI siècle (1523–1598)*, E.J. Brill, Leiden, 1981, p. 343.

However, according to Peter Stephens and René Bornert, Bucer's sacramental thinking divides into two periods. From 1524 until 1530, there is this sharp dualism, but between 1530 and 1551 he began to rethink his theology of sacraments, and the inward and outward were brought into closer association.[19] Already in 1527 Bucer had started to use the term *exhibere/fürtragen*, which became for him a key term, and which as David Wright notes, can only mean 'confer', 'impart' and 'bestow'.[20] Bornert commented:

> The sacraments, he says, are not only external signs, but also instruments, channels, implements of the interior reality which they signify. They present (*praesentare, zustellen*), they offer (*offere, anbieten*), they give (*dare, reichen, darreichen, dargeben, schenken*), they communicate (*communicare, übergehen*) the spiritual gift which the faithful receive (*recipere, empfangen*) by faith.[21]

From the mid-1530s, Bucer was attributing to the rite of baptism what he had previously reserved for the baptism of Christ or in the Spirit. In the *Gospels* (1536), he wrote about

> ... the sacraments, which are as it were visible gospels, instituted by Christ the Lord, so that he may communicate his redemption to us through them. Thus it is quite clear that they are in a certain way instruments and channels of the Spirit and of his grace.[22]

In his *Brief Summary of the Christian Doctrine and Religion Taught at Strasbourg* (1548), he wrote:

> We confess and teach that holy baptism, when given and received according to the Lord's command, is in the case of adults and of young children truly a baptism of regeneration and renewal in the Holy Spirit, whereby those who are baptized have all their sins washed away, are buried into the death of our Lord Jesus Christ, are incorporated into him and put on him for the death of their sins, for a new and godly life and the blessed resurrection, and through him become children and heirs of God.[23]

A new order of baptism was issued for Strasbourg in 1537, and although it does not contain any of the technical sacramental language, it is more confident that the rite does impart something.[24] An opening prayer asks God to bestow the Holy Spirit

> ... and grant that by thy operation we, as thy ministers and ministers of the new covenant, may by this thy holy baptism truly impart to and bestow upon this child

---

[19] Peter Stephens, *The Holy Spirit in the Theology of Martin Bucer*, Cambridge University Press, Cambridge, 1970; Bornert, *Le Reforme Protestante*.

[20] David Wright, 'Infant Baptism and the Christian Community in Bucer', in David Wright (ed.), *Martin Bucer: Reforming Church and Community*, Cambridge University Press, Cambridge, 1994, p. 99.

[21] Bornert, *Le Reforme Protestante*, p. 317.

[22] 53.B.3, cited in Stephens, *The Holy Spirit*, p. 217.

[23] Cited in Wright, 'Infant Baptism', p. 98.

[24] Fisher, *Christian Initiation: The Reformation Period*, pp. 38ff; Hubert, *Die Strassburger Liturgischen*, pp. 44ff.

in thy name and according to thy command and promise the inner renewing of the Spirit and a true rebirth as thy child. [25]

A second prayer picks up the idea of circumcision and the promise to Abraham, and Jesus receiving the children, and mentions the grace given to us in baptism. A short exhortation before the Gospel reading asks that we 'recognize and perceive the work of the Lord in this holy sacrament'. A statement after the Gospel reading notes 'It is [the Lord's] baptism, we are only his ministers and instruments, through whom he will dispense the mystery.' After the Creed an exhortation to the godparents says, 'We all through my ministry which I shall perform here on behalf of the whole community of the church may incorporate him now in the Lord by holy baptism.' The child is undressed, and named, and water is poured on three times with the Matthean formula. A post-baptismal prayer thanks God for having granted the child new birth through holy baptism, and incorporated him/her into the body of Christ.

Although Bucer had tried to steer a moderate course between Luther and Zwingli, Lutherans regarded him as Reformed, and were suspicious of his sacramental theology and liturgical forms. In 1548 Bucer left for England, a casualty of the Interim. Under the leadership of Johann Marbach, Strasbourg would become a Lutheran stronghold with Lutheran forms.

The Rites of Basel, Bern and Neuchâtel

The Reformed baptismal rite for Basel, *Form des Tauffs*, was mainly the work of Oecolampadius and was published in 1526. Oecolampadius' sacramental views were akin to those of Zwingli, and his baptismal rite was partly inspired by the Zurich form and the 1525 Strasbourg form. It began by asking the name of the child, and continued with the *votum* from Psalm 121. There followed an exhortation explaining baptism and salvation, a prayer, and then the reading of the Gospel from Mark 10. A further explication came next, referring to the faith of Abraham and the covenant with God. The Lord's Prayer was recited, together with a prayer adapted from a Strasbourg rite of 1525. Then came a renunciation of Satan and a trinitarian confession of faith, and after the baptism the child was clothed in a white robe. The rite concluded with part of Psalm 116.

It was Zwingli who was responsible for organizing the Disputation at Berne in 1528, which won Berne for the Reformed cause. Present at the Disputation, in addition to Zwingli, were Oecolampadius from Basel and Bucer from Strasbourg. Two liturgies were issued for Berne within two consecutive years. In 1528 *Ein Kurtze gmeine form* was published, and was possibly the work of Kasper Megander who had come to Berne from Zurich. It had a similar title to the Zurich liturgy, and the baptismal rite was identical to that of the 1525 Zurich rite, with the exception that the Berne rite had

---

[25] Fisher, ibid., pp. 38–9.

a brief exhortation after the Gospel, and included the Lord's Prayer and the *Ave Maria*.

In 1529 a second Berne liturgy appeared, *Ordnung und satzung*. The baptismal rite departed considerably from that of 1528. It began with a statement regarding the fact that oil, salt and consecrated water are no longer to be used, and warned that grace is not dependent upon baptism in water. This language appears to rely upon the statement found in the Strasbourg rite. In the liturgy itself, the opening *votum* is retained. There is a request as to whether baptism is being sought, and then a brief explication explaining that God is asked to give the child faith so that the exterior baptism will be inwardly effectual by the Holy Spirit. The Lord's Prayer followed, and the Creed. Then came the following prayer:

> Almighty God, heavenly Father, who has promised to be our God and the God of our children, no less than the God of Abraham and of his kin: we beseech earnestly that you may grant your Holy Spirit to this infant, and take him up into the covenant of your mercy, according to the immutable principle of your choice, that he may in his time, and according to your will, know you as his God, and honour, live and die for you, so that this our baptism and the acceptance of the child into your community, according to your will, shall not be in vain, but that the child shall be baptized through the death of your son to a new life which pleases you, in the name of the same, your Son, our Saviour Jesus Christ. Amen.

The gospel reading could be from either Matthew 19, Mark 10, or Luke 8. There follows a brief admonition, a charge to the parents, a second request that baptism is sought, together with the name, the baptism with formula, and dismissal.

After the Berne Disputation, Guillaume Farel (1489–1565) was charged with making the German texts available to the French-speaking areas around Berne. If these were published, they have not survived. But Farel did publish his liturgy for Neuchâtel, *La Maniere et fasson*, in 1533. Although Elfriede Jacobs has argued that Farel's sacramental theology is a genuine Farelian position in its own right, Farel tended towards the Zwinglian and early Bucerian view on sacraments.[26] Farel prefaced his rite with a Declaration, which is a doctrinal statement. In this he denied that grace is bestowed through the outward ceremony, noting that good and bad receive the outward rite, as did Simon Magus and Paul. He drew a sharp distinction between the outward ceremony and the inward baptism of grace by the Holy Spirit. This latter is not bound by time, place or ceremony. The outward ceremony is entry into the Church, and it is hoped that at some stage the candidate will receive the baptism of the Spirit. This sharp separation certainly reflects Zwingli's firm division between the spiritual and the physical.

The actual rite begins with the *votum*, followed by a first request that baptism is sought, and then an admonition from the Berne rite of 1529, with the Lord's Prayer. After this comes the prayer from the Berne rite, quoted above, with reference to

---

[26] Elfriede Jacobs, *Die Sakramentslehre Wilhelm Farels*, Theologischer Verlag, Zurich, 1978.

Abraham and his kin. The Gospel reading followed, from Matthew 19, and then the Berne 1529 admonition. There is a second query concerning baptism being sought, an explication and the Ten Commandments, and the Creed, together with a recitation of the duties of the Christian life. The parents are asked, 'Do you promise?' There followed a further admonition, a third request that baptism is being sought, the name of the child, and the baptism. After this a rubric directs that pure and neat water shall be placed on the head with the hand with the following formula:

> Our Lord God by his grace and goodness make this child, who was made and formed in his image and likeness, to be a true member of Jesus Christ his son, bearing fruit worthy as a child of God. Amen.

The rite ended with the dismissal from the Berne rite, with a command to guard the child well.

John Calvin and Geneva

Calvin was a French scholar, who fled France and for a while took refuge in Basel. It was there that he completed the first edition of the *Institute* (1536). He passed through Geneva in 1536, and Guilliame Farel, who by now was a pastor in Geneva, persuaded Calvin – with threats of God's punishment – to stay and assist. Both Farel and Calvin were expelled in 1538, and Calvin became pastor to the French-speaking congregation in Strasbourg. He returned to Geneva in 1541. He compiled a liturgy for use at Strasbourg in 1540, and revised it slightly for use in Geneva in 1542.

In his *Institute* of 1536, Calvin gave the following definition of sacraments:

> On the nature of sacraments, it is very important for us that some definite doctrine be taught, to learn from it both the purpose for which they were instituted and their present use. First, what is a sacrament? An outward sign by which the Lord represents and attests to us his good will toward us to sustain the weakness of our faith. Another definition: a testimony of God's grace, declared to us by an outward sign. From this we also understand a sacrament never lacks a preceding promise but is rather joined to it by way of appendix, to confirm and seal the promise itself, and to make it as it were more evident to us.[27]

This seems to take over Luther's idea of promise, and to downplay Zwingli's definition. Indeed, throughout this edition of the *Institute*, the Zurich doctrine is held at arm's length. Calvin launched an attack on those who believe that faith, once given, is complete, arguing that God teaches us through his Word, confirms it by the sacraments, and illuminates our minds by the Holy Spirit. He also attacked those who 'dared to write that baptism is nothing but a token and mark by which we confess our religion before men, as soldiers bear the insignia of their commander as a mark

---

[27] Calvin, *Institutes of the Christian Religion, 1536 Edition*, trans. Ford Lewis Battles, Eerdmans, Grand Rapids, MI, 1975, p. 87.

of their profession'. Although Willem Balke interpreted this as rejection of the anabaptist position, it seems more likely to be rejecting the more extreme remarks of Zwingli.[28]

The influence of Farel in Geneva may account for the fact that Calvin's writings between 1537 and 1539 show an increased tendency to distinguish between the outward and the inward. The 1539 *Institute* added a very lengthy discussion on circumcision, baptism and infant baptism. Gone is any reference to Luther's idea of child faith. Instead we have an approach similar to Zwingli's, justifying infant baptism on analogy with circumcision. Calvin notes that, although circumcision and baptism are two different signs, the promise of each is the same, namely God's fatherly favour, forgiveness of sins, and eternal life. Children share the covenant and the sign and eternal life. Infants receiving the sign of regeneration and renewal, if they depart from the world before coming of age of knowledge, are regenerated and renewed by God's Spirit, according to his hidden and unknown way. Calvin wrote in his 1540 *Commentary on Romans*, commenting on Romans 2:25:

> The Jews thought that circumcision was of itself sufficient for the purpose of obtaining righteousness ... Circumcision, therefore, requires perfection. The same may also be said of our baptism. If anyone puts his trust in the water of baptism alone, and thinks he is justified, as though he had obtained holiness from the ordinance itself, we must adduce in objection to this the end of baptism, which is that the Lord thereby calls us to holiness of life. The grace and promise, which baptism testifies and seals to us, would not in this case be mentioned, because we have to deal with those who are content with the empty shadow of baptism, and neither regard nor consider what is of real importance in it.[29]

Once in Strasbourg, however, it seems that Calvin came under Bucer's influence, and adopted or extended Bucer's terminology of instrument and exhibit. In the 1559 *Institute* he explained:

> God uses the means and instruments which he sees to be expedient, in order that all things may be subservient to his glory, he being the Lord and disposer of all. Therefore, as by bread and other aliment he feeds our bodies, as by the sun he illumines, and by fire gives warmth to the world, and yet bread, sun, and fire are nothing, save inasmuch as they are instruments under which he dispenses his blessings to us; so in like manner he spiritually nourishes our faith by means of the sacraments, whose only office is to make his promises visible to our eye, or rather, to be pledges of his promises.[30]

The sacraments are instruments through which God works as he pleases and through which he gives us the reality he promises. Christopher Elwood summarizes Calvin's view thus:

---

[28] Willem Balke, *Calvin and the Anabaptists*, trans. William J. Heynen, Eerdmans, Grand Rapids, MI, 1981, p. 54.

[29] Ross Mackenzie, *The Epistles of Paul the Apostle to the Romans and to the Thessalonians*, Oliver and Boyd, Edinburgh, 1961, p. 55.

[30] Calvin, *Institute*, 4.14.12.

In the notion that the sacraments are instruments of God's grace we have the real hallmark of the Calvinist doctrine. Calvin invokes instrumentality as a way of distinguishing sacramental signs from the communicative power that proceeds from and is the exclusive prerogative of God. The signs are efficacious not because of an inherent capacity but in the sense that they are instruments God has chosen to attest to the genuine operation of the Spirit's power to unite believers with the body of Christ.[31]

For Calvin, what is promised is also offered or exhibited. Writing specifically on baptism, in the *Genevan Catechism* (1541), he taught that baptism is the entrance into the Church. It consists in the forgiveness of sins, and it figures 'spiritual regeneration', though it is by the blood of Christ, not the water itself, that this is accomplished. The *Catechism* holds together the objectivity of the sacrament and personal faith:

> Master: But do you attribute nothing more to the water than that it is a figure of ablution?
>
> Scholar: I understand it to be a figure, but still so that the reality is annexed to it; for God does not disappoint us when he promises us his gifts. Accordingly, it is certain that both pardon of sins and newness of life are offered to us in baptism, and received by us.
>
> Master: Is this grace bestowed on all indiscriminately?
>
> Scholar: Many precluding its entrance by their depravity, make it void to themselves. Hence the benefit extends to believers only, and yet the sacrament loses nothing of its nature.[32]

And,

> Master: How are these blessings bestowed upon us by baptism?
>
> Scholar: If we do not render the promises there offered unfruitful by rejecting them, we are clothed with Christ, and presented with his Spirit.

Although for his Morning Service and Communion rite, Calvin drew heavily on Martin Bucer's Strasbourg rite of 1539, in a letter of 1564 Calvin suggested that he had himself authored the baptismal rite:

> I was constrained also to make the formula of baptism, whilst at Strasbourg, and when infants of Anabaptists were brought to me from five and ten leagues round about to baptize them. I made then this rough formula, but the fact remains I advise you not to change it.[33]

However, this 'rough formula' was certainly not Calvin's own *creatio ex nihilo*, but was based firmly on Farel's 1533 rite for Neuchâtel, and behind that, the 1529 rites of Berne, those of Basel and Zurich, and earlier rites of Strasbourg. Calvin's only

---

[31] Christopher Elwood, *The Body Broken. The Calvinist Doctrine of the Eucharist and the Symbolism of Power in Sixteenth-Century France*, Oxford University Press, Oxford, 1999, p. 71.

[32] Jean Calvin, *Tracts and Treatises on the Doctrine and Worship of the Church,* trans. H. Beveridge, reprinted, ed. T.F. Torrance, Oliver and Boyd, Edinburgh and London, 1958, Vol. 2, pp. 85–9.

[33] 'Discourse d'adieux aux ministres', 28 April 1564, in *Corpus Reformatorum* ix, 894.

contribution seems to have been in shortening some of Farel's prayer material, and replacing Farel's explications with his own.[34]

His 1540 Strasbourg rite may be tabulated as follows:

- The *votum*, 'Our Help is in the Name of the Lord, who made heaven and earth' (cf. Farel, Berne, Zurich)
- Request for baptism (cf. Farel)
- An explication (Calvin replaced Farel's)
- Prayer and Lord's Prayer (cf. Farel, Berne)
- Second request concerning baptism (cf. Farel)
- Admonition with paraphrase of Creed, Ten Commandments, and call to live the Gospel life, put as a promise with response, 'yes'
- Matthew 19 (cf. Farel and Berne)
- Third request concerning baptism, and request for name (cf. Farel)
- Baptism with triune formula and rubric (cf. Farel)
- Dismissal: possible laying on of hands? (cf. Farel)

Calvin replaced a much longer explication on baptism which Farel had written. Farel had tended to explain what baptism did not do. Calvin presented a more positive theology: we must be born again; when we have been shown our wretched state, God promises that he will regenerate us by the Holy Spirit into a new life; we renounce ourselves, and obey his will as shown in his Holy Word, and he will direct us by the Spirit. The explication taught that the fulfilment is in Jesus Christ, whose death and passion has such power and efficacy. He remits our sins, and graces are conferred on us, and we are incorporated into the Church. For this God has appointed the sign of water. Our sins are washed in his blood. Infants belong to the covenant, and are therefore baptized. The reading from Matthew 19 is used as a Gospel mandate.

After this explication comes the first prayer. This prayer is found in a longer form in the 1529 Berne rite in German, and then appears in French translation in Farel's rite of 1533. In the latter two versions, there is a reference to the God of Abraham and his kin, to link in with the concept of covenant, with baptism replacing circumcision. The thrust of that prayer is that God is asked to grant the Holy Spirit to the infant and take him/her into the covenant, and that by making the child a member of the community through this baptism, God will later make him/her be baptized through the death of Jesus so the Church rite will not have been in vain. This is an interesting distinction between two baptisms, God's and the Church's. Calvin changed the prayer. He omitted reference to Abraham, and asked God to confirm the grace of the promise to be our God in this infant. God is asked to give protection, and to remit original sin, and then afterwards to sanctify him/her with the Holy Spirit. Petition is made that when the infant comes of age he/she may obtain remission of sins, and God is asked

---

[34] See further Bryan D. Spinks, 'Calvin's Baptismal Theology and the Making of the Strasbourg and Genevan Baptismal Liturgies 1540 and 1542', *Scottish Journal of Theology* 48 (1995), 55–78.

to incorporate the infant into the fellowship of the Church. The prayer has a much more positive focus than in its Berne and Neuchâtel original, where there is a hesitation about the rite achieving anything.

The Lord's Prayer, and Creed followed, with instructions that the infant must be taught these. Then came promises about instruction in doctrine and way of life, and the paraphrase of the commandments. The act of baptism followed and, as in Farel's rite and that of Berne, Calvin's Strasbourg rite had a formula, which perhaps included laying-on of hands.[35] The final rubric asserted:

> We know that elsewhere many other ceremonies are used, which we do not deny to have been very ancient; but because they have been invented at will, or at least for some slight consideration, whatever it may be, since they have not been founded upon the word of God, and furthermore seeing that so many superstitions have arisen out of them, we have no hesitation in abolishing them.

In the 1542 Genevan rite the Creed was restored in full, but the second and third requests for baptism disappeared, together with the Gospel (which was already paraphrased in the Gospel explication), and the dismissal (and hand-laying, if it had accompanied the formula).

John Knox: Geneva and Scotland

During the Catholic reign of Mary Tudor, a number of English exiles came to reside in Frankfurt. Desiring a liturgy more Reformed than the English *Book of Common Prayer* of 1552, John Knox, William Whittingham, Anthony Gilby, William Cole and John Foxe drew up a rite, based on Calvin's Strasbourg rite. But when more English exiles arrived, a majority wished for a version of the 1552 *Book of Common Prayer*. Knox, Whittingham, Cole and Gilby with their supporters left Frankfurt and settled in Geneva, and there printed their liturgy, the *Genevan Form of Prayers*, subsequently styled 'Knox's liturgy'.[36] On his return to Scotland in 1559, Knox took this rite with him, and it was formally adopted by the Church of Scotland in 1562.

In 1556 Knox had attacked the 'popish' view of baptism as 'an adulteration and profanation', and he considered that parents in offering their children for Catholic baptism were offering them to the devil. However, he was against re-baptism, 'for the spirit of regeneration, which is freely given to us by Christ Jesus our all-sufficiency, hath purged us from that poison which we drank in the days of our blindness'.[37] Knox added:

> We have some respect also, that no more be given to the external sign, than is proper to it, that is, that it be the seal of justice and the sign of regeneration, but

---

[35] Old, *The Shaping of the Reformed Baptismal Rite*, p. 164.

[36] Text in Fisher, *Christian Initiation: The Reformation Period*, pp. 119–23.

[37] 'Answer to some Questions concerning Baptism', in John Knox, *Works*, David Laing (ed.), Edinburgh, 1855, Vol. IV, pp. 119–22, quoted by Fisher, ibid., p. 118.

neither the cause, neither yet the effect and virtue. The seal once received is durable, and needeth not to be iterate, lest that iteration and multiplication of the sign, the office of the Holy Spirit, which is to illuminate, regenerate, and to purge, be attributed unto it ... [38]

Here Knox seems to have sharply divided the outward from the inward, in a way reminiscent of Bullinger. The *Scots Confession* of 1560, drawn up by John Knox, John Willock, John Winram, John Spottiswoode, John Row and John Douglas, taught the following:

> And this we utterlie damne the vanitie of thay that affirme Sacramentes to be nathing ellis bot naked and baire signes. No, wee assuredlie beleeve that be Baptisme we ar ingrafted in *Christ Jesus*, to be made partakers of his justice, be quhilk our sinnes ar covered and remitted.[39]

Although the baptismal rite of the *Genevan Form of Prayers* is based directly on Calvin, the language echoes in places the *Book of Common Prayer* of 1552, and the compilers made the wording of the explication and the prayers their own English Reformed rite.[40]

The rite was prefaced by a rubric prohibiting private baptism and women (midwives) from baptizing. The minister enquires: 'Do you present this child to be baptized, earnestly desiring that he may be ingrafted in the mystical body of Jesus Christ?' The explication/exhortation which follows picks up on Calvin's final prayer, but grounds baptism in the Reformed defence of infant baptism – that in the Old Testament circumcision was a sacrament, and in the New Testament it is baptism:

> ... our infants appertain to him by covenant and therefore ought not to be defrauded of those holy signs and badges whereby his children are known from infidels and pagans. Neither is it requisite that all those that receive this sacrament have the use of understanding and faith, but chiefly that they be contained under the name of God's people: so that the remission of sins in the blood of Christ Jesus doth appertain to them by God's promise.

Further support is gained from St Paul and Jesus' command. Water is commanded to be used outwardly, but inwardly it is the blood of Christ that purges our souls from our 'infection', 'whose venomous dregs, although they continue in this our flesh, yet by the merits of his death are not imputed unto us, because the justice of Jesus Christ is made ours by baptism'.

The explication makes clear that there is no virtue or power in the water, but rather that it is the Holy Spirit who works inwardly in the hearts of the elect. God will guide us through the journey of life which is 'encumbered with many enemies'. Because of this the godparents must provide guidance and instruction.

---

[38] Ibid. in Fisher, ibid., p. 119.

[39] Schaff, *Creeds of Christendom*, Vol. 3, pp. 467–8.

[40] G.J. Cuming, 'John Knox and the Book of Common Prayer: a short note', *Liturgical Review* 10 (1980), 80–81.

After the explication, the father or godfather says the Creed, and this is followed by an adaptation of Calvin's prayer, itself adapted from Farel, and then the Lord's Prayer. The baptism with traditional trinitarian formula follows; the minister takes 'water in his hand and layeth it upon the child's forehead'. Then, unlike Calvin's liturgy, the rite concludes with a thanksgiving for the benefits which God gives, and asks that the candidates do not fall and 'lose the force of baptism'. The rite was administered during the Morning Service.

Zacharias Ursinus, the Heidelberg Catechism and the 1563 Palatine Liturgy

Zacharias Ursinus and Caspar Olevianus were the architects of the German Reformed tradition. Ursinus was regarded by the Lutherans as a crypto-Calvinist. In 1560 he moved to Zurich, and in 1561 received a call to Heidelberg. In addition to being a chief author of the *Catechism*, Ursinus also wrote an exposition or explication of its propositions. The Heidelberg theologians are also credited with drawing out and making more systematic the concept of the covenant of grace. Zwingli had used the concept of covenant to defend infant baptism, and this was taken up by Calvin, who spoke in his liturgy of the covenant of salvation (*l'alliance de salut*). The Heidelberg theologians developed a distinction between the covenant of works which God made with Adam, and the covenant of grace which he made through the work of Christ.[41]

The *Catechism* defined sacraments as 'visible, holy signs and seals appointed by God'.[42] Baptism was treated under questions 69 to 74. Question 69 asked: 'How is it signified and sealed unto thee in holy baptism that thou hast part in the one sacrifice of Christ on the cross?'

The answer given was that Christ had appointed an external washing with water to which he added a promise that those baptized are washed by his blood from all sin. To be so washed is to have remission of sins, to be renewed by the Holy Spirit, and be sanctified as members of Christ (Q. 70). It is also called 'the washing of regeneration' (Q. 71). Infants are baptized 'as a sign of the covenant, to be ingrafted into the Christian Church, and distinguished from the children of unbelievers, as was done in the Old Testament by Circumcision, in place of which in the New Testament Baptism is appointed' (Q. 74).

In his discussion of the *Catechism*, Ursinus states the ends of baptism as 'a sealing of the promise of grace, that is, of our justification and regeneration, and a declaration of the will of God, to this effect, that he here grants these gifts to those who are

---

[41] See D.A. Weir, *The Origins of the Federal Theology in Sixteenth-Century Reformation Thought*, Clarendon Press, Oxford, 1990; Lyle D. Bierma, *German Calvinism in the Confessional Age. The Covenant Theology of Caspar Olevianus*, Baker Books, Grand Rapids, MI, 1996.

[42] Text in Schaff, *The Creeds of Christendom*, Vol. 3, pp. 328ff.

baptized, and that he will for ever grant them'. [43] Like circumcision, baptism is never to be performed more than once. Regeneration and salvation do not depend on baptism, but are signified and sealed by the external, which is always joined with it in its 'proper use'.[44] As the minister 'applies the sign outwardly, so God by virtue of his applies inwardly the thing signified to all those who receive the sign with true faith'.[45] Furthermore,

> ... in the proper use of the sacraments the exhibition and reception of the signs, and things signified, are inseparably connected. And hence the Holy Ghost interchanges the terms, attributing what belongs to the thing signified to the sign, and what belongs to the sign to the thing, to teach us what he gives, and to assure us that he does really give it.[46]

This is forcefully summarized in a series of 'Theses concerning Baptism':

> 3. Baptism has the power to declare or seal according to the command of God, and the promise which Christ has joined to it in its lawful use; for Christ baptizes us by the hand of his ministers, just as he speaks through them.

> 4. There is, therefore, in baptism a double water; the one external and visible, which is elementary; the other internal, invisible and heavenly, which is the blood and spirit of Christ. There is, also, a double washing in baptism; the one external, visible, and signifying, viz: the sprinkling and pouring of water, which is perceptible by the members and senses of the body; the other is internal, invisible, and signified, viz: the remission of sins on account of the blood of Christ shed for us, and our regeneration by the Holy Spirit and engrafting into his body, which is spiritual, and perceived only by faith and the Spirit. Lastly, there is a double dispenser of baptism: the one an external dispenser of the external, which is the minister of the church, baptizing us by his hand with water; the other an internal dispenser of the internal, which is Christ himself, baptizing us with his blood and Spirit.[47]

In defence of infant baptism, Ursinus cites the baptism of households in the New Testament. He notes that, although Christ does not expressly command the baptism of infants, 'He commands that all who are included in the covenant and church of God should be baptized, of whatever age, sex, or rank they may be.'[48] He draws on the by-now common Reformed argument by comparing baptism of children to circumcision of infants.

The rite of baptism in the Palatinate liturgy of 1563 was prefaced by a theological rationale and rubrical/canonical instructions.[49] Children of believers are in the

---

[43] G.W.Williard, *The Commentary of Dr. Zacherias Ursinus on the Heidelberg Catechism*, Eerdmans, Grand Rapids, MI, 1954, p. 358.

[44] Ibid., p. 361.

[45] Ibid., p. 365.

[46] Ibid.

[47] Ibid., p. 372.

[48] Ibid., p. 368.

[49] German text in *Kirchen-Formularien der Evangelische-Reformirten Gemeinen*, Germantaun, 1798; English translation in J.H.A. Bomberger, 'The Old Palatinate Liturgy of 1563', *Mercersburg Review* 2 (1850), 277–83.

covenant and so may be partakers of baptism; administration of baptism is reserved to preachers of the Word; the sacrament shall be administered in the Church after the sermon on Sundays, or holy days, or a public weekday service; the father or friend must request baptism and list the sponsors, and the father must attend the baptism (and in the case of illegitmate children, the mother's name will be entered, and the authorities informed so that suitable Christian discipline may be exercised).

The rite follows the pattern already found in Zurich, Neuchâtel, Geneva and Scotland. It opens with the *votum* from Psalm 121:2, followed by an explication. It has a lengthy trinitarian section on the triune name, setting forth salvation wrought by Christ. This is followed by the 'obligations' of baptism as response to the salvific work of God, noting that there are two parties to a covenant (*Bunde*). By his grace we should confess his name, and forsake sin. It made explicit reference to the covenant made with Abraham, and taught:

> Now our Lord Jesus Christ came into the world, not to diminish the grace of God, but rather to extend the covenant of grace (*Gnadenbund*) in which the people of Israel were previously included over the whole earth, and hath appointed Baptism in the place of circumcision, as a sign and a seal of this covenant unto us and our children.

The explication concludes:

> From all this it is evident, that our children are also included in the kingdom and covenant of God, and should therefore receive Baptism, as a seal of the covenant, although they may not understand its holy mysteries; even as those infants were blessed by Jesus Christ, in word and deed, and in the Jewish Church children were circumcised on the eighth day; although neither the one nor the other was understood by them.

There then followed a version of the *sindflutgebet* of Luther, perhaps witnessing to the wide influence of this prayer, as well as Ursinus' earlier Lutheranism. The Lord's Prayer followed, and then the Apostles' Creed. A single question is addressed to the sponsors, and a rubric indicates that the head only was sprinkled with water with the triune formula. Then comes a Thanksgiving, in which Christ's threefold ministry of Prophet, Priest and King is mentioned. An address to the sponsors followed, and finally came the Aaronic blessing. This rite, with little change, was preserved through to the nineteenth century, and was used by the German Reformed Church in the USA.

The Dutch Rite: From Jan Laski to Petrus Datheen

The earliest Dutch Reformed liturgy is Marten Micron's translation or Dutch version of Jan Laski's (John à Lasco) *Forma ac Ratio*. The English Edwardian Church placed the 'Stranger' (that is, Reformed foreign congregations in England) under the Superintendency of the Polish-born Laski; these included Dutch, French, Flemish and Italian congregations. Although some of the French congregations outside London used a version of Calvin's Strasbourg liturgy published by Valerand Poullain,[50] those in London used the rites drawn up by Laski. The Latin forms were not published until 1556, after Laski had left England, but the Dutch, French and Italian versions seem to confirm the claim of the *Forma ac Ratio*, that it was drawn up in 1550, even though the details and texts were still evolving.[51] Prior to coming to London, Laski had been Superintendent of the Church in East Friesland, which, although seemingly Lutheran, was in fact Reformed in its theology. It seems that the *Forma ac Ratio* was partly inspired by the rites of East Friesland.[52]

Laski's sacramental theology seems to place him nearer to Bullinger and Farel than to Calvin. In his *Epitome Doctrinae Ecclesiarum Phrisiae Orientalis* of 1544, and *Brevis et Dulucida de sacramentis Ecclesiae Christi Tractatio* of 1552, he stressed that sacraments are seals, and they attested to something already established. They do not give grace. Baptism attests our justification and the divine goodwill towards us.

The *Forma ac Ratio* provides that baptism takes place at the end of the Morning Service, before the final psalm.[53] An admonition on the administration of baptism gave a theological defence of infant baptism. A prayer for the candidates followed, and then three questions were put to the sponsors. After this came the baptism with the triune formula, and then a prayer giving thanks that 'us and our seed' have been freed from death to eternal life. A short exhortation, psalm, blessing, and commendation of the poor concluded the rite.

Although Micron had put this rite, or a version of it, into Dutch, this liturgy was not to be the one finally adopted for the Netherlands Church.[54] In 1566 Petrus Datheen published *Ceremonien ende Ghebeden*, together with a catechism, both of which were translated from the Palatinate liturgy and the Heidelberg Catechism. This rite began with the *votum*, followed by an explication giving three principal parts of baptism. Then came the Palatinate *sindflutgebet*, slightly modified, a three-fold question to the sponsors (expanding the Palatinate version), the baptism, and then the Palatinate thanksgiving prayer. Datheen deleted the Lord's Prayer and the Creed. It would seem that for a few years Micron's rite and Datheen's rite may have been in use together in different areas. However, Datheen's rite was to replace Micron's. Datheen's form continued to be modified until the adoption of its final form as *The Netherlands Liturgy* at the Synod of Dordt in 1619. The main

---

[50] A.C. Honders, *Valerandus Pollanus. Liturgica Sacra (1551–1555)*, E.J. Brill, Leiden, 1970.

[51] See Bryan D. Spinks, *From the Lord and 'The Best Reformed Churches'*, CLV, Rome, 1984. See also the discussion in Andrew Pettigree, *Foreign Protestant Communities in Sixteenth-Century London*, Clarendon Press, Oxford, 1986; Dirk W. Rodgers, *John à Lasco in England*, Peter Lang, New York, 1994.

[52] A. Sprengler-Ruppenthal, *Mysterium und Riten nach der Londoner Kirchordnung der Niederländer*, Böhlau Verlag, Köln, 1967. For baptism, see pp. 19–58.

[53] Text in A. Kuyper, *Joannis a Lasco Opera*, 2 vols, F. Muller, Amsterdam, 1866, 2, pp. 107–14.

[54] W.F. Dankbaar and Marten Micron, *De Christlicke Ordinancien der Nederlantscher Ghemeinten Te Londen (1554)*, Martinus Nijhoff, s-Gravenhage, 1956, pp. 73–9.

modifications were to the opening explication, which was shortened, and the exhortation, which was expanded.[55]

What do these Reformed rites have in common, in addition to their liturgical antecedents in Zurich, Berne, Neuchâtel and Strasbourg? One feature throughout is theology by explication rather than through the liturgical text and actions. The theological self-consciousness found in medieval scholastic theology finds its early modern Protestant counterpart in these rites. The rite must be prefaced by the theology as teaching.

The second common factor is the concern to defend infant baptism by extending the link with circumcision and the covenant. Against Anabaptist movements, infant baptism is defended on the grounds that children of the New Covenant are not less privileged than those of the Old Covenant, and so on the grounds that the parents are in the covenant, infants qualify. As a result, the parents – usually the father – were given the main role in the rite, and sponsors become a mere adornment.

Reformed Orthodoxy and Baptism

By the end of the sixteenth century and through into the seventeenth, Reformed theology, like Lutheran theology, entered a period of scholasticism, or orthodoxy, when belief was codified. Richard Muller gives a list of Reformed divines who qualify, and these range from Theodore Beza, who worked alongside Calvin in Geneva, to Thomas Ridgley in England who died in 1734.[56] What marked out these codifiers was their acceptance and use of Aristotelian terminology, which Luther and Calvin consciously tried to avoid, albeit not with total success, and their tendency to summarize theology in a series of propositions.

William Ames (1576–1633) was an English Cambridge theologian, and an habitual Nonconformist. He eventually fled England for the University of Franekar, where he published his work *The Marrow of Sacred Divinity* in 1623. His system of theology could be summarized in chart form in accordance with Ramist methodology.[57] Ames defined a sacrament as a sign, and held that a sign serves three functions: it informs (*notificans*), it reminds (*commonefaciens*) and it seals (*obsignans*). A sacrament does not include the spiritual thing it refers to, but it does seal the whole covenant of grace to believers.

---

[55] See Daniel James Meeter, *'Bless the Lord, O my Soul'. The New-York Liturgy of the Dutch Reformed Church*, 1767, Scarecrow Press, Lanham, MD, 1998 for details of the development.

[56] Richard Muller, *Post-Reformation Dogmatics. Vol.1. Prolegomena to Theology*, Baker Book House, Grand Rapids, MI, 1987, pp. 13–52.

[57] William Ames, *The Marrow of Theology*, English translation John Dykstra Eusden, Baker Books, Grand Rapids, MI, 1997. For a discussion of Ramist method, see Bryan D. Spinks, *Two Faces of Elizabethan Anglican Theology. Sacraments and Salvation in the Theology of William Perkins and Richard Hooker*, Scarecrow Press, Lanham, MD, 1999, pp. 35–7.

At this point in his work, Ames turned to discuss ecclesiastical discipline and the administration of the covenant of grace, returning later to discuss more briefly baptism and the Lord's Supper. Ames defined baptism as the sacrament of initiation or regeneration.[58] It confirms our ingrafting into Christ, and stands for the remission of sins and for adoption, in that we are consecrated by it to the Father, Son and Holy Spirit, whose names are pronounced over the baptized. It should be administered to all those who are in the covenant of grace – and here we see that what Ames means by baptism as a 'seal'; being in the covenant of grace is prior to baptism. The sign is water, chosen because nothing in common use more fitly represents the spiritual washing in Christ's blood. Ames defended infant baptism thus:

> The infants of believers are not to be forbidden this sacrament. First, because, if they are partakers of any grace, it is by virtue of the covenant of grace and so both the covenant and the first seal of the covenant belong to them. Second, the covenant in which the faithful are now included is clearly the same as the covenant made with Abraham, Rom.4:11; Gal.3.7–9 – and this expressly applied to infants. Third, the covenant as now administered to believers brings greater and fuller consolation than it once could, before the coming of Christ. But if it pertained only to them and not to their infants, the grace of God and their consolation would be narrower and more contracted after Christ's appearing then before. Fourth, baptism supplants circumcision, Col.2:11, 12; it belongs as much to the children of believers as circumcision once did. Fifth, in the very beginning of regeneration, whereof baptism is a seal, man is merely passive. Therefore, no outward action is required of a man when he is baptized or circumcised (unlike other sacraments); but only a passive receiving. Infants are, therefore, as capable of participation in this sacrament, so far as its chief benefit is concerned, as adults.[59]

Johannes Wollebius (1586–1629) studied at Basel, and was later Old Testament professor there. He set out his theological system in *Compendium Theologiae Christianae* (1626). Chapter XXII was entitled 'The Seal or Sacraments of the Covenant of Grace in General', suggesting a preference for the term 'Seal'. He defined a sacrament as 'a divinely instituted act of worship, in which the grace promised by God to the people of the covenant is sealed by visible signs, and the people of the covenant are at the same time bound to obedience to him'.[60]

Formerly, noted Wollerbius, the term 'sacrament' was used for a soldier's oath. It is also called a mystery, because it signifies something hidden and supernatural set forth in signs or types. Although applied to the entire act, sign and signified, by synecdoche it is applied simply to the thing signified. The principal efficient cause is the entire Holy Trinity. The agents are legitimately called ministers. The means by which a sacrament is performed is the word of institution. The latter does not effect any change in substance or quality, but only use.[61]

---

[58] Ames, *Marrow of Theology*, pp. 210ff.

[59] Ibid., p. 211.

[60] In John W. Beardslee III (ed. and trans.), *Reformed Dogmatics: J. Wollebius, G. Voetius [and] F. Turretun*, Oxford University Press, New York, 1965, p. 120.

[61] Ibid., pp. 120–21.

When Wollebius turns specifically to baptism, he discusses its meaning as both immersion and sprinkling. He identifies four types of baptism: in water, in teaching, with fire, and in blood, or martyrdom. The principal efficient cause of baptism is Christ, and the instrumental cause is the minister; lay baptism is regarded as invalid. Sprinkling is used because of the cold climate, and the sprinkling may be once or three times. The words are the triune formula. The purpose of baptism is to confirm being ingrafted into the Church; the subject of baptism is all the people of the covenant. Children of believers may be baptized, but not those of unbelievers. Amongst his conclusions, Wollebius stated:

> Baptism is not necessary in the absolute sense, but because of the commandment of Christ; nor is it to be understood as necessary in the sense that children baptized by one other than a minister, or dying without baptism, are excluded from the number of the blessed.[62]

Francis Turretin (1623–87) studied at Geneva, Leiden, Utrecht, Paris, Samur, Montauban and Nîmes, becoming professor of theology in Geneva in 1653. His background gave him a wide spectrum of international Reformed theology, the fruits of which were set forth in his *Institutes of Elenctic Theology* (1679–85). The section on sacraments was the nineteenth topic extended over thirty-one questions.

A great deal of attention was given to the definition of the word 'sacrament', tracing it to the word 'mysterion', but defining its 'matter' as a sign and a thing signified, which has a form (the relation of the sign to the thing signified), and an efficient (God). A sacrament also has an end, or principal purpose, which is 'the confirmation of the covenant of grace and the sealing on the part of God of our union with Christ (promised in the covenant) and of all his benefits; and on our part the testification of our deep gratitude to God and of love towards our neighbor'.[63]

In Turretin we see the Protestant emulation of the medieval scholastic theology, with generic definitions. The discussion of baptism commences at the eleventh question.[64] It is the sacrament of regeneration, and the meaning of the word 'baptism' is given thorough discussion. The author of this sacrament is God; the external matter is twofold – the element of water and the ceremony of administering it. Turretin defended the use of sprinkling. The internal matter or thing signified is Christ with his benefits. Just as water washes the body, so the blood of Christ cleanses us. The subjects of baptism are all the covenanted, and the end is to aid our faith and to aid our confession amongst men. As to the necessity, Turretin stated:

> Our opinion, however, is that baptism is indeed necessary according to the divine institution as an external means of salvation (by which God is efficacious in its legitimate use), so that he who despises it is guilty of a heinous crime and incurs eternal punishment. But we believe it is not so absolutely necessary that he who

---

[62] Ibid., p. 131.

[63] Francis Turretin, *Institutes of Elenctic Theology*, English translation George Giger, James T. Dennison (ed.), 3 vols, Presbyterian and Reformed Publishing Company, Phillipsburg, NJ, 1997, Vol. 3, pp. 341–2.

[64] Ibid., pp. 377–420.

is deprived of it by no fault of his own is to be forthwith excluded from the kingdom of heaven and that salvation cannot be obtained without it.[65]

Lay-administered baptism was considered null and void. The formula is that of Matthew 28:19, though he saw both the Western and Eastern forms as valid. Infants are baptized because they are in the covenant.

A particular expression of this Reformed Orthodoxy was the English *Westminster Confession and Catechisms* (1647), together with their liturgical counterpart, *A Directory for the Public Worship of God* (1644). These documents date from the English Civil War, when Parliament abolished the Church of England as an episcopal church, and the national church operated on a loose presbyterian system. A group of divines, mostly ordained clergy in the Church of England, together with some Scottish Commissioners, formed the Westminster Assembly of Divines, who drew up theological documents for the Parliamentary rulers. The *Thirty Nine Articles* of the Church of England were replaced by the *Westminster Confession*, and the *Book of Common Prayer* was replaced by the *Directory*. These documents reflect the prevailing theology in England and Scotland at the time. They were disowned by the Church of England at the Restoration in 1660, but would later find refuge in the Church of Scotland.

Chapter XXVII of the *Westminster Confession* defined sacraments as 'holy signs and seals of the covenant of grace', instituted by God, representing Christ and his benefits, and to confirm our interest in him. Section III noted:

> The grace which is exhibited in or by the sacraments, rightly used, is not conferred by any power in them; neither doth the efficacy of a sacrament depend upon the piety or intention of him that doth administer it, but upon the work of the Spirit, and the word of institution, which contains, together with a precept authorizing the use thereof, a promise of benefit to worthy receivers.[66]

Chapter XXVIII expounded baptism. It is a sacrament of the New Testament, ordained by Christ, and is a sign and seal of the covenant of grace. The outward element is water, with the trinitarian formula. Dipping is not necessary; pouring and sprinkling water suffices. Believers and the infants of one or both believing parents are to be baptized. Grace and salvation are, however, not tied to the sacrament, nor is its efficacy tied to the moment of administration.

The *Directory* for worship was compiled by a sub-committee, almost half of whom did not believe in set forms of worship.[67] The result was not a prayer book, but a set of instructions and suggestions for the order of worship, as well as the content of the prayer formulae. The provisions for the baptismal rite began by ruling out private baptism and lay administration of baptism. The initial exhortation, or 'Instruction',

---

[65] Ibid., p. 387.

[66] Schaff, *Creeds of Christendom*, Vol. 3, p. 661.

[67] Text, Westminster Assembly, *The Westminster Directory*, Ian Breward (ed.), Grove Liturgical Study 21, Grove Books, Bramcote, 1980. See Bryan D. Spinks, *Sacraments, Ceremonies and the Stuart Divines, Sacramental Theology and Liturgy in England and Scotland 1603–1662*, Ashgate, Aldershot, 2001, pp. 126–7.

described baptism as a 'Seale of the Covenant of Grace, of our Ingrafting into Christ, and of our Union with him'. It is the seal of remission of sins, regeneration, adoption and life eternal. Appeal was made to the covenant of grace for infant baptism, because children are 'federally holy before Baptisme'. The Instruction also noted that the inward grace and virtue of baptism is not tied to the moment of baptism. In many ways, the 'Instruction' is a quasi-liturgical rehearsal of the section found in the *Confession*.

Once the 'teaching' was complete, the minister was to pray that God would bless and sanctify the ordinance, and join the outward to the inward. After the child was named, it was baptized with the triune formula. Afterwards the minister was to give thanks 'to this or the like purpose':

> Acknowledging with all thankfulnesse, that the Lord is true and faithfull in keeping Covenant and Mercy; That hee is good and gracious, not onely in that he numbreth us among his Saints, but is pleased also to bestow upon our children this singular token and badge of his love in Christ: That in his truth and speciall providence, hee daily bringeth some into the bosome of his Church, to be partakers of his inestimable benefits, purchased by the blood of his dear Son, for the continuance and increase of his Church.

Entirely omitted are the recitation of the Lord's Prayer, and the Apostles' Creed.

Some Eighteenth-Century Developments

According to Muller, Thomas Ridgley (1667–1734) represents an example of eighteenth-century Late Reformed Orthodoxy. An independent minister, he was awarded a DD by Aberdeen University for his work *A Body of Divinity*, which was a commentary on the *Westminster Larger Catechism*. Naturally, he defines sacraments as signs and seals of the covenant of grace.[68] They are an effectual means of salvation, though not by any power in themselves; 'the sacraments become effectual means of salvation only by the working of the Holy Ghost, and the blessing of Christ, by whom they were instituted'.[69] They are channels through which grace is conveyed, but it is Christ who conveys grace by his Spirit. In baptism, there must be the application of water by dipping, pouring or sprinkling.[70] It is to be performed in the name of the Father, the Son and the Holy Ghost, for 'in this solemn act of dedication, there is a professed acknowledgment of the divine Trinity'.[71] It is a sign and seal of the covenant of grace. However, there are two ways of being in the covenant:

> There is a being in covenant professedly or visibly; and to exhibit persons as thus in the covenant, is the immediate intent and design of this ordinance. But there is

---

[68] Thomas Ridgley, *A Body of Divinity*, 2 vols, Robert Carter and Brothers, New York edn, 1855, Vol. 2, p. 486.

[69] Ibid., p. 488.

[70] Ibid., p. 492.

[71] Ibid., p. 493.

also a being in covenant, as laying hold on the grace of the covenant, when we give ourselves up to Christ by faith, and, in consequence, lay claim to the blessings of his redemption.[72]

Baptism is a sign and seal of both. However, there are privileges expected, and obligations acknowledged. In the case of infant baptism, children are under an indispensable obligation to perform the duties which are incumbent on all those baptized; nevertheless, infants are to be 'consecrated or devoted to God in baptism' because they are included in the covenant.[73] Ridgley gave the usual Reformed defence of infant baptism by analogy with circumcision. He also expended several pages considering the mode of baptism, and how to 'improve' our baptism – that is, by a disciplined life.

An example of one Reformed baptismal rite from the early eighteenth century is that of Jean Frederick Ostervald. Ostervald was a Swiss French-speaking Reformed minister, and wrote a liturgy for use in Neuchâtel and Vallangin in 1713. Ostervald had a keen interest in the Church of England, and for his liturgical rites drew on the *Book of Common Prayer* of 1662 of the Church of England, though the baptismal rite shows little signs of this source.

Ostervald outlined his theology of baptism in his *Compendium of Christian Theology*. He noted that the word 'sacrament' was not found in Scripture, but was a word used to describe certain rites and ceremonies instituted by God for the confirmation of his covenant. He stressed that the word applied not to the signs alone, but to the entire action with words. There was a need to know the rite, and then its signification. Here Ostervald sounds almost postmodern, suggesting that there is no generic sacrament, but only sacramental rites. For Ostervald, sacraments are 'public pledges, and seals of the divine covenant, both on God's part, and on ours. For by them, God offers, and confirms his grace unto us, and we testify, and bind over our faith and obedience unto him'.[74] The efficacy is twofold: the objective, or moral, which presents us the grace of God and our duty; and the subjective, which is the grace of the Holy Spirit. Concerning baptism he wrote:

> The rites of Baptism are very simple, viz. immersion into pure water, and sprinkling, with the pronunciation of certain words; besides, the persons to be baptised made a profession of their faith, and renounced the world and the Devil. The Holy Spirit was invoked upon them, they were conducted to the font, descended into the water, and were baptised by the Minister. Afterwards they were delivered to their sponsors, milk and honey were offered them to be tasted, they were confirmed by imposition of hands, cloathed [*sic*] with a white garment, and at length were admitted to the Eucharist. In subsequent times, other rites were superadded, as salt, spittle, exorcism, which Bellarmin describes, upon the Sacrament of Baptism.[75]

---

72 Ibid., p. 95.

73 Ibid., p. 500.

74 J.F. Ostervald, *A Compendium of Christian Theology*, English translation and editor John McMains, Nathaniel Patten pub., Hartford, CT, 1788, p. 344.

75 Ibid., p. 351.

The significance of the rite, says Ostervald, is that it admits us into the divine covenant and the Church of God. God confirms and confers certain benefits, and we give a public declaration of our faith. Children have the right of baptism because they are under the covenant. Ostervald warned pastors that baptism was not a trivial matter, for in it God receives people into the covenant and pours his Holy Spirit upon them; they in turn are called to lead a holy life, for otherwise baptism is of no avail.[76]

The liturgical rite he composed in 1713 opened with the usual *votum*, and a question asking if the child is presented to God and the Church for baptism. The congregation are briefly exhorted to join in the following prayer:

> Almighty God, heavenly Father, who has promised through your goodness to be our God and that of our children, as you were to Abraham and his; we pray you to give your Holy Spirit to this child, receiving it into the Covenant of your Mercy, and into the participation of your Grace. To the end that when he comes to the age of reason, he will know you as his God, that he will adore you and serve you only, that he will live and die in you; so that the baptism by which we receive him into your Holy Church, is not administered to him in vain; but that he will be truly baptised into the death of your Son, and a New Life which is acceptable to you, through Jesus Christ our Lord. Amen.

A Gospel reading from Matthew 19 followed, with a series of questions to the parents and sponsors regarding their duties, with a final question of ' Do you promise these things?' The minister then said, 'The Lord give you grace to faithfully accomplish this promise.' Baptism with the triune formula followed.

In 1724 and in 1743, the Church in Geneva published liturgical forms[77] in *Les Prieres Ecclesiastiques* and *La Liturgie* respectively. The baptismal rite of 1724 retained Calvin's structure, though after the *votum* and request if baptism is desired, a new, shorter exhortation followed, which took as its main theme the Johannine idea of being born again in order to enter the Kingdom of God, omitting Calvin's stress on original sin. It also regarded infant baptism as a consecration of the infant to God. The prayer 'Lord God, Father eternal' has theological changes. Instead of asking God to confirm his grace on the infant, God is asked to accomplish his promise. Although the reference to Adam and corruption is retained, reference to original sin is dropped in favour of a request that the infant be received into the covenant. The father and godparents are told their duties, and after their affirmative response the minister asks that God grant them the grace to accomplish their promise. The baptism with triune formula follows. The rite of 1743 had only minor stylistic changes.

---

[76] Ibid., pp. 352–4.

[77] My thanks to Professor Bruno Bürki for kindly supplying me with the texts of these two rites.

Some Developments in Nineteenth-Century Reformed Baptismal Theology and Rites

John Riggs has observed that the forces of orthodoxy, pietism and the Enlightenment coalesced in the life of the most influential Reformed theologian of the nineteenth century, Friedrich Daniel Schleiermacher.[78] Schleiermacher (1768–1834) found traditional religious doctrine difficult to believe, though he regarded being religious an essential part of being human. This feeling of absolute dependency he termed 'God-consciousness', and the supreme mode of this God-consciousness was revealed in Jesus Christ. He wrote:

> If it be the essence of redemption that the God-consciousness already present in human nature, though feeble and repressed, becomes stimulated and made dominant by the entrance of the living influence of Christ, the individual on whom this influence is exercised attains a religious personality not his before.[79]

Rejecting the Chalcedonian concept of Christ's two natures, Schleiermacher argued that Christ had perfect 'God-consciousness'. However, given that this was something already present in human nature, there is a sense in which Schleiermacher can be perceived to be doing anthropology rather than theology. God-consciousness is 'activated' when Christ enters the person, and results in regeneration and sanctification, and in our participation in the Spirit:

> Being taken up into living fellowship with Christ includes at the same time being conscious both of our sonship with God and of the Lordship of Christ; and both in scripture are ascribed to the indwelling of the Holy Spirit.[80]

However, because regeneration is both Christological and pneumatological,

> It is evident enough that one can all too easily lapse unawares into the region of magic, if regeneration be brought into connexion with our particular method of administering the sacrament of baptism.[81]

Schleiermacher in fact was reluctant to use the word 'sacrament', but did so 'for convenience'.[82] He held that any change in a person occurs by the work of the Spirit quite apart from baptism. According to Schleiermacher, faith was 'the appropriation of the perfection and blessedness of Christ', and this was a precondition of baptism.[83] He therefore questioned infant baptism. True to the Bullinger line of thought, he wrote:

> There will always be some regenerate persons who are not yet baptized but who might well have claimed to be received earlier into the Church; similarly, there

---

[78] John W. Riggs, *Baptism in the Reformed Tradition*, Westminster John Knox Press, Louisville, KY, 2002, p. 90.

[79] F. Schleiermacher, *The Christian Faith*, T&T Clark, Edinburgh, 1989 edn, p. 476.

[80] Ibid., p. 574.

[81] Ibid., p. 490.

[82] Ibid., pp. 658–9.

[83] Ibid., p. 631.

will be baptized persons who are not yet regenerate but in the most active way are being commended to divine grace for regeneration by the prayers of the Church.[84]

He opined that the baptismal formula could be changed without affecting the validity of the baptism.[85] Infant baptism only becomes a complete baptism when a profession of faith comes later; in other words, confirmation completes infant baptism.[86]

Though it is difficult to pinpoint any particular direct liturgical influence, Schleiermacher's questioning of infant baptism, together with his idea of God-consciousness, did bring into question whether or not infants should be dedicated rather than baptized, and how much prominence the notion of sin should be given in the rite.

Many rites of the eighteenth century simply preserved the inherited forms. The 1835 Vaud liturgy presented the rite of 1725. Nevertheless, there were particular places and persons in the Reformed tradition from which and from whom more comprehensive liturgical provisions emerged.

Scotland

The Church of Scotland worshipped with the memory of the *Westminster Directory*.[87] That something more than a tradition of memory was needed is evidenced by the publication in 1802 of *The Scotch Minister's Assistant*, published at Inverness by Harry Robertson, Minister of Kilteran. A second and revised edition was published at Aberdeen in 1828 under the title *The Presbyterian Minister's Assistant*. An opening prayer of thanksgiving to God waxed eloquently, praying for the Holy Spirit to be poured down upon 'our seed, and thy blessing upon our offspring, that they may spring up as Willows by the water courses'. The minister then asked if the child was being presented for baptism and for admittance to the visible church. There followed a long discourse which included the phrase 'into a covenant transaction'. It explained that the first covenant was broken by disobedience and apostasy of our first parents, but that God entered into another covenant 'whereof Jesus Christ is the surety and mediator'. He bestows pardon of sin, regeneration and sanctification. Because humans are forgetful of spiritual things, God has appointed certain outward visible signs and symbols 'to represent the blessings of his covenant'. It notes:

> Such is the element of water used in the sacrament of Baptism, which points out and leads us to reflect upon the guilty and polluted state by nature; the necessity of washing implying uncleanness ...

---

[84] Ibid., pp. 622–3.

[85] Ibid., p. 629.

[86] Ibid., pp. 633ff.

[87] See for example Walter Steuart of Pardovin, *Collections and Observations Methodiz'd Concerning the Worship, Discipline, and Government of the Church of Scotland in Four Books*, Edinburgh, 1709, pp. 126ff.

The sprinkling teaches the person to shun filthiness and pollution of flesh and spirit, and to maintain holiness of life. The baptized are dedicated to the Trinity, and are admitted to the privileges of the Church.

This explanation of the meaning of baptism was followed by a creedal interrogatory section, including belief in the Confessions of Faith and Catechisms of the National Church. A prayer followed which included the petition:

> Deny us not thy presence on this solemn occasion, O our God, deny us not thy grace. Sanctify the element of water which is now exhibited and applied as a sign and symbol of thy grace. Let the outward Baptism with water be accompanied with the inward Baptism of the Holy Spirit.

Baptism with the triune formula followed, and then a concluding prayer for the child and parents, though since it outlined the duties of the parents in bringing up the child in the faith, it seems more directed to the parents than to God.

This liturgical rite was a private undertaking, and it was followed by a number of others such as W. Liston of Redgorton who published *The Service of God's House or Forms for the guidance of Ministers and Heads of families, to the proper conducting of Public and Private Worship, according to the practice of the Church of Scotland* (1843), Alex Brunton, *Forms for Public Worship in the Church of Scotland* (1848), and James Anderson, *The Minister's Directory or Forms for the Administration of the Sacraments and other Rites and Ordinances, according to the Church of Scotland* (1856). The latter adds the words 'one God' to the triune baptismal formula.

Another important compilation was that of Robert Lee of Greyfriars, Edinburgh, in 1857. However, the most important compilation was the *Euchologion* of the Church Service Society. Although this, too, was a private endeavour, it was used by many ministers and came to be something of the unofficial 'official' rite of the Church of Scotland. The *Euchologion* was published first in 1867, and went through a number of revised editions to the definitive form of the seventh edition in 1896. The 1867 edition contained two rites of baptism, the first being that of the 1564 *Book of Common Worship*, or Knox's Genevan rite; and the second being based on the *Westminster Directory* and Richard Baxter's Savoy Rite.[88] The second of these reappeared with modification in the 1869 second edition. The rite itself began with asking if the parents present the child for holy baptism. This was followed by a reading of Mark 10:13ff., with a very brief exhortation. Then came an admonition to the sponsors, with two forms being provided, and the creed asked as an interrogative. That in turn was followed by:

> Do you promise that if it shall please God to spare this child, you shall, as soon as *he* is able to understand them, instruct *him* [or cause *him* to be instructed] in these truths, and in the meaning of the baptismal covenant; and according to your best ability, by good example, and with prayer to God on *his* behalf, train *him* up in the nurture and admonition of the Lord?[89]

---

[88] See Chapter 3.
[89] *Euchologion*, 2nd edn, Blackwood and Sons, Edinburgh, 1869, p. 192.

A prayer followed, which included the petition

> May it please Thee to sanctify this element of water to this spiritual use; and to join the inward baptism of Thy Spirit to the outward baptism of water, making it to this child the seal of remission of sins, of adoption, regeneration, and eternal life ...[90]

A second alternative prayer was provided. The child was named, and then baptized with the triune formula, and blessed with the Aaronic blessing. Intercession for the child and its parents followed, concluded with the Lord's Prayer and the Grace.

In the absence of an official liturgy other than the memory of the *Directory*, there was evidently a need to clothe a rite with prayer, and restore the credal confession. Explication remained an important element in the rite, and as in *The Scotch Minister's Assistant*, the authors of this rite felt it necessary to articulate the symbolic parallelism of Bullinger – that the outward and inward did not necessarily coincide.

Also from Scotland, but from the Congregationalist tradition, came John Hunter's *Devotional Services for Public Worship*. Hunter was minister of Trinity Church, Edinburgh, though the nucleus of *Devotional Services* was formed when he was a minister in York. The book increased in size and scope until its final seventh edition in 1901. In that year Hunter became minister at the King's Weigh House Chapel, London, and his book became an extremely popular resource for English Congregational ministers.

In the fifth edition (1892), the provision for baptism was entitled 'The Baptism or Dedication of Children'. After some introductory Scripture sentences, an 'Address' defined the service as one of thanksgiving, testimony, recognition and dedication. It was a thanksgiving for the child, recognition of God as source of life, testimony that children are children of God and that he claims them as his, and dedication of the child to the will of God, and the consecration of the parents to new and holier fidelities. The triune baptismal formula was used, but if the service was one of dedication, then the minister said, 'I dedicate thee to the will and service of God in the name of the Father, the Son, and the Holy Spirit. Amen.'[91] A brief intercessory prayer followed, and the Grace.

The United States: Mercersburg

The Mercersburg theology is associated with the names of John Nevin and Philip Schaff as developed at Mercersburg Seminary, Pennsylvania, in the mid-nineteenth century. Nevin had been brought up in the Presbyterian Church and had trained in theology at Princeton under Charles Hodge. However, alarmed at liberalism, individualism and subjectivism, he came into the German Reformed Church in America. The liturgy in use was that derived from the 1563 Palatinate rite. Nevin had a passion for history as developmental, and in this he was joined by his younger

---

[90] Ibid., p. 193.
[91] *Devotional Services for Public Worship*, Maclehouse, Glasgow, 1892, p. 108.

colleague from Germany, Phillip Schaff. Though not always in complete agreement on detail, they recalled the German Reformed Church to its Calvinist and Catholic roots, which was expressed both in their writings on theology, and in their part in the 'provisional' or 'Mercersburg' Liturgy of 1857, proposed for adoption by the German Reformed Church. In the event, it was a modified form which was adopted.

For Nevin, sacraments were objective and convey the presence of God. He wrote:

> If sacraments are regarded as in themselves outward rites only, that can have no value or force except as the grace they represent is made to be present by the subjective exercise of the worshipper ... it is hard to see on what grounds infants, who are still without knowledge or faith, should be admitted to any privilege of the sort. If there be no objective reality in the life of the church, as something deeper and more comprehensive than the life of the individual believer separately taken, infant baptism becomes necessarily an unmeaning contradiction.[92]

Nevin was particularly critical of the teaching of the New England Congregationalist, Horace Bushnell. Although he agreed with Bushnell's attack on American individualism, he felt that Bushnell based Christian nurture on human nature rather than grace and the supernatural work of God.[93] Nevin argued that baptism has an objective force whose efficacy rests not on the minister or the parents of the child, but upon Christ. He felt that Bushnell underplayed the doctrine of original sin. John Payne remarks of Nevin's defence of infant baptism, 'it is remarkable how small a role that argument with its analogy of baptism to circumcision played in his thinking'.[94]

The rite of infant baptism in the provisional liturgy began with the invocation of the Trinity.[95] An exhortation which included Matthew 28:19 and Mark 10:13ff. followed, noting that in baptism God is asked to grant the child 'that which by nature he cannot have' – possibly reflecting Nevin's reaction to Bushnell. Following the Palatinate rite, the Provisional Liturgy included a version of Luther's *sindflutgebet*, though the version of the Anglican *Book of Common Prayer* was the one used. An exhortation to the parents, echoing the Anglican rite, led into the renunciation of the devil and the confession of the Creed. The baptism was followed by the Thanksgiving prayer from the Anglican rite, the Lord's Prayer, an exhortation to the parents or sponsors, and concluded with the words: 'The peace of God, which passeth all understanding, keep your hearts and minds, through Christ Jesus. Amen.' Thus the liturgy combined elements from the Palatinate rite with material from the Anglican rite, and downplayed entirely the concept of covenant.

---

[92] John W. Nevin, *The Mystical Presence: A Vindication of the Reformed or Calvinistic Doctrine of the Holy Eucharist*, Philadelphia, 1846; reprint in *The Mystical Presence and Other Writings on the Eucharist*, Bard Thompson and George H. Bicker (eds), Lancaster Series on the Mercersburg Theology 4, United Church Press, Philadelphia, PA, 1966, p. 143.

[93] See John B. Payne, 'Nevin on Baptism', in Sam Hamstra and Arie J. Griffion (eds), *Reformed Confessionalism in Nineteenth-century America. Essays on the Thought of John Williamson Nevin*, Scarecrow Press, Lanham, MD, 1995, pp. 125–51, p. 129.

[94] Ibid., p. 138.

[95] *A Liturgy: or, Order of Christian Worship*, Philadelphia, PA, 1865, pp. 203ff.

Eugène Bersier's Paris rite

Bersier was Anglo-Swiss by birth, and spent his entire ministry at L'Eglise de l'Etoile in Paris. His *Liturgie à l'usage des Réformées* was published in 1874. In the baptismal rite, Bersier retained the traditional Reformed *votum*, followed by an explication of why the Church baptizes – it was instituted by Jesus who proclaimed the Kingdom of God, and who himself was baptized, and in Matthew 28 commanded the disciples to baptize. In the explication Bersier wrote:

> The invisible grace which baptism represents is the double grace of redemption: in the first place, the pardon of sins by the sacrifice of Jesus Christ, then, regeneration and purification of the soul by the Holy Spirit. The water is the image of the divine grace which effaces our sins; but this grace, to be efficacious, must be received by faith that the Holy Spirit produces ... [96]

The explication explained that, though an infant cannot take for himself the pledge (covenant) of being consecrated by God, the minister gives the sign of redemption, praying that God will fulfil the work of grace in the soul. The explication ends with the parents and sponsors being asked whether they believe the Gospel and the Creed, and renounce the world and its desires. A further brief exhortation follows before the first prayer. This is followed by the Lord's Prayer, the baptism, and the Aaronic grace and peace.

Zurich: Alois Emanuel Biedermann

In a recent study Theodore Vial has drawn attention to the struggle that occurred in Zurich between 1864 and 1868 over revision of the baptismal liturgy – a struggle between conservatives and a more liberal group who had been influenced by the theology of David Friedrich Strauss.[97] An earlier struggle had already resulted in the conservatives taking control in 1830, but a more liberal Great Council came into office in 1846. The Board of Education offered an opening on the theology faculty to the liberal Biedermann. A revised liturgy was adopted in 1854, but by 1864 the Great Council requested the Church Council of Zurich to consider whether the liturgy needed expansion. Vial notes that the membership on the Liturgy Commission included Professor Kesselring and Heinrich Hirzel, minister of Zurich's St Peter's Church as leading spokesmen for the liberal theological point of view; Rudolph Wolfensberger and George Rudolf Zimmermann, minister of Zurich's Fraumünster Church, representing the conservatives; and Professor Alexander Schweizer and Church Councilman Georg Finsler, who in 1866 became Antistes, as proponents of mediating theology.[98] Much of the struggle was over the place of the Apostles' Creed in the rite of baptism. Biedermann had objected to a

---

[96] *Liturgie à l'usage des Réformées*, Paris, 1874, p. 185.

[97] Theodore M. Vial, *Liturgy Wars. Ritual Theory and Protestant Reform in Nineteenth-century Zurich*, Routledge, New York, 2004.

[98] Ibid., pp. 17–18.

number of clauses in the Creed, and the liberal members of the Liturgical Commission wanted the Creed replaced with a credal statement which did not tax the intellectual integrity of the liberals. The final outcome was the provision of two baptismal rites in 1868.[99] The first rite, the 'conservative rite' began with the invocation of the Trinity and the traditional Reformed votum. There was a brief exhortation, mentioning that baptism was the means of admitting the child to the community (*Gemeinde*) and that it is a symbol of the covenant (*Bundeszeichen*) of the New Testament. The Apostles' Creed followed, and then a lengthy prayer, and the Lord's Prayer. After a very brief exhortation to the sponsors, the child was baptized, and the congregation dismissed. The second, 'liberal rite' began with the votum, and had a lengthier exhortation, which regarded baptism as a consecration of the child to God, and as a blessing. There was no credal profession. After the exhortation came a prayer, the Lord's Prayer, baptism with the triune formula, and dismissal. A similar provision of dual rites for conservative and liberal views is also to be found in the *Aargauische Liturgie*, 1903, which Karl Barth would have known when pastor of Safenwil.

Concluding remarks

Although there are nuanced differences in the teaching of the foundational Reformed theologians, such as Zwingli, Bullinger, Calvin and Ursinus, nevertheless, the rites which stem from them show a certain uniformity in theology and structure. Covenant began to be the overriding theological concept. The defence of infant baptism on the grounds of the covenant meant that the emphasis on original sin and remission of sins, together with exorcisms, were excised from the rite. Rites regarded as superstitious and without biblical warrant, such as the use of oil, the white garment, and the giving of a candle, also disappeared. Following northern European pragmatism, sprinkling was the mode of baptism. The need to explain a reformed understanding of baptism led to the incorporation of lengthy explications to explain what little ritual action was left in the rite. Where the stone font was disused and a bowl attached to the side of the pulpit, the focus moved from ritual to word. Since covenantal theology stressed that the right to baptism of infants was justified only by biological reasons, parental faith and promises began to make sponsors theologically redundant, though the force of custom meant that the practice continued. However, in some Reformed churches sponsors had no place in the rite. Will Costen has pointed out how this breached the social ritual. The infant had been handed to the midwife, who presented the child at the door of the Church; the baptized child was handed to the godparent, symbolizing the role of nurturing and care, physical and spiritual, of godparents. Now a child was handed over by and returned to the father.[100] In the nineteenth century we find a

---

[99] English texts in ibid., pp. 117–21.
[100] Will Coster, *Baptism and Spiritual Kinship in Early Modern England*, Ashgate, Aldershot, 2002, p. 51.

prominent and influential theologian questioning infant baptism and also the unfailing use of the trinitarian formula; however, we also find moves by some Reformed churchmen to expand the short rites which they had inherited, and in others, provision for liberals who had problems with some traditional Christian beliefs.

CHAPTER 3

The Anglican Tradition:
From Thomas Cranmer to F.D. Maurice

The Anglican Communion is a fellowship of those churches which trace their ancestry to the Reformation in England, and to the creation of the Church of England and the Church of Ireland. It includes those Scottish bishops and clergy who were expelled from the Church of Scotland in 1689. All trace their liturgical ancestry to the *Book of Common Prayer*, whose main architect was Archbishop Thomas Cranmer.

The First Cranmerian Rites, 1549 and 1552

The English Reformation as a juridical separation from Rome began in the 1530s with Henry VIII's marital problems. Although a certain 'liberal catholicism', in accordance with the humanism of the age, flowered, and the cult of the saints was seriously reduced, there was little official change doctrinally or liturgically until after Henry's death and the succession to the throne of his young son, Edward.[1] Henry had promoted a number of evangelically minded bishops, and after his death these, together with members of the council who ruled on behalf of the young king, pursued a Protestant course. In 1549, all Latin rites other than those for ordination were replaced by a vernacular *Book of Common Prayer*, enacted with an Act of Uniformity. This book, in which some of the services were little more than a vernacular translation of the Latin services, was short lived, and was replaced in 1552, with a new Act of Uniformity, by a more obviously Protestant book.

The precise immediate origins of the 1549 *Book of Common Prayer* are unclear. It is known that there was a committee of bishops. Whatever the parts played by this committee, though, the major work and inspiration behind the vernacular rites came from Archbishop Thomas Cranmer. We may assume that the rites he compiled were not incompatible with his theology.[2] As archbishop, the former Cambridge don had little time or leisure to write extensive theological works, and his theology of baptism is particularly hard to glean.[3] The recent work of Ashley Null on his doctrine of repentance assists in setting his theology of baptism in a broader setting.[4]

---

[1] Eamon Duffy, *The Stripping of the Altars*, Yale University Press, New Haven, CT and London, 1992.

[2] Diarmaid MacCulloch, *Thomas Cranmer*, Yale University Press, New Haven, CT and London, 1996.

[3] See Gordon Jeanes, 'Signs of God's Promise: Thomas Cranmer's Sacramental Theology and Baptismal Liturgy', Ph.D. dissertation, University of Wales, Lampeter, 1998.

[4] Ashley Null, *Thomas Cranmer's Doctrine of Repentance*, Oxford University Press, Oxford, 2000.

Furthermore, Cranmer had helped compile a book of doctrine called *The King's Book* in 1543, and he was the author of some of the homilies in the *Book of Homilies* (1547). From these we have some idea of the theological framework within which he worked. His work of 1550, *A Defence of the True and Catholic Doctrine of the Sacrament of the Body and Blood of our Saviour Christ* also yields something of his general view on sacraments.

Drawing on Cranmer's unpublished *Common Places* and the *Croydon Commentary*, Ashley Null argues that Cranmer initially shared the Scotist theology of John Fisher, but that his reading of Luther took him back again and again to a point where both Scotus and Fisher seemed semi-Pelagian. Cranmer accepted the Reformation concept of the imputation of righteousness, and by the 1540s had rejected the idea of a sacramental context for justification. In justification God grants both faith and love. The believer's faith lays hold of the extrinsic righteousness of Christ, on which basis sins are forgiven. Good works and acts of charity certify to the believer's conscience that he is justified; they also serve as certification for the Christian community. To protect the utter gratuity of this saving faith Cranmer appealed to Augustine's teaching on the unconditional predestination of the elect to eternal life. In other words, the doctrine of election was fundamental.[5] The implication is that no sacramental rite can confer or guarantee grace.

As Geoffrey Cuming observed, *The King's Book* suggested a considerable amount of phraseology for the rites in the *Book of Common Prayer*.[6] Further, this work gives some indication of teaching on the sacrament in the 1540s. The summary statement at the end of the 'Seven Sacraments' asserted:

> For by baptism we be incorporated into the body of Christ's Church, obtaining in that sacrament remission of sins, and grace, wherewith we be able to lead a new life.

To these three effects of baptism – remission of sins, incorporation and grace – a fourth was listed in the section on Confirmation:

> … all such as had duly received the sacrament of baptism were by virtue and efficacy thereof perfectly regenerated in Christ, perfectly incorporated and made the very members of his body, and had received full remission of their sins, and were endued with graces and gifts of the Holy Ghost.

These four effects of baptism all find liturgical expression in the 1549 baptismal rite. However, *The King's Book* made a distinction between the sacrament of baptism and the sacrament of the altar. By the late 1540s, Cranmer was no longer able to share this distinction, or the view that the sacraments necessarily conveyed grace. In the *Defence* he wrote:

> And whensoever two or three be gathered together in his name, [Christ] is there in the midst among them, by whose supernal grace all godly men be first by him

---

[5] Ibid.

[6] G.J. Cuming, *A History of Anglican Liturgy*, Macmillan and Co., London, 1969, p. 53.

spiritually regenerated, and after increase and grow to their spiritual perfection in God, spiritually by faith eating his flesh and drinking his blood.[7]

Gordon Jeanes aptly observes that there is no reference here to the sacraments at all, nor are they deemed necessary; with or without the sacraments, regeneration and growth are the path to life in Christ.[8] In his *Answer* to Stephen Gardiner's *Explication*, Cranmer wrote:

> Although the sacramental tokens be only significations and figures, yet doth Almighty God effectually work in them that duly receive his sacraments, those divine and celestial operations which he hath promised, and by the sacraments be signified. For else they were vain and unfruitful sacraments, as well to the godly as to the ungodly.[9]

And in refuting the doctrine of transubstantiation in the eucharist, Cranmer urged:

> The third example is of the water in baptism, where the water still remaineth water, although the Holy Ghost come upon the water, or rather upon him that is baptized therein.[10]

When we turn to the 1549 baptismal rite, we find that the main theological thrust is a traditional Augustinian theology of baptism, with an emphasis on original sin and regeneration, and also that baptism is reception into the Ark of the Church. Cranmer shows no interest in the Reformed Covenant theology, but instead uses the idea of promise.[11] The rite was in two parts and, as in the medieval Sarum rite on which it was mainly based, the first part took place at the church door, and the second at the font. However, in addition to the Sarum rite, Cranmer drew on contemporary theological debate, Hermann von Wied's *Consultation*, the Brandenburg-Nürnburg rite of 1533, and a Gallican/Mozarabic blessing of the font. Some ceremonies were discarded, but signing the forehead, exorcism of the devil, anointing of the head and giving the white robe were retained.

Opening rubrics noted that the ancient custom was to baptize at Easter or Whitsuntide, and that, although this custom cannot be restored, baptism as a public event should be. Godfathers and godmothers play their traditional role in the rite, and they, with the children, must assemble at the church door, 'either immediately afore the last canticle at Mattins or else immediately afore the last canticle at Evensong, as the curate by his discretion shall appoint'.[12] The rubrics and some of the brief opening exhortation were suggested by the baptismal rite for Hermann's *Consultation*, though the latter, stressing that all are 'conceived and born in sin', also draws on the third

---

[7] Defence 3.2. in *Writings and Disputations of Thomas Cranmer relative to the sacrament of the Lord's Supper*, J.E. Cox (ed.), Parker Society, Cambridge, 1844, p. 89 (cited as PS I).

[8] Jeanes, 'Signs of God's Promise', p. 243.

[9] *Answer*, 3; PS I, p. 148.

[10] *Defence*, PS I, p. 320.

[11] See Jeanes, 'Signs of God's Promise', pp. 235–42.

[12] Text; Fisher, *Christian Initiation: The Reformation Period*, pp. 89ff. For the social implications of godparents, see Coster, *Baptism and Spiritual Kinship*.

section on baptism in *The King's Book*.[13] Next came a version of Luther's *sindflutgebet*. Cranmer added:

> We beseech thee (for thy infinite mercies) that thou wilt mercifully look upon these children, and sanctify them with thy Holy Ghost, that by this wholesome laver of regeneration whatsoever sin is in them may be washed clean away, that they, being delivered from thy wrath, may be received into the ark of Christ's Church, and so saved from perishing.

Here, unlike Luther, Cranmer invokes the Holy Spirit on the candidates, though with Luther he shared the importance of the concept of sin.

The prayer is followed by a consignation with the sign of the cross on the child's forehead with a formula using military imagery. This is followed by a prayer, an exorcism, the Gospel reading from Mark 10, and an exhortation, Lord's Prayer, Creed and a short collect. However, the Markan Gospel reading appears to have been central and crucial for Cranmer at this point. In a seminal article, Gordon Jeanes has suggested that a manuscript in Lambeth Palace Library, *De Sacramentis* MS 1107, is the work of Thomas Cranmer.[14] The section of this manuscript which defends infant baptism reads thus:

> … for Christ ordered infants to be brought to him. (1) he takes them in his arms. (2) he lays his hands on them. (3) he blesses them, that is, he sanctifies them, by forgiving their sins and imparting the Holy Spirit.

This clearly has the Markan passage in mind, and something very similar is found in the exhortation/explication which follows the Gospel reading:

> Ye perceive how by his outward gesture and deed he declared his good will toward them. For he embraced them in his arms, he laid his hands upon them, and blessed them: Doubt ye not, therefore, but earnestly believe, that he will likewise favourably receive these present infants, that he will embrace them with the arms of his mercy, that he will give unto them his blessing of eternal life: and make them partakers of his everlasting kingdom.

This, and not covenant theology, was Cranmer's justification for infant baptism.

The second part of Cranmer's rite commenced with the rubric:

> Then let the priest take one of the children by the right hand, the others being brought after him. And coming into the church toward the font, say … .

There is, then, a ritual action in that the priest emulates in some way Christ's action of taking the children. The exhortation which follows reiterated the theme:

> … ye have prayed for them that our Lord Jesus Christ would vouchsafe to receive them, to lay hands upon them, to bless them, to release them of their sins, to give them the kingdom of heaven, and everlasting life.

---

[13] Bryan D. Spinks, 'Treasures Old and New: A Look at Some of Thomas Cranmer's Methods of Liturgical Compilation', in Paul Ayris and David Selwyn (eds), *Thomas Cranmer: Churchman and Scholar*, The Boydell Press, Woodbridge, 1993, pp. 175–88; p. 182.

[14] Gordon Jeanes, 'A Reformation Treatise on the Sacraments', *Journal of Theological* 46 (1995), 149–90.

The exhortation was followed by the renunciation of the devil, and the recitation (again) of the Creed. Baptism is with the triune formula, and was followed by the giving of a white robe, and an anointing with a formula which is found in the Sarum Confirmation rite. The rite concluded with a charge to the godparents.

A service was provided for Private Baptism, 'in time of necessity', and at the end of this rite was located a prayer for the blessing of the water, to be carried out each month. This blessing was adapted from Mozarabic or Visigothic sources, though precisely where Cranmer had found it remains a puzzle.[15] It included the petition:

> Send down we beseech thee the same thy Holy Spirit to assist us, and to be present at this our invocation of thy holy Name: Sanctifie this fountain of baptism, thou that art the sanctifier of all things, that by the power of thy word, all those that shall be baptized therein, may be spiritually regenerated, and made the children of everlasting adoption. Amen.

The blessing, which was series of petitions, was followed by a collect.

A separate service of Confirmation was included, being an almost word-for-word translation from the Sarum rite, except that anointing with oil was replaced by the laying-on of hands, and the concluding prayer came from Hermann.

The 1549 *Book of Common Prayer* was criticized by the conservative as being too Protestant, and by those of Protestant persuasion as being too conservative and Roman. Martin Bucer, the former Strasbourg Reformer, was by now Regius Professor of Divinity at Cambridge, and the Italian Reformer, Peter Martyr Vermigli, was Regius Professor of Divinity at Oxford. Both were invited to submit critiques of the 1549 book. Martyr's critique does not seem to have survived, but that of Bucer, his *Censura*, has. He criticized such things as the white robe, anointing and exorcism. He approved the use of the sign of the cross, but not the formula which accompanied it. He was also critical of blessing the font.[16]

The 1549 baptismal rite was simplified in the Prayer Book of 1552. In this book, the 'staged' rite was discontinued; now the whole rite took place inside the church. The exorcism, white robe and anointing were removed. The 1549 'Blessing of the Water of the Font' was heavily modified and relocated to the main baptismal rite. Apparently no blessing of the water was needed since, as Luther's *sindflugebet* made clear, Christ's baptism in the Jordan had sanctified all water for the purpose of baptism. Bucer had been critical of the blessing, but Cranmer too seems to have had second thoughts by 1550. In *A Defence* he wrote:

> Consecration is the separation of any thing from a profane and worldly use unto a spiritual and godly use. And therefore when usual and common water is taken from other uses, and put to the use of baptism in the name of the Father, and of

---

[15] H. Boone Porter, 'Hispanic Influences on Worship in the English Tongue', in J. Neil Alexander (ed.), *Time and Community. In Honor of Thomas Julian Talley*, Pastoral Press, Washington, DC, 1990, pp. 171–84.

[16] Fisher, *Christian Initiation: The Reformation Period*, pp. 96-105.

the Son, and of the Holy Ghost, then it may rightly be called consecrated water, that is to say, water put to an holy use.[17]

In the Preface to his *Answer* to Gardiner's *Explication*, Cranmer had written:

> And sometimes by this word 'sacrament' I mean the whole ministration and receiving of the sacraments, either of baptism, or of the Lord's supper: and so the old writers many times do say, that Christ and the Holy Ghost be present in the sacraments; not meaning by that manner of speech, that Christ and the Holy Ghost be present in the water, bread or wine (which be only the outward visible sacraments), but that in the due administration of the sacraments according to Christ's ordinance and institution, Christ and his holy Spirit be truly and indeed present by their mighty and sanctifying power, virtue, and grace, in all them that worthily receive the same.[18]

In the 1552 Prayer Book, the 1549 'Blessing of the Water of the Font' was rewritten to exclude any blessing of the water, and rather than the water being renewed and blessed once a month, the modified version was a constituent prayer to be recited at every baptism.

The sign of the cross was removed from its 1549 position to a point immediately after baptism, replacing the 1549 anointing with oil and the English-language Sarum prayer which had been retained. Following a number of seventeenth-century commentators, Marion J. Hatchett has argued that what was once conveyed in the medieval rite of Confirmation was now placed to follow baptism:

> The anointing is gone but its place is taken by a signation on the forehead, the site of the medieval confirmation anointing (in contrast to the baptismal anointing on the crown of the head), accompanied by a text which echoes the medieval confirmation anointing form and is related to Thomas Aquinas' definition of the medieval rite called confirmation.[19]

From this, Hatchett and others have proposed that for Cranmer, Christian initiation was complete in baptism. However, Gordon Jeanes has seriously questioned this interpretation. Jeanes noted that it is hard to imagine what might have led someone of Cranmer's theology and outlook to try to patch a piece of the confirmation service into baptism, and if a formula for signing is to be used, there is a certain limit on what the wording is likely to be. Jeanes suggested that

> It is better by far to invoke a Biblical reference, to those who have the sign of God on their foreheads (Rev. 7:2ff, 9:4). In short, there is nothing which need distract us from seeing Cranmer as altering the traditional pre-baptismal signing on the forehead and placing it later in the service in order to convey the importance of the whole Christian life.[20]

---

[17] PS I, p. 177.

[18] Ibid., p. 3.

[19] M.J. Hatchett, 'Prayer Books', in S. Sykes and J. Booty (eds), *The Study of Anglicanism*, London, SPCK, 1988, p. 128.

[20] Jeanes, 'Signs of God's Promise', pp. 354–5.

Furthermore, Cranmer certainly did not regard Christian initiation as complete in baptism; rather he saw catechesis and confirmation as part of instilling faith and Christian godly living.[21] Noting how the rite has a narrative element to it, and the deliberate repetition of the words 'promise', 'believe', 'receive', 'graft' and 'incorporate', Stephen Sykes explains of the 1552 baptismal liturgy:

> The Christian 'profession' entails a journey 'in Christ,' which begins with a dying to sin. This in itself presupposes that humanity apart from Christ is in a state of sin, the information appropriately conveyed by the words with which the liturgy begins ... Delivery of sin through the atoning death of Christ brings the Christian into the company of those undertaking the journey of sanctification, a constant further dying to sin and growth in obedience and godliness. The final state is that of enjoyment of the kingdom and eternal life, Thus, deliverance from sin, sanctification and entry into the kingdom constitutes a comprehensive summary of life 'in Christ.' Because the self-same promises of the Gospel accompany the Christian throughout his or her entire life, Baptism is a reminder of the Christian profession, a structure and framework for the whole of Christian living.
>
> It is not, therefore, accidental that in the pivotal address to the godparents before they make their promises, what is entailed in Christ's reception of and blessing of children is spelt out as follows: 'To release them of theyre synnes ... to geue them the kingdom of heaven, and euerlasting lyfe.' This pattern is constantly reiterated ... .[22]

Sykes concludes:

> ... this liturgy is characterised by a structure and a pattern of repetitions expressive of the way in which a Christian becomes involved in the divine plan, and the consequences of having done so. The structure focuses the drama upon the child, deploying the powerful thought of divine tenderness towards small children, but at the same time addresses adult participants through the metaphor of growth to maturity. It deliberately sets out to remind all present of the fundamental character of their own baptism, and to reinforce and encourage Christians in the profession of their faith.[23]

From the Elizabethan Settlement to the Westminster Directory

Edward VI died in 1553, and the Protestant experiment in England was temporarily halted by the accession of Mary, who took steps to restore Catholicism and the Catholic rites. Amongst the English Protestant exiles in Frankfurt, 'A Liturgy of Compromise' was drafted, which sought to bring the 1552 rites more in line with

---

[21] Bryan D. Spinks, 'Cranmer, Baptism, and Christian Nurture; or, Toronto Revisited', *Studia Liturgica* 32 (2002), 98–110.

[22] Stephen Sykes, 'Baptisme doth represente unto us oure profession', in Margot Johnson (ed.), *Thomas Cranmer, Essays in Commemoration of the 500th Anniversary of his Birth*, Turnstone Ventures, Durham, 1990, pp. 122, 143, 134.

[23] Ibid., p. 136.

Reformed practice. In the rite of baptism the questions to godparents were abbreviated, and the post-baptismal charge was directed mainly to the father of the child. The signing with the cross and its formula was omitted.[24] This rite already hinted at objections which would be articulated by the 'godly' or Puritan members of the Church of England throughout the sixteenth and seventeenth century.

Mary's death in 1558 resulted in the accession of Elizabeth I, and a return to a Reformation Church of England. The 1559 *Book of Common Prayer* was essentially that of 1552, and the baptismal rite remained the same. However, despite the Church of England's adoption of Articles of Faith, there was a wide latitude of theological interpretation of baptism. On the one hand, the great Cambridge pastor William Perkins used the terminology of sacraments as seals of the covenant and moral instruments. He wrote:

> Baptisme is appointed by God, to bee no more but a seale annexed unto, and depending upon the covenant: therefore wee must put a difference betweene it, and the covenant.
> The Covenant of grace, and our beeing in Christ, is absolutely necessary: for no man, woman, or childe, can bee saved, unlesse they have God for their God.[25]

On the other hand Richard Hooker regarded sacraments as powerful instruments of God, which, in addition to being moral instruments, are also mystical. Baptism gives regeneration, and is a sign of prevenient grace.[26]

Perkins was one of the 'godly' or Puritan wing of the Church of England. Amongst these were a number who wished for further liturgical reform. In the rite of baptism, they objected to the use of godparents, the frequent use of the word 'regenerate', the sign of the cross, and the custom of private baptism by midwives. On Elizabeth's death, James VI of Scotland succeeded to the English throne, and since he came from the Presbyterian Church of Scotland, many of the godly hoped for further reform of the Prayer Book. On his journey to London, James was presented with the Millenary Petition which, amongst other things, requested:

> ... that the cross in baptism, interrogatories ministered to infants, confirmation, as superfluous, may be taken away; baptism not to be ministered by women, and so explained ... .[27]

As a result of this petition, James summoned the Hampton Court Conference in 1604, where representatives of the 'godly' argued their case before a larger number of bishops and deans. There has been some disagreement amongst scholars as to what was actually achieved at the conference, since the account given by Dean William

---

[24] *The Liturgy of the Frankfurt Exiles 1555*, Robin Leaver (ed.), Grove Books, Bramcote, 1984, pp. 9–11.

[25] William Perkins, *Works*, 3 vols, printed by J. Legatt and C. Legge, Cambridge, 1616–18, 2:74. See further Spinks, *Two Faces of Elizabethan Anglican Theology*.

[26] See ibid.

[27] Henry Bettenson, *Documents of the Christian Church*, Oxford University Press, Oxford, 1979, p. 282.

Barlow is rather different from an anonymous account by Patrick Galloway (a Scottish minister in attendance); and the unpublished account of Laurance Chaderton for the 'godly'.[28] The resulting 1604 *Book of Common Prayer* contained only minor changes. A new rubric ruled out baptism by midwives and laity. Arnold Hunt observed:

> The consequent alteration of the Prayer Book rubric to forbid lay baptism was of considerable doctrinal significance, since it effectively denied the absolute necessity of baptism as a precondition of salvation.[29]

One significant addition was made in the catechism, which now included a section on baptism and the Lord's Supper. This was the work of John Overall, Dean of St Paul's, and was based on the 1570/73 catechism of Alexander Nowell. Sacraments were described as 'an outward and visible sign of an inward and spiritual grace, given unto us, ordained by Christ himself, as a means whereby we receive the same, and a pledge to assure us thereof'. The inward spiritual grace of baptism was explained as death unto sin, and a new birth to righteousness, and being made children of grace.

Although the liturgical text remained unchanged, there were a variety of theological views on the theology of sacraments and baptism. In the sixteenth century Richard Greenham, pastor at Dry Drayton, had been given permission by the bishop of Ely to omit the sign of the cross in baptism.[30] There were those such as Arthur Hildersham, John Downame and Bishop William Bedell who used the Reformed terminology of seals of the covenant, and those such as Samuel Ward and Thomas Bedford who, influenced by Richard Hooker's work, taught that sacraments were channels of grace and instruments which convey grace.[31] Cornelius Burges wrote a lengthy work in 1629 defending the phraseology of regeneration in the baptismal rite. He differentiated between 'initial' regeneration and 'actual' regeneration. The initial regeneration, rather like a seed, is given in baptism. In God's time it grows into actual regeneration.[32]

Whereas the Millenary petitioners had hoped that King James would reform the Church of England along Scottish lines, the king in fact attempted the reverse. He reintroduced bishops into the Church of Scotland, and also, in 1615, requested a revision of the liturgy of John Knox. Three drafts were made, and the second and third of these (*c.* 1616–17 and 1618–19) contained baptismal rites, and seem to have been

---

[28] Arnold Hunt, 'Laurance Chaderton and the Hampton Court Conference', in Susan Wabuda and Caroline Litzenberger (eds), *Belief and Practice in Reformation England*, Ashgate, Aldershot, 1998, pp. 207–28. See also Mark H. Curtis, 'Hampton Court Conference and its Aftermath', *History* 46 (1961), 1–16; Fred Shriver, 'Hampton Court Re-Visited: James I and the Puritans', in *Journal of Ecclesiastical History* 33 (1982), 48–71.

[29] Hunt, 'Laurance Chaderton', p. 224.

[30] Kenneth L. Parker and Eric J. Carlson, *'Practical Divinity'. The Works and Life of Revd. Richard Greenham*, Ashgate, Aldershot, 1998; John H. Primus, *Richard Greenham. The Portrait of an Elizabethan Pastor*, Mercer University Press, Macon, GA, 1998.

[31] For fuller details, Spinks, *Sacraments, Ceremonies, and the Stuart Divines*.

[32] Cornelius Burges, *Baptismall regeneration of Elect Infants, Professed by the Church of England, according to the Scriptures, the Primitive Church, the present reformed Churches, and many particular Divines apart*, London, 1629.

authored by William Cowper, bishop of Galloway.[33] Opposition to even introducing kneeling for communion and observance of Christmas and Easter resulted in these drafts being shelved. However, James' son, Charles I, allowed the Scottish bishops to go ahead with revision in 1636. The result was an unsuccessful attempt to impose on the Scottish Church a Prayer Book which used material from the 1549 rite. In the baptismal liturgy of the proposed Book the 1552/1559/1604 version of the *sindflugebet* added the petition, 'sanctify this fountain of baptism, thou which art the sanctifier of all things', and in the prayer immediately before the baptism the words were added of the water, 'which we here bless and dedicate in thy Name to this spiritual washing'. The book proved impossible to implement, and the resulting events snowballed and tipped over into the crisis which caused the English Civil War and the compilation of the *Westminster Directory*.[34]

From Taylor and Baxter to the Eighteenth Century

During the Cromwellian period an elegant liturgy was authored by Jeremy Taylor, a Royalist Episcopal chaplain, which was, at least in theory, permitted by the generous rubrics of the *Westminster Directory*. Taylor's contemporary, Richard Baxter, of Presbyterian persuasion and a Parliamentary chaplain, produced the *Reformed Liturgy* in 1661 as an alternative to the *Book of Common Prayer*. The theology of these two clergymen, and their liturgical proposals, give an interesting insight as to where the divergent theologies of the Church of England were heading.

Taylor's baptismal rite represents a revision of the *Book of Common Prayer* rite, augmented with his own exhortatory material and theology, together with some material borrowed from the Roman rite. In his work *Unum Necessarium*, Taylor set forth a controversial doctrine of original sin, which seemed to suggest that it was mortality rather than a sinful nature *per se* that was inherited from Adam.[35] In a later work, *Deus Justificatus*, Taylor distanced himself from Calvin, the Supralapsarians, the Sublapsarians and the Westminster Confession chapter on original sin. The result is that in his baptismal rite, Taylor played down the idea of original sin. His opening exhortation stated:

> ... it is necessary that every man who is reckoned in Adam should be also reckoned in Christ, that every one who is born of the flesh, be also born again, and born of the Spirit, that every son of man by nature may become the son of God by Adoption.[36]

---

[33] See Spinks, *Sacraments, Ceremonies and the Stuart Divines*, appendix 3; G.W. Sprott, *Scottish Liturgies of the Reign of James VI*, William Blackwood, Edinburgh, 1901.

[34] See Chapter 2.

[35] *Works* (Heber-Eden edition, London 1847–52), Vol. 7. See Bryan D. Spinks, 'Two Seventeenth Century examples of *Lex Credendi, Lex Orandi*: The Baptismal and Eucharistic Liturgies of Jeremy Taylor and Richard Baxter', *Studia Liturgica* 21 (1991), 165–89.

[36] Text in H. Boone Porter, *Jeremy Taylor, Liturgist*, Alcuin Club/SPCK, London, 1979.

Here we seem to have the idea of natural man becoming supernatural by adoption. On the question of justification, Taylor departed from the notion that the righteousness of Christ was imputed to the believer. Rather, he felt, it is because of the righteousness of Christ that the faith of the believer counts for justification. For Taylor, obedience precedes justification, and justification and baptism are but the gate and portal towards pardon. They are conditional, depending for their efficacy upon previous obedience and a subsequent holy life.

Taylor adopted what by the seventeenth century was common theological parlance, namely, the Reformed terminology of the Covenant of Grace. But he seems to have nuanced it with his view of justification and holiness. The opening exhortation of his rite expressed the hope that the child 'may all his life walk in this Covenant of grace and holiness'. His exhortation to the godparents explained, 'It is a Covenant of grace and favour on God's part and of faith and obedience on ours.' Faith and works are held together in justification. Taylor also utilized the common Reformed defence of infant baptism. After readings from Matthew 3:13–17 and Mark 10:13–17, in a second exhortation Taylor included an optional passage which discussed circumcision in the Old Testament, and explained:

> [... so Baptisme which is now the seal of the same faith and the same righteousness, and a figure like unto the former is to be administred to infants although they have no more actual faith then the children of Israel had; our Blessed Saviour having made Baptisme as necessary in the New Testament as Circumcision in the Old. For because little children can receive the kingdome of God, and in infants there is no incapacity of receiving the mercies of god, the adoption to be children of God, a title to the promises, the covenant of repentance and a right to pardon; whosoever shall deny to baptize infants when he is justly required, is sacrilegious and uncharitable. Since therefore the Church of God hath so great, so cleer, so indubitable a warrant to baptize infants, and therefore did alwaies practice it,] let us humbly and charitably give thanks to God ... .[37]

In the Cromwellian Church, certain ministers were persuaded against infant baptism, such as John Tombes of Bewdley, and hence the reference to sacrilegious and uncharitable refusal.[38]

In his *Great Exemplar*, Taylor wrote:

> The holy Ghost descends upon the waters of baptism, and makes them prolifical, apt to produce children unto God: and therefore St. Leo compares the font of baptism to the womb of the blessed Virgin, when it was replenished with the holy spirit.[39]

In the opening exhortation of his liturgical rite he wrote:

---

[37] Porter, facsimile reproduction between pp. 40–41, in *Jeremy Taylor, Liturgist*.

[38] Spinks, *Sacraments, Ceremonies and the Stuart Divines*; E. Brooks Holifield, *The Covenant Sealed. The Development of Puritan Sacramental Theology in Old and New England, 1570–1720*, Yale University Press, New Haven, CT and London, 1979.

[39] Taylor, *Works*, 2:240.

Let us humbly and devoutly pray unto God in the name of our Lord Jesus Christ
that he will be pleased to send down his holy Spirit upon these waters of Baptisme;
that they may become to this infant [all that shall be washed in them] a laver of
regeneration, and a well of water springing up to life eternal.

Two prayers of blessing were included, based on the Roman blessing of the font. The
second included the words, 'he blesse and sanctifie by his holy Spirit this water, that
it maybe instrumental and effective of grace, of pardon and sanctification'. Taylor
also believed that at baptism each person was assigned a guardian angel. He gave this
liturgical expression in a blessing before the final charge to the godparents.

Richard Baxter represented the 'godly' or Presbyterian party in the Church of
England. Like Taylor, Baxter's views on original sin were suspect to many of his
friends; in the 1640s he had adopted the Amyraldian view of grace and 'hypothetic
universalism'. In Adam the first sin was actual, and thence followed the 'habitual
pravity'. Adam's sin is imputed to us. But there were degrees of sin, and Baxter was
much more concerned with actual sin than with original sin. He openly espoused the
Reformed concept of the covenant of works and the covenant of grace, and in fact the
term 'covenant' occurs some twenty-one times in his rite. In 1649 he had published
his *Aphorisms of Justification*, which seemed to some to teach Arminianism
condemned at the Synod of Dort in 1619. Baxter seems to have adopted the idea of a
bilateral covenant, requiring not only faith, but piety and holiness on the part of the
believer, and thus is not too distant from Taylor on this matter.

Baxter saw no place for godparents, and in his proposed rite of 1661, which
combined some Prayer Book elements with Scripture and his own interpretation of
the *Westminster Directory*, exhortations and questions were addressed only to the
parents. The opening exhortation explained that the child is 'solemnly entered a visible
member of Christ and his Church, a child of God, and an heir of heaven'. The prayer
before baptism asked God: ' be reconciled to him, and take him for thy child, renew
him in the image of thy Son, and make him a fellow citizen with the saints, and one
of thy household'. The prayer after baptism thanked God that he has 'now received
this child into thy covenant and church, as a member of Christ by this sacrament of
regeneration'. Unlike Taylor, Baxter saw no need to include a blessing of the water
or a petition that God will use the water. And there was no signing with the sign of
the cross. Thus Baxter presented a rite which was based on the structure and themes
of the provisions in the *Westminster Directory*, though the interrogations and
confession of faith were suggested by the *Book of Common Prayer*.[40]

Though the prose of these two rites is very different, they both tone down original
sin, use covenant theology, and stress the need for an obedient and holy life. However,
the Restoration Settlement resulted in a *Book of Common Prayer* which was only a
mild revision of the former book. Because during the Cromwellian period a number
of people had not been baptized in infancy, and to meet the need of Native American

---

[40] The Savoy Liturgy is to be found in Baxter, Richard, *The Practical Works of Richard Baxter*, William
Orme (ed.), 23 vols, J. Duncan, London, 1830, vol. 1.

converts in the new American colonies, a new rite of baptism for those of 'Riper Years' was provided. Here was a certain irony in that the old Catholic rites had been rites for adults, used by adaptation for infants. The Reformation had turned these rites into rites for infant baptism, requiring a new rite for adults to be authored.

The changes made in the rite of public baptism were mainly cosmetic and stylistic. Because of the separate rite for adults, this was now styled as the ministration of public baptism *of infants*. A rubric required three godparents, two of which must be of the same sex as the child. The *sindflugebet* was slightly altered, and the reference to Christ sanctifying the Jordan 'and all other waters' was changed to 'didst sanctifie water to the mystical washing away of sin'. This theme was picked up in the prayer over the font immediately before baptism, which now had the additional words 'sanctifie this Water to the mysticall washing away of sin'. A rubric at the end of the former rite which commanded that the children be taught the Creed, Commandments and Catechism, was now set as a direct admonition. The liturgical rites in the Restoration *Book of Common Prayer* retained basically the text of the sixteenth century, even though theological discussion, as evidenced by Perkins and Hooker, Ward and Burgess, Taylor and Baxter, had moved well beyond that text and its theology.[41] And public baptism seems to have become an exception rather than the norm. William Sherlock of St Paul's wrote in 1682:

> Public baptism is now very much grown out of fashion; most people look upon it as a very needless and troublesome ceremony, to carry their children to the public congregation, there to be solemnly admitted into the fellowship of Christ's church. They think it may be as well done in a private chamber, as soon as the child is born, with little company and with little noise.[42]

Noise may have been thought inappropriate at the baptism, but not at the celebrations afterwards.[43] Samuel Pepys had recorded his attendance at a baptism at the house of Michael Mitchell, a liquor-seller, in 1667:

> His little house full of his father and mothers and the kindred, hardly any else, and mighty merry in this innocent company; and Betty mighty pretty in bed, but her head aching, not very merry; but the company mighty merry, and I with them; and so the child was christened, my wife, his father, and her mother the witnesses, and the child's name Elizabeth. So we had gloves and wine and wafers, very pretty, and talked and tattled.[44]

With private baptism becoming the norm, Cranmer's ritual actions within the rite became obscured.

No official revision of the rite took place in the Church of England until the twentieth century. In 1689 an attempt was made to bring in moderate Presbyterians

---

[41] Spinks, *Sacraments, Ceremonies and the Stuart Divines*.

[42] Cited in David Cressy, *Birth, Marriage and Death. Ritual, Religion, and the Life-Cycle in Tudor and Stuart England*, Oxford University Press, Oxford, 1997, p. 192.

[43] See ibid. for the social customs.

[44] Ibid., p. 191.

who had left in 1662, and a revised liturgy known as the *Liturgy of Comprehension* was drafted, but it came to nothing.[45] In this proposed revision, the *sindflugebet* would have been emended again to read 'didst *appoint water to be used in this sacrament for* the mystical washing away of sin', and although the rite retained the cross in baptism, a rubric at the end of the rite allowed for it to be omitted by those of tender conscience.

In the eighteenth century a number of private proposals were made. William Whiston succeeded Isaac Newton in the Lucasian Chair of Mathematics at Cambridge, and like Newton, held heterodox views on the Trinity. Newton's views were not published in his lifetime, but Whiston published his views and was deprived of the Cambridge Chair. Whiston proposed using material from the *Apostolic Constitutions*, in the conviction that these were the work of the Apostles.[46] Dr Samuel Clarke, another Newtonian disciple, also set forth what was regarded as a heterodox theology of the Trinity. He expressed the view that all prayer should really be directed only to the Father. In an interleaved Prayer Book of 1724 he entered his suggested amendments to the *Book of Common Prayer* to bring it in line with his theology. These suggestions were expanded and published after his death by Theophilus Lindsey. In this rite the Prayer Book service was considerably truncated. The baptismal formula was rendered after Zwingli's observations, 'I baptize thee into the name of the Father, and of the Son, and of the holy Spirit.'

The first official revision outside England was the 1789 *Book of Common Prayer* of the Protestant Episcopal Church of the United States of America. In this rite parents may serve as sponsors, the Credal confession is abbreviated, and the sign of the cross could be omitted.[47]

The Nineteenth-Century 'Angry Controversy'

From the sixteenth century, with William Perkins and Richard Hooker, there had existed within the Church of England divergent views on sacraments, and this divergence continued through the seventeenth and eighteenth centuries. Apart from the Cromwellian period when the *Book of Common Prayer* had been replaced by the *Westminster Directory*, the varying theological opinions were held together by a common liturgical ritual. In the mid-nineteenth century disputes between the High Churchmen, the Evangelicals and the Broad Churchmen became more vitriolic, and

---

[45] Timothy Fawcett, *The Liturgy of Comprehension 1689*, Mayhew-McCrimmon, Southend-on-Sea, 1973.

[46] Bryan D. Spinks, 'Johannes Grabe's Response to William Whiston', Bart Day et al. (eds), *Lord Jesus Christ, Will You Not Stay. Essays in Honor of Ronald Feuerhahn on the Occasion of His Sixty-Fifth Birthday*, Concordia Publishing House, St Louis, MO, 2002, pp. 91–104.

[47] Marion Hatchett, *The Making of the First American Book of Common Prayer*, Seabury Press, New York, 1982, pp. 124–5.

the meaning of baptismal regeneration – already a point of debate and dispute in the seventeenth century – became 'a subject of angry controversy', which has been documented by Peter Jagger.[48]

In 1848 the bishop of Exeter, Henry Phillpotts, refused to induct George Gorham as incumbent of Speke on the grounds that his teaching on baptismal regeneration was unsound. Phillpotts was a High Churchman, and in an Episcopal Charge of 1845 had stated:

> Baptism is not merely the seal of a new covenant, but also God's method of giving to us a new nature, wherein we are born of the Spirit, and are thus really, though mystically, made one with Christ, and, through Christ, with the Father.[49]

Gorham, in contrast, seems to have taught that infants were not worthy recipients of baptism unless they had received prevenient grace; if they were lacking this, no spiritual grace was conveyed in the baptismal ritual. The court case which resulted eventually gave the victory to Gorham, in that he was instituted to the living (by the Archbishop of Canterbury) and his teaching was declared to be not incompatible with the teaching of the Church of England.

The High Church view of baptismal regeneration was set forth by Edward Pusey in the Oxford *Tracts for the Times*, Tracts 67, 68 and 69, which were later published as *Scriptural View of Holy Baptism*. Defending the idea that in baptism we are regenerated, Pusey wrote:

> The plain letter of Scripture says, 'We are saved by baptism', and men say, 'We are not saved by baptism': our Lord says, 'A man must be born of water and the Spirit'; man, that he need not, cannot be born of water: Scripture, that 'we are saved by the washing of regeneration'; man, that we are not, but by regeneration, which is as a washing … Surely they have entered into a most perilous path, which, unless they are checked in pursuing it, must end in the rejection of all Scripture truth which does not square with their own previous opinions.[50]

He argued:

> Baptismal regeneration, as connected with the Incarnation of our Blessed Lord, gives a depth to our Christian existence, an actualness to our union with Christ, a reality to our sonship to God, an interest in the presence of our Lord's glorified Body at God's right hand, a joyousness amid the subduing of the flesh, an overwhelmingness to the dignity conferred on human nature, a solemnity to the communion of saints who are the fulness of Him who filleth all in all, a substantiality to the indwelling of Christ, that to those who retain this truth the school which abandoned it must needs appear to have sold its birthright.[51]

---

[48] Peter J. Jagger, *Clouded Witness*, Pickwick Publications, Allison Park, PA, 1982. The section of this chapter is greatly indebted to Jagger's studies of this period. The reference to angry controversy is in a sermon by Bishop John Kaye, cited by Jagger, p. 9.

[49] H. Phillpotts, *A Charge 1845*, 30, cited in Jagger, ibid., p. 8.

[50] Edward Pusey, *Tracts for the Times*, 3 vols, Charles Henry, New York, 1839–40, Vol. 2, 69, p. 198.

[51] Ibid., 67, p. 12.

The *Tracts* gave rise to the name Tractarians, though not all High Churchmen shared all the ideas set forth by the Tractarians. Another High Churchman, J.B. Mozley, in his *The Primitive Doctrine of Baptismal Regeneration* (1856), asserted that although the regeneration of adults cannot be ascertained with certainty, 'in the case of infants we can assert … infants … are certainly regenerate after baptism and if they die as infants are certainly saved'.[52]

Whereas baptismal regeneration became the watchword of the Tractarians and other High Churchmen, the Evangelical party were more concerned with conversion, and were concerned with the distinction between the visible and invisible Church. Charles Simeon held that baptism is necessary for all who embrace the faith of Christ, and is full of blessings for those who receive it aright. The outward ritual gives us a title to the blessing of the Christian covenant, but if we receive it 'not aright', we will be like Simon Magus. We must have both the sign and the thing signified. Baptism brings a change of state rather than a change of nature; it begins a process whereby change may come about.[53] The evangelical Canon Frederick Meyrick expressed it as a 'change of federal relation and of spiritual condition but not of moral disposition'.[54] Another representative of the Evangelical wing was William Goode, who held:

> Baptism is the formal act of incorporation into Christ's Body, the Church; not merely the visible Church, but (when God acts in the ordinance) the true Church, the mystical Body of Christ. And therefore it may justly be said, that, where it is efficacious, that we are regenerated by it. For whereas, before, we were only the children of Adam, and so of wrath; we are hereby made children of grace, members of Christ. But it must be remembered that as in the natural birth, there was life previously; so in the spiritual new birth, life, a living principle of faith must have been implanted to make the birth by baptism effectual to the production of a being spiritually alive.[55]

In his study of this period, Peter Jagger also identified a 'Broad Church' position, and cited Frederick Temple as a representative. Temple described baptism as 'the bestowal of a germ of spiritual vitality which, if cultivated, will grow with a child's feebler impulses of his humanity to triumph over those lower selfish ones, which are unhappily the stronger'.[56] In the process of regeneration, Temple saw two powers at work: natural conscience and the grace of God. At baptism an infant is promised grace, but this will come at a time best for the infant, and it may be rejected by him. Similarly Connop Thirlwall held that the gift of the Spirit is given according to the capacity of the recipient, not immediately, but according to God's good pleasure. Thirlwall appealed

---

52   J.B. Mozley, *The Primitive Doctrine of Baptismal Regeneration*, London, 1856, pp. 129–30, cited by Jagger, p. 10.

53   Summary in Jagger, *Clouded Witness*, pp. 17–18.

54   Ibid., p. 23.

55   William Goode, *The Doctrine of the Church of England as to the effects of Baptism in the case of Infants*, 1849, pp. 21–2; see Peter Toon, *Evangelical Theology 1833–1856. A Response to Tractarianism*, John Knox Press, Atlanta, GA, 1979.

56   Jagger, *Clouded Witness*, p. 34.

to the idea of covenant, and noted that the gift depended on the fulfilment of the baptismal contract.[57]

The rise of the Tractarian movement led to the formation of the Free Church of England, and, in the USA, the Reformed Episcopal Church. One of the hallmarks of its baptismal rite in its version of the *Book of Common Prayer* was the removal of references to regeneration and the blessing of the water.[58]

A quite distinct contribution was made by F.D. Maurice. It is difficult to place Maurice in any party, though perhaps he could be termed 'Broad Church'. Of Maurice's theology William J. Wolf has written:

> The basic principle of Maurice's theology is that God has created and redeemed the whole human race in Christ. The heart of the Gospel, as he understood it, is that Christ, the Eternal Son of God, is 'the Head and the King of our entire race.' He believed this to be the witness of the creeds and behind them of the biblical revelation. He interpreted every Christian doctrine, and the human situation as well, in the light of the doctrines of the Incarnation and Atonement, placed in a Trinitarian setting.[59]

Indeed, this is the context of his teaching on baptism. Since the work of Christ was cosmic, baptism simply declared the actual relationship of humanity to God. Humans by right are children of God, and baptism is the means by which they are set within the circle of light which had been always shining for all humanity and was gradually to lead it into the fullness of truth. There are perhaps some correspondences here with Schleiermacher's idea of God Consciousness. For Maurice, baptism is the sacrament of 'constant union' and the pledge that every human is a child of God. Baptism creates unity with Christ, and a unity with the church and all humanity:

> Thou belongest to the head of thy race, thou art a member of His Body ... thou hast the nature of the Divine Son, thou art united to Him in whom is life, and from whom the life of thee and of all creatures comes.[60]

Elsewhere Maurice summed up his teaching on baptism thus:

> We are baptised into the Name of Father, and of Son, and of Holy Ghost. The Spirit with whom we are taken into covenant accompanies us through all our pilgrimage. If we accept the teaching of our Baptism Service and of our Catechism, we must ascribe to Him all the good thoughts of the child, its perceptions of the unrealised world in which it is dwelling, its intuitions of a spiritual world with which it has to do, its power of receiving and returning affection, its capacity of understanding and of making itself understood. To the same source we must trace the awakening of conscience in the boy, his acknowledgement of a law against

---

[57] Ibid., p. 35.

[58] John Fenwick, *The Free Church of England. Introduction to an Anglican Tradition*, T & T Clark, London, 2004.

[59] William J. Wolf, 'Frederick Denison Maurice', in William J. Wolf, John E. Booty and Owen C. Thomas (eds), *The Spirit of Anglicanism*, T & T Clarke, Edinburgh, 1979, p. 74.

[60] F.D. Maurice, *Sermons Preached in Lincoln's Inn Chapel*, 6 vols, 1891, Vol. 1, p. 81, cited by Jagger, *Clouded Witness*, p. 31.

which his inclinations are struggling, his sense of powers which are to wrestle with the earth and to subdue it, his faculties of learning, his craving for fellowship.[61]

For Maurice, baptism discloses the status of all humanity which is inherent in the incarnation – a view shared by neither the High Churchmen nor the Evangelicals.

Concluding Remarks

The baptismal rite in the foundational *Books of Common Prayer* 1549–1662 was derived from the Sarum medieval rite, but with Lutheran inspiration in places, as well as Thomas Cranmer's own theological and liturgical ideas. The omission in 1552 of an explicit blessing of the water was regarded as a defect which was corrected in 1662. According to Stephen Sykes, Cranmer's rite can be regarded as the making of a covenant.[62] Although this is a legitimate reading of the rite, this should not be confused as implying that Cranmer promoted the concept of baptism as covenant. As we have noted, he avoided this terminology, and the emphasis in the rite is on remission of sins and entry into the (ark of) the Church. Later seventeenth and eighteenth-century divines would use covenant in their theological writings about baptism, but this was imported from the Reformed theological vocabulary, and found no verbal support in the liturgical text. The doctrinal wars which erupted in the nineteenth century bequeathed to Anglicanism in England and elsewhere the question of the relationship of conversion and faith to infant baptism, and the meaning of the language of regeneration in the rite. In England itself, it would raise the question of whether in fact anyone should or could be baptized – particularly as the trend found in the 1851 Religious Census of declining allegiance to the Established or any Church would continue into the twentieth century. In an Established Church, any parishioner could demand baptism for their child, regardless of their own allegiance to the Church. The question of whether infant baptism should be restricted to active church members would begin to surface in the twentieth century, and this would indirectly affect revision of the baptismal ritual.

---

[61] F.D. Maurice, *The Faith of the Liturgy and the Doctrines of the Thirty-nine Articles. Two Sermons*, Cambridge, 1869, pp. 19–20.

[62] Sykes, 'Baptisme doth represente'.

CHAPTER 4

The Radical Reformation Tradition: Anabaptists, English Separatists, Baptists and Quakers

Luther, we have observed, made no liturgical reforms until 1523, and when he did, it was in reaction not primarily against his Catholic opponents, but against those he regarded as dangerous fanatics who had rushed ahead, and, so he claimed, had misunderstood him. Andreas Karlstadt, taking Luther's use of the word 'faith' in a subjective manner, had by the end of 1523 rejected infant baptism, insisting that water without faith was no more efficacious than a bath. Another 'fanatic' to Luther's mind was Thomas Müntzer of Allstedt.

Thomas Müntzer and Anabaptism

Müntzer is a strange figure, who developed an apocalyptic revolutionary theology, and was executed for his part in the peasants' uprising. Müntzer aligned himself with emerging groups who advocated restricting baptism to adults, though he himself did not abandon infant baptism. In his Protestation or Proposition of 1524 he declared that initiation in the Christian Church had become 'crude monkey-play', because infant baptism was unknown in the early Church.[1] According to Müntzer, 'water' in John 3:35 should be read in the light of John 7:37, and is really referring to the Holy Spirit.[2] He held that a covenant was created within by the Spirit of God, which was inward baptism. However, this was linked with the suffering which must be undergone in the Christian life. He wrote, 'We have covenanted ourselves in baptism; a Christian should, and must suffer.'[3]

As pastor at Allstedt he issued liturgies in the German language, including an outline for a baptismal rite in which godparents were first exhorted to pay heed to what baptism means. Psalm 68 was read in German, and then Matthew 3. Salt was presented to the child, though its exorcistic role was spiritualized: '*N*, receive the salt of wisdom, so you may learn to distinguish good and evil in the spirit of wisdom, and never be trodden down by the devil.'

---

[1] Peter Matheson, *The Collected Works of Thomas Müntzer*, T & T Clark, Edinburgh, 1988, p. 191.

[2] Ibid., p. 192.

[3] Ibid., p. 102, in a letter to Hans Zwiss, 25 July 1524. See also Rollin Stely Armour, *Anabaptist Baptism*, Wipf and Stock, Eugene, OR, 1998, pp. 59–62.

The child was invited to become a member of the people of God. The Creed was spoken, the devil renounced, and the child anointed. The priest asked if the parents wished baptism for the child. Then the child was baptized with the following formula:

> I baptize you in the name of the Father, and of the Son and of the Holy Spirit. Amen. May God who has conceived you of his eternal love, grant that you may avoid the oil of the sinner.

Then a bonnet or garment was put on, and a lighted candle given to the infant with the words:

> *N.*, let Christ be your light; see that your light is not darkness, but let the life of Christ be your mirror, that you may live to all eternity. Amen.

Though aligned with the emerging Anabaptist groups, Müntzer was not himself one of their leaders. Anabaptism does not have one single origin, though it does have interconnections. Anabaptist movements emerged in Switzerland, South Germany and the Netherlands, with different theologies. What was held in common was the concept of a believers' church, and the insistence on believers' baptism. For the developed teaching of the movement we must turn to some of the leading figures of early Anabaptism.[4]

Balthasar Hubmaier

Hubmaier was born *c.* 1480, became a Catholic priest and gained a doctorate and taught in the University of Ingolstadt. In the 1520s he read works by Luther, Zwingli and Erasmus, and this changed his life. He allied himself with Zwingli, but felt that Zwingli had failed to have the courage of his convictions on the issue of infant baptism. Hubmaier aligned himself with the Anabaptist groups which were emerging – and which had indirect links with the social unrest underlying the peasants' uprisings. On Holy Saturday, 15 April 1525, Wilhelm Reublin, a Catholic priest who rejected infant baptism, rebaptized sixty people, including Hubmaier. On Easter Sunday Hubmaier rebaptized some three hundred people, resigned as a parish priest, and became pastor of the newly formed Anabaptist congregation in Waldshut. All churches – Catholic, Lutheran and Reformed – recoiled in horror at this movement, and all made Anabaptism a crime punishable by death, though in fact some areas, such as Strasbourg, were tolerant and allowed congregations to exist openly. Hubmaier was burnt at the stake in Vienna on 10 March 1528.

Where did Hubmaier part company with Zwingli? Zwingli was a Swiss patriot, and believed in a state church under the Magistrate. He also believed that one is born into a covenanted community, and original sin was not a great issue for him. Hubmaier held that one is born into sin and must choose consciously to be part of the Church. Therefore faith is needed. In reply to Zwingli he wrote:

---

4 Much of what follows is indebted to the important study of Armour, *Anabaptist Baptism*.

You ask, 'what or how much must I know if I want to be baptized?' The answer is that you must know this much of the Word of God before you receive baptism: you must confess yourself a miserable sinner and consider yourself guilty; you must believe in the forgiveness of your sins through Jesus Christ and begin a new life with the good resolution to improve your life and to order it according to the will of Christ in the power of God the Father, the Son, and the Holy Ghost; and, if you err therein, you must be willing to accept discipline according to the rule of Christ in Matthew 18: [15–20], so that you may grow in faith from day to day like a mustard seed, even up into the clouds of heaven. That much you must know. To know and to believe this is to believe that Jesus is the Christ, which belief is necessary before baptism.[5]

Even more sharply than Zwingli, Hubmaier drew a distinction between inward baptism and the outward ritual action, and in words quoted almost word for word from Zwingli, asserted, 'No physical element or external thing in this world can cleanse the soul; but faith cleanses the hearts of men. Thus it follows that baptism can wash away no sin.'[6] Against Zwingli he argued that if baptism is a sign of a pledge, the pledge must come before the sign. Hubmaier complained that the priest,

> … mumbles over the infant in Latin (it could as well be German, for infants know one as well as the other; it is an error either way). Then the priest asks: 'Credis in deum patrem omnipotentem, creatorem celi et terre? Say, "I believe."' Now if it is in the Word of God that the godparents are to answer for the infant, 'I believe,' prove it with clear Scripture. But if it were in Scripture, why would the priest not say to the godmother and godfather: 'You godparents, say "We believe?"' … ' What they say should be said by the infant.[7]

Hubmaier's charge illustrates the fact that the Latin rite assumed adult baptisms, but it also illustrates why the Reformed tradition sat lightly to the tradition of godparents, and placed the theological weight on covenant holiness and parental promises.

Rebaptism became the visible sign of this ecclesiological distinction. Like the Donatists, Hubmaier believed that there was no salvation outside the true church. He also argued for a distinction between the baptism of John and of Jesus in his ministry, and baptism after the resurrection which now depended on the gift of the Spirit. Thus infant baptism was not baptism at all, and rebaptism was not rebaptism but real baptism. Hubmaier explained:

> In receiving water baptism, the baptizand confesses publicly that he has yielded himself to live henceforth according to the rule of Christ. In the power of this confession he has submitted himself to the sisters, the brethren, and the church, so that they now have the authority to admonish him if he errs, to discipline, to ban, and to readmit him … Whence comes this authority if not from the baptismal vow?[8]

---

5 *Von der christlichen Taufe der Gläugigen*, 1525, cited in Armour, ibid., p. 29.
6 Ibid., cited in Armour, ibid., p. 30.
7 Ibid., cited in Armour, ibid., p. 42.
8 Cited in Armour, ibid., p. 43.

Hubmaier also spoke of three baptisms, based on 1 John 5:6–8: of external water baptism on confession of faith before the Church, of blood in martyrdom, and of suffering.

In 1527 Hubmaier wrote three liturgical texts, one of which was a rite for baptism. It obviously presupposes adult candidates. The bishop gave an examination of the candidates' faith and then the congregation prayed for the person. A prayer asked for the coming of the Spirit, followed by the threefold interrogation – traditional, based on the Creed. But some other promises were added: a short renunciation of evil, a promise to follow the Word of Christ, and then a promise to uphold the teaching in Matthew's Gospel regarding a brother sinning. This 'ban' was important to Hubmaier's theology of the Church.

Then the candidate was asked if he/she desired baptism which brings incorporation into the visible Church (hence the denial of the efficacy of a previous infant baptism) and remission of sins. The traditional baptismal formula was retained. After the baptism prayer was made, the bishop or chief pastor lay his hand on the head of the new member and gave a formula of admission to the Church. One might also note that there was no insistence on submersion – indeed, Hubmaier baptized with a milk pail balanced on top of the old font in his church. The move to submersion was a later development.

In a letter to Oecolampadius, Hubmaier described a dedication service for infants in place of baptism. The infant would be brought before the assembled congregation, the minister would explain the Gospel passage, 'Let the children come unto me', the child would be named, and then the Church would pray that Christ would be gracious to the child.

Hans Hut

Hans Hut had been associated with Müntzer and the peasant uprising at Frankenhausen. Released by the authorities, he returned to his home at Bibra and attempted to stir up a revolution. The peasant revolutionaries were crushed, and Hut fled. It was at this stage that Hut seemed to have developed a concept of eschatological baptism in anticipation of the return of Christ. One Hermann Anwald testified:

> Hut took two fingers, dipped them in water, and made the sign of the cross on his forehead. Whoever does not have this cross will find God sending His angel who will strike him dead. And all who are unbaptized will be slain by the angel.[9]

In his work *True Baptism*, Hut wrote:

> Water baptism is a sign only, a covenant, a parable and a memorial of desire, which the person can remember daily in expectation of the true baptism. This baptism is, as Christ said, the waters of tribulation by which the Lord makes us clean, washes and saves us from all carnal lusts, sins and unclean works and behaviour. Just as we recognize that no creature can justify itself and come to its true purpose without

---

[9] Cited in Armour, ibid., p. 87.

becoming subject to humans, so also no person can justify himself and come to his true purpose, that is, to blessedness, but by accepting the baptism of affliction which God has shown and worked in the person and to which the person is subjected as justification. If a person is to be justified by God he must be still before the Lord his God and to allow God to work in him as God wills. For as David said, trust in the Lord and place your hope in him, for He does all things well.

Therefore, the water of tribulation is the real essence and power of baptism, by which the person is swallowed up in the death of Christ.

This baptism was not first instituted in the time of Christ. It has been from the beginning and is a baptism with which all friends of God, from Adam to the present, are baptized, as Paul said. Jesus accepted this covenant with God in the Jordan river. Here he demonstrated love to all people, in obedience to the Father, even unto death and became an example of one upon whom the baptism of tribulation was richly poured out by the Father. That is why the sign and the essence of baptism must be clearly distinguished from each other. The Christian community administers the sign of the covenant of baptism through one of her true servants, just as Christ received it from John. The true baptism then follows. God administers it through the waters of tribulation and in return He offers the comfort of the Holy Spirit. God lets no one founder in this baptism, for it is written, 'He leads into hell and out again, he makes dead and then brings to life again'. This is the baptism with which the Lord was baptized. Whoever would be a disciple of the Lord must be baptized and made pure in the Holy Spirit and be united by the bonds of peace into one body.[10]

Once again, suffering becomes an instrumental part of this Anabaptist understanding of baptism. The sign of water baptism is retained, almost as the outward trigger which anticipates the baptism of tribulation, during which the Holy Spirit will be the comforter.

Melchior Hoffman (d. 1543)

Melchior Hoffman was one of the Strasbourg Anabaptists. Hoffman adopted a theology of universal atonement, with freedom of the human will to accept faith.[11] He saw regeneration in two stages: the birth of the 'letter', in which a person became a child of God, and the birth of the spirit, when a person became an elect one of God. Baptism in water was the making of a covenant pledge to struggle to achieve full spiritual birth. Hoffman used the analogy of a vow to a king, but he also likened it to a nuptial vow. Like other Anabaptist leaders, however, Hoffman also linked baptism with struggle and suffering. His typological approach to Scripture enabled him to see water baptism as a dedication towards entrance into a wilderness experience of testing and cleansing. The Exodus story pointed to a time when the Church would be led into the wilderness in preparation for the end of the world and the establishing of the

---

[10] Hans Hut, *True Baptism*. English translation from: <http://www.anabaptist.org/Baptism.htm>.
[11] Armour, *Anabaptist Baptism*, pp. 97ff.

Kingdom of God. At the end of time there would be two special witnesses – Elijah and Enoch; Hoffman saw himself as Elijah.

Hoffman left no details of how baptism was administered, though according to a Lutheran source, he had administered the rite in a room of a church building which served as a vestry, and 'out of a barrel', which suggests that it was by pouring. During imprisonment in 1539 he is reported to have recanted and accepted infant baptism, but it may be that this simply meant that he was able recognize infant baptism as the first baptism.

Pilgram Marpeck

Marpeck was one of the most reflective interpreters of Anabaptist belief. He argued that there were two biblical covenants. The old covenant made in eternity and renewed with Noah, Abraham and Moses, lacked the power to bring salvation. In Jesus Christ, the old covenant 'figura' gave place to the reality, which Marpeck pinpointed as being when Christ descended into Hades and preached to the Old Testament dead. The new covenant brings the covenant of a good conscience, and a heart cleansed from sin. Regeneration had three stages. Marpeck wrote:

> First, one must be born through the Word as he dedicates himself to it in full faith. Second, he is born through water. At that time power is present to become a child of God [which begetting will take place later as the third birth] both here and in the life to come. 'He who endures to the end will be saved,' if he accepts Christ and desires to become a child of God and do His will.[12]

As with other Anabaptist teachers, Marpeck emphasized that suffering was an important ingredient in redemption, and that water served as the symbol, 'for wherever water is spoken of in Scripture, it means affliction, anguish, woe, and suffering, and the watery deep means bodily death'.[13] This suffering was both an inner spiritual suffering as well as physical suffering in the world.

Marpeck argued that there were two steps in the process of new birth. First was birth through the Word as Law and Gospel and then birth through Water and Spirit. Regeneration took place after these, which was demonstrated by keeping the commandments and sharing the sufferings of Christ. Marpeck also spoke of the covenant pledge. The Spirit created a good conscience – in fact, the Strasbourg Anabaptists spoke of a 'covenant of good conscience'.[14] According to Armour, what was significant about Marpeck was the way he held together the outward sign with what he believed to be the inner reality. He wrote:

> As in all other matters, the reality must precede its own witness, so that the sign can be rightly taken or given. When otherwise, the sign is false and a vain

---

12 *Glaubensbekenntnis*, quoted in Armour, ibid., p. 116.
13 Ibid., cited in Armour, ibid., p. 116.
14 Armour, ibid., p. 118.

mockery. If the reality is there and is known, then the sign is truly and wholly useful, and everything signified by the sign is [then] to be given to the sign, for it is no more a sign, but a reality.[15]

The unity of the action was described in three ways by Marpeck. First, the Spirit was a 'co-witness' in the believer; second, the three persons of the Trinity were deeply involved, and third, the soul and body were united as are the inward and outward baptism. He also spoke of three types of baptismal witness: water, Spirit and blood.

Marpeck rejected infant baptism, arguing that infants remain in 'creaturely innocence' until they come of age. He did, however, envision the dedication of infants. He left no indication of the baptismal ritual he and his Church followed, though in his writings the common use of the term 'pour' suggests that this was the mode of baptism used.

Menno Simons

Menno Simons (1496–1561) was a Catholic priest, ordained in 1524 in the Netherlands. He later became an Anabaptist elder. He attacked infant baptism, and defended rebaptism. In his *Foundation of Christian Doctrine*, Simons wrote that:

> … baptism is a sign of obedience, commanded by Christ, by which we testify when we receive it that we believe in the Word of the Lord, that we repent of our former life and conduct, and that we desire to rise with Christ unto a new life, and that we believe in the forgiveness of sins through Jesus Christ.[16]

Vincent G. Harding notes that here are the major strands of Simons' understanding of baptism – obedience to a command, testimony of belief, and pledge to live in newness of life – and that the believer is the active subject in this process.[17] Elsewhere Simons could assert that 'those who are regenerated, renewed and converted; who hear, believe and keep all the commandments and will of God …' and, 'In the outward ceremonies as such God takes no pleasure, but he has commanded them because he requires of us faithful obedience.'[18] For Simons, baptism was a command – Matthew 28:19 and Mark 16:16 – a command which must faithfully be obeyed. Indeed, this is why Jesus was baptized, as an act of obedience. Simons wrote, 'My dear sirs, we seek nothing in this baptism other than to obey our beloved Lord Jesus Christ, who has taught and commanded us this with His own blessed mouth.'[19]

Those who were disobedient gained no benefit from water. In fact, he held that we are received into God's covenant by faith and obedience; hence, infants cannot be in the covenant. He argued:

---

[15] Armour, ibid., p. 121.

[16] John C. Wenger, *The Complete Writings of Menno Simons*, Herald Press, Scottdale, PA, 1956, p. 125. See also pp. 120–42 for Simons' exposition of baptism and rejection of infant baptism.

[17] Vincent G. Harding, 'Menno and the Role of Baptism', *Mennonite Quarterly Review* 33 (1959), 323–34, p. 324.

[18] Wenger, *The Complete Writings*, p. 234.

[19] Ibid., p. 236.

> ... Abraham was circumcised, and we baptized, because it is thus commanded by God. Whatsoever disobeys and opposes the voice of the Lord commanding these ceremonies and despises the performance of them because of their uselessness and triviality, not observing that it was commanded by God, excludes himself from the precious covenant of grace by his disobedience; neither does he prove his faith to be fruitful and living, but on the contrary he proves that it is unfruitful and dead before God.[20]

However, Harding pointed out a contradiction in Simons. Of new birth Simons had said that it

> ... consists, verily, not in water nor in words; but it is the heavenly, living, and quickening power of God in our hearts which flows forth from God, and which by the preaching of the divine Word, if we accept it by faith, quickens, renews, pierces, and converts our hearts, so that we are changed and converted from unbelief to faith, from unrighteousness to righteousness ... from the wicked nature of Adam to the good nature of Jesus Christ.[21]

Those persons so regenerated are then baptized. This means that regeneration, salvation and conversion all come before baptism. However, he also asserted, 'We must receive this baptism ... Otherwise we cannot obtain remission of sins nor the Holy Ghost. For who has ever received the remission of sins contrary to the Word of God?'[22] This suggests that, to Simons, baptism was first in the order of salvation.

In a later work, *The New Birth*, Simons explained how the covenants and Spirit and water come together:

> In baptism they bury their sins in the Lord's death and rise with Him to a new life. They circumcise their hearts with the Word of the Lord; they are baptized with the Holy Ghost into the spotless, holy body of Christ; as obedient members of His church, according to the true ordinance and Word of the Lord. They put on Christ and manifest his Spirit, nature and power in all their conduct.[23]

Once more the emphasis is subjective: we desire to die and to rise. Yet at other times he suggested a more reciprocal understanding: 'The Lord has bound himself with us in His Grace, through His Word', and 'We henceforth bind ourselves by the outward sign of the covenant in water ... that we will no longer live according to the evil, unclean lusts of the flesh, but walk according to the witness of a good conscience before Him.'[24]

Simons provided no summary of the ritual he presupposed, though according to John Horsch, the word *doopsel* in Simons, which has sometimes been translated as 'dipping', simply means baptism, and his reference to 'a handful of water' suggests pouring rather than immersion as the mode which he presupposed.[25]

---

[20] Ibid., p. 262.

[21] Ibid., p. 265.

[22] Ibid., p. 244.

[23] Ibid., p. 93.

[24] Ibid., p. 125.

[25] John Horsch, 'Did Menno Simons Practice Baptism by Immersion?', *Mennonite Quarterly Review* 1 (1927), 54–6.

The Anabaptist leaders, like the Reformed, did not all share precisely the same ideas and theology. What we do find in common is use of the concept of covenant as a pledge, and the belief that humanity is given some capacity to actively make a pledge to God. The ritual of baptism comes afterwards, as a mature act of obedience to the prior faith. Yet it also testifies to further baptisms – particularly of suffering. As to the mode of baptism, in the sixteenth century, pouring seems to have been as acceptable as immersion.

Anabaptist Baptismal Rituals

The most notable successors of the sixteenth-century Anabaptists were the Mennonite and Amish communities, along with the German Brethren. The Mennonites were Swiss in origin but, together with Anabaptist groups in the Netherlands, took their name from Menno Simons. The Amish were a group that broke away from the Mennonites in 1693, under Jacob Amman, who wished to implement stricter discipline. The German Brethren began in 1708 in Schwarzenau, Germany. Subject to persecution, a large number migrated from Europe to the USA beginning in the eighteenth century. It is the baptismal rites of some of these groups which are considered here. The communities are by nature conservative, and thus their rituals conserve an earlier *traditio*. They tend to divide on a number of issues, including the mode of baptism. The Mennonite Brethren and some other small groups only immerse, and immersion is once and backwards; the Krimmer Mennonite Brethren immerse three times forward; and the Old Mennonites only pour water on the candidate's head.[26]

An Amish statement of belief and description of practice is preserved in Bishop Nafziger's Letter to the Ministers in the Netherlands, and is dated 1781. In the section on baptism, the letter explains:

> When we have applicants who desire to be received into the church of Christ and the congregation of God, whether young men or young women, the same come to us in council before the meeting (services) where they are instructed and are told of the almighty power of God, the creation of heaven and earth and all things visible … .[27]

Several paragraphs summarizing the catechesis follow. It includes the work of the triune God, and 'Further they are told about the new birth and the improvement of life, etc.'[28] At the end of the instruction (the period of time is not specified) the candidates are asked if they believe, and catechesis ends with a reading from Acts 2:22ff. The ritual is outlined as follows:

---

[26] For the various groups see Abraham P. Toews, *American Mennonite Worship*, Exposition Press, New York, 1960, Chapter IV. See p. 177 for the different practices.

[27] (Harold S. Bender ?), 'An Amish Church Discipline of 1781', *The Mennonite Quarterly* 4 (1930), 140–48, p. 141.

[28] Ibid., p. 142.

With these words the applicants are requested to come before the ministers and when they have fallen on their knees the story of Philip and the Ethiopian eunuch is told them, how he was reading the prophet Isaiah but did not understand it and how then Philip preached the Gospel to him, so that he desired to be baptized, and Philip baptized him. Then the applicant for baptism is asked: Do you believe from your whole heart that Jesus Christ is the Son of God ? Answer, yes. Do you believe that God has raised him from the dead, and are you willing to be obedient to God and the Church, whether to live or to die? Answer, Yes.

When then the head has been uncovered, whether young man or young woman, the bishop places his hands on the head and a fully ordained deacon pours water on his hands, whereupon the bishop calls him by name and says: 'On this confession of faith which thou hast confessed, thou art baptized in the name of God the Father and the son and the Holy Ghost'. Then the bishop gives him his hand and raises him up, pronounces peace and says: 'The Lord continue the good work which he hath begun in you and complete it unto a blessed end through Jesus Christ'. He then dismisses him in the name of God.

If no fully ordained deacon is present, another minister is permitted to pour the water into the hands of the bishop.[29]

Another manuscript 'Minister's Manual', which is undated, but perhaps also late eighteenth century, notes that instruction takes place, and describes the ritual of baptism as follows:

When the usual chapters have been read and explained with still other fitting words and speeches then one speaks at last of Philip and the official from Ethiopia out of the eighth chapter of Acts. Afterwards one presents the articles of faith to the applicants, not entirely according to the written letter indeed, but one explains them a little more briefly, otherwise it lasts altogether too long.

Afterward when everything has been presented fully and completely then as already mentioned above they are asked what then belongs to a true Christian faith whereupon the answer is to be, Baptism and Communion. Then one tells them to kneel down in the name of God. In all such cases of kneeling it is fitting that the bishop should say, 'This kneeling is not to be before me but before the all-highest and all-knowing God and his church.' Then they are asked, 'You also believe then that Jesus is the Son of God who has come into the world to save repentant sinners?' Whereupon the answer is, 'Yes'. Then baptism is administered according to the commandment of the Gospel.

When the ceremony of baptism is ended, then one extends his hand to one applicant after the other, raises them up and says, 'May the dear God who has begun this good work in you also help to complete it in you and to strengthen and comfort you therein to a blessed end, through Jesus Christ, Amen.' Also I do not consider it unfitting to give them the kiss [of fellowship] and to wish them peace.[30]

---

[29] Ibid., p. 143.

[30] John Umble, 'An Amish Minister's Manual', *The Mennonite Quarterly* 15 (1941), 95–117, 106–07.

Present-day descriptions of various Amish communities give only minor variations. Thus the *Amish County News*[31] gives the customs of the Lancaster County Amish. Catechesis classes are usually nine in number. Baptism take place as part of the normal church service, usually two services prior to the autumn communion:

> After the hymns and sermons, the young people kneel. They are reminded that this is a promise to God, witnessed by those at the church service. Each is asked four questions, signaling their commitment to join the church. Then the prayer coverings are removed from the head of each girl, and the bishop raises each applicant's head. He is assisted by the deacon who holds a wooden bucket. With a cup, the deacon pours some water from the bucket into the bishop's hands and onto each applicant's head three times, in the name of the Father, the Son, and the Holy Ghost.
>
> The hand of each applicant is taken and they are helped to their feet as the bishop, in the Pennsylvania German dialect, says these words, 'In the name of the Lord and the Church, we extend to you the hand of fellowship. Rise up, and be a faithful member of the church'. The boys are greeted as members with the Holy Kiss. The girls receive this blessing from the deacon's wife.[32]

The Old Mennonite Church, in its Church Polity statement published in 1944, describes the following ritual after instruction:

> Addressing the applicants, the minister says:
> 'And now if it is still your desire to be baptized and to be received into church fellowship, you will rise ... then asking them:
> Do you believe in one true, eternal, and almighty God?
> Do you believe in Jesus Christ, as the only begotten Son of God, that he is the Only saviour of Mankind, that he died upon the cross and gave himself a ransom for our sins that through him we might have eternal life?
> Do you believe in the Holy Ghost?
> Are you truly sorry for your past sins, and ... willing to renounce Satan, and the world?
> Do you promise by the Grace of God, and the aid of his Holy Spirit, to submit yourself to Christ?'
> Candidates kneel, while the congregation stands ... the minister prays ...
> The deacon or some other brother now brings a vessel with water, and the minister laying his hands upon the head of the subject for baptism, says:
> 'Upon the confession of thy faith, which thou hast made before God and these witnesses (he now with both hands takes a quantity of water from the vessel, and pours it upon the head ...) I baptize thee with water, in the name of the Father, and of the Son, and of the Holy Ghost.'
> When the baptism takes place in an outside body of water the subject kneels and the minister takes the water from the stream.
> After all the applicants are thus baptized ... the minister gives them his hand and says 'Arise! And as Christ was raised up by the glory of the father, even so thou

---

[31] *Amish Country News*, Brad Igou (ed.), 2005 <http://www.amishnews.com/amisharticles/religioustradi tions.htm>.

[32] Ibid., pp. 3–4 of 8.

... shalt be acknowledged as a member of the body of Christ, and a brother (or sister) of the church.'[33]

The rite of the Evangelical Mennonite Church, published in 1949, is very similar in structure, and in substance. The recent study by Daniel B. Lee examines the ritual of baptism of the Weaverland Mennonites as contained in their Confession of Faith of 1996.[34] Candidates study the Eighteen Articles of the Dortrecht Confession of Faith of 1632. They are asked three long interrogatory questions. The first is a paraphrase of the Apostles' Creed; the second is a renunciation of Satan, and the third asks them to accept the discipline of the church. The bishop then prays over them, and recites the Lord's Prayer. He lays hands on the head of each candidate, saying:

> 'Upon thy confession of faith, which thou hast confessed before God and many witnesses, thou art baptized with water, in the name of the Father, and of the Son and of the Holy Ghost.'

> As the bishop says 'baptized with water,' the deacon pours a small amount of water on the head of each candidate.

> When all are baptized, the bishop then approaches the first baptized person and extends him the right hand of fellowship and says, 'In the name of the Lord, in the name of the church, I offer thee my hand; arise, to a new beginning, to a new life. The Lord strengthen you that you may be able to finish your newly started work, and be his disciple; acknowledge the truth and the truth shall make you free.'

The rite concludes with the giving of the kiss of peace to the candidates, the bishop's wife greeting the women.[35]

Thus, we find a stable ritual: instruction, confession of faith, laying-on of hands and baptism with the triune formula, and the kiss of peace. The words spoken by the bishop vary from community to community, reflecting a time when the rite was probably extemporized but had been committed to textual summary in the various groups. It is interesting that the main differences tend to be over the mode of baptism. However, the intricate theologies of the founding teachers do not seem to be articulated in the rite – for example, there appears to be no reference to a baptism of suffering. On the whole the emphasis is on baptism as ecclesiological – admission to a community of faith.

---

[33] Given in Toews, *American Mennonite Worship*, pp. 178–9.

[34] Daniel B. Lee, *Old Order Mennonites. Rituals, Beliefs, and Community*, Burnham Inc., Chicago, IL, 2000.

[35] Ibid., pp. 68–71.

English Separatists and Baptists

Although some members of the Church of England felt that the English Church was in need of further Reformation, they nevertheless remained members. A few, however, felt that it was so like the Roman Catholic Church that it was not a church at all, and they seceded to form their own small churches. Those of the sixteenth century are generally known as Separatists, and amongst their leaders were Robert Brown, Robert Harrison, Henry Barrow, John Penry and John Greenwood – though the groups certainly did not always recognize one another. Their teaching was regarded as seditious, and they were prosecuted by the authorities. In *A Booke which sheweth the life and manners of all true Christians* (1582), Robert Brown expounded his theology and beliefs. On baptism he certainly supported infant baptism, and defended it by reference to covenant. The minister was to preach the word, and then apply the sign:

> The bodies of the parties baptised must be washed with water, or sprinckled or dipped, in the name of the Father, and of ye Sonne, and of the holy Ghost, unto the forgevenes of sinnes, and dying thereto in one death and burial with Christ.
>
> The preacher must pronounce them to be baptised into ye bodie and governement of Christ, to be taught & to professe his lawes, that by his mediation & victorie, they might rise againe with him unto holines & happines for ever.
>
> The church must geve thankes for the partie baptised, and praye for his further instruction, and traininge unto salvation.[36]

According to the deposition made by Daniel Bucke to the magistrate, the Barrowist Church which had removed to the Netherlands practised baptism as follows:

> … they had neither god fathers nor godmothers, and he tooke water and washed the faces of them that were baptised: the Children that were there baptised were the Children of Mr. Studley Mr. Lee with others beinge of severall yeres of age, sayinge onely in the administracion of this sacrament I doe Baptise thee in the name of the father of the sonne and of the holy gost withoute usinge any other cerimony therin as is now usually observed according to the booke of Common praier …[37]

The Separatists were isolated congregations, but their radical separation from the national Church set a precedent for others to follow. By the seventeenth century a number of groups had seceded to covenant together and advocate believers' baptism. The two main groups were the General Baptists and the Particular Baptists.

The leaders of the *General Baptists* included John Smyth, Henry Denne, Thomas Grantham and Joseph Wright. The name 'General' reflects their belief that Christ's redemption extended to all, and humans have not lost the faculty of willing the good.

---

[36] Robert Harrison and Robert Browne, *The Writings of Robert Harrison and Robert Browne*, Albert Peel and Leland H. Carlson (eds), Allen and Unwin, London, 1953, p. 260.

[37] C. Burrage, *The Early English Dissenters*, 2 vols, Cambridge University Press, Cambridge, 1912, Vol. 1, p. 143.

John Smyth was a Cambridge graduate and was ordained in the Church of England, but fell foul of the authorities. At Gainsborough the parish priest was neglectful of his duties, and Smyth attempted to upstage and replace him in the parish, but without a licence, so he came under episcopal displeasure. He then separated from the Church, and gathered his own congregation which eventually settled in the Netherlands. In a short confession of faith Smyth listed as the fourteenth article, 'That baptism is the external sign of the remission of sins, of dying and of being made alive, and therefore does not belong to infants.'[38] It was in the Netherlands that

> ... Mr. Smyth, Mr. Helwys and the rest having utterly dissolved, and disclaimed their former church, state, and ministry, came together to erect a new church, by baptism. Unto which they also ascribed so great virtue, as they would not so much as pray together, before they had it. And after some straining of courtesy as to who should begin ... Mr.Smyth baptized first himself, and next Mr. Helwys, and so the rest, making their particular confessions.[39]

Thus baptism was dependent upon a confession of faith. It appears that pouring was the mode of baptism until 1642 when total immersion came to be the normative ritual. Edward Barber wrote *A small Treatise of Baptisme or Dipping* (1642), and assumed without argument that 'baptism' meant 'dipping', and taught that 'those immersed are "visibly sealed to the day of redemption", have a "right to communion" and are "crucified, dead and buried, and risen again with Christ"'.[40] As in other Separatist groups, no written liturgies were used, and, in the 1650s, a dispute broke out as to whether the baptismal ritual needed a laying-on of hands.[41]

The leaders of the *Particular or Calvinist Baptists* included John Tombes and Henry Jessey. Like Smyth, they tended to be clergy of the Church of England who eventually came to reject infant baptism, though they also rejected the episcopal hierarchy and other elements of the English Church such as written forms of prayer. They held firmly to a doctrine of election. Tombes of Bewdly sparked off considerable controversy over baptism during the first days of the Westminster Assembly.[42] Henry Jessey seems to have left the Church of England *c*. 1635 to pastor the Separatist congregation of Samuel Eaton (*d*. 1639). In 1638 the question of the validity of infant baptism surfaced, and the congregation split. One spin-off from this was the group brought together by John Spilsbury and William Kiffin.

In 1640 Richard Blunt joined Spilbury's congregation, and he raised the question of the correct mode of baptism: 'Mr Richard Blunt ... being convinced of Baptism yet also it ought to be by dipping ye Body into ye Water, resembling Burial & rising

[38] In William L. Lumpkin, *Baptist Confessions of Faith*, Judson Press, Valley Forge, PA, 1969, p. 101.

[39] John Robinson, *Of Religious Communion*, Leiden, 1614, cited in O.K. Armstrong and Marjorie Armstrong, *The Baptists in America*, Doubleday, New York, 1979, p. 39.

[40] E. Barber, *A Small Treatise of Baptisme or Dipping*, London, 1642, pp. 11ff.

[41] B.R. White, *The English Baptists of the Seventeenth Century*, Baptist Historical Society, Didcot, 1996, pp. 40ff.

[42] Spinks, *Sacraments, Ceremonies and the Stuart Divines*, pp. 114ff.

again … Col 2:12, Rom 6:4, had sober conference about in ye Church.'[43] Henry Jessey moved to a position whereby he immersed infants, but Blunt eventually persuaded the congregation to adopt believers' baptism. Several of the leaders of these associated congregations drew up the First London Confession in 1644. This document insisted that baptism should be only administered to 'persons professing the faith'. It taught: 'The Way and manner of the dispensing of this Ordinance the Scripture holds out to be dipping or plunging the whole body under the water.' The meaning of baptism was explained as:

> … the washing of the whole soule in the blood of Christ: Secondly, that interest the saints have in the death, buriall, and resurrection; thirdly, together with a confirmation of our faith, that as certainly as the body is buried under the water, and riseth againe, so certainly shall the bodies of the Saints be raised by the power of Christ, in the day of the resurrection, to reigne with Christ.[44]

Most of the Particular Baptists held much in common with the authors of the Westminster Confession, though in polity they sided more with the Independents. Many of the ministers gathered in association authored a new confession based on the Westminster Confession. It was published in 1677, and again in 1688. In it baptism is termed an 'ordinance' with the Lord's Supper, and is defined as a sign to the party baptized of fellowship with Christ in his death and resurrection, of being engrafted into him, and remission of sins. Only those who profess repentance and obedience are the proper subjects of this ordinance. Baptism is in the triune formula, and 'Immersion, or dipping of the person in water, is necessary to the due administration of this ordinance.'[45]

A description of a baptism at Whittlesford in 1767 gives some idea of the ritual as commonly used:

> Dr Gifford, at ten o'clock, mounted a moveable pulpit near the river in Mr Hollick's yard, and, after singing and prayer, preached a suitable sermon on the occasion from Psalm cxix.57. After sermon, the men retired to one room, the women to two others, and the baptizer, Mr Gwennap, to another, to prepare for the administration. After about half an hour, Mr Gwennap, dressed as usual (except a coat, which was supplied by a black gown made like a bachelor's) came down to the waterside. He was followed by the men, two and two, dressed as usual, only, instead of a coat, each one had a long white baize gown, tied round the waist with a piece of worstead-binding, and leaded at the bottom that they might sink; they had on their heads white linen caps. The women followed, two and two, dressed as usual, only all had white gowns, Holland or dimitty. Their upper-coats were tacked to their stockings, and their gown leaded, lest their clothes should float. Mr Gwennap sang a hymn at the waterside, spoke about ten minutes on the subject, and then taking the oldest man of the company by the hand, led to a convenient depth in the river. Then pronouncing the words, I baptize thee in the

---

[43] Cited in Michael A.G. Haykin, *Kiffin, Knollys and Keach – Rediscovering our English Baptist Heritage*, Reformation Today Trust, Leeds, 1996.

[44] *London Confession*, 1644, in Lumpkin, *Baptist Confessions*, p. 167.

[45] *Second London Confession*, 1677, in Lumpkin, ibid., p. 291.

name of the Father, of the Son, and of the Holy Ghost, he immersed the person once in the river. Robinson stood in a boat, and, with other assistants, led the rest in, and, having wiped their faces after their baptism, led them out. Mr Gwennap added a few words after the administration at the water-side, and concluded with the usual blessing.[46]

Quaker Baptism in the Spirit

Quakers, or the Society of Friends, emerged in the mid-seventeenth century; quite a few had been Baptists before becoming Quakers. T.L. Underwood has pointed out that in many ways, the Quaker view of baptism was a logical extension of what he regards as the weak initiatory, outward and Godward qualities of the seventeenth-century Baptists.[47] Baptists stressed the outward as response to the inward, but it was the inward which was all important. The Baptist John Bunyan had declared that someone who was dead to sin and lived to God had something better than the ritual act:

> The best of Baptisms he hath; he is Baptized by that one spirit; he hath the heart of Water-baptism, he wanteth only the outward shew, which if he had would not prove him a truly visible Saint; it would not tell me he had grace in his heart.[48]

Friends agreed, claiming that they had Christ's Spirit direct, and so had no need of outward ordinances. George Fox (1624-91), one of the founders of the Friends, recorded:

> When all my hopes in them ['separate preachers'] and in all men were gone, so that I had nothing outwardly to help me, nor could tell what to do, then, Oh then, I heard a voice which said, 'There is one, even Christ Jesus, that can speak to thy condition,' and when I heard it my heart did leap for joy … So he it was that opened to me when I was shut up and had not hope nor faith. Christ it was who had enlightened me, that gave me his light to believe in, and gave me hope, which is himself, revealed himself in me, and gave me his spirit and gave me his grace, which I found sufficient in the deeps and in weakness.[49]

Edward Burrough thus claimed that ordinances 'as they are performed in the Power of God by the leadings of his Spirit we own, but where such things are done out of the power or leadings of that Spirit in mans wills, they are but formal, dead and empty, and as such to be denied'.[50]

---

[46] K.A. Parons (ed.), *Church Book: St. Andrews' Street Baptist Church, Cambridge, 1720–1832*, Baptist Historical Society, London, 1991, pp. 41–2.

[47] T.L. Underwood, *Primitivism, Radicalism, and the Lamb's War. The Baptist–Quaker Conflict in Seventeenth-Century England*, Oxford University Press, Oxford, 1997.

[48] John Bunyan, *The Miscellaneous Works of John Bunyan*, ed. Roger Sharrock, 13 vols, Clarendon Press, Oxford, 1976–94, Vol. 4, p. 172.

[49] George Fox, *The Journal of George Fox*, ed. John L. Nickalls, Religious Society of Friends, London, 1975, pp. 4, 11–12, cited in Underwood, *Primitivism*, pp. 9–10.

[50] Edward Burrough, *The Son of Perdition*, London, 1661, pp. 23–4, cited in Underwood, ibid., p. 69.

The great spokesman for the Friends, William Penn, explained, 'The time of the Baptism of the Holy Ghost, Christ's only Baptism, therefore called the One Baptism, has been long since come; Consequently the other, which was John's, was fulfilled, and as becomes a Fore-runner, ought to cease.'[51] According to John Fox, whoever comes into the baptism of the Spirit, comes into the one in which all the other ends, the greater.[52] Justification and sanctification are inward spiritual states – they are Baptism in the Spirit – and thus no outward rite is necessary at all.

Thus, the split between outward and inward, developed by Zwingli and Bullinger, and further separated in the Radical wing of the Reformation, was taken to its conclusion in the Friends, who saw themselves in the position of the first Christians, prior to Scripture being written down. Their testimonies reveal a particular vocabulary to describe their conversion experience. From a miserable state they passed to a period of waiting, in which they eventually encountered Christ. This was followed by a time of inward and spiritual judgement. Enlightenment, or a 'Disciples state', followed, resulting in the internalization and spiritualization of the work and person of Christ. Christ within becomes the inner light, and God, Christ, Spirit and light became interchangeable. As Penn explained:

> Whatever is to be obtained and enjoyed within, is originally and chiefly ascribable to the Discoveries, Convictions and Leadings of the blessed Light of Christ within through every Generation, however variously the Principle may have dominated; as, the Word of God nigh, Wisdom, Light, Spirit, &c. under the Old Testament; and Light, Grace, Truth, Christ, Spirit, Anointing, Gift of God, &c. under the New Testament.[53]

The pneumatological/Christological is strongly discernable, though this branch of the Radical Reformation, having its own theology of indwelling and the inner light, abolished the ritual act of baptism.

Concluding Remarks

The Radical Reformation developed certain Reformation principles to what the heirs of the Reformation regarded as unnecessary extremes. In the Anabaptist tradition we find a stress on faith as a conscious undertaking, and therefore the need for those baptized in infancy to be (re)baptized. The ritual is stripped to a bare minimum in accordance with scriptural norms: instruction, confession of faith/commitment, and baptism with the triune formula. The mode was not of immediate importance amongst the Anabaptists, but division on this matter developed later. The ritual was regarded as mandated by Scripture, but rather than conveying grace, was a response to grace,

---

[51] William Penn, *Reason Against Railing*, London, 1673, p. 107, cited by Underwood, ibid., p. 74.

[52] George Fox, *The Great Mystery of the Great Whore Unfolded*, London, 1659, p. 112, cited in Underwood, ibid., p. 76.

[53] Penn, *Reason Against Railing*, cited by Underwood, ibid., p. 107.

and, at least in terms of Zwingli's definition of a sacrament as an oath or pledge, was the rite of pledging oneself to the community of believers. In the English separatist tradition there was no objection to infant baptism, but the rite was simple. In the English Baptist tradition, both General and Particular, the term 'sacrament' came to be replaced by the term 'ordinance', and although believers' baptism was insisted upon, the rite was not regarded as conveying any spiritual gifts. At most it was a faithful response to the gift of faith and the Spirit. This was taken even further by the Quakers, for whom inner enlightenment was all that was needed. Here the Zurich theology which had stressed the difference between the outward and inward was taken to its ultimate conclusion. Only the inward is necessary. The ritual of baptism, however basic, can be entirely dispensed with.

CHAPTER 5

Some New Churches of the Eighteenth and Nineteenth Centuries

The eighteenth and nineteenth centuries witnessed a number of revivalist movements which resulted in the foundation of new churches. For this chapter, six have been selected: the Moravians, Methodists and the Swedenborgians belonging to the eighteenth century; and the Disciples of Christ, the Catholic Apostolic Church and the Church of Jesus Christ of Latter Day Saints, from the nineteenth century. These have been chosen either because of their distinctive theology and practice, or, in the case of Methodism and Mormonism, their growth to be a mainline and/or world-wide denomination. The first three have the common link of Pietism, and their founder figures, Count Zinzendorf, John Wesley and Emmanuel Swedenborg met one another, and both Wesley and Swedenborg at one time worshipped with the Moravians in London.[1] However, Swedenborg claimed to receive visions and revelations of heavenly things and a 'New Church', and the new church which was founded upon his writings was a Restorationist Church. The three nineteenth-century churches are all examples of Restorationist Churches, which believed they were refounding the Apostolic Church, and preparing for the Second Coming of Christ.

Three Eighteenth-Century Churches of the Pietist Tradition

The Moravians

In one sense the Moravian Church was not a New Church, since it traces its roots to a sub-group of the Bohemian Brethren or Hussites of the fifteenth century, the *Unitas Fratrum*.[2] This group thrived until the Battle of White Mountain in 1620, when Catholic forces defeated its army, and the group was then subjected to persecution. It continued as an underground movement, calling itself 'The Hidden Seed'. In 1722 some of the families emigrated to Saxony as refugees and settled on land belonging to Count Nikolaus Ludwig von Zinzendorf. Under Zinzendorf's patronage, the church was 'refounded' at Herrnhut, and developed extensive missionary work in the New World. In order to facilitate this work in British colonies, the Moravians founded a

---

[1] For a general survey, Mark A. Noll, *The Rise of Evangelicalism. The Age of Edwards. Whitefield and the Wesleys*, Intervarsity Press, Downers Grove, IL, 2003.

[2] I am indebted to Colin Podmore for his help with this section, particularly with recent German works. See also Colin Podmore, *The Moravian Church in England, 1728–1760*, Clarendon Press, Oxford, 1998.

settlement in Fetter Lane, London, in 1742. The Church claimed to have bishops in an unbroken succession from the Catholic Church, and this claim, together with the faith of the Church, was set out for the British Government in the *Acta Fratrum Unitatis in Anglia* (1749). Zinzendorf had been brought up as a Lutheran in a Pietist household, and the 'refounded' Moravian Brethren had a Lutheran Pietist stamp to it. The *Acta Fratrum* included the Lutheran Augsburg Confession of 1530. However, the Pietist concern with devotion to the passion of Christ and his sacred wounds also became central in Moravian devotion. Francis Okely wrote:

> It is impossible to utter any divine truth, or to speak anything, which one might call complete without mentioning the LAMB, our Saviour. This must be the anointing, and the salt, the principal ingredient of every matter, of every sigh, of every writing, of every sermon, yea of every thought.[3]

Zinzendorf, who preached and wrote on theological topics, and steered the theology of the refounded Church, taught that 'To love Jesus without his Blood and Wounds, by which all has been purchased for us, is an empty Love, not productive either of Life or Chearfulness.'[4] And as a Pietist, he emphasised the 'Feeling in the Heart'.[5] Affirming the Protestant recognition of two sacraments, he wrote:

> These two Mysteries are sufficiently distinguish'd from any thing else ... But holy Baptism is a general Entrance into the Kingdom of Jesus Christ; and the blessed Communion is a general Means of Grace for his Soldiers. Now concerning the former, we should pray, that the Water may be tinged with Christ's Blood, to the Healing of all Sin whether Original or Actual ... .[6]

For Zinzendorf, the baptized person finds his or her life in the wounds of the Lamb:

> For to be baptized out of the side of Jesus, and to pour the whole stream of the death-water and heart's blood of Jesus Christ upon a soul, and to make her to swim in the sea of the wounds and to place her whole future life, indeed all that is hers, and all that will occur with her in the future, even until the last day and beyond the last day, under the 'bed' of the baptismal waters and in the sea of grace, so that the soul, when she eats, drinks, weeps, laughs, whether she is within or outside of the congregation, when she only enjoys herself or communicates: all of this she does, so to speak, several fathoms under the sea of grace, under the ocean of grace, under the stream from the side, so that the streams of grace go far above her head and cover the souls as the sea covers the earth – according to the prophetic description.[7]

---

[3] Francis Okely, *Dawnings of the Everlasting Gospel-Light,* Northampton, 1775, p. 12, cited in A.J. Lewis, *Zinzendorf the Ecumenical Pioneer,* SCM Press, London, 1962, p. 64.

[4] Nikolaus Ludwig von Zinzendorf, *Maxims, Theological Ideas And Sentences out of the Present Ordinary of the Brethren's Churches: His Dissertations and Discourses From the Year 1738 till 1747.* Extracted by J. Gambold, London, 1751, p. 7.

[5] Ibid., p. 61.

[6] Ibid., p. 54. See also Theodor Wettach, *Kirche bei Zinzendorf,* Theologischer Verlag Rolf Brockhaus, Wuppertal, 1971, pp. 119–29.

[7] *Ein und zwanzig Discurse,* pp. 125–6, cited in Arthur J. Freeman, *An Ecumenical Theology of the*

However, validity rested on the disposition of the recipient: 'For 'tis the Intention of the Receiver, not the Minister, which can determine the Grace to be more or less.'[8]

Zinzendorf believed strongly that humanity was in one of two states: either being saved by grace, or 'still married to the Life of Sin'.[9] Baptism was the sacrament of total absolution:

> The Lamb's Death, and his Blood shed on the Cross, has adorned us once for all. As we by the Fall have put on Satan's Stamp and Nature; so we put on the Lord Jesus, his Blessing, his Merit, every holy and glorious Thing belonging to him. Which I will not scruple to compare the making of Base-born Children legitimate, by spreading the Cloke over them.[10]

The 'Cloke' seems to be a reference to the atoning work of Christ, the covering with his blood. Elsewhere Zinzendorf commented that when Pilate brought Jesus forth in the robe which he had placed upon him, which was dripping with blood, he resembled a newly baptized person 'cloath'd with his baptism Vestment'.[11] However, baptism leaves a mark which the Spirit should make visible:

> Baptism ought to leave such a signature, that we could proceed like People mark'd with the Blood of Christ, in Covenant with God, who were Masters over Sin, and could make the Devil fly before us: But since People forget that Mystery, they cannot lay Claim to the Glory of it, till it is visible once more that they have another Spirit within them.[12]

He believed that baptism made a person more receptive to the Gospel and softened hardened hearts: 'in baptized Persons there is a certain Tenderness, that they must assent to the Word; and the Divine Faithfulness keeps hold of them by some Corner, as it may be possible'.[13]

Zinzendorf was fond of the image of the Trinity as family, with Christ as our husband, the Father our father, and the Holy Spirit our mother. Thus he explained:

> If we date the Holy Ghost's Office as Mother from hence, it will be particularly clear. For how could we have either Father or Mother, till we first had the Lamb? But now we can say to the Holy Spirit, 'Because Thou hast once form'd and overshadowed Jesus in the Womb, therefore Thou certainly art our Mother; for in the first place we belong and are related to Him, and secondly He has also committed us to thy Care. Thou art to form these *animulae*, little Souls, who are espoused to Him the *Animas*, the original and Bridegroom-Soul, into a good sort of Spirit, in their small Degree resembling Thyself.' Accordingly He not only concern'd himself with Jesus in the Womb, but also with *John*, Luk.11.41 and still

---

Heart: The Theology of Count Nicholas Ludwig von Zinzendorf, The Moravian Church in America, Bethlehem, PA, 1998, p. 283.

[8] Zinzendorf, *Maxims*, p. 177.

[9] *Maxims*, p. 13.

[10] Ibid., p. 38.

[11] Ibid., pp. 342–3.

[12] Ibid., pp. 11–12.

[13] Ibid. p. 12.

does the like; in which Case, Baptism is a Confirmation of the Grace already in some respect begun, and also a general Washing-away of the Filth which notwithstanding cleaves to us from the Fall. Afterwards he cleanses us from casual Spots in the same Blood of the Lamb, and goes on adorning us as his own Daughter, according to his Mind for whom we are intended.[14]

Because he believed the benefits of the atonement are heart-felt, and not necessarily mind-felt, Zinzendorf had no problem at all with infant baptism:

Our little children, who are baptized in the name of the Father, of the Son, and of the Holy Spirit, who grow up where they were hatched (born from his holy side), who know nowhere to go but to him; to whom a thousand *notiones* [notions] prevailing in the world remain hidden; but who day and night live [*umgehen*] with the dear Lamb, and are accustomed to live [*umgehen*] with him and who even at their third and fourth year cleave to him with heart and mind, closer than to their own life, in a way which could not be brought about with ever so much effort and *studio* [study] in fifty years even if it was to be presented continuously, or if one was to bring the matter *mechanismum* [mechanically] into his own mind. These little scholars of the Holy Spirit, I say, doubtless get acquainted with their divine Papa and Mama at the same time, as soon as they are capable of thinking; this is quite natural.[15]

In the *Acta Fratrum*, the Augsburg Confession was included as a standard of Moravian belief. In the same work, under the title 'Rationale of the Brethrens Liturgies', the fourth of six propositions explained that the Apostle Paul ordained that baptism should be in the Name of the Lord, 'which in other Places intimates to be a mysterious Dipping into the Death of Jesus'.[16] Elsewhere Zinzendorf noted that baptism was first administered in the name of Jesus, but later the disciples used the triune name 'as we do now'.[17] However, Zinzendorf's emphasis on the blood of Christ, the wounds of the Lamb, and being baptized into the death of Jesus resulted in the use of the baptismal formula, 'Into the death of Jesus I baptize thee *N.N.* in the name of the Father, and of the Son, and of the Holy Ghost.'

The liturgy provided in the *Acta Fratrum* was basically Luther's German Litany, which the Moravians chanted, and which, together with hymns, provided the main Sunday worship service. In the section on the liturgies it states that all the ceremonies used in the Moravian Churches are joined in one aim, 'namely, the deepest Impression of the Washing from our natural Impurity with a Covenant Water certainly impregnated with the Blood of Christ; and the Cloathing [*sic*] with the mystical Garment of Jesus Christ, in a manner as real as inexpressible'.[18] According to A.E. Peaston, baptism occurred at the words of the Litany, 'Regenerate our children through water and the Holy Spirit.'[19] However, at some stage separate baptismal rites were drawn up.

---

[14] Ibid., pp. 276–7.

[15] *Ein und zwanzig Discurse*, p. 67, cited in Freeman, *An Ecumenical Theology*, p. 285.

[16] *Acta Fratrum Unitatis in Anglia*, London, 1749, p. 94.

[17] Zinzendorf, *Maxims*, p. 232.

[18] *Acta*, p. 97.

[19] A.E. Peaston, *The Prayer Book Tradition in the Free Churches*, James Clarke, London, 1964, p. 101.

That of the German edition of 1770 was translated into English in 1793.[20] Section XII provided two liturgies for the baptism of children, one for adults, and one for adults who were 'From Among the Heathen'. The first of the two for children was to come after the singing of some suitable verses and a short discourse. Much of it was chanted, being divided between the *Liturgus*, the choir, and the congregation (signified by the letters L,C, A). After initial versicles and responses (the first of which is 'Christ thou Lamb of God, which taketh away the sin of the world'), a hymn verse was sung:

> An infant, Lord, we bring to thee,
> As thy redeemed property,
> And thee especially intreat,
> Thyself this child to consecrate
> By baptism, and its soul to bless,
> Out of the fulness of thy grace.

A series of interrogatories followed, with a stress on the saving work of the blood of Christ. The congregation interrupted the questions with the following verse:

> The eye sees water, nothing more,
> How it is poured out by men;
> But faith alone conceives the pow'r
> Of Jesu's blood, to make us clean;
> Faith sees it as a cleansing flood,
> Replete with Jesu's blood and grace,
> Which heals each wound, and makes all good,
> What Adam brought on us, his race,
> And all, that we ourselves have done.

The *Liturgus* might offer a prayer before the actual baptism, or sing a suitable verse such as:

> Be present with us, Lord our God,
> This water can't make clean,
> But whilst we pour it, cleanse by blood,
> This infant from all sin.

Immediately before the baptism the *Liturgus* asks the congregation:

> Ye, who are baptized into Christ Jesus, how were ye baptized?
> Answer: Into his death.

Then the children were baptized with the triune formula prefaced by the words 'Into the death of Jesus I baptize thee' (*In den Tod Jesu taufe ich nun auch dich*).[21] After

---

[20] *Liturgic Hymns of the United Brethren, Revised and Enlarged. Translated from the German*, London, 1793.

[21] More recent English and American Moravian rites have dropped this distinctive preface to the triune formula, for example, *The Liturgy and Canticles authorized for use in the Moravian Church in Great Britain and Ireland*, Moravian Publication Office, London 1914. Also the 1960 and 1987 rites; for these see Fred Linyard and Phillip Tovey, *Moravian Worship*, Grove Books, Bramcote, 1994.

the baptismal act, there was a laying-on of hands with the words, 'Thus art thou now buried with him by baptism into his death.' Then a verse was sung,

> His death and passion ever,
> Till soul and body sever,
> Shall in thy heart engrav'd remain.

And the *Liturgus* declared,

> Now therefore live, yet not thou, but Christ live in thee. And the life, which thou now livest in the flesh, live by the faith of the Son of God, who loved thee and gave himself for thee.

The second order has different versicles and responses, different catechetical questions, different hymns and formula for the imposition of hands, but the core baptism material is the same. The baptismal rite of adults includes the Lord's Prayer recited in parts by the *Liturgus*, the choir and all. The credal questions give a good summary of the Moravian understanding of baptism:

> L. Dost thou believe in Jesus Christ, the only begotten Son of God, by whom are all things and we through him?
> *Answer*: I do.
> L. Dost thou believe, that he is thy Lord, who redeemed thee, a lost and undone human creature, purchased and gained thee from all sin, from death and from the power of the Devil, not with gold or silver, but with his holy precious blood, and with his innocent suffering and dying?
> *Answer*: I verily believe it.
> L. Dost thou desire to be cleansed from sin in the blood of Jesus Christ, and to be buried into his death by holy baptism?
> *Answer*: That is my sincere desire.
> L. Dost thou desire to be embodied into the congregation of Christ, by holy baptism, which is the laver of regeneration, and renewing of the Holy Ghost, and in his kingdom to live under him and serve him in eternal righteousness, innocence, and happiness?
> *Answer*: That is my sincere desire.

The credal questions differ in the baptism of adults 'From Among the Heathen', but contain nothing which could not have been in the first order of adult baptism.

The mode of baptism seems to have been by pouring water. Engravings of various Moravian baptisms were published in 1757.[22] One for an infant shows the child being held by the parent, and the pastor pouring water over the baby's head from a basin on a (communion?) table. That of a Negro shows a rite of exorcism before the baptism, for which there was a large tub of water on the floor. An engraving of Native Americans being baptized shows them kneeling over a tub, and water is poured on their heads, and similarly an engraving of baptisms in Greenland has three male and

---

[22] *Kurze, zuverlässige Nachricht von der, unter dem Namen der Böhmisch-Mährischen Brüder bekanten, Kirche Unitas Fratrum Herkommen, Lehr-Begrif, äussern und innern Kirchen-Verfassung und Gebräuchen,* n.p., 1762 edition by David Cranz. I am indebted to Colin Podmore for drawing my attention to these engravings.

two female candidates kneeling around a large tub on the floor, and the pastor pouring water over their heads. Another plate indicates that the kiss of peace was exchanged after the baptism of adults.

The Lutheran Pietism of Zinzendorf, with his emphasis on the passion of Christ as the sacrificed Lamb of God, and the need for the benefits to be heart-felt, gave rise to the Moravian rite of baptism which stressed the Pauline idea of baptism into the death of Christ. However, it was not so much concerned with being 'dead' in terms of being buried, but of being baptized into the cleansing blood of the sacrificed Lamb. This emphasis gave rise to the preface to the triune formula, 'In the death of Jesus I baptize thee ...', and there are references throughout the rite to the wounds of Christ and his blood. Baptism here is firmly soteriological, and centres on the atonement.

John Wesley and Methodism

John Wesley met Moravians on his journey to Georgia, and in May 1738 was at the Aldersgate Moravian meeting when his heart was 'strangely warmed'. For a time he was associated with the Fetter Lane Society, which was 'Moravian in foundation and character, even if initially Anglican in membership'.[23] He visited Herrnhut, and knew Zinzendorf. He also met Swedenborg, though he certainly did not share the latter's later theology. Thus the Methodist tradition, though to become considerably larger world-wide, and more well-known than the Moravians, shared a common Pietist origin.

There has been considerable discussion over what exactly Wesley taught on baptism since some of his statements seem ambiguous. Gayle Felton has suggested that, although there may be ambiguity, confusion has been often due to a failure to understand Wesley's distinctions. Felton notes:

> Significant examples are his differentiation between the outward and inward aspects of a sacrament, his two-fold understanding of the nature of regeneration, and his divergent interpretations of the infant and adult baptism. An attempt to elucidate his theology of baptism must also be grounded in a Wesleyan understanding of salvation as a lifelong, dynamic process rather than a fixed, achieved state.[24]

To further complicate efforts to pin down a 'Wesleyan' understanding of baptism, Wesley's followers did not feel bound by his teaching or his liturgical rites.

Wesley was influenced in his Oxford days by High Church Anglican views, and had read and accepted some of the principles of the Non-jurors, particularly that only a minister with valid episcopal ordination could effect a valid baptism. He read works by Daniel Brevint and the Non-juror, Robert Nelson, on sacraments, and William

---

[23] Podmore, *The Moravian Church*, p. 40.

[24] Gayle Carlton Felton, *This Gift of Water. The Practice and Theology of Baptism Among Methodists in America*, Abingdon Press, Nashville, TN, 1992, p. 48.

Wall's *The History of Infant Baptism*. From the Moravians he learned a new understanding of adult regeneration.[25]

Wesley wrote a number of short works and sermons relating to baptism, but his most famous treatise on the subject, *A Treatise on Baptism* (1756), was based on the baptismal section of his father Samuel's work, *The Pious Communicant* (1700). He eventually produced rites of baptism in his liturgy for America and then for England, but both were based heavily on the *Book of Common Prayer*.

In his 1756 *Treatise on Baptism* Wesley defined baptism as 'the initiatory sacrament, which enters us into covenant with God'. It is a sign and seal of God's covenant. The matter used is water, and the rite is performed by washing, dipping, or sprinkling; Wesley noted that Scripture does not determine the mode. He listed five benefits of baptism: it washes away the guilt of original sin by the application of the merits of Christ's death; it enters a person into covenant with God; it admits to the Church, so that the person is made a member of Christ, its head; it makes children of God – regeneration; and it makes a person an heir to the Kingdom. Wesley argued that baptism is the ordinary means of salvation: 'In the ordinary way, there is no other means of entering into the church or into heaven.' He defended infant baptism, demonstrating to his satisfaction that children are the proper subject of baptism.

Controversy over Wesley's understanding of baptism has mainly centred on his meaning of regeneration. As noted earlier, Bernard Holland argued that the Moravians had taught Wesley of a two-fold regeneration: in infancy, and in later life. As early as January 1739, Wesley wrote in his journal:

> Of the adults I have known baptized lately, one only was at that time born again, in the full sense of the word; that is, found a thorough, inward change, by the love of God filling her heart. Most of them were only born again in a lower sense; that is, received the remission of their sins. And some (as it has since too plainly appeared) neither in one sense nor the other.[26]

Ole Borgen notes that Wesley shied away from a static relationship between the *signum* and the *res* of sacraments; they may coincide, but are not necessarily tied together.[27] Thus in his sermon on 'The New Birth', John Wesley wrote:

> And, First, it follows, that baptism is not the new birth; They are not one and the same thing ... Nothing, therefore, is plainer than that, according to the Church of England, baptism is not the new birth ... as the new birth is not the same thing with baptism, so it does not always accompany baptism: They do not constantly go together ... There may sometimes be the outward sign, where there is not the inward grace. [28]

---

[25] Bernard G. Holland, *Baptism in Early Methodism*, Epworth Press, London, 1970, p. 51.

[26] *The Journal of the Rev. John Wesley*, N. Curnock (ed.), 6 vols, Epworth Press, London, 1938, Vol. ii, p. 135.

[27] Ole E. Borgen, *John Wesley on the Sacraments*, Francis Asbury Press, Grand Rapids, MI, 1972, 1985. In this Wesley follows one strand in Church of England tradition. See Spinks, *Sacraments, Ceremonies and the Stuart Divines*.

[28] *The Works of the Rev. John Wesley*, 15 vols, John Mason, London, 1856, Vol. 6, pp. 73–4.

Yet equally he could write:

> By water then, as a means, the water of baptism, we are regenerated or born again; whence it is called by the Apostle, 'the washing of regeneration.' Our Church therefore ascribes no greater virtue to baptism than Christ himself has done.[29]

Wesley held Arminian beliefs, allowing for human free will and endeavour in holiness. He seems to have rejected his father's idea of federal holiness, but accepted that baptism was a baptism into God's covenant. Regeneration was something that God did in infant baptism, but actual sin meant that a second regeneration or new birth was needed in adult life. This was a 'conversion' on God's part, and the need for a holy life on our part. Bernard Holland explains:

> It thus seems certain that Wesley considered infant regeneration to be applicable only to the first years of life, prior to the beginning of actual sin (at about nine or ten years of age) at which stage adult re-birth becomes necessary. The two regenerations are placed in separate compartments of life, and the dividing wall between them is the onset of conscious sin. In baptism, infant regeneration restores the child to favour with God, but his first acts of conscious sin break this relationship so that a new atonement is now required, and this is effected when (and if) conversion occurs.[30]

Although Charles Wesley did not agree on every issue with his brother, he seems to have held similar views as regards baptism. Charles recorded:

> I prayed at Islington with Anne Gates, believing we had the petitions we asked. I then baptized a child and her. We all felt the descent of the Holy Ghost. Before, she was in the spirit of heaviness and bondage. The moment the water touched her, she declares she felt her load removed, and sensibly received forgiveness. Sorrow and sighing fled away. The Spirit bore witness with the water, and she longed to be with Christ. We gave glory to God, who so magnified his ordinance.[31]

In one of his hymns Charles wrote:

> Let the Promised Inward grace
> Accompany the Sign;
> On her new-born Soul impress
> The glorious Name Divine:
> Father, all thy name reveal!
> Jesus, all thy Mind impart!
> Holy Ghost, renew, and dwell,
> Forever in her heart![32]

As with John's views, for Charles the inward and outward may coincide, and that is what is prayed for. Another baptismal hymn asks:

---

[29] Ibid., Vol. 10, p. 192.

[30] Holland, *Baptism in Early Methodism*, p. 66.

[31] *The Journal of the Rev. Charles Wesley*, 2 vols, John Mason, London, 1849 (Baker Book Reprint, Grand Rapids, MI, 1980), Vol. I, p. 223.

[32] Cites in Holland, *Baptism in Early Methodism*, p. 167.

Jesus, with Us thou always art,
Effectuate now the Sacred Sign,
The Gift Unspeakable impart,
And bless the Ordinance Divine.

Eternal Spirit! Descend from high,
Baptizer of our Spirits thou!
The Sacramental Seal apply,
And witness with the Water Now!

O! that the Souls baptized therein,
May now thy Truth and Mercy feel;
May rise, and wash away their sin –
Come, Holy Ghost, their Pardon seal![33]

In 1784 John Wesley had printed *The Sunday Service of the Methodists in North America*. This was based firmly on the 1662 *Book of Common Prayer* which Wesley loved, though with concessions to ideas of reform which were in circulation, and to the missionary needs in America. An edition for the British Methodists was printed in 1786. In the 1784 rite, references to baptismal regeneration before the baptism were retained, but those concerning after the baptism were removed. Wesley also removed references to godparents. In his work *Serious Thoughts concerning God-fathers and Godmothers* (1752), he argued that they were highly expedient. However, he expressed unease about the renunciations and promises made by godparents, explaining:

> I did not insert them, and should not be sorry had they not been inserted at all. I believe the compilers of our liturgy inserted them because they were used in all the ancient liturgies. [34]

Instead of godparents, the rite spoke of 'friends of the child'. In his British version the 1662 reference to 'the mystical washing away of sin' was removed, and in place of 'grafted into the body of Christ's Church', the infant is 'admitted into the visible body of Christ's Church' – suggesting that they might not be part of the invisible Church. In both editions, the signing with the cross was omitted.

It would thus appear that, although Wesley retained much of the Church of England baptismal rite for infants, he gave expression to his understanding of regeneration. That regeneration is part of the benefits of baptism is expressed by retaining it in references prior to the baptism; uncertainty as to whether the *signum* and *res* coincided for each particular infant would seem to account for its omission in the rite after the baptism. However, the early Methodists were concerned by preaching to arouse the second regeneration, or conversion; and in the American context, this led to adult converts. Wesley included an emended version of the 1662 rite for 'such as are of Riper Years', but again, since regeneration might not coincide with the rite, references to it after the baptism were dropped. The emphasis of Wesley's rite would seem to be

---

[33] Cites in ibid., p. 166.
[34] *Works*, 10, p. 508.

soteriological – saving from sin, and ecclesiological – being with the visible Church, which allowed for the possibility of regeneration and following a holy life.

Already in Wesley's lifetime he had split from his early partner in ministry, George Whitefield, since Whitefield was Calvinist in theology, whereas Charles and John were Arminian. After John Wesley's death, Methodism divided into a number of groups, such as the Methodist New Connexion, the Bible Christian Connexion, and the Primitive Methodist Connexion. Although the main group, Wesleyan Methodism, stayed closer to the ideals of Wesley than other groups, none felt absolutely bound to Wesley's theology of baptism or his love of the *Book of Common Prayer*.

The Reverend Richard Watson (1781–1833) was a second-generation Methodist. His father had been a member of a Chapel of the Countess of Huntingdon's Connexion, but had subsequently joined a Methodist Society. Richard became a lay preacher, but then joined one of the breakaway groups, the Methodist New Connexion.[35] He became an ordained minister in the New Connexion, only to return later in 1811 to the Wesleyan Methodists. Between 1821 and 1826 he wrote his *Theological Institutes*.[36] The fourth part included treatment of the sacraments of baptism and the Lord's Supper. We find little of Wesley's concern about new birth, and the Holy Spirit. In fact, although Watson cited many authorities, Wesley is not amongst them. Watson argued that the practice of baptism rests on the example of Christ in Matthew 28:19, and that baptism and the Lord's Supper are 'federal rites' or 'federal transactions'.[37] Much of his discussion is taken up with the covenant of grace made with Abraham, and its continuity in baptism, where baptism is 'the sign and seal of the covenant of grace under its perfected dispensation'. It is a mutual covenant:

> In this respect it binds us, as, in the other, God mercifully binds himself for the stronger assurance of our faith. We pledge ourselves to trust wholly in Christ for pardon and salvation, and to obey his laws.[38]

Baptism is more than circumcision, since it belongs to the new covenant:

> Of this great new-covenant blessing, baptism was therefore eminently the sign; and it represented the pouring out of the Spirit, the descending of the Spirit, the falling of the Spirit upon men, by the mode in which it was administered, the pouring of water from above upon the subjects baptized.[39]

Like Wesley, Watson rejected the need for credal confession and renunciation of the devil, 'for, ancient as these questions may be, they are probably not so ancient as the time of the Apostle'.[40]

---

[35] For the views on infant baptism amongst ministers of the Methodist New Connexion, see Bernard G. Holland, 'The Doctrine of Infant Baptism in Non-Wesleyan Methodism', Wesley Historical Society Occasional Publication 1, n.p., 1970, cyclostyled, no pagination, but pp. 1–5.

[36] In *The Works of the Rev. Richard Watson*, 12 vols, London 1834–38, Vol. XII.

[37] Ibid., pp. 214, 224.

[38] Ibid., p. 241.

[39] Ibid., pp. 240–41.

[40] Ibid., p. 236.

Ceremonies such as the sign of the cross and anointing with oil and triple immersion were first mentioned by Tertullian, and so are attributed to the invention of men like himself who added superstition to the simple baptismal rite.[41] Watson noted that in the Church of England the meaning of regeneration in the liturgy was a matter of debate, but it was a matter of debate with much discussion for him. He expends many pages on the mode of baptism, and on justifying infant baptism, but his discussion on benefits is brief and to the point. In addition to giving the grace of the covenant, baptism

> ... conveys also the present blessing of Christ, of which we are assured by his taking children in his arms and blessing them; which blessing cannot be merely nominal, but must be substantial and efficacious. It secures, too, the gift of the Holy Spirit in those secret spiritual influences, by which the actual regeneration of those children who die in infancy is effected; and which are a seed of life in those who are spared, to prepare them for instruction in the word of God, as they are taught it by parental care, to include their will and affections, and to begin and maintain in them the war against inward and outward evil, so that they may be divinely assisted, as reason strengthens, to make their calling and election sure. In a word, it is, both as to infants and to adults, the sign and pledge of that inward grace which, although modified in its operations by the difference of their circumstances, has respect to, and flows from, a covenant-relation to each of the three Persons in whose name they are baptized ... .[42]

Though the mention of regeneration is brief, it does seem to reflect Wesley's position. However, rather like Reformed theologians, it is covenant that occupies much of Watson's discussion.

The baptismal rite contained in *Service Book: Including Chants and Hymns with Devotional and Sacramental Services for use in Wesleyan-Methodist Congregations* (Manchester, 1889), illustrates the freedom these communities felt to develop Wesley's provisions. The rite began with a short exhortation, centering on Matthew 28:19 and the obedient response to this injunction (compare Watson). Four short readings followed: Matthew 28:18–20, Mark 10:13–16, Genesis 17:7 and Isaiah 44:13. A longer exhortation followed, echoing that of the *Book of Common Prayer* (and the New Church) and making reference to the arms of God's mercy. It exhorted that we should pray to God that

> ... of His bounteous mercy, His Holy Spirit may be given to *this child*: and also *his* parents, who here present *him* in this holy sacrament; that they may be enabled to fulfil the solemn covenant into which they are now entering ... .

A prayer asked that the Holy Spirit be given that the infant may be born again and made an heir of everlasting salvation. A prayer also invoked the Holy Spirit for the parents so that they might bring the child up in the nurture and admonitions of the Lord. Wesley's 1786 version of the *sindflutgebet* was included, together with a prayer

---

[41] Ibid., p. 267.
[42] Ibid., pp. 266–7.

that the child may become a true disciple and receive grace. After the minister asked the name of the child, the baptism with the classical formula followed. Following the baptism, the minister said an emended version of the Prayer Book's and Wesley's affirmation:

> We receive this child into the congregation of Christ's flock, that he may be instructed and trained in the doctrines, privileges, and duties of the Christian religion, and trust that he will be Christ's faithful soldier and servant unto his life's end.

The series of short prayers beginning 'Grant' from before the baptism in the Prayer Book and Wesley now followed as post-baptismal prayers. The rite ended with the Grace. The concept of 'regeneration' was expressed as 'may be born again', but the word 'regeneration' itself is absent from the rite.

Other Methodist groups felt free to simplify and change even further. Amongst the Bible Christians, for example, the baptismal rite commonly consisted of a Bible reading, a baptismal hymn, extempory prayer and the triune formula.[43] In the early nineteenth century some of its leaders were suspicious of infant baptism, and an early Conference asserted of baptism, 'We believe it has been generally used as an initiating ordinance into the Christian Church.'[44] Later in the century, infant baptism was defended, and baptism, with the Lord's Supper, was called a sacrament, but suspicion of regeneration remained, and infant baptism was regarded as a dedication of the child to God.

Amongst the Primitive Methodists, Hugh Bourne put forward a quite distinctive teaching. Basing baptism on the Old Testament, he emphasized the gift of the Spirit, and regarded the Church as the 'guardian parents' of all children.[45] Later in the century, the denomination moved nearer other Non-Wesleyans, regarding baptism as a dedication of the child to God. A similar pattern is found in America, with some groups trying to maintain loyalty to Wesley's forms and regarding baptism as sacramental, bestowing some benefit, and others using simplified forms, while others regarded the rite as a dedication of the child.[46]

---

[43] See J.C.C. Probert, *The Worship and Devotion of Cornish Methodism*, cyclostyled, n.p., 1978 (copy in the Bodleian Library, Oxford), p. 97.

[44] See Holland, 'The Doctrine of Infant Baptism', p. 6.

[45] Hugh Bourne, *A Treatise on Baptism, in Twelve Conversations, with Five Original Hymns,* 1823, cited in Holland, *The Doctrine.*

[46] See Gayle Felton, *This Gift of Water*, and Karen Westerfield Tucker, *American Methodist Worship*, Oxford University Press, New York, 2001.

The Swedenborgians or New Church 'signified by the New Jerusalem in the Revelation'

Emanuel Swedenborg was born in Stockholm in 1688.[47] His father, Jesper Swedberg, was Bishop of Skara and Westgothland in the Church of Sweden, and a Pietist. Emanuel was educated at Uppsala, London, Paris and Utrecht. A Latinist and mineralogist, he was appointed by Charles XII of Sweden as Assessor of the Swedish Mining Board. He was a prolific writer, and published works on physiology and anatomy. He visited England with some frequency, and in 1744 had lodged in Fetter Lane and worshipped with the Moravians. In the mid-1740s he was drawn to consider more seriously things spiritual, and between 1747 and 1756 published the *Arcana Caelestia*, which was a detailed interpretation of Genesis and Exodus. Further writings included *The Divine Love and Wisdom, The Divine Providence, Conjugal Love* and *The True Christian Religion*.

These writings were controversial, and Swedenborg had the works published in London and Holland, under an assumed name. Controversy erupted when his name was appended to *Conjugal Love,* published in Amsterdam in 1768. As a result of the furor Swedenborg left Stockholm, and settled first in Amsterdam, and then, in 1771, in London. He died in 1772 and was buried in the Swedish Church in Wapping, London. Remembered in Sweden for his scientific knowledge, his remains were later interred in Uppsala Cathedral. Swedenborg lived and died as a member of the Lutheran Church of Sweden. His religious ideas, one of which was that there was an invisible 'New Church', were unorthodox, but at his death they remained simply his ideas. However, by the 1780s certain people began to meet to discuss his writings, and from these meetings in England, the visible New Church was founded.

What, then, was distinctive about Swedenborg's religious ideas? Swedenborg claimed to have had direct revelations from God, who commanded him to write down the revelations. The writings claim to give a spiritual interpretation of the Word, and represent an allegorical, and at times quasi-scientific, interpretation of Scripture. He taught that there were five great epochs of divine history. The first was the time until the Great Flood, and the second was the time of the great ancient civilizations. The third was the Israelite, or Jewish, hegemony, and the fourth is the time of world-wide Christianity. A fifth epoch was the time of the New Church, which followed the Last Judgement, which Swedenborg suggested had taken place in 1757.

He had distinct ideas concerning the absolute unity and singleness of God, who embraces himself as a trinity. The Trinity for him was not a Trinity of persons, but of activities of the one God. The Father is creative love, the Son is the immanent Word of truth, and the Holy Spirit is the living power of God in everything that exists. In Jesus, God and humanity are completely united. Heaven and Hell are realities, and

---

[47] G. Trobridge, *Swedenborg. Life and Teaching*, Swedenborg Society, London, 1935; Dennis Duckworth, *A Branching Tree. A Narrative History of the General Conference of the New Church*, The General Conference of the New Church, London, 1998.

opposite, not reserved for the future, but present experiences. The atonement should not be regarded as 'satisfaction', but the bringing back of the lost, and requires reformation of character. Salvation requires human voluntary cooperation. The 'New Church' is composed of all those who accept these principles of truth.

Swedenborg's understanding of baptism was set out in the second volume of *The True Christian Religion* (1770). He observed that acts of washing were enjoined upon the Israelites – Aaron, Levites, and the bronze sea and many basins – and these were representative to prefigure the Christian Church which was to come: 'The washing of a person's spirit is meant by the washing of his body; and the internals of the Church were represented by such external rituals as were practised by the Israelite Church.'[48] But acts of washing and baptisms are no more effective unless the person's internal nature is purified from evil and falsities. Baptism replaced circumcision, but both rites were only given as a sign and memorial that people should be purified from evils, and so become the chosen people.[49]

The first purpose of baptism is as a sign which enables people to be recognized, in the same way that ribbons are tied on the babies of two mothers as a sign to tell them apart.[50] John the Baptist baptized in the Jordan, which, says Swedenborg, was the entrance to the land of Canaan, and this stands for the Church. Swedenborg explained:

> In the heavens, however, children are by baptism brought into the Christian heaven, and have angels there allotted to them by the Lord to take care of them. So as soon as children are baptised, angels are put in charge of them, who keep them in a state in which they can receive faith in the Lord. But as they grow up and become their own masters and think for themselves, they abandon their angel tutors, and choose for themselves such spirits as are at one with their life and faith. These facts show plainly that baptism is being brought into association with Christians in the spiritual world too.[51]

A second purpose of baptism is 'getting to know the Lord, the Redeemer and Saviour Jesus Christ'.[52] The third and 'real purpose behind baptism', is redemption and regeneration. But baptism without faith is of no avail. Drawing on his Swedish Lutheran tradition, Swedenborg contended:

> Every Christian ought to be fully aware that baptism involves purification from evils and so regeneration, for when he is baptised as an infant, the priest makes the sign of the cross with his finger on his forehead and chest as a token of the Lord, and then turning to the godparents asks whether he renounces the devil and all his works, and whether he accepts the faith. To which the godparents answer in place of the child: 'Yes, indeed.' The renouncing of the devil, that is,

---

[48] Emanuel Swedenborg, *The True Christian Religion*, Swedenborg Society, London, 1988 edn, Vol. 2, p. 715.

[49] Ibid., p. 719.

[50] Ibid., p. 720.

[51] Ibid., p. 721.

[52] Ibid., p. 723.

of the evils which come from hell, and faith in the Lord, bring about regeneration.[53]

Swedenborg believed that regeneration is signified in heaven by white and purple clothing. He concluded his treatment of baptism with experiences of his heavenly conversations or revelations.

Swedenborg spoke of a New Church, but he did not found a New Church. Those who met to read and discuss his writings called themselves 'The Theosophical Society'.[54] Some of those who were persuaded by his writings, such as John Clowes, Rector of St John's Church, Deansgate, Manchester, believed that they should remain within their own churches and by preaching let the New Church truth permeate. Others such as James and Robert Hindmarsh, who were Methodists, believed that a separate, visible New Church should be founded, and did so. James Hindmarsh had been a schoolmaster at Kingswood School and was commissioned by John Wesley as a lay preacher. His son Robert was a printer living in London, and was printer to the King. In 1787 the 'separation' group met, and after Communion James Hindmarsh baptized five others, including Robert, into the New Church. Robert Hindmarsh recorded:

> Tuesday, 31 July 1787, met at No. 6, in the Poultry, at Wright's.
> Those present participated in a celebration of the Holy Supper at which James Hindmarsh was selected by lot to officiate. After Holy Supper, Robert Hindmarsh was called, and the Faith of the New Haven and New Church, from Emanuel Swedenborg's Universal Theology, being read to him, he was questioned whether he firmly believed the same, and was desirous of being Baptised into that Faith. On his answering in the affirmative, he was marked with the sign of the Cross on his Forehead and Breast, and baptised in the name of the Father, and of the Son, and of the Holy Ghost.[55]

It is interesting that the signing is the one outlined by Swedenborg from his experience of the Swedish Lutheran baptismal rite.

James Hindmarsh became the first minister of the New Church in Great East Cheap in January 1788, but later the congregation chose Robert as first ordained priest of the New Church. Robert then ordained his father James and Samuel Smith. In April 1789 the first General Conference was held. Resolution XXII of the first General Conference stated:

> Resolved Unanimously: That it is the Opinion of this Conference, that as Baptism in the Old Church is a Baptism into the Faith of Three Gods … so Baptism in the New Church, being a Baptism into the Faith of the One God … is highly necessary, inasmuch as the Person baptized thereby takes upon him the Badge and Profession of genuine Christianity, and is at the same time inserted among Christians in the Spiritual World.

---

[53] Ibid., p. 726.

[54] See Duckworth, *A Branching Tree*, pp. 48–9. It has no connection with the Theosophical Society founded by Madame Blavatsky in 1875.

[55] Robert Hindmarsh, *The Rise and Progress of the New Jerusalem Church*, Hodson & Son, London, 1861, p. 58.

It is therefore recommended to all who desire to become Members of the New Jerusalem Church, to be baptized, both themselves and their Children, in the Faith of that Church; and in case they have already been baptized in the faith of the Old Church, to be re-baptized in the Faith of the New.[56]

Whether to insist on rebaptism, or simply to encourage it but not insist upon it, was a subject of discussion at a number of succeeding General Conferences, and the latter became the practice.

The traditional triune formula was not questioned, but rather the understanding in the 'Old Church' of three persons of God, which sounded like 'the Faith of Three Gods'.[57] We also note that at the Third General Conference of 1791, ministerial dress was suggested, consisting of a purple cassock with gold cord and a white surplice, two of the colours Swedenborg linked with the regenerate in Heaven.

The Minutes of the Second General Conference of April 1790 refer to 'the Forms for the Administration of Baptism and the Lord's Supper', which were read, corrected and passed unanimously. Indeed, *The Liturgy of the New Church signified by the New Jerusalem in the Revelation* was printed by Robert Hindmarsh in 1790, with apparently three editions, a fourth in 1791, and a fifth in 1797 for use at Cross Street, Hatton Garden, where Hindmarsh's congregation had relocated. However, when *The Liturgy of the Lord's New Church, (signified by the New Jerusalem in the Revelation) formed upon the plan of that of the Church of England* (Manchester, 1793) and *The Order of Worship of the Society of the New Church (signified by the New Jerusalem in the Revelation) Meeting in Red Cross Street, near Barbican* (London, 1794), are compared with one another and with Hindmarsh's rites, it appears that in the 1790s the rites were fluid and the text was not uniform. This may be directly related to the fact that there was for a while a split between Hindmarsh and other London ministers.[58]

The baptismal rite in the 1790 third edition of Hindmarsh's work began with a rubric directing that a basin of water is placed on the table, and the minister begins with the Lord's Prayer. An exordium followed which unfolded the three uses of baptism outlined in Swedenborg's *The True Christian Religion*, including a reference to guardian angels. It concluded thus:

> Now, whereas these three Uses follow each other in Order, and join with each other in the ultimate or last Use, and consequently in the Idea of Angels cohere together as one, therefore whensoever Baptism is performed, or read in the Word, or named, the Angels who are present do not understand Baptism, but Regeneration. Wherefore by these Words of the Lord, 'Whosoever believeth, and is baptized, shall be saved,' is understood by the Angels in Heaven, that whosoever acknowledgeth the Lord, and is regenerated, will be saved. Be it known therefore to every Christian, that whosoever doth not believe on the Lord, and keep his

---

[56] I am indebted to the Revd Norman Ryder for the extracts from the General Conference minutes.

[57] For the late seventeenth and eighteenth-century (mis)understanding of the classical Trinitarian term 'person', see Philip Dixon, *Nice and Hot Disputes. The Doctrine of the Trinity in the Seventeenth Century*, Continuum, New York, 2003.

[58] See Duckworth, *A Branching Tree*, for details.

> Commandments, cannot be regenerated, notwithstanding his having been baptized; and that being baptized, without Faith in the Lord, is of no Avail; for Baptism itself neither giveth Faith, nor Salvation, but is a Testimony to such as are baptized, that they may receive Faith, and that they may be saved, if they are regenerate.

A prayer followed, in which God is asked to admit the infant into the fellowship and communion of 'thy New Church' and embrace him 'with the Arms of thy Divine Mercy', a text improvised from the liturgical text of the 1662 *Book of Common Prayer*. A credal form was addressed to the parents:

> *Minister.* Dost thou believe, that God is One both in Essence and in Person, in whom there is a Divine Trinity, consisting of Father, Son and Holy Spirit; and that the Lord and Saviour Jesus Christ is He?
> *Answer.* I do.
> *Minister.* Dost thou believe, that in Order to Salvation Man must live a Life according to the Ten Commandments, by shunning Evils as Sins against God?
> *Answer.* I do.
> *Minister.* Art thou desirous to have this Child baptized into this Faith?
> *Answer.* I am.

A prayer then followed, which included the words

> We beseech thee to be present in this Assembly, and to sanctify this Water to the Use which thou hast ordained in thy Word, that *this Child* now to be baptized may hereafter be cleansed from all *his* Impurities, and by a living Faith in thy DIVINE HUMANITY be prepared to dwell with thee in thy eternal Kingdom. Amen.

The baptismal formula was 'I baptize thee in the Name of the Lord Jesus Christ, who is at once the Father, Son, and Holy Spirit. Amen.' A statement of reception into the Church followed, an exhortation/charge to the parents, thanksgiving, Lord's Prayer and the Grace. Swedenborg's signing of the forehead and breast does not seem to have found its way into the rubrics.

The Manchester 1793 rite was entitled 'The Administration of Baptism to Infants'. It commenced with a reading from Matthew 28:18–20 and Mark 10:13–16. An address to the parents emphasized that in God's Name or Person there is a divine trinity, and that humanity must follow its commandments. The credal questions are the same as Hindmarsh's, but the baptismal formula is 'I baptize thee into the Name of the Father and the Son and the Holy Spirit. Amen.' The declaration of reception was followed by the Aaronic blessing, and then came the exhortation/charge to the parents, a thanksgiving, Lord's Prayer and the Grace.

The Red Cross Street Church, Barbican, London was pastored by the Revd Manoah Sibly, who disagreed with Hindmarsh on compulsory rebaptism. The baptismal rite of the 1794 liturgy was entitled 'The Order of the Administration of Baptism for Children'. It began with the reading from Mark 10, followed by the Lord's Prayer. The credal questions had rather different wording:

> *Q.* Dost thou believe, that God is one in essence, person, and operation; in whom is contained the divine trinity of Father, Son, and Holy Spirit? That in essence he

is love, in person the Lord the saviour Jesus Christ, and in operation the creator and redeemer?

A. I do.

Q. Dost thou believe, that evil actions ought not to be done, because they are of the devil, and from the devil; and that good actions ought to be done, because they are of God, and from God; and that they should be done by man as of himself; nevertheless that he ought to believe, that they are with him, and by him, from the Lord?

A. I do.

Q. Art thou desirous to have this infant baptized in this faith?

A. I am.

The prayer which followed picked up the themes of Matthew 28:19 and Mark 10:13–16, and prayed:

> We humbly implore thee favourably to receive *this infant* now presented before thee, admit *him* into the fellowship and communion of thy new church, embrace *him* with the arms of thy divine mercy, and let thy divine influx continually guide *him*; that being enrolled by baptism among the number of those who acknowledge thee in thy Divine Human to be the only God of heaven and earth, the creator, redeemer, and regenerator ... We beseech thee therefore to sanctify and bless this water to the use which thou hast ordained in thy word, that *this infant* now to be baptized may hereafter retain the substance of which baptism is the sign, and be cleansed from all *his* impurities, that by a living faith in thy Divine Human, and a life agreeable to thy commands, *he* may be habitually prepared to dwell with thee in thine eternal kingdom. Amen.

Baptism by sprinkling followed, with the formula, '*N,* I baptize thee in the name of the Lord Jesus Christ, who in one person is Father, Son, and Holy Spirit.' After a statement of reception came the Aaronic blessing, using 'Jehovah' in place of Lord, an exhortation/charge to the parents, thanksgiving and Grace. A rite for adults was almost identical, though it omitted a charge to the parents.

A more uniform rite in terms of text and order seems to have been established by the 1800s, where *The Liturgy of the New Church, as used in York Street Chapel, St. James' Square, Westminster* (printed by J. Hodson, Hatton Garden, 1800), and *The Liturgy of the New Church, Hatton Garden* (1805) are practically identical. The rite began with the Lord's Prayer, Mark 10:13–16, and then an abbreviated form of the 1793 introduction and interrogations. The prayer was that of 1793, but the baptismal formula in both was 'I Baptize thee into the name of the Lord Jesus Christ, who is Father, Son, and Holy Spirit.' A standard text for the New Church seems to have been established by the General Conference in 1828. The rite began with Matthew 28:18–19 and Mark 10:13–16 and the Lord's Prayer (cf. 1794). An address based on Swedenborg's teaching followed, with interrogatories, prayer with blessing of the water (cf. 1793), the triune formula of 1800/1805, declaration of reception, Aaronic blessing, and admonition for the child to learn the Lord's Prayer, Ten Commandments and the Creed of the New Church, the Prayer of Thanksgiving and the Grace. A more meagre rite was provided in the *Book of Public Worship* of the General Convention at Boston, USA in 1850. It outlined the nature and use of baptism, the doctrines of charity and faith, the classical Trinitarian baptismal formula, Aaronic Blessing, Lord's Prayer and Grace.

This heterodox Church thus provided a baptismal rite with an emphasis on Swedenborg's understanding of the Trinity and, indirectly, his Christology. The emphasis was also soteriological, ecclesiological and eschatological – saving from sin, but by admission to the New Church through belief in Swedenborg's teaching, particularly concerning the Trinity, in the New Age.

Three Nineteenth-Century Restorationist Churches

The Catholic Apostolic Church

The origins of the Catholic Apostolic Church can be traced to a series of meetings held at Albury Park, the home of the wealthy banker and MP, Henry Drummond (1786–1860). These meetings brought clergy and laity of different denominations together to discuss biblical passages about prophecy, and the delegates were of the opinion that the return of Christ would precede a millennium, and that Christ's return was imminent. One of the signs of the approaching *parousia* would be the outpouring of prophecy and gifts of the Spirit. Amongst the group was Edward Irving, minister of a Scottish congregation at Cross Street, Hatton Garden, London (cf. one of the New Church congregations) which later relocated to Regent Square. Several of the Albury Park group were members of Irving's church.

In 1830 reports of the miraculous healing of Mary Campbell in Port Glasgow, and of the prophecies which accompanied it, reached the Albury group, and delegates were sent to investigate. Mary Campbell moved to London and became a member of Irving's congregation. They prayed for the manifestations of the Spirit, and in 1831 'tongues' and other gifts of the Spirit became part of public worship at Irving's church. Not all members of the church were enthusiastic about this, and Irving, already under suspicion for holding unorthodox Christological views, was declared unfit to be minister. He and some 800 of the congregation left the Regent Square building. In 1833 the Church of Scotland deposed Irving from the ministry.

Meanwhile, as a result of the London manifestations and prophecies given by Robert Baxter, prayer meetings were held at Albury Park, and John Cardale and Henry Drummond emerged as leaders of what would become the Catholic Apostolic Church. Prophecies led to the calling and setting-apart of twelve Apostles who in turn instituted a ministry of Angels (bishops), Elders (priests) and Deacons, and the founding of the new Church.[59] As the community believed that they were living in the last days, no provision was made for filling the places of the Apostles as they

---

[59] See Columba Flegg, *Gathered Under Apostles. A Study of the Catholic Apostolic Church*, Clarendon Press, Oxford, 1992.

died. With the death of the last Apostle in 1901, there could be no further ordinations, and the Church gradually entropied.

Initially this Church inherited a Church of Scotland pattern of worship, and directions for worship were issued in 1838. However, under the direction of the Apostles, a liturgy with increasing ceremonial began to evolve. The first printed rite was published in 1843, and it continued to evolve until 1880. The liturgiographer of the Church was John Cardale, who also wrote a commentary on the liturgical rites.[60]

As a worshipping congregation rather than a meeting of delegates interested in prophecy, the Catholic Apostolic Church had its roots in Edward Irving's Church of Scotland congregation in London, and its theological foundations were Irving's. Irving published a series of homilies on baptism in 1828.[61] Although he worked with the Reformed Confessions of the Church of Scotland, Irving had also been influenced by the sacramental teaching of the sixteenth-century Church of England divine, Richard Hooker, and he also expected, or hoped for, a new outpouring of the Spirit. His homilies, therefore, represent a blend of the Augustinian emphasis on original sin and baptism as remission of sin, covenant theology, and concern for the work of the Holy Spirit. As regards the first of these, he wrote:

> … as the rite is emblematical of purification, and there is no outward impurity to be washed away, the impurity signified must be inward, or spiritual impurity. But this child hath not yet been conscious of good or ill, and cannot have contracted any guilt, being admissible to this ordinance as soon as born: it cannot, therefore, be intended against actual impurity contracted by itself: it must be for the sake of some impurity which it hath brought with it into the world, that Christ hath appointed it to be washed with the waters of Baptism. Here, then, to any mind which reflecteth upon the rite of Baptism, is revealed the fundamental doctrine of revealed Religion, that we are shapen in sin, and brought forth in iniquity, and are transgressors from the womb of our mother.[62]

Following traditional Reformed theology, Irving also appealed to the idea of covenant to justify infant baptism. On analogy with circumcision,

> … so do I argue now, that our parents, having had faith, and made profession of the same upon every occasion in the presence of the church, had likewise the righteousness which is by faith, and transmitted a holy seed unto their children; in the sign of which they also are, by the seal of Baptism, set apart for a holy people unto the Lord. The sacrament of Baptism signifieth, therefore, that we were born in covenant, and free to inherit all the privileges of the covenant, whereof the two principal are the remission of sins and the receiving of the Holy Ghost.[63]

---

[60] John Cardale, *Readings in the Liturgy and Divine Offices of the Church*, 2 vols, Thomas Bosworth, London, 1874–75.

[61] Edward Irving, *Homilies on the Sacraments*, Vol. 1, *Baptism*, Andrew Panton, London, 1828.

[62] Ibid., pp. 140–41.

[63] Ibid., pp. 170–71.

The last mention of the Holy Spirit draws attention to another emphasis of Irving's. Although he expected outpourings of the Spirit, he was suspicious of evangelical ideas of conversion:

> I observe, first, That there is no ground from any part of Scripture, to speak thus slightingly of Baptism, thus peremptorily to separate from it the Holy Ghost, thus to magnify conversion into the importance of a sacrament, and thus to date Christian experience from the time of conversion, and thus to exclude a portion of the baptized from the table of the Lord, instead of freely inviting them all.[64]

He thus argues that those who are baptized are regenerated and die and rise with Christ, though in terms of the gift of the Spirit, this is to be expected at any age of life, and not confined to the years of reason and thought.[65] He was conscious of the accusation of teaching an *ex opere operato* doctrine regarding regeneration, and was at pains to distance himself from this. He contended that in baptism seeds of a spiritual nature are conveyed, which the Spirit may bring to fruitfulness, and that parents should trust that the Spirit will do this.[66] The homilies on baptism, however, were written prior to the manifestations of the Spirit of 1830 and 1831. In subsequent writings Irving made a formal separation between regeneration and baptism with the Holy Spirit.[67]

Irving's theological writings were the foundation of the original congregation, but it was Cardale and the Apostles who gave liturgical expression and change in theology to the newly founded church. There is a certain irony in that the Apostolate was founded on the basis of prophecy, but subsequently prophecy and charismatic ecclesiology became subjugated to the Apostolate. The rites of initiation of the Catholic Apostolic Church as developed between 1838 and 1880 have been the subject of a detailed study by Paul Roberts.[68] The 1838 instructions for baptism were found in a letter from J. Thompson, Chief of Elders. The rite consisted of a confession of sin and unworthiness, absolution, and reading from either Mark 10:13–16, John 3:1–8, or Romans 6:1–11. The reading was followed by an optional address to the Church, and then prayer 'for the blessing and presence of God in His ordinance'. Baptism in the triune formula followed, and a blessing of the infant, a declaration of admission into the Church, thanksgiving, a charge to the parents or sponsors, and a psalm and blessing. [69]

---

[64] Ibid., pp. 414–15.

[65] Ibid., p. 343.

[66] Ibid., pp. 149, 151.

[67] Edward Irving, *The Day of Pentecost, or the Baptism with the Holy Ghost*, John Lindsay, Edinburgh, 1831.

[68] Paul J. Roberts, 'The Pattern of Initiation: Sacrament and Experience in the Catholic Apostolic Church and its implications for modern liturgical and theological debate', Ph.D. thesis, University of Manchester, 1990. The discussion which follows is indebted to Paul Robert's study, and I am grateful to him for the loan of a copy of the thesis. He also discusses some significant differences in the Scottish editions of the liturgy.

[69] Text in ibid., pp. 113–14, cited from P.E. Shaw, *The Catholic Apostolic Church*, Kings Crown Press, New York, 1946.

The terminology and structure is still in the orbit of the Church of Scotland. However, each of the Apostles was assigned jurisdiction over particular countries, and were sent out to 'spy out the land', to 'dig for gold' and to 'seek gates for entrance'. Cardale also undertook theological and liturgical study. The result was that a more elaborate liturgy evolved, drawing on liturgical practices ancient and modern, and Eastern and Western. The 1843 liturgy contained a single rite of baptism. By 1851 a number of rites had been added to reflect stages of admission to the Church. This liturgy included a rite of Receiving of a Catechumen, Dedication of Catechumens, Baptism, Committing to Pastorship, Benediction, Renewal of Vows, and Laying-on of Hands. It is remarkable that nothing like these staged rites would emerge in other Western churches until the Liturgical Movement of the twentieth century.

Roberts suggests three reasons for the provision of a rite for Receiving a Catechumen in 1851: Cardale's exhaustive reading of liturgical sources; missionary work in countries the Apostles visited, and urban life in Britain, where many adults were unbaptized.[70] The Dedication of Catechumens seems to have been inspired by the ancient scrutinies and the 'Opening of the Ears of the Elect', but Cardale rejected the use of salt, spittle and exsufflation.[71] The definitive rite for baptism falls into two parts. The first part was inspired by the *Rituale Romanum*, and is basically the reception of a catechumen designed for adult candidates. It includes the delivery of the Apostles' Creed and the Lord's Prayer.

Much of the second part of the rite uses material from the *Book of Common Prayer,* as well as material inspired by Eastern rites. An exhortation was followed by interrogatories of belief and renunciation of evil. A version of the *sindflutgebet* followed, and other material from the *Book of Common Prayer*. The prayer over the water was changed to ask God to 'sanctify + this water, *and by Thy mighty power and presence make it effectual* to the mystical washing away of sin, and to the sanctifying of the spirit of this child'. Cardale commented, 'We have no doubt that the water to be used in Baptism ought to be set apart or consecrated by prayer, invoking the power and presence of the Lord.'[72] Baptism in the triune name followed, and the remainder of the rite used slightly emended *Book of Common Prayer* material.

The Form of Committing to Pastorship was an official liturgical act in which candidates were transferred from an Angel-Evangelist (instructor) to the Angel of the local church. The rite of Benediction was a rite of admission to communion for those who had been baptized, but before they received the more formal 'Sealing' or Laying-on of Hands by the Apostles. The service of Renewal of Vows formed the bridge between baptism and the Laying-on of Hands. The latter, as Roberts notes, marks a fundamental change in the theology of initiation in the Catholic Apostolic Church. In 1847 it was determined that the Apostles were the unique conveyors of the gift of the Holy Spirit. The scriptural justification for this rite of Sealing was Acts 8 and Acts 19. However, this

---

[70] Roberts, 'The Pattern of Initiation', pp. 134–5.

[71] Cardale, *Readings*, Vol. 2, p. 348.

[72] Ibid, p. 351.

was not 'Confirmation', which in other churches bishops administered; this was the revival of a rite reserved for Apostles. According to Cardale, Jesus was conceived by the Holy Spirit, but then later anointed for ministry; in Christian initiation, this is represented in baptism and then the Apostolic sealing. In defining baptism, Cardale wrote:

> ... the sacrament of holy Baptism is the basis and root of all the other sacraments and ordinances for the ministration of the Spirit. It is the door of entrance into the house of God, which is the temple of the Holy Ghost. It is the manner and means ordained by God for our being born again, that we may live the new and eternal Life of manhood brought to us by Jesus Christ: and those only who are quickened with that new life can be made partakers of the Holy Ghost, as He was given on Pentecost. It is, therefore, the means of admission into that blessed company, among whom the gifts of the Holy Ghost are bestowed and distributed.[73]

Although not immediately apparent, there is here a division between baptism into the house of God and, on admission, the gifts of the Holy Spirit. In baptism the Spirit regenerates:

> The Lord communicates His life, to those who hear and obey His Gospel, through the Sacrament of Baptism. He supplies the food and nourishment of His life by communicating to the quickened spirit His own Divine Nature, through the Sacrament of His Body and Blood. He ministers health and strength and growth through all the divers ministries and ordinances of His House. Through these means the Spirit of life is bestowed and ministered continually to the children of God, who have been born from above of water and of the Spirit.'[74]

But there is a second operation of the Spirit which is the anointing power:

> As the Lord and Spirit of power He dwells personally in the creature spirit; and there He rests in His sevenfold fullness. By His indwelling presence, power and grace, the manifold gifts which He imparts are exercised; and in the exercise of them the spirit is inspired and the spiritual faculties are energized by Him. These gifts of the Holy Ghost (both those enumerated by the apostle Paul in the Epistle to the Corinthians, and those subordinate gifts mentioned or referred to in other parts of the Epistles of the apostles) are not only gifts bestowed or divided by Him; but also they are the manifestation, through the organs of the men, of Himself, the indwelling Spirit.[75]

This second endowment of the Spirit, coming through the hands of the Apostles, enables the believer to fulfil his or her ministry and place in the Body of Christ.[76] Although in some editions of the liturgy chrism is mentioned, it is clear that the primary ritual action of this rite was the laying-on of hands.

Quite apart from the elaborate liturgical rites, Roberts notes that a shift in theology has taken place between Irving and the later Catholic Apostolic Church. Baptism becomes an indelible act of God, and the Church is the visible community in which

---

[73] Ibid., p. 235.

[74] Ibid., p. 410.

[75] Ibid., p. 382.

[76] For full discussion, see Roberts, 'The Pattern of Initiation', pp. 187–208.

dwells the Spirit, of which the Apostles are the bestowers and guarantors. The Holy Spirit is always active in baptism, and regeneration always takes place. Those who do not persist in the faith are not unregenerate, but apostates. In a document addressed to the leaders of the world churches, composed in 1836, the leaders of the Catholic Apostolic Church had stated:

> (Sacraments) are not empty signs of unreal things; neither are they merely the most suitable forms devised by God or adopted by convention of men for the expression of spiritual truths; nor yet are they merely commemorative of blessings otherwise or collaterally obtained, or invisibly enjoyed; but they are present actings of Christ in the midst of His people, and do operate that which they express; they are sacraments, sure pledges of His love and faithfulness in bestowing the blessings by them, the which He ordained them to convey. They seal by their very administration the covenant of God, the blessings contained in that covenant, and the responsibilities involved therein; so that every baptized man shall be judged by the covenant as one who have received the life of God, and every one who has partaken of the bread and of the wine shall be judged as a partaker of the body and blood of the Lord, and can find no retreat, but only a progress onward, either to perfect salvation, or to utter and eternal apostasy.[77]

The theology of baptism certainly retained the idea of original sin and remission of sins, but the emphasis was on sacramental grace, reinforced by a stress on ecclesiology – the restored Apostolic Church, and pneumatology, though the gifts of the Spirit became less and less about prophecy and tongues and more and more a sacramental gift guaranteed by the hands of the Apostles.

The Disciples of Christ

In 1832, at the time when Edward Irving's Church was experiencing manifestations of the Spirit, another Church across the Atlantic was founded: the Disciples of Christ. Just as Irving was a minister of the Presbyterian Church of Scotland, so the leading ministers in this new Church in America were former Presbyterians – Barton W. Stone (1772–1844), Thomas Campbell (1763–1854), and his son, Alexander Campbell (1788–1866). The Disciples were an amalgamation of congregations under the leadership of Stone, and those under the leadership of the two Campbells. It was a Restorationist Church and one which, like the Catholic Apostolic Church, believed itself to be refounded on the basis of the Apostolic Church of the New Testament.[78] However, its interpretation of this was rather different than that of the Catholic Apostolic Church.

In 1801 a Presbyterian camp meeting at Cane Ridge, Kentucky attracted thousands of frontier people, and ministers present included Baptists and Methodists as well as Presbyterians. Barton Stone recorded:

---

[77] Cited in ibid., p. 251, from *Testimony to the Bishops of the Church and to the Princes of Christendom* in E. Miller, *History and Doctrines of Irvingism*, 2 vols, C. Kegan Paul & Co, London, 1878.

[78] For further discussion, see Max Ward Randall, *The Great Awakenings and the Restoration Movement*, College Press Publishing Company, Joplin, MO, 1983.

> I saw the religion of Jesus more clearly exhibited in the lives of Christians then
> than I had ever seen before or since ... We all engaged in singing the same songs
> of praise – all united in prayer – all preached the same things – free salvation
> urged upon all by faith and repentance.[79]

There were certainly manifestations of the Spirit not dissimilar to those in some
Methodist revival meetings and in Irving's church. Stone found the Westminster
Confession and Presbyterian polity too constricting, and in 1803 he and four other
Presbyterian ministers were charged before the Synod of Kentucky with departing
from the Westminster standards. Before they came to trial, they rejected the authority
of the Synod of Kentucky, and formed their own Synod. In a document entitled 'The
Last Will and Testament of the Springfield Presbytery' (1804), they appealed to the
Bible as the only sure guide to heaven. Later some members of this Church became
persuaded that believer's baptism was the correct New Testament practice.

In 1807 another Presbyterian minister, Thomas Campbell, who had come from
Northern Ireland, wrestled with similar problems regarding the strict interpretation of
the *Westminster Confession*, and relationships with ministers of the already fragmented
Presbyterian groups in the USA. Campbell too was charged with departing from
Westminster standards, and eventually left both his Presbytery and Synod. Campbell
had a vision of a single Church, whose authority would be the Bible only, and which
would transcend the Presbyterian divisions. His principles were set out in 1809 in 'A
Declaration and Address', in which he made a strong plea for Christian unity on the
basis of New Testament faith and practice.[80]

In a frontier situation, both Stone and Campbell had followers who had not been
baptized, as well as families who expected infant baptism. In 1811 Campbell inquired
as to why three members of his church at Brush Run, Kentucky had not taken part in
the Lord's Supper. They replied that they had not been baptized. On 4 July 1811, in
Buffalo Creek, Kentucky, Campbell baptized the three men, dipping the head of each
and pronouncing the triune formula. Campbell had been joined by his family, and his
son, Alexander, became his assistant. When Alexander's son was born, questions
surfaced about whether the infant should be baptized. After a study of the New
Testament passages, and the Greek words translated as baptism, Alexander came to
the conviction that only believers were the proper subject of baptism, that the proper
mode was immersion, and that therefore his own baptism as an infant by sprinkling
was invalid. A Baptist preacher (re)baptized him by immersion on 12 June 1812 in
Buffalo Creek, together with Thomas, their wives, and some other adults.[81]

For a period of time, the Campbell congregations aligned themselves with an
Association of Baptist Churches, but there were too many differences in their theologies

---

[79] Lester G. McAllister and William E. Tucker, *Journey in Faith*, Bethany Press, St Louis, MO, 1975, pp. 61–2, 73.

[80] For the 13 principles see Randall, *The Great Awakenings*, pp. 113–14.

[81] Recorded in Robert Richardson, *Memoirs of Alexander Campbell*, 2 vols, Standard Publishing Company, Cincinnati, OH, 1913, Vol. 1, pp. 396–8.

for this to last. Finally, in 1832, Stone's congregations and the Campbell congregations joined to form the new Church as an ecumenical one, founded on the New Testament, with weekly celebration of the Lord's Supper, believer's baptism by immersion, and an ordained ministry regarded as a representative ministry on behalf of the priesthood of all believers. Campbell was also a strong post-millennialist, though his associate until 1830, Sidney Rigdon, who later joined the Mormons, was a pre-millennialist.[82]

The foundational theology of the Disciples of Christ was set forth by Alexander Campbell in *The Christian System, in Reference to the Union of Christians, and the Restoration of Primitive Christianity* (1866). However, the section on baptism is a summary of a longer treatise defending believers' baptism by immersion, *Christian Baptism: with its Antecedents and Consequences* (1851). In this earlier work, Campbell examined first what he called 'Antecedents', which included a discussion of how to interpret Scripture, and a consideration of faith, or repentance, and covenants of promise. A second section considered the 'Action' of baptism, examining the root meaning of *bapto,* and *baptizo*, and establishing that it means to dip, not to pour or to sprinkle. In a third section he examined the subjects of baptism, arguing that these are limited to believing people, and infants are excluded. In the fourth section Campbell set out his beliefs on the 'design' of baptism. It is, so he argued, first and foremost for the remission of sins, and it brings unity with Christ. He wrote:

> Baptism, a new institution, is an ordination of great significance, and of the most solemn and sublime importance. It is a sort of embodiment of the gospel; and a solemn expression of it all in a single act. Hence the space and the place assigned it in the commission. It is a monumental and commemorative institution, bodying forth to all ages the great facts of man's redemption as developed and consummated in the death, burial, and resurrection of the Lord Jesus Christ. Hence, immediately upon the first constitutional promulgation of it on the part of the Christian Lawgiver and Saviour, he adds, '*He that believeth and is baptized shall be saved.*'[83]

The 'consequents' of baptism are listed as adoption, justification and sanctification.

In his theological work, *The Christian System*, Campbell reiterated that baptism means immersion in water, not pouring or sprinkling. The subjects of baptism are '*Penitent believers* – not infants nor adults, not males nor females, not Jews nor Greeks; but professors of repentance towards God, and faith in Christ – are the proper subjects of this ordinance.'[84] The rite is for the remission of sins, and introduces subjects to the blessings of the death and resurrection of Christ. However, Campbell warned:

> But it has no abstract efficacy. Without previous faith in the blood of Christ, and deep and unfeigned repentance before God, neither immersion in water, nor any

---

[82] Hiram J. Lester, 'Alexander Campbell's Millennial Program', *Discipliana* 48 (1988), 35–9.

[83] Alexander Campbell, *Christian Baptism: with its Antecedents and Consequents*, Alexander Campbell, Bethany, VA, 1851, p. 257.

[84] Alexander Campbell, *The Christian System*, Standard Publishing Company, Cincinnati, OH, 1901 edn, p. 41.

other action, can secure to us the blessings of peace and pardon. It can merit nothing. Still to the believing penitent it is the *means* of receiving a formal, distinct, and specific absolution, or release from guilt. Therefore, none but those who have first believed the testimony of God and have repented of their sins, and that have been intelligently immersed into his death, have the full and explicit testimony of God, assuring them of pardon. To such only as are truly penitent, dare we say, 'Arise and be baptized, and wash away your sins, calling upon the name of the Lord,' and to such only can we say with assurance, 'You are washed, you are justified, you are sanctified in the name of the Lord Jesus, and by the Spirit of God.'[85]

In contrast to the Catholic Apostolic Church, which restored the liturgical rites of what it believed to be the pattern of the early Church, with an ecclesiological and pneumatological emphasis, the Disciples of Christ stressed prior belief, immersion as the mode of baptism, and a soteriological emphasis, with an unscripted rite derived from the Presbyterian inheritance of the *Westminster Directory* and adapted to the needs of frontier believers' baptism.

The Church of Jesus Christ of Latter-day Saints

The very name of the church popularly called the Mormon Church is a reminder that it was one of the nineteenth-century Restorationist churches, and, like the Catholic Apostolic Church, was founded on Pre-millennial beliefs.[86] The prophet Joseph Smith is purported to have received his first vision (cf. Swedenborg) in 1820:

> I saw a pillar of light exactly over my head, above the brightness of the sun, which descended gradually until it fell upon me.
>   It no sooner appeared than I found myself delivered from the enemy which held me bound. When the light rested upon me I saw two personages, whose brightness and glory defy all description, standing above me in the air. One of them spake unto me, calling me by name, and said – pointing to the other – THIS IS MY BELOVED SON, HEAR HIM.[87]

The subsequent visions of an angel and the delivery to Smith of the *Book of Mormon* was regarded as a fulfilment of Revelation 14:6–7, and the Latter-day Saints believed that they were living on the eve of the Second Coming. Prophecy held an important place in the life of the new Church, and the Restoration included the Aaronic and Melchizedek priesthoods. In 1835 Smith appointed Twelve Apostles and 'the Seventies'. The former, unlike the Twelve of the Catholic Apostolic Church, could have successors. It was while translating the *Book of Mormon*, in May 1829, that

---

[85] Ibid., p. 42.

[86] Grant Underwood, *The Millenarian World of Early Mormonism*, University of Illinois, Urbana and Chicago, 1993. See also Douglas J. Davies, *An Introduction to Mormonism*, Cambridge University Press, Cambridge, 2003.

[87] Cited in Ivan J. Barrett, *Joseph Smith and the Restoration*, Brigham Young University Press, Provo, UT, 1973, p. 48.

Joseph Smith and Oliver Cowdery discovered that the Nephite prophets of old taught, like the contemporary Campbellites, that baptism was for the remission of sins. When at prayer at the Susquehanna River in Pennsylvania, Smith and Cowdery had a vision of John the Baptist, and he laid hands on them to confer upon them the Aaronic priesthood.[88] John the Baptist then commanded the young men to baptize each other in the river, and afterwards they were instructed to lay hands on one another.

Ivan Barrett explains that 'Immediately upon emerging from the water, Joseph Smith and Oliver Cowdery experienced the glorious influence of the Holy Ghost – each enjoyed the spirit of prophecy and prophesied many things that would shortly come to pass.'[89] Any doubts about understanding baptism as being primarily for the remission of sins was removed when Sidney Rigdon, an associate of Campbell, joined the emerging Mormon Church, and endorsed this Restorationist understanding of the ordinance. In 1830 Smith later baptized his parents and others as the new Church began to be organized. Some who had previously been baptized in other churches desired to join the Church without further baptism. It was then revealed to the Church:

> Wherefore, although a man should be baptized an hundred times it availeth him nothing, for you cannot enter in at the strait gate by the law of Moses, neither your dead works. For it is because of your dead works that I have caused this last covenant and this church to be built up unto me, even as in days of old. Wherefore, enter ye in at the gate, as I have commanded, and seek not to counsel your God. Amen.[90]

Like the Catholic Apostolic Church, Smith taught that baptism consisted of two distinct elements: baptism in water, and a baptism of fire and the Holy Spirit. People who had previously been baptized had not received the true Holy Spirit, and so rebaptism was insisted upon.

Baptism was administered by immersion in pools or lakes. Specific Mormon scriptures establishing the basis for baptism are found in Mosiah 18:12ff., where Alma took Helam and the immersion is linked with entering a covenant and reception of the Spirit of the Lord, and Moroni 8, which condemns infant baptism, and stresses, 'Behold, baptism is unto repentance to the fulfilling the commandments unto the remission of sins.' The ritual for baptism is set forth in 3 Nephi 11:23–8:

> Verily I say unto you, that whoso repenteth of his sins through your words, and desireth to be baptized in my name, on this wise shall ye baptize them – Behold, ye shall go down and stand in the water, and in my name shall ye baptize them. And now behold, these are the words which ye shall say, calling them by name, saying: 'Having authority given me of Jesus Christ, I baptize you in the name of the Father, and of the Son, and of the Holy Ghost. Amen.'

---

[88] At some point the Melchizedek priesthood was restored, though the date was not recorded, ibid., p. 125.

[89] Ibid., p. 122.

[90] *Doctrine and Covenants*, 22:2–4 (Mormon texts are all cited from <http://scriptures.lds.org>).

> And ye shall immerse them in the water, and come forth again out of the water. And after this manner shall ye baptize in my name; for behold, verily I say unto you, that the Father, and the Son, and the Holy Ghost are one; and I am in the Father, and the Father in me, and the Father and I are one. And according as I have commanded you thus shall ye baptize.

The formula for baptism includes the traditional Trinitarian formula, though the Mormon understanding of the Trinity is more akin to that of Swedenborg than to the classical orthodox understanding.[91]

One of the doctrinal works requested by the Mormon Church is *The Articles of Faith* by James E. Talmage, who held the office of an Apostle in the Church. Here water baptism is regarded as an essential ordinance: 'The candidate for admission into the Church and kingdom, having obtained and professed faith in the Lord Jesus Christ, and having sincerely repented of his sins, is properly required to give evidence of this spiritual sanctification by some outward ordinance, prescribed by authority as the sign and symbol of the new profession.'[92] Baptism is defined as 'a sign of the covenant entered into between the repentant sinner and his Maker, that thereafter he will seek to observe the Divine commands', echoing the Reformed tradition with which the founding prophets were acquainted. Talmage notes its description in the Mormon scriptures – Alma, Moroni and, in The Pearl of Great Price: Moses 6, Adam is recorded as being baptized. The purpose of baptism is 'to afford admission to the Church of Christ with the remission of sins'.[93] Since this requires the exercise of faith, baptism is restricted to those who are capable of exercising the faith. Talmage quoted from the prophet Joseph Smith as recorded in *Doctrine and Covenants*:

> In a revelation on Church government given through Joseph the Prophet, April, 1830, the Lord specifically states the conditions under which persons may be received into the Church through baptism: these are His words: – 'All those who humble themselves before God, and desire to be baptized, and come forth with broken hearts and contrite spirits, and witness before the Church that they have truly repented of all their sins, and are willing to take upon them the name of the Jesus Christ, having a determination to serve him to the end, and truly manifest by their works that they have received of the Spirit of Christ unto the remission of their sins, shall be received by baptism into his Church'.[94]

Infant baptism is regarded, says Talmage, 'to be sacrilege in the eyes of God'. Like Alexander Campbell, Talmage insists that the word 'baptism' means immersion, and not pouring or sprinkling, and that the symbolism of the rite is preserved in no form other than immersion.[95] However, like the Catholic Apostolic Church, the Mormon

---

[91] See Owen F. Cummings, 'Is Mormon Baptism Valid?', *Worship* 71 (1997), 146–53. See also Davies, *Introduction to Mormonism*, pp. 67–76.

[92] James E. Talmage, *The Articles of Faith* [1890], *The Deseret News* edn, Salt Lake City, 1919, p. 122.

[93] Ibid., p. 124.

[94] Ibid., pp. 126–7.

[95] Ibid., p. 140.

Church also regards baptism as two-fold: first, water baptism, and then, administered by those endowed with the Melchizedek priesthood, comes the baptism of fire and the Holy Ghost. Again, as in the Catholic Apostolic Church, the symbolic gesture is the laying-on of hands. Talmage explained:

> The Bestowal of the Holy Ghost is effected through the ordinance of an oral blessing, pronounced upon the candidate by the proper authority of the Priesthood, accompanied by the imposition of hands by him or those officiating. That this was the mode followed by the apostles of old is evident from the Jewish scriptures; that it was practiced by the early Church Fathers is proved by history; that it was the acknowledged method among the Nephites is plainly shown by the Book of Mormon records; and for the same practice in the present dispensation authority has come direct from heaven.[96]

There are other 'initiatory rituals', particularly ceremonial washings and anointings performed only in the Temples. And, peculiar to the Mormon Church, the rite for Baptism for the Dead is administered in the Temples. In the early 1830s Mormonism did not differ greatly from other American Protestant frontier groups, other than in its claim to have new revealed Scriptures. However, the influence at one point of Masonic rituals, together with the restoration of Old Testament concepts, led to the establishing of Temples with special rituals.[97] The first was at Kirtland, Ohio. It was dedicated in 1836, but had to be abandoned because of local hostility to Mormonism. The second at Nauvoo, Illinois, was begun in October 1840. Earlier in 1840, at the funeral of Colonel Seymour Brunson, Joseph Smith spoke on the subject of baptism of the dead in 1 Corinthians 15, and Jane Neyman asked to be baptized in the Mississippi River for her dead son. In October 1840 Smith wrote to the Twelve Apostles:

> The Saints have the privilege of being baptized for those of their relatives who are dead, whom they believe would have embraced the Gospel, if they had been privileged with hearing it, and who have received the Gospel in the Spir[i]t, through the instrumentality of those who have been commissioned to preach to them while in prison.[98]

In January 1841 he announced that it had been revealed to him that the Nauvoo Temple should have a baptismal font for baptism for the dead. In October 1841 he announced the suspension of baptisms for the dead until they could be performed in the font in the Temple. One month later a temporary structure had been built:

> The baptismal font is situated in the center of the basement room, under the main hall of the Temple; it is constructed of pine timber, and put together of staves tongued and grooved, oval shaped, sixteen feet long east and west, and twelve feet wide, seven feet high from the foundation, the basin four feet deep, the moulding of the cap and base are formed of beautiful carved work in antique style.

---

[96] Ibid., pp. 170–71.

[97] See Davies, *Introduction to Mormonism*; David John Buerger, *The Mysteries of Godliness: A History of Mormon Temple Worship*, Smith Research Associates, San Francisco, CA, 1994.

[98] Cited in Barrett, *Joseph Smith*, pp. 489–90.

The sides are finished with panel work. A flight of stairs in the north and south sides lead up and down into the basin, guarded by side railing.

The font stands upon twelve oxen, four on each side, and two at each end, their heads, shoulders, and fore legs projecting out from under the font; they are carved out of pine plank, glued together, and copied after the most beautiful five-year-old steer that could be found in the country … The water was supplied from a well thirty feet deep in the east end of the basement.[99]

This was to be temporary until one could be cut from stone. The imagery is suggested by the basin on the back of bulls in Solomon's Temple (2 Chronicles 4:1–4), and is replicated in other subsequent Temples, such as Salt Lake City, though more recently it is reported that smaller temples have had six oxen.[100] These lavish fonts are only used for the rite of baptism for the dead. Although it has been pointed out that this practice was found in America in the eighteenth century amongst a Seventh Day German Baptist group in Ephrata Cloister in Pennsylvania, there seems to be no direct link with its adoption by Smith. It rests, of course, on the single reference in 1 Corinthians 15:29, though appeal is also made to 1 Peter 3:19. Although it is almost impossible to know what Paul understood by the practice he mentions in passing in 1 Corinthians 15:29, and the practice, if ever widespread outside the Corinthian community, quickly died out, it remains a fact that only the Mormon Church has attempted to deal positively in considering the possible meaning of the verse. In Mormon thought, this of course is part of the Restoration, and is a salvific rite which is necessary for one to be admitted amongst the elect. In both Mormonism's rite of water baptism and proxy baptism for the dead, the emphasis is on soteriology; indeed, even baptism with fire and the Holy Spirit is seen less as a gift of the Spirit than as a further means to salvation amongst the elect.

Concluding Remarks

The Moravian and Methodist Churches were both influenced by the Pietism of their founding figures, Count Zinzendorf and John Wesley. For both these men, the Atonement was a crucial aspect of understanding baptism, and both gave importance to heart-felt faith, or conversion. Because of this, in the rite of baptism in water, the benefits of the atonement are proclaimed and applied as a seed in infants, but a second regeneration comes with personal faith.

Swedenborg also came from a Pietist background, and had found some initial affinity with the Moravians in London. However, his visions and revelations which

---

[99] Joseph Smith Jr., *History of the Church of Jesus Christ of Latter-day Saints*, 7 vols, Deseret Book Co, Salt Lake City, UT, 1976, Vol. 4, p. 446.

[100] See Sandra Tanner, 'Baptism for the Dead and the Twelve Oxen Under the Baptismal Font', <http://www.utlm.org/onlinersources/twelveoxenbaptismalfont.htm>, p. 2. It reports that a mirror will be used to give the image of twelve oxen.

he recorded, with the belief that the Last Judgement had taken place and there was a 'New Church' for the last age, places him as a Restorationist. The subsequent founders of the New Church held that baptism was into the faith as expounded by Swedenborg (particularly his understanding of the Trinity and Christology), and hence Hindmarsh was reluctant to accept the validity of baptism in other churches.

This was true also of the Disciples of Christ and the Mormons; for both of these baptism is by immersion (the mode becomes a doctrinal matter) for the remission of sins. Infant baptism for these two churches becomes invalid (sacrilege according to Talmage), and for Mormons, as for Hindmarsh, all other baptisms are invalid (even of adults by immersion) because they are not baptisms into the Restored Church and its distinct understanding of the Godhead. For both the Catholic Apostolic Church and the Mormons, the hand-layings in Acts are seen as a distinct apostolic rite which must be restored, and which conveys the Spirit through the hands of the new apostles. In all the Restorationist churches baptism becomes an eschatological sign of the new age and the new restored Church.

PART II
CONVERGING STREAMS

Cross-currents: Some Baptismal Theologies of the Twentieth Century

Theological thinking about baptism in the first decade of the twenty-first century is still dominated by certain influential twentieth-century theologians, particular theological schools of thought, and particular theological documents. The latter half of the twentieth century has been a time of considerable ecumenical activity. Theologians have tended to write for an ecumenical audience, or have sought to bring their denomination or tradition into dialogue with other denominations and traditions, seeking areas of agreement, as well as pinpointing areas of disagreement. This chapter considers some of these theological contributions, the issues which have been raised by them, and the possible implication for the rituals of baptism composed or revised over the last few decades.

Baptism as Ethical Response

One of the most influential giants of twentieth-century theology was the Swiss Reformed theologian, Karl Barth. Barth had touched on baptism indirectly in a number of his earlier works from 1919, but the publication of his Gwatt lecture of May 1943 indicated a departure from what had been the traditional Reformed understanding of baptism, and its defence of infant baptism.[1] In this work Barth called for 'responsible baptism' in place of 'half baptism', which he felt had become the norm of Christendom. Barth carefully distinguished between the temporal act in the church and the eternal act of Christ of which it is a depiction or representation (*Abbild*):

> Baptism is holy and hallowing, though we have yet to see why and how far. But it is neither God, nor Jesus Christ, nor the covenant, nor grace, nor faith, nor the church. It bears witness to all these as the event in which God in Jesus Christ makes a man His child and a member of His covenant, awakening faith through His grace and calling a man to life in the Church. Baptism testifies to a man that this event is not his fancy but is objective reality which no power on earth can alter and which God has pledged Himself to maintain in all circumstances. It testifies to him that God has directed all His words and works towards him and does not cease so to do.[2]

---

[1] For more detailed discussion, see Bryan D. Spinks, 'Karl Barth's Teaching on Baptism: Its Development, Antecedents and the "Liturgical Factor"', *Ecclesia Orans* 14 (1997), 261–88, upon which this section is based.

[2] Karl Barth, *The Teaching of the Church Regarding Baptism*, English translation Ernest Payne, SCM Press, London, 1948, p. 14.

Barth could describe baptism as a representation, a picture, a witness, and a sign, and following Augustine and Calvin, it can be called a *signum visibile*. However, the ritual act is not itself the cause of regeneration; it only points back to what was already achieved by Jesus Christ in AD 30 on Golgotha, and the covenant of grace.[3] It is 'baptism with the Holy Spirit' which unites a person with the work of Jesus Christ and accomplishes full justification before God. Men and women are covenant partners, and consecrated for God:

> These things a man becomes because he believes in Jesus Christ and in his own renewal as a child of God through Him, and because he confesses this his faith, becoming by reason of this confession a responsible partner in the divine grace, a living member of the Church of Jesus Christ. All this – that is, everything accomplished in the death and the resurrection of Jesus Christ, right up to and including the last thing of all, namely, the praise of God which breaks from the lips of the forgiven sinner and is accepted by grace – is the reality which is portrayed in water-baptism.[4]

Water-baptism is the visible sign of the invisible *nativitas spiritualis*. Its power lies in the fact that it comprehends the whole movement of sacred history. However, Barth makes it quite clear that as such it is a human act, a part of the Church's proclamation, and like all activities of the Church, sacramental. The Church obeys the mandate of her Lord. Only Jesus Christ can testify of Jesus Christ. He is Lord of baptism, and the chief actor. Barth criticized Zwingli for holding that the potency of baptism is a symbol of the faith of the Church and of the faith of her individual members, and that its performance is an act of remembrance and therefore an act of confession, and thus something which confirms faith.[5]

Barth seemed fearful lest any efficacy should appear to be attributed to the water, and noted that the power of Jesus Christ is not dependent upon carrying out baptism; the free word and work of Christ can make use of other means. Water-baptism is thus a symbol of the fact that we have been redeemed, and not itself the means of redemption. It is because baptism is an active obedient response, needing in man an active partner, that infant (passive) baptism must be deplored. One is not brought to baptism; one comes. Thus the arguments of Luther and Calvin (and Zwingli?) in support of infant baptism will not hold water (as it were!). Quoting Schleiermacher, Barth agrees that 'Infant Baptism is complete Baptism only when the profession of faith which comes after further instruction is regarded as the act which consummates it.'[6] Infant baptism is thus 'half baptism'. Behind this lurks Barth's suspicion of the *Volkskirche* in all its forms, but particularly as manifested in the German Christian Movement.

---

[3] Ibid., pp. 11, 21.

[4] Ibid., p. 13.

[5] Ibid., p. 20.

[6] Ibid., p. 47. Schleiermacher, *The Christian Faith*, p. 633.

In this work, Barth is still able to appeal to what may be termed the Augustinian-Calvinian terminology of baptism.[7] Yet at the same time, there is a clear distinction made between water-baptism and Spirit-baptism. The former is the active response to what already has been achieved by Spirit-baptism, itself accomplished on the Cross in time, and in the election of Jesus Christ in eternity.

Barth's criticism of infant baptism led to a number of theological replies through the next two decades. Defence of infant baptism came from F.-J. Leenhardt and Oscar Cullman, and the Lutheran New Testament scholar, Joachim Jeremias, though Kurt Aland supported Barth's critique.[8]

In the short fragment of *Church Dogmatics* (*CD*) IV.4, Barth's earlier objection to infant baptism was pursued and expanded, though as a logical conclusion to the meaning of water-baptism, which is quite distinct from Spirit-baptism.[9] The great change was Barth's rejection of the term 'sacrament' for baptism, and his refusal to allow that sacraments – other than the One Sacrament, Jesus Christ – can be channels of divine grace. According to Barth himself, it was his son Markus' work on baptism in the New Testament which changed his mind.[10] In his book, *Die Taufe – Ein Sakrament?*, Markus Barth had outlined four theories of the origin of Christian baptism: the Hellenistic Mystery cults; Jewish proselyte baptism; the baptism of John the Baptist; and Old Testament prophecies. He rejected the supposed influence of the first two, though he allowed a role for the latter two. He then subjected passages in the New Testament associated with baptism to a lengthy and detailed exegesis.

His overall conclusions were that the New Testament statements concerning water-baptism are remarkably unified and harmonious: 'Complete obedience (*Ganzer Gehorsam*) is impossible without the act figuratively described as baptism.'[11] In the whole of the New Testament, baptism is a work which God commands men to do; with it they answer to the saving work of God and the proclamation of this saving work. In the performance of baptism, the person who is baptized and the baptizer, together with the whole congregation, confess before God and the world their knowledge of the significance and effect of the death of Christ, and the working of the

---

[7] For the legitimacy of this term see Charles C. West, 'Baptism in the Reformed Tradition', in Ross T. Bender and Alan P.F. Sell (eds), *Baptism, Peace and the State in the Reformed and Mennonite Traditions*, Wilfrid Laurier Press, Waterloo, IA, 1991, pp. 13–36. Calvin quotes Augustine, defining sacraments as testimonies of divine grace towards us, confirmed by an outward sign or visible form of an invisible grace. For Calvin's use of Augustine on the sacraments, see Joseph Fitzer, 'The Augustinian Roots of Calvin's Eucharistic Thought', *Augustinian Studies* 7 (1976), 69–98.

[8] F.-J.Leenhardt, *Le Baptême chrétien, son origine, sa signification*, Delachaux & Niestlé, Neuchâtel, 1946; Oscar Cullman, *Baptism in the New Testament*, English translation J.K.S. Reid, SCM Press, London, 1950; Joachim Jeremias, *Infant Baptism in the First Four Centuries*, English translation D. Cairns, Westminster Press, Philadelphia, PA, 1963; Kurt Aland, *Did the Early Church Baptize Infants?*, English translation, G.R. Beasley-Murray, Westminster Press, Philadelphia, PA, 1963.

[9] *CD* IV.4, pp. 165ff.

[10] Ibid., p. x. 'In face of the exegetical conclusions in my son's book, I have had to abandon the "sacramental" understanding of baptism, which I still maintained fundamentally in 1943.'

[11] Markus Barth, *Die Taufe – Ein Sakrament?*, Evangelischer Verlag: Zollikon-Zurich, 1951, p. 522.

Spirit of God. They confess in water-baptism their desire for the baptism of the Spirit and their sure hope or trust that the baptism of the Spirit will occur. Baptism is a 'work' in the sense of an offer, a motion, an affirmation, an attestation, a genuine divine service: in its meaning, its nature and its working, it is nothing else but prayer.[12]

The ultimate theological point which Markus Barth made was that baptism is not an unfailing tool which effects what it portrays, but is to be understood as confession, obedience, hope and prayer. It is not a sacrament, but a rite which indicates what has already been effected by the free work of God. This thinking provided concepts and views which Karl Barth was to adopt in *CD* IV.4, namely, that water-baptism is not a sacrament, but a human work and act of obedience, and that the theological baptism with the Holy Spirit is sharply distinct from the anthropological baptism in water:

> A man's turning to faithfulness to God, and consequently to calling upon Him, is the work of this faithful God which, perfectly accomplished in the history of Jesus Christ, in virtue of the awakening, quickening and illuminating power of this history, becomes a new beginning of life as his baptism with the Holy Spirit.

> The first step of this life of faithfulness to God, the Christian life, is a man's baptism with water, which by his own decision is requested of the community and which is administered by the community, as the binding confession of his obedience, conversion and hope, made in prayer for God's grace, wherein he honours the freedom of this grace.[13]

Under the title 'Baptism with the Holy Spirit', Barth immediately took up the question of how what took place in the saving work of Christ *extra nos* and *pro nos* can be also *in nobis*; that is, going from the ontological to the ontic and to the noetic. For Barth the change necessary for the *in nobis*, faith, is the divine change wrought by the Holy Spirit:

> We thus maintain that the power of the divine change in which the event of the foundation of the Christian life of specific men takes place is the power of their baptism with the Holy Ghost.[14]

This is a form of grace, but the same cannot be said for the rite of water-baptism:

> Baptism with the Spirit does not take place in a man either with or through the fact that he receives water baptism. He also becomes a Christian in his human decision, in the fact that he requests and receives baptism with water. But he does not become a Christian through his human decision or his water baptism.[15]

Through the initiative of God's grace, baptism of the Spirit justifies and sanctifies, and summons to obedient gratitude.

---

[12] Ibid., p. 524. Compare Markus Barth, 'Baptism', in *The Interpreter's Dictionary of the Bible*, Supplementary Volume, Abingdon, Nashville, TN, 1972, pp. 85–9.

[13] *CD* VI.4, p. 2.

[14] Ibid., p. 30.

[15] Ibid., pp. 32–3.

As John Webster diagnoses, underneath this whole section is the concern that no account of baptism is adequate if it allows the creaturely action (whether of the candidate or the community) to trespass upon the unique, finished work of Jesus Christ the reconciler, or upon the self-communication of that work through the Holy Spirit.[16]

When Barth turns to 'Baptism with Water', he notes that baptism with the Holy Spirit does not exclude baptism with water, nor render it superfluous; rather, it makes it possible and demands it.[17] Water-baptism is an obedient response to the grace of God which has come upon a man or woman by the history of Jesus Christ which has taken place for him or her. It is thus a human response to the *in nobis* of the work of the one sacrament, Jesus Christ. Water-baptism responds to the mystery, but is not itself a mystery.[18] It has a basis, a goal and a meaning. The basis is not Matthew 28:19, but the baptism of Jesus himself in the Jordan by John, which he freely undertook. In this he began the fulfilment of his mission, entering upon his office as Messiah, Saviour and Mediator. In his baptism he confessed both God and men, and he took up his life as the Messiah. He did so in an act of obedience, but his baptism of the Spirit was not dependent upon the baptism in water. The goal is that baptism looks beyond itself to the coming kingdom, the coming judgement and coming grace:

> ... it looks to Him who has already done this, and it does so in the expectation that He will do it again in the future to and in those who are baptised ... Hence Christian baptism, as it is the form of the petition for the coming of the kingdom, is far from being itself in any sense the baptism of the Spirit. It is a form of the petition for this – that the outpouring of the Spirit might take place again, and especially on these newcomers to faith.[19]

For Barth, baptism is a human work that derives from and hastens towards the work of God.[20]

Having established the basis and goal, Barth moved to the meaning of baptism. He rejected the sacramental approach of Roman Catholicism, Lutheranism and his own Reformed tradition, because they all perceive baptism as in some way a divine action, a consensus he believed was in need of demythologizing.[21] He embarked on an examination of New Testament passages to test whether the idea of water-baptism as sacramental is found there. Although some passages could be taken in this way, he found that no passage *has* to be taken so:

> According to what the New Testament says concerning baptism, it is highly and even supremely probable that this Christian action is not to be understood as a divine work or word of grace which purifies man and renews him.[22]

---

[16] John Webster, *Barth's Ethics of Reconciliation*, Cambridge University Press, Cambridge, 1995, p. 117.

[17] *CD* IV.4, p. 41.

[18] Ibid., p. 102.

[19] Ibid., p. 77.

[20] Ibid., p. 73.

[21] Ibid., p. 105.

[22] Ibid., p. 128.

Here Barth followed the conclusions of his son, but in contradistinction to Markus, he asserted that the 'mystery' idea of baptism was imported from the Mystery religions, and he appealed to Zwingli for the interpretation of *sacramentum* as an oath. His own view, so he suggested, might be termed 'Neo-Zwinglian', though 'Neo-Anabaptist' might be more appropriate.[23]

Because water-baptism is an act of obedience, infant baptism is excluded for Barth, as is any use of baptism as a general, natural, historical or social rite belonging to the pattern of human life.[24] Water-baptism must be responsible baptism. Webster is surely correct in identifying three issues which drive Barth to these conclusions: first, the nature of sacramental mediation, where Christ alone is the one sacrament; secondly, his critique of religion, in which religion is man's attempt to do God's saving work; and third, an insistence on safeguarding the integrity of human action.[25] Though this may be the case, and fully logical to its context, it placed Barth in direct opposition to traditional Reformed understanding of sacraments and baptism. Coming from a respected theologian, Barth's view of the ritual of water-baptism and his suspicion of infant baptism, particularly where it was bound up with a state church, called churches to think seriously about what they were doing in both.

Baptism as Eschatological Sign of Repentance and Hope

Coming to faith as a prisoner of war, Jürgen Moltmann was influenced by Barthianism when he studied at Göttingen University. After he served as a pastor in the Evangelical Church of Bremen-Wasserhorst, he returned to an academic career. Moltmann is called the 'theologian of Hope', and his writings have placed the eschatological context of the Gospel and the trinitarian history of God centre-stage. He has not written a separate work on baptism, but in his *The Church in the Power of the Spirit*, he treats sacraments in general, and baptism and the Lord's Supper in particular.[26]

Moltmann begins his discussion of sacraments by reminding readers that the Latin word *sacramentum* was chosen to render the Greek word *mysterion*, and that a *mysterion* is a divine eschatological secret. It is

> ... an apocalyptic term for the future already resolved on by God, for the end of history. The mystery is the divine resolve. Its revelation in history has the character of a veiled announcement, of a promise of the future, and of anticipation. Its revelation at the end of history takes place when it is openly put into effect.[27]

---

[23] Ibid., p. 130.

[24] Ibid., p. 133.

[25] Webster, *Barth's Ethics*, p. 126. Cf. George Hunsinger, *How to read Karl Barth*, Oxford University Press, New York, 1991, pp. 138ff. Barth argues against existential soteriology of the indirect type, the social type, and the sacramental type.

[26] Jürgen Moltmann, *The Church in the Power of the Spirit. A Contribution to Messianic Ecclesiology*, English translation SCM Press, London, 1977.

[27] Ibid., pp. 203–04.

In addition, this divine secret or revelation has a trinitarian dimension or concept. This includes the eschatological history of God's dealings with the world in the signs and wonders of the Holy Spirit, and signs of the End. Together with proclamation of the Word and *charismata*, sacraments are the signs and wonders 'of the history of the Spirit who creates salvation and brings about the new creation, and who through Christ unites us with the Father and glorifies him'.[28] Whereas the proclamation of the Gospel calls the Church into being, baptism calls it to the freedom of the messianic era:

> Through baptism in Christ's name believers are publicly set in Christ's fellowship; and through baptism in the name of the triune God they are thereby simultaneously set in the trinitarian history of God ... we understand baptism as a sign bound up with the gospel which is also the public sign of life of the Holy Spirit, who unites believers with Christ and brings about the new creation.[29]

Baptism thus proclaims this promise. However, according to Moltmann, when baptism is understood in the context of this promise, the present baptismal practice and theology of the churches becomes problematical. Like Barth, he sees infant baptism as a particular problem – particularly where it is the basic pillar of the *corpus christianum*, the Christian society. Like Barth, Moltmann writes from the background of a state church, and church tax, where the right of infant baptism is bound up with nationality and culture. Moltmann argues that faith and baptism commit one to service in the natural relations of life, but they are not themselves passed on through these natural relations.

Again, apparently in agreement with Barth, he notes that justification and prevenient grace come about when a person believes, not directly at baptism. Here again, *res* and *signum* are kept separate. Indeed, argues Moltmann, 'If baptism were to effect grace *ex opere operato*, as an unconditionally effective means of salvation, then all children without distinction would have to be baptized.'[30] However, infant baptism is not a token of prevenient grace, but a sign of the prevenient faith of the parents. Infant baptism is seen as the first act of pastoral care. Yet,

> Baptism cannot be without faith. Faith commits us to representative service, but it cannot be taken as being representative for the faith of another person or as a temporary substitute for that faith.[31]

Turning to the positive aspects of baptism, Moltmann underlines its New Testament origins with John the Baptist, the desert preacher:

> It was not an initiation rite for an existing society; it was the eschatological sign of the setting forth out of present oppression towards the immediately imminent freedom of the divine rule.[32]

---

[28] Ibid., p. 206.
[29] Ibid., p. 226.
[30] Ibid., p. 230.
[31] Ibid.
[32] Ibid., p. 233.

Whereas John's was an eschatology of judgement, Jesus' was one of grace and forgiveness. The Church's baptism follows from the eschatology of Jesus, though it preaches John's baptism too. Christian baptism is a sign of the coming of God into a person's life and the person's turning to the future. Christology and eschatology are intertwined. But the Spirit is so woven into the person and work of Christ that baptism must be seen in trinitarian terms as part of the eschatological history of God's dealings with the world.[33]

Moltmann points out, however, that the New Testament itself presents a variety of differing emphases on baptism: in Mark the link between baptism and the death of Jesus is important, whereas for Matthew baptism is based upon the missionary charge of the resurrected Lord. For Luke, it is Pentecost which illuminates baptism as for the remission of sins and the reception of the Spirit, and for Paul it gives tangible form to Christ's fellowship of believers. Ultimately, though, Moltmann stresses that its meaning is best found in the trinitarian sense – as 'representation' and 'recognition' of the reconciliation brought about through Christ's death 'for us', baptism manifests the creative power of the Spirit.[34] He concludes:

> Baptism points to the liberation of man which took place once and for all in the death of Christ. At the same time it reveals the crucified Lord's claim to new life and anticipates in man the future of God's universal glory. In this context there can be no talk about the efficacy of baptism *ex opere operato*. Baptism is efficacious *ex verbo vocante*. Its word of promise is the word through which it calls. But the calling gospel is a call to faith, to the new obedience of righteousness, to freedom and to hope. It is hence perceived by faith and laid hold of in hope. It is a creative event, but it creates nothing without faith. In so far as faith is a call, baptism is necessary. But we cannot say that it is necessary for salvation.[35]

Moltmann offers suggestions for a new practice, though he makes no recommendations of how his theology and recommendations might impinge upon the rite itself. Adult baptism should be the norm, and infant baptism replaced by the blessing of children, with prayers for the parents, since parenthood is a *charisma*. Baptism should be freed from associations with birth rites and giving of names, and seen as a call event. It is a call to be there for others:

> It is the sign of the dawn of hope for this world and of messianic service in it. It is a missionary sign. Through a baptism of this kind the meaning of one's own life is comprehended in the wider framework of God's history with the world. Baptism joins a fragmentary and incomplete human life with the fullness of life and the perfect glory of God.[36]

Baptism becomes not initiatory but vocational, and is a liberating event in a person's life, corresponding to a Church which spreads the liberty of Christ.[37]

---

[33] Ibid., p. 236.
[34] Ibid., p. 239.
[35] Ibid., p. 240.
[36] Ibid., p. 241.
[37] Ibid., p. 242.

Moltmann, like Barth, calls the churches which practice infant baptism to look closely at their practice, and consider what a vocational baptismal rite may imply. He reminds the Church of the trinitarian history of God, and says that simply to baptize in the traditional formula may not be sufficient to claim a baptism as trinitarian. Above all, whatever baptism may point back to in the past, and do in the present, Moltmann reminds the Church that it is also an eschatological sign, pointing to the future history of God. If these views are at all valid, then one may ask how they might be articulated in rite and practice.

Baptism as a Divine Gift

Like Moltmann, with whom he was at one time a colleague in the same university, Wolfhart Pannenberg was influenced by Barthianism. Whereas Moltmann leans towards the German Reformed tradition, Pannenberg represents more the Lutheran strain in the German Evangelical Church tradition. He treats baptism extensively in his *Systematic Theology*, following his discussion of our adoption as God's children, and justification.[38] In his discussion of justification, Pannenberg stresses that one result of justification is the believer's participation by faith in the atoning death of Christ, and thus being in unbreakable fellowship with him.[39] So for him there is a close link between faith, baptism and justification:

> For the forgiveness of sins as an effect of Christ's atoning death, whose reception by believers is the basis of their righteousness before God (Rom.3:25) that God confirms by declaring them righteous, was conferred on individuals by baptism according to a general early Christian conviction. Hence baptism has a place when we think about the basis of justification.[40]

The same applies to regeneration, which is also a work of the Holy Spirit in baptism. This means, suggests Pannenberg, that the link between justification and baptism needs to be made clearer in the Reformation Churches. He argues:

> According to the NT witness, however, the event of the regeneration of believers takes place in baptism. Here again, then, we see the mediation of the faith fellowship of individuals with Christ by the church ... The Christian life of individuals takes concrete form in the believing appropriation of baptism. The appropriating process of regeneration in baptism continues throughout the Christian life. An ongoing part of it is the renewed penitence of Christians and their turning (conversion) to the God revealed in Jesus Christ and consequently to their own new existence in Christ on the basis of the act of baptism.[41]

---

[38] Wolfhart Pannenberg, *Systematic Theology*, English translation G.W. Bromiley, Volume 3, Eerdmans, Grand Rapids, MI, 1998.

[39] Ibid., pp. 231–2.

[40] Ibid., pp. 232–3.

[41] Ibid., p. 237.

Baptism constitutes a new identity; it is a new birth with lasting effect, and can never be undone. It gives 'character', and all of the baptized are thus permanently other than they were before. Here Pannenberg contrasts considerably with both Barth and Moltmann; for him baptism is not just a sign, but also signifies something. Indeed, he argues, the early Church quickly came to relate baptism to the forgiveness of sins, the atoning effect of the death of Jesus, and also to the eschatological gift of the Spirit.[42] In the form of an enacted sign baptism sets up the relation to Jesus Christ in his death and resurrection. However, as a sign it does more than point to something signified; it also sets people moving in the direction to which it points. Thus it is more than a visible and public expression of faith in Christ; it 'has an objectivity that by its very content and meaning claims the baptized'.[43]

Baptism is also closely interwoven with conversion and penitence. Turning to God and baptism go together, and the New Testament, argues Pannenberg, does not separate coming to faith and baptism (*contra* Moltmann); only by baptism do those who rely on the apostolic message in faith 'objectively' receive once and for all fellowship with Jesus Christ and consequently the forgiveness of sins that is based on the atoning death of Jesus Christ. Faith in the gospel without baptism is not yet Christian saving faith in its full sense. Furthermore, following Luther, Pannenberg links penitence with baptism – we daily drown the old Adam, which is true contrition. If Christians fall from grace, they can always regain it, for baptism is always there throughout our lives.[44]

Having stated that faith, conversion and penitence are all linked to baptism, Pannenberg turns to consider the question of infant baptism. If baptism is simply an expression and public confession of a turning to faith, then we have to reject infant baptism. However, once more Pannenberg stresses the objectivity of the sign:

> But if baptism does something that even those already converted before baptism cannot do for themselves but have to receive, namely, the definitive linking of the baptized to the destiny of Jesus, then the matter is obviously much more complex than those who espouse believers' baptism have often assumed.[45]

Baptism can no longer be regarded as simply a human act, because at its core it is a divine action on the candidates. Faith does not make baptism, but receives it, for baptism is the means by which the abiding promise of personal belonging to Jesus Christ is given to believers. Thus infant baptism is not precluded:

> If we understand baptism as a 'gift' whose reception is not tied to a specific stage of the power of human judgment and decision but simply presupposes the absence of opposition and a readiness in principle, why should baptism be denied to infants? [46]

---

[42] Ibid., p. 240.
[43] Ibid., p. 243.
[44] Ibid., p. 253.
[45] Ibid., p. 260.
[46] Ibid., p. 262.

Pannenberg insists that this does not mean that all infants without distinction should be baptized. But it does mean that infant baptism is one possible form of baptism, just as adult baptism is another form. Pannenberg goes on to consider the development of the rite of confirmation, noting that baptismal confession by candidates at confirmation is not the end but the beginning of personal appropriation of the faith. The personal confession is not the core of the rite, but the strengthening of the Spirit.

Finally Pannenberg turns to consider the institution of the rite and its symbolism. Whatever the historico-critical method makes of Mark 16:16 and Matthew 28:19, he claims, the real basis of Christian baptism is the fact that Jesus was baptized, and his baptism with the Father and the Spirit present is the model for all Christian baptisms.

In Pannenberg we find an emphasis on the objective nature of baptism, in that it is something which God does, and in which God gives, and we receive. It is an enacted sign which places the individual in the community of the Church and in Jesus Christ. In so far as the model for baptism is the baptism of Jesus, the event is always a trinitarian one. The enacted sign looks back to what the triune God has done, but stresses also the divine action *hic et nunc*, as well as pointing to God's future action.

Baptism Into the One Vicarious Baptism of Christ

T.F. Torrance is a theologian and former Moderator of the General Assembly of the Church of Scotland, who taught systematic theology at Edinburgh. He was Convener of the Special Commission on Baptism, 1955–62, and was responsible for drafting much of the material for the reports that were published. He has also written important essays on baptism. Here we will consider the 1955 Interim Report, 'The New Testament Doctrine of Baptism', and Torrance's essay, 'The One Baptism Common to Christ and His Church'.[47]

The 1955 report considered first the then-current position of biblical studies which, common in the era of 'biblical theology', contrasted the Hebraic and Hellenistic minds. However, even at this stage the report grounded baptism in Christology:

> The doctrine of Baptism is grounded in the Person and Work of Christ. What He was, what He taught, and what He did are the facts that determine and shape the Sacrament of Baptism and give it its significance.[48]

This statement becomes the hermeneutical key which unlocks the rest of the report.

---

[47] The report is found in *Reports to the General Assembly*, Edinburgh, 1955, abbreviated as *RGA*; see also Bryan D. Spinks, '"Freely by His Grace": Baptismal Doctrine and the Reform of the Baptismal Liturgy in the Church of Scotland, 1953–1994', in Nathan Mitchell and John Baldovin (eds), *Rule of Prayer, Rule of Faith. Essays in Honor of Aidan Kavanagh*, OSB, Liturgical Press, Collegeville, MN, 1996, pp. 218–42. T.F. Torrance, 'The One Baptism Common to Christ and His Church', in Thomas Torrance (ed.), *Theology in Reconciliation*, Geoffrey Chapman, London, 1975, pp. 82–105.

[48] *RGA*, 1955, p. 611.

The institution of baptism was addressed with a stress on its trinitarian dimension. At the Jordan the Word of the Father is heard addressing the Son; the Spirit of God descends upon him, confirming his Sonship. Thus baptism into the name of Christ and baptism into the name of the Trinity are alternative ways of referring to the same thing. The report also seized upon the New Testament use of *baptisma* rather than *baptismos*, suggesting that it is similar to *kerygma*, and describes an event of God. *Baptisma* refers not only to the ritual action in water, but is used of Christ's impending death:

> In the New Testament the sacrament of Baptism and the Vicarious Baptism of Christ are spoken of so indivisibly that it is impossible to distinguish what has been done for us by the Cross and resurrection and what by the Sacrament of that Baptism.[49]

The section of the report dealing with baptism in the Apostolic Church spoke of the Spirit bringing redemption and creation together. Jewish proselytes baptized themselves, but children were baptized by someone else; in Christian Baptism all are baptized as though they are dependent children. Baptism is also in the Name, which means into the sphere where the mighty acts of God in the incarnation, birth, life, death, resurrection and ascension are operative for our salvation:

> This does not mean, of course, that the Sacrament of Baptism automatically saves us, but that it places us in Christ, where His death and resurrection are operative, though we may fall away from Him with terrible consequences (1 Corinthians 10:1–12). Baptism requires the response of faith, and a whole life of faith, for we cannot be saved without faith; yet Baptism tells us that it is not our faith that saves us but Christ Himself alone.[50]

Infant baptism is defended with the appeal to Acts 2:38, the promise to you 'and your children', on the grounds that baptism is not the sacrament of our repentance, nor of our faith, but of God's adoption and his promise of the Spirit. The strong Christological approach of this report was further strengthened in a section on 'The Apostolic Interpretation of Baptism'. Here baptism was described as a sacrament of the Incarnation:

> In the actual administration of Baptism by the Apostolic Church the candidates descended into the waters, and after being immersed in them in death, they ascended out of them in resurrection to newness of life. That language of descent and ascent described the descent of Christ into the death of the Cross and His ascent out of it in His resurrection, but it was also used to describe the descent of the Son of God into our mortal humanity and His ascent in our resurrected humanity to the right hand of God the Father Almighty. Thus behind Baptism into Jesus Christ lies the whole Incarnation and Ascension of the Son of God, spoken of as the Descent and Ascent of the Son of Man (for example, in John 3:13; Ephesians 4:9ff.).

---

[49] Ibid., p. 618.
[50] Ibid., p. 626.

Ultimately the Sacrament of Baptism is grounded in the Incarnation, in which the Eternal Son of God immersed Himself in our mortal humanity and assumed it into oneness with Himself that He might heal it and through the whole course of His obedience reconcile us to God.[51]

A final section of the report noted two aspects needing further elucidation: the relation between God's Covenant faithfulness and our faith, and the Christological pattern of the doctrine. The ground of our baptism is not our faith, but the faithfulness of Christ. In him God has kept covenant and faith with his people and the promise is to us and our children. In baptism Christ stands surety for us. As to each of us, he demands different responses:

> We can be sure that He does act in Baptism and will act precisely as He acted during His ministry in Judea and Galilee, sometimes requiring prior faith, sometimes acting through the faith of a parent or even master, and sometimes without any prior response to His Word of re-creation and blessing of peace.[52]

Since this report was to be the cornerstone of the Commission's work, it was rewritten and published in book form under the title *The Biblical Doctrine of Baptism*. Though this perhaps had less of Torrance's stamp on it, it nevertheless forcefully stated Torrance's position:

> Our salvation ultimately depends upon something other than our faithfulness within the covenant relationship: that would be a salvation by works, and who then would be saved? To be baptized is to be baptized out of self and into another, into Christ. It is He who saves us, and He alone. The ground of Baptism is therefore not our faith, but the faithfulness of Christ.[53]

Many of the arguments of this report are presupposed and reiterated in Torrance's essay, 'The One Baptism Common to Christ and His Church'. Agreeing with Barth and Rahner that the primary *mysterium* or sacrament is Jesus Christ himself, Torrance stresses that baptism is into the *koinonia* or participation in the mystery of Christ and his Church. It cannot be interpreted as a flat event in itself – either as a ritual event or ethical event, but in a dimension of depth going back to the saving work of God in Christ, for,

> … when the Church baptises in his name, it is actually Christ himself who is savingly at work, pouring out his Spirit upon us and drawing us within the power of his vicarious life, death and resurrection.[54]

Torrance here unfolds again the distinction between *baptisma* and *baptismos*, noting that *baptisma* includes Christ's incarnation, birth, life, death and resurrection:

> It was of course the preparatory baptism of John, initiation by water into the messianic age and community, that supplied the Christian Church with its ritual act,

---

[51] Ibid., p. 637.
[52] Ibid., p. 660.
[53] Church of Scotland, Special Commission on Baptism, *The Biblical Doctrine of Baptism*, Saint Andrew Press, Edinburgh, 1958, p. 58.
[54] *Theology in Reconciliation*, p. 83.

but it was transformed and filled with content through Jesus' submission to John's baptism and his fulfilment of it in the whole course of his vicarious obedience.[55]

Jesus was baptized with the baptism of repentance not for his own sake but for ours, and in him it was our humanity that was anointed by the Spirit and consecrated in sonship to the Father. He received a baptism meant for sinners on our behalf, and received divine judgement on our behalf. Baptism is always into his one vicarious *baptisma*. Baptism is administered to us in the name of the Triune God, and all we can do is to receive it, for we cannot add anything to Christ's finished work. Through baptism we are united to him through the Spirit and participate in his saving life:

> It is not a separate or a new baptism but a participation in the one all-inclusive
> baptism common to Christ and his Church, wrought out vicariously in Christ alone
> but into which he has assimilated the Church through the baptism of one Spirit,
> and which he applies to each of us through the same Spirit. It is *baptisma* in the
> Name of the Triune God.[56]

The one *baptisma* brings together the baptism of Jesus in water and the Spirit at the Jordan, his baptism in blood on the cross, and the baptism of the Church in his Spirit at Pentecost. When we receive baptism, we are granted God's grace to participate in the one all-inclusive incarnational *baptisma* of Jesus Christ and to become members of his Body and children of the heavenly Father. The baptism of the Spirit may precede or follow baptism with water, but the focal point of both is the invocation of the name of Christ, for it is in him that both baptisms find their unity. In baptism it is not so much that we confess Christ as that he confesses us before the Father. We are presented before God as subjects of his saving activity, and are initiated into a mutual relation between the act of the Spirit and the response of faith. Baptism is in, with and through Christ.

According to George Hunsinger, Torrance brings Calvin and Barth together in a brilliant new synthesis; like Calvin, Torrance holds that sacraments are vehicles of testimony that impart the very Christ they proclaim, but like Barth, he claims that salvation must be spoken of in the perfect tense.[57] He does so by using a Christocentric soteriology. In his own words:

> Here the grace of God is not simply the relation between God and the creature
> construed in terms of efficient causality but the out-going of God himself towards
> the creature, and the personal self-giving of God to man which takes place only
> by way of Incarnation. It is such a self-communicating of God to man that man
> is given access to, and knowledge of God in his own inner life and being as Father,
> Son and Holy Spirit. This profound reciprocity in word and act is fulfilled in Christ
> and in the Spirit: *in Christ*, for it is in hypostatic union that the self-giving of God
> really breaks through to man, when God becomes himself what man is and

---

[55] Ibid., pp. 84–5.

[56] Ibid., p. 88.

[57] George Hunsinger, 'The Dimension of Depth: Thomas F. Torrance on the Sacraments of Baptism and the Lord's Supper', *Scottish Journal of Theology* 54 (2001), 155–76, p. 159.

assumes man into a binding relation with his own being; and *in the Spirit*, for then the self-giving of God actualises itself in us as the Holy Spirit creates in us the capacity to receive it and lifts us up to participate in the union and communion of the incarnate Son with the heavenly Father.[58]

The emphasis we find in Torrance, then, is that baptism is grounded objectively in the saving work of Christ, which is also the work of the divine Trinity. Baptism is an act of God in his Church, and the faith confessed is Christ's obedient faithfulness in his saving ministry and mission. Thus a trinitarian dimension is crucial, as is the Christological/incarnational soteriology, which allows us to participate in the life of the divine.

Baptism as Covenant

The concept of baptism as covenant, of which echoes can be found in the New Testament, was the main hermeneutical concept developed in the Reformed tradition. It can also be found in late sixteenth and seventeenth-century Anglican theology, adopted from Reformed thinking, though it was not a concept used in the classical Anglican rites. In a book called *Believing in Baptism*, Archdeacon Gordon Kuhrt of the Church of England stated that the purpose of his study was to 'enquire carefully into the biblical theology of baptism', and argued that 'covenant' is the crucial concept for understanding the theology of baptism.[59] He sets forth a 'biblical theology' rather than one concerned with church policy, church history (including liturgical history) or sacramental theology.

More specifically, rather than start with John's baptism, or baptism in the early Church in Acts, Kuhrt begins with the epistles, where he finds two features: the ethical consequences of baptism and the Old Testament covenant context of baptism. Of the nine passages he selects, four draw a parallel with an Old Testament covenant episode – Galatians 3:26–9, Colossians 2:11–13, 1 Peter 3:18–21 and 1 Corinthians 10:1–4: 'These four references to Abraham's seed, circumcision, Noah and to Moses are quite explicit associations of baptism with Old Testament covenant episodes.'[60] He cites other passages where a reference to baptism is probable, and there finds the metaphors of washing, sealing, anointing, promise, inheritance, redemption and bridegroom-bride imagery, though behind all of them he finds an Old Testament covenant reference:

> The Old Testament covenant imagery is overwhelmingly apparent in all these passages that probably or possibly refer to baptism, just as they were in key passages that spoke explicitly of baptism. This is a matter of cardinal importance because it clearly indicates that baptism is understood by the letter writers against

---

[58] *Theology in Reconciliation*, p. 100.
[59] Gordon Kuhrt, *Believing in Baptism*, Mowbray, London, 1987.
[60] Ibid., pp. 22–3.

this background, and furthermore, this background is not just incidental to understanding baptism – it is *the* theological context.[61]

Having set this scene, Kuhrt then examines God's covenants in the Old Testament: Noah (covenant introduced), Abraham (covenant clarified), Moses (covenant developed), David (covenant preserved), the prophets (covenant broken and renewed), the Messiah (covenant fulfilled) and heaven (covenant consummated). He holds that this is the context in which the New Testament writers understood the nature and meaning of Christian baptism.[62] It is from this context that Kurht then turns to consider the baptism of John. According to Kuhrt, the word *baptizo* has a variety of possible meanings, and cannot be used to offer a conclusive answer on the mode of baptism. However, when turning to consider washing in the Old Testament, Kurht insists that each is concerned with covenant law or is in the context of God's covenant promise of grace. John's baptism

> ... was essentially preparatory, and pointing towards the supreme salvation-events of the cross, Pentecost and ultimately the Parousia of the Messiah. In this sense he brings down the curtain on the Old Testament era of 'promise,' and stands at the doorstep of the new covenant Messianic era of 'fulfillment.'[63]

Jesus in his baptism identifies with sinners, and in his death makes a new covenant. Christian baptism brings the blessings of forgiveness, belonging to Jesus Christ, and sharing his death and resurrection. It also gives the Holy Spirit, new birth, and membership in the Body of Christ – 'God's covenant community'.[64] Christian baptism takes place in the context of the Gospel, and requires faith and the covenant of God's promise. It requires living a holy life:

> Baptism is not simply a sign of God's saving action in the *past* (in Jesus' death, resurrection and gift of the Spirit) or God's saving action in the *present* (in the application of that eternal covenant plan to an individual's experience through regeneration and conversion), but also God's saving action in the *future* (in the Spirit's outworking of fruit of character and gifts of service, and pledge of final redemption) ... Having been initiated, the convert is called to live accordingly. Become what you are – baptized, believer, set apart for God, recipient of the covenant promise. [65]

According to Kuhrt:

> Baptism is a covenant sign that God gives to confirm and seal his promise of salvation.
> It effects what it signifies, in the context of faith.
>
> Baptism requires conversion i.e. repentance and faith.

---

[61] Ibid., p. 29.
[62] Ibid., p. 50.
[63] Ibid., p. 60.
[64] Ibid., p. 77.
[65] Ibid., p. 80.

Baptism shapes conversion i.e. in terms of washing, death and new life, and anointing with the Spirit.
Baptism tests conversion i.e. ensuring it is 'into Christ.'

The language of efficacy which the New Testament writers use with respect to baptism is sacramental language, covenant language. It is not unconditional for it presupposes the context of faith – sacramental language must always be faith language.[66]

In subsequent chapters, Kuhrt notes that infant baptism makes sense only within a Christian household, where parents are regular church members. He has in mind the practice in England where folk religion alongside an established Church often results in 'indiscriminate' baptism, where infants of non-practising parents are baptized. Covenant requires response, and thus parents need to live up to promises (here Kuhrt had in mind the promises of the baptismal rite in the 1980 *Alternative Service Book* of the Church of England). He argues:

The blessings of baptism embrace the entire gospel of God's grace, but it can only be known in the context of the covenant-pattern and in the context of the word of the gospel received by faith. *Efficacy there is* – as a sacrament, a covenant-sign from God, it is a gift of loving grace; *unconditional it is not* – as a sacrament, a covenant-sign from God, it is to be received with faith.[67]

The implications are that, for adults, this requires a mature confession of faith, and in the case of infants, the outward observance of Christian practice by their parents.

Kuhrt's book certainly asks those who practice indiscriminate baptism to examine carefully what they are doing. Ecclesiology is in the forefront, stressing continuity with the covenant people of God. In contrast to Torrance, Kuhrt's view has Christ less at the centre of the ritual: Christ seems to be a subheading of the concept 'covenant'. Also, the implication seems to be that in infant baptism it is the parents – their ecclesiastical commitment – which is central, suggesting contract rather than covenant of grace.[68]

Baptism as Efficacious Divine Command for Remedy for Original Sin

In his book entitled *Baptism*, David Scaer, writing from a Confessional Lutheran viewpoint, defends the Augustinian-Lutheran position that baptism is God's work and remits original sin. Scaer argues that baptism is the foundational sacrament, commanded, or mandated, by God. Essential to baptism is its origin in Christ's death and resurrection, since his death was a death to sin and his resurrection was for his

---

[66] Ibid., p. 91.

[67] Ibid., p. 101.

[68] See further Bryan D. Spinks, 'Luther's Timely Theology of Unilateral Baptism', *Lutheran Quarterly* 9 (1995), 23–45.

vindication (justification). Thus in baptism the faithful die to sin in his death, and are raised to justification in his resurrection.

Baptism is necessary for salvation. It is based on the Divine Command, and here Matthew 28:19 is regarded as a command to the Church. Furthermore, Christ not only commands baptism, but he also does the baptizing: 'Baptism is in its entirety a christological event, since Christ is the one who commands it, is present in it as the one who performs it, and is the one who is believed.'[69]

After discussing the biblical origins of baptism, Scaer considers its efficacy. In contrast to Barth, Scaer notes that in Lutheran theology baptism is always complete in itself, as containing the totality of the Christian life. Faith receives the benefits, but faith does not belong to its essence.[70] Forgiveness of sins is present in baptism as an accomplished and completed reality demanding and creating faith. Here Scaer appeals to the reference in 1 Corinthians regarding baptism on behalf of the dead. It is not that he wishes to restore this practice, as in Mormonism, but he suggests that it shows that the Corinthians believed that baptism did something – it effected salvation on the recipients. Likewise, Ephesians 5:25–7 presents baptism not as the rite of individual initiation, but as that act which makes the entire church acceptable to Christ. Scaer also stresses the importance of the traditional trinitarian formula.

Much of Scaer's study on baptism is taken up with reiterating and restating both Luther and the Lutheran *Confessions*, and defining the Lutheran position over against Roman Catholic, Baptist and Reformed views – which is what we would expect from a series on Confessional Lutheran Dogmatics. The book is a reminder that the Augustinian view as understood by Luther is still considered important in some Lutheran circles. Scaer reminds us that we cannot escape the New Testament concern that baptism is for the remission of sins, and that too is bound up with the old Adam/ New Adam typology. Soteriology is crucial. However, the concept of sacraments as God's promises also ensure that the *res* and *signum* are not sundered. Baptism is Christ's trinitarian act, giving justification, and it is efficacious. Here, at least, Scaer and Torrance seem to agree on an objectivity of the sacrament, its Christological focus and the grace it offers.

Baptism Amongst Baptists

Baptists were loosely affiliated, and although sharing a common conviction on believers' baptism, they have tended to divide amongst themselves on other issues, and generated breakaway groups, and hence Primitive Baptists, Regular Baptists, Free Will Baptists, and Missionary Baptists represent just a few of the smaller distinctive groups. Some smaller groups baptize in the name of Jesus Christ rather than with the

---

[69] David P. Scaer, *Baptism. Confessional Lutheran Dogmatics*, Vol. XI, The Luther Academy, St Louis, MO, 1999, p. 25.

[70] Ibid., p. 43.

triune formula. However, larger groups representing the Calvinistic or Particular Baptists are federated together. The Baptist Union of Great Britain and Ireland had its origin in a general Union in 1813; in the United States the largest Baptist bodies are the American Baptists and the more conservative Southern Baptists. However, within what are federations, with considerable congregational freedom, it is difficult to determine what constitutes normative teaching. The American Baptist Convention's *A Baptist Manual of Polity and Practice* (1963) sets out the following as regards 'official' teaching.[71] It commenced by noting two general tendencies in the history of the Church – either to stress that in the ceremony God does something to a passive individual, or a human active role in the ritual act. While Baptists have sought to keep in sight both God's grace and the human response, the emphasis has always been to emphasize baptism as an act of obedient response. Even so, it is closely related to what God has done in Christ. The *Manual* picks up on the idea found in Zwingli of an oath; in baptism we say something to God, and say it before humans: 'Thus, Baptists are numbered among those who think of baptism as primarily a response made by man. In baptism a person signifies his repentance toward God, his trust in God's mercy, and his surrender to obey God's will.'[72]

Baptism is a confession to God before men, but is more than a private affair, and its administration takes place before the visible Church: 'It is the view of Baptists that the baptized person has already become regenerate by the work of the Spirit prior to baptism, and that baptism is a public acknowledgment of that fact.'[73] Baptism itself does not confer the Holy Spirit, bring remission of sins, or regeneration; however, that does not mean it is an empty form, and should be an occasion of blessing: 'Baptism, then, may be thought of as a rite ordained by Christ as the means by which his disciples are to express the humble confession, the faith, and the willing obedience required of them.'[74]

Two recent discussions on baptism from theologians of the Baptist tradition which are considered here are those of James McClendon, Jr (USA) and Christopher Ellis (UK).

James McClendon discusses the doctrinal aspects of baptism in the second volume of his *Systematic Theology*, and in the context of signs of salvation.[75] In discussing Christian worship, McClendon says:

> … understood as interactive response, the human responding by God's grace to the divine, worship is a communicative practice. In a broad but true sense, all worship is prayer. This communication, carried on in the public language of Christian liturgy, is not confined to Hebrew or English or to any natural language. Instead, God has provided for it an inclusive sign-language. To communicate with God we are expected to learn that language. The signs fall into three classes: the

---

[71] Norman H. Maring and Winthrop S. Hudson, *A Baptist Manual of Polity and Practice,* Judson Press, Valley Forge, PA, 1963, pp. 129–36.

[72] Ibid., p. 130.

[73] Ibid., p. 131.

[74] Ibid., p. 133.

[75] James McClendon, Jr, *Systematic Theology: Doctrine*, Abingdon Press, Nashville, TN, 1994.

great historic signs that created the people of God, the remembering signs set in the local assemblies of that people, and various providential signs that guide particular journeys.[76]

Amongst these signs of salvation, baptism is one of the remembering signs. These remembering signs declare the present presence of Christ with his people, and they call the Church to remember the great story of salvation and expectation at its end.[77] McClendon suggests that primitive Christian discipleship began with a future-oriented rite, which emphasized entrance to the community, conversion, and God's forgiveness of the sins of the people. Two additional elements also appeared in baptism: the name of Jesus was invoked (and later, the triune name) and the gift of the Spirit to the baptized person and to the community. McClendon suggests that in the Baptist heritage baptism is not just a symbol, but also a sign, and signs not only betoken something, but do something, and convey something.[78] He identifies two New Testament models of baptism. First, there is Saul, who was converted and became Paul; second, there is Jesus, whose baptism was not a conversion but a fulfilment. Christians have both models:

> Through the centuries, I believe, many more have found it possible to come in faith to baptism's waters as Jesus did, not converted *from* a flagrant opposition to him, but turning *with* him toward a life of full faithfulness. Both stories are conversion stories, turning stories; in both stories baptism is a commissioning, metaphorically an 'ordination' to service, and although these two have different pasts, their stories converge – at the cross.[79]

Because baptism is a sign of salvation, no one in good faith seeking this sign is turned away. However, McClendon argues, when ancient Christians began to include infants, they denied the inclusiveness of both the New Testament models, and invented an infant baptism ritual. He writes:

> Thus the privilege of Christian initiation was effectively revoked, this time not for Gentiles or barbarians or women or slaves, but for the child of many a Christian home. By this rule such a one is told she may not ever ask for baptism; nor is she permitted to remember her baptism; whatever else she may do in faith, she may not stand with a faith of her own in the baptismal waters and hear the glad words, 'Upon the profession of your faith I baptize you, my sister, in the name of the Father, and of Jesus God's Child, and of the Spirit of God'.[80]

Two additional models of initiation follow. The first is infant baptism, followed later by instruction (conversion) and communion; the other is baptism and infant communion. Although faith is present in both – of the church and family – the requisite faith of the child is missing. Although noting ecumenical advances on understanding

---

[76] Ibid., p. 383.

[77] Ibid., p. 386.

[78] Ibid., p. 388.

[79] Ibid., pp. 390–91.

[80] Ibid., p. 391. It is unclear whether McClendon promotes this paraphrase of the traditional formula.

between believer's baptism churches and paedobaptist churches, nevertheless McClendon views infant baptism as impaired, and suggests that since signs may be repeated, those baptized as infants who later seek admission to a believers' Baptist Church, should have some baptismal ritual:

> The appropriate remedy for an impaired baptism is not its utter details ('this is no baptism'), but its *repair*: we may 'repeat' a wedding, an ordination, or a baptism, furnishing what had earlier been lacking (for example, this time a church for the wedding, collegial acknowledgment for the ordination, or the candidate's confession in baptism), and by this repetitive act regularize *the original one* rather than deny its (impaired) existence. Moreover, a wedding ten years later will not deny the existence of offspring but may incorporate them into the ceremony; baptismal repair can likewise acknowledge the earlier rite and the genuine faith that has appeared. While a baptism too late is almost as strange as one too early, brought together they may just fill the bill. In any case, let the guiding principle still be welcome to each and every seeker, so that 'whatsoever will' may come.[81]

Recent studies have documented how in British Baptist circles, since the 1940s, there has been a growing 'sacramentalism'.[82] Christopher Ellis sets out his ideas on baptism in a collection of essays entitled *Reflections on the Water. Understanding God and the World through the Baptism of Believers* (1996). Ellis begins by noting that there is a wide variety of belief amongst Baptists, and that generally Baptists do not refer to baptism as a sacrament, but as an ordinance, which is carried out in obedience to the command of Christ. He notes that in contrast to those who speak of baptism conferring grace, Baptists speak of baptism as either a response to God's grace, or a means of grace in so far as grace comes through faith. Coming out of the radical tradition, Ellis asserts that any theological claims must be tested by Scripture; second, the Church is conceived of as a fellowship of believers, and so the subjects of baptism are believers. Most Baptists agree that the usual mode is by immersion. However, Baptists insist that God is beyond the control of the Church (and State), and thus are suspicious of theologies which suggest that grace is tied to the outward signs. Salvation comes by relationship to Jesus, not submission to sacramental rites. Thus salvation comes prior to the act of baptism:

> ... this prior reality of faith can encourage us to view salvation as a process within which baptism plays a significant part. Baptism may be seen as a medium of the Spirit who has already impinged on the person and led him or her to a confession of faith and a life of discipleship. Now the symbolism of water, burial, and resurrection; the invoking of the triune Name; and the partnership of the people of God all lead to a new stage of life in the Spirit, in union with Christ and amongst the company of his people.[83]

---

[81] Ibid., p. 396.

[82] Anthony R. Cross, *Baptism and the Baptists. Theology and Practice in Twentieth-century Britain*, Paternoster Press, Carlisle, 2000; Stanley K. Fowler, *More Than a Symbol. The British Baptist Recovery of Baptismal Sacramentalism*, Paternoster Press, Carlisle, 2002.

[83] Christopher Ellis, 'Baptism and Sacramental Freedom', in Paul S. Fiddes (ed.), *Reflections on the*

Ellis suggests that one objective aspect of baptism is that it is the visible means by which a believer is made a member of the people of God, and notes that some Baptist divines, such as John Gill in the eighteenth century, and Andrew Fuller in the early nineteenth century, taught that the sign, when rightly used, leads to the thing signified. However, many Baptists have been and are suspicious of ritual acts. Ellis suggests that ecumenical studies which emphasize baptism as part of a process are helpful to Baptists in understanding how baptism can operate as a sign; while not wanting to attribute any magic to the water, he suggests that the subjective experiences of believers are grounded in objective causes and consequences.[84] Baptists can agree that baptism is a sacrament (ordinance) of proclamation, not just of one's personal faith, but of the saving work of Christ; that it is a sacrament of partnership, where the human response works with the Holy Spirit – the Spirit stirs and beckons, and we respond; it is a sacrament of presence in the sense that the *mysterion* of God's salvation is offered in an embodied form, and where physical water is a reminder that God in the incarnation uses the physical; it is a sacrament of prophecy, pointing beyond the here-and-now in warning and promises; and it is a sacrament of promise, being a pledge of what is in store for the people of God.[85] Freed from 'mechanical sacramentalism' we are freed to approach baptism as an opportunity for celebration and fruitfulness where the Spirit moves powerfully amongst a praising and responsive people: 'Here is the freedom of one who freely loves and freely forgives and who promises to meet us both in the waters of baptism and in the world to which we are sent.'[86]

Thus amongst English-speaking Baptists, and especially certain British Baptist theologians, there is a tendency to find new emphasis in the divine action in the ritual of baptism, though without abandoning the emphasis on personal faith. There is a trend to view baptism as part of a journey of faith, and thus some Baptists are prepared to acknowledge the validity of infant baptism when it is part of an on-going process of growth in faith and commitment.

Baptismal Formula as Negotiable Metaphor

Feminist theologians have been critical of what they perceive to be patriarchal language, from the male authorship and interests of Holy Scripture to its translation and, in the English language, use of engendered nouns and pronouns. Some feminist writers have been critical of the overuse and, in some cases, any use at all of 'Father', 'Son', and 'Lord'. This criticism has encompassed not only translation of Scripture,

---

Water. Understanding God and the World through the Baptism of Believers, Regent's Park College, Oxford, 1996, pp. 23–45, p. 31.

[84] Ibid., p. 36.
[85] See ibid., pp. 37–41.
[86] Ibid., p. 42.

but more especially hymns and liturgical texts.[87] Not surprising, the classical trinitarian formula used in baptism has come in for criticism.

In her study *Gender and the Name of God*, Ruth Duck argued that for the first few centuries the formula of Matthew 28:19 was not used as a formula, but was more a summary of the theology of baptism.[88] Therefore it is not only possible, but desirable (in the interests of avoiding metaphors which are patriarchal) to find alternatives to the Matthean formula. Arguing that in the so-called *Apostolic Tradition* (which she accepted as authentic Roman usage *c.* 215) baptism was thrice in response to the three-part recitation of the Creed, she suggests the following as a possible alternative:

> Do you believe in God, the Source, the fountain of life?
> I believe.
> Do you believe in Christ, the offspring of God embodied in Jesus of Nazareth and in the church?
> I believe.
> Do you believe in the liberating Spirit of God, the wellspring of new life?
> I believe.[89]

Other alternatives to the 'patriarchal' formula are 'I baptize you in the name of God the Source of all being, of the Eternal Word of God, and of the Holy Spirit', and 'in the name of the Creator, Sustainer, and Redeemer', though she notes that the latter has been widely criticized because it relies too much on functions that are appropriated to the persons of the Trinity, but which are actions of the Trinity as a whole.[90] She also cites with approval the formula suggested by James Kaye and adopted by the Riverside Church, New York: 'I baptize you in the name of the Father and of the Son and of the Holy Spirit, one God, Mother of us all.'

The recent reappraisal of the so-called *Apostolic Tradition* somewhat weakens Duck's argument, since she makes it a normative text. As she notes, the earliest indisputable witness is seventh century (not eighth century as she claims elsewhere).[91] But other earlier witnesses she cites are ambiguous, and an earlier date than the seventh century for use of the Matthean formula can be established in some of the Eastern sources.

However, feminist critique does not ultimately stand or fall on historical argument. Much of it centres on 'Father' and 'Son' being metaphors, and on what constitutes a metaphor. Many feminists seem to understand metaphor in a loose literary manner, as synonymous with 'figure of speech', and are critical of its univocal use, whereas often other theologians use metaphor in a more philosophical manner, and regard the

---

[87] The literature is legion, but see for example, Ruth Duck and Patricia Wilson-Kastner, *Praising God. The Trinity in Christian Worship*, Westminster John Knox Press, Louisville, KY, 1999.

[88] Ruth Duck, *Gender and the Name of God. The Trinitarian Baptismal Formula*, Pilgrim Press, Cleveland, OH, 1991.

[89] Duck and Wilson-Kastner, *Praising God*, p. 54.

[90] Ibid., pp. 54–5.

[91] Ibid., p. 54. Cf. *Gender and the Name of God*, p. 131.

use of 'Father' and 'Son' in the Gospels as equivocal.[92] This of course is a discussion in its own right, reaching beyond the baptismal formula. In terms of baptism it does raise the question of why one would wish to change the classical formula (cf. Moravians, Swedenborgians and Mormons), particularly if, in an ecumenical context, some churches would deem a baptism as irregular or invalid if the formula was changed. It also sidesteps the issue of whether 'patriarchal' language is better tackled by expansive language rather than use of feminine words, which may only exacerbate the very problem it claims to address.

Baptism in Ecumenical Convergence

One of the most stimulating 'overviews' on the theology of baptism has been the 1982 Lima Statement of the World Council of Churches *Baptism, Eucharist and Ministry* (*BEM*). Whereas individual theologians and individual denominations advance a particular understanding or understandings of baptism, this document represents an overview of denominational consensus in so far as denominational theologians, working together on a common task, were able to reach the consensus, or convergence, expressed in the statement. Churches were invited to prepare official responses, particularly as to how far the text expresses the faith of the Church through the ages. Not only did the document give a theology of baptism; it also gave some implications for the rites of baptism.

The document contains 23 paragraphs interspersed with commentary, and is divided into five main sections. The first brief section on the institution of baptism notes that it is rooted in the ministry, death and resurrection of Christ, and is incorporation into Christ. It is entry into the New Covenant. It is a gift of God.

Under the heading 'The Meaning of Baptism', *BEM* notes that a variety of images are used in Scripture to express the significance of baptism. The document singles out five:

a   *Participation in Christ's Death and Resurrection.* Baptism means participation in the life, death and resurrection of Jesus Christ. By baptism Christians are immersed in the liberating death of Christ, where the old Adam is crucified, and the power of sin is broken. We are raised now, confident that we will ultimately be one with Christ in his resurrection.

b   *Conversion, Pardoning and Cleansing.* Baptism as administered by John was for the forgiveness of sins. Those baptized are pardoned, cleansed and sanctified in Christ.

---

[92] See Janet Martin Soskice, *Metaphor and Religious Language*, Clarendon Press, Oxford, 1985. See also Thomas J. Scirughi, *An Examination of the Problems of Inclusive Language in the Trinitarian Formula of Baptism*, Edwin Mellon Press, Lewiston, NY, 2000.

c *The Gift of the Spirit.* The same Spirit who revealed Jesus as the Son and empowered the disciples at Pentecost is at work in the lives of the baptized.

d *Incorporation into the Body of Christ.* Baptism is a sign and seal of our common discipleship. The one baptism of Christ's Church unites us to Christ.

e *The Sign of the Kingdom.* Baptism initiates the reality of a new life which is a sign of the Kingdom of God and the life of the world to come.

Here the Christological, soteriological, pneumatological, ecclesiological and eschatological dimensions of baptism are combined.

In the section on 'Baptism and Faith', *BEM* states that baptism is both God's gift and our human response, thus combining the emphasis found in Barth with that of Torrance and Pannenberg, and expressed by Kuhrt as he unfolds his idea of Covenant. Baptism is life-long growth into Christ (as Luther said, restated by Scaer). The Christian life is one of struggle, yet continuing in the experience of grace.

In the section on practice, *BEM* discussed the differences between believers' and infant baptism. It attempted to find the common ground between churches which practice only believers' baptism and paedobaptist churches, by stressing that all baptisms are rooted in the faithfulness of Christ and within the faith and life of the believing community. It called on believer baptists to consider how to express the fact that children are placed under the protection of God's grace; and paedobaptists to guard themselves against indiscriminate baptism, and to take seriously the need for Christian nurture.

In the final section, *BEM* turned to implications for the celebration of baptism. It is to be administered with water in the Name of the Father, the Son and the Holy Spirit – implying that the Matthean Naming is expected to be present somewhere in the ritual. It suggests that the symbol of water should not be minimalized, and encourages immersion. Other gestures such as laying-on of hands, anointing, and the sign of the cross can be vivid signs. The document noted:

> Within any comprehensive order of baptism at least the following elements should find a place: the proclamation of the scriptures referring to baptism; an invocation of the Holy Spirit; a renunciation of evil; a profession of faith in Christ and the Holy Trinity; the use of water; a declaration that the persons baptized have acquired a new identity as sons and daughters of God, and as members of the Church, called to be witnesses of the Gospel. Some churches consider that Christian initiation is not complete without the sealing of the baptized with the gift of the Holy Spirit and participation in holy communion.[93]

It provided that normally baptism was administered by an ordained minister, that it should be administered during public worship, and it is appropriate to certain great festivals as Easter, Pentecost and Epiphany. The document tries to hold together the various scriptural emphases on the meaning of baptism, without favouring one

---

[93] *Baptism, Eucharist and Ministry*, Faith and Order Paper No. 111, World Council of Churches, Geneva, 1982, p. 6.

particular emphasis to the exclusion of others, and offers churches a document of convergence which can form a base for assessing their rituals of baptism.

Concluding Remarks

Churches reflecting on their teaching on baptism and compiling baptismal rites have been prompted to consider a whole series of issues raised by recent theologians, and particularly by the convergence document of the World Council of Churches. Churches have been challenged regarding the indiscriminate practice of infant baptism; the need to hold together baptism as God's act, and baptism as human response; how to hold together the Christological and soteriological, as well as how to express the pneumatological and eschatological. Equally important is the emphasis that baptism is trinitarian in that it is about community of the Church within the *koinonia* of the triune God.

Above all, churches are challenged to see the rite of baptism in a wider context of the journey of faith in the community of faith. Thus baptism points back to what God has done, proclaims what God is doing, and looks towards what God will do. The convergence is perhaps illustrated by recent Baptist reflections and the *Catechism of the Catholic Church* – two Church bodies which traditionally have seemed diametrically opposed on their understanding of sacraments. Reflecting what seems to be a position accepted by a good number of British Baptists, Paul Fiddes wrote:

> Baptists should in fact be quite willing to recognize that there are elements of *both* faith and divine grace in the act that is called infant baptism. There is the prevenient grace of God, already at work deep in the being of the child, giving life and wholeness, and enticing it towards a personal response of faith to Himself in due time. There is the faith of parents and the Christian community, supporting and nurturing the child as it grows. Most Baptists will also recognize that the completed sequence of infant baptism and later personal faith in Christ sealed in confirmation constitutes initiation into the church as the body of Christ, and many Baptist churches in Britain do not therefore require baptism of believers in this situation. When salvation is seen as a process or a journey, as the World Council of Churches report *Baptism, Eucharist, and Ministry* urges, many Baptists can readily perceive different combinations of grace and faith at different stages of the journey and can find various ceremonies appropriate to mark the stages.[94]

In the *Catechism of the Catholic Church*, the section on baptism states that from the time of the apostles, becoming a Christian has been accomplished by a journey and initiation in several stages, and the journey can be covered rapidly or slowly.[95] Considering the question of who can receive baptism, it treats adult baptism first, and then infant baptism. For both it states:

---

[94] Paul Fiddes, 'Baptism and Creation', in *Reflections on the Water*, p. 60. For other similar views see Anthony R. Cross, *Baptism and the Baptists*. Stanley K. Fowler, *More Than a Symbol*.

[95] *Catechism of the Catholic Church*, Liberia Editrice Vaticana, para. 1229.

It is only within the faith of the Church that each of the faithful can believe. The faith required for Baptism is not a perfect and mature faith, but a beginning that is called to develop.[96]

The whole ecclesial community bears some responsibility for the development and safeguarding of the grace given at baptism.[97] The *Catechism* also notes, 'God has bound salvation to the sacrament of baptism, but he himself is not bound by his sacraments' – thus allowing for both the objective work of God, and the need for human response or appropriation.

---

[96] Ibid., para 1253.
[97] Ibid., para 1255.

CHAPTER 7

Tidal Marks:
Some Contemporary Baptismal Rites

The last fifty years have witnessed an unprecedented industry of liturgical revision in the mainline Western churches, most notably the revised rites in the Roman Catholic Church which resulted from the Second Vatican Council. Called by Pope John XXIII, the Council began its work under his successor in 1963, and the revision of the liturgy was the first major task undertaken by the Council. The principles underlying the liturgical revisions were shared and became influential in other churches.

The revisions in the Roman Catholic Church were the fruits of what is called the Liturgical Movement. This movement, often traced to particular Benedictines in the first decade of the twentieth century in France, Germany and Austria, was concerned that the Catholic liturgy should be understood by the laity, and that they should participate in and be formed by it.[1] Later, Catholic scholars pressed for alterations and reforms of the Tridentine forms in use, appealing to earlier rites in the history of the development of liturgies. Already in the 1950s, prior to the Second Vatican Council, the special rites for Holy Week had been reformed and restored, and provision made for the renewal of baptismal vows at the Easter Vigil on Holy Saturday night.

The insights of the Roman Catholic Liturgical Movement were shared by liturgical scholars and pastoral liturgists in many other mainline Western churches. The 1951 Report of the Faith and Order Commission on Worship, under the auspices of the World Council of Churches, noted, 'In the course of this enquiry we have been struck by the extent to which a "liturgical movement" is to be found in churches of widely differing traditions.'[2] At this time the common opinion of liturgical scholars was that the so-called *Apostolic Tradition* was the work of Hippolytus *c.* 215, and that it provided churches with liturgical paradigms which pre-dated Reformation disputes and polemic, and which thus might help the churches to grow together in their worship forms. Indeed, there tended to be considerable agreement between liturgists of the different churches on what appropriate liturgical ideals might be. With the continuing growth of ecumenism through the work of the World Council of Churches, and the keen interest in ecumenism which came from the Second Vatican Council in the Roman Catholic Church, much liturgical scholarship was pursued ecumenically, and

---

[1] Bernard Botte, *From Silence to Participation*, Pastoral Press, Washington, DC, 1988; John Fenwick and Bryan Spinks, *Worship in Transition. The Liturgical Movement in the Twentieth Century*, Continuum, New York, 1995; Alcuin Reid, *The Organic Development of the Liturgy*, Saint Michael's Abbey Press, Farnborough, 2004.

[2] P. Edwall, E. Hayman and W.D. Maxwell (eds), *Ways of Worship*, SCM Press, London, 1951, p. 16.

spread as if by osmosis. The result can be seen in agreement on use of common texts, common structures, and frequent borrowing of material between churches. This has had an impact on the revision of baptismal rites in the latter part of the twentieth century.

Liturgical scholars have been mainly concerned about earlier precedents in structures and texts. However, revision of the baptismal rites has also been influenced by pastoral situations and theological issues. The twentieth century saw the continued decline of the influence of the Christian church in European countries. Many of those countries had a state, national, or majority church – the Church of England in England, the Dutch Reformed Church in the Netherlands, the Lutheran Church in Sweden, and the Roman Catholic Church as a majority church in France. Instead of the older Christendom model, where national identity and church membership were often synonymous, churches have been faced with a new identity as a minority but distinct people of God in a secular society. Thus there has been a marked concern for ecclesiology, as we have seen in some of the theologians discussed in the previous chapter.

Closely connected with this has been a renewed questioning of infant baptism, particularly of the practice identified as 'indiscriminate baptism'. As infant baptism became the norm, the Western Catholic rite was the old adult/child/infant process, telescoped and slightly adapted for infant baptism. The Reformation Churches revised and devised forms of baptism which acknowledged the pastoral reality, and were thus rites for infant baptism. Only later, in connection with missionary work, did these churches produce rites for adult baptism. In Europe, baptism became seen as part of national identity, and both as a birth rite and birth right. As we have said, Karl Barth and Jürgen Moltmann both questioned whether infant baptism should continue, and we have noted the intense discussion which followed Barth's criticisms. Much of the debate stemmed from the fact that in European societies, although active church membership was declining, many people brought their infants for baptism, while neither they nor the children were actively taking up their Christian status.

In England it was an 'Anglican' problem. Already in a 1939 report of the Church of England, doubts were voiced about 'indiscriminate baptism'. This report recommended that instruction for parents applying for their child's baptism be tightened up, and even that the sacrament be deferred in families whose older children were not going to church. Reports in 1944, 1949, 1954 and 1965 made the same observations. Most baptisms were performed on a Sunday afternoon as a private service for the families, and not during normal public worship. In some quarters it was suggested that godparents should be vetted, that parents should undergo instruction, and even that perhaps baptism of infants should be restricted only to those whose parents were active members of the Church. In France, the Roman Catholic Church had a similar problem. A.M. Rouget wrote of indiscriminate infant baptism:

> One might ask oneself, as do many priests today in anguish, if such baptisms should be celebrated at all; if they are not doing more harm than good, by weighing down the Church with a multitude of Christians who are so only in name, and who do harm to the Church by confirming unbelievers in their opinion that, far from

being a living society, a leaven that should raise the world's mass, the Church is a worn-out institution, ineffective, unreal, surviving only by custom.[3]

Another French Roman Catholic scholar, A.G. Martmort, stressed that adult baptism by immersion is the norm of the Church, and not infant baptism, which is always a derivation from the norm.[4] In the presbyterian Church of Scotland the same questioning was behind the Reports of the Special Commission issued from 1955 to 1962.[5] The result has been a concern in the revision of baptismal rites to show adult baptism as the norm from which infant baptism is derived, and that baptisms should take place within normal Sunday public worship.

A further concern – and one linked with both ecclesiology and the discussion on infant baptism – has been the relationship of confirmation to baptism. Confirmation has been a Western development (anointing in the Eastern rites is not 'Eastern Confirmation'), and although the Roman Catholic Church has kept it as a separate sacrament, most Reformation Churches retained or restored a rite of confirmation which was an adult affirmation of baptism, and normally required for admission to communion. The theological question has been: what is confirmation – does it confer further graces and gifts of the Spirit, or is it the conscious confession of faith which completes infant baptism? If the former, then do those baptized as adults need confirmation? If adult baptism is the norm, how can confirmaton be reintegrated into the rite of baptism? Is it necessary for reception of communion, or is baptism alone sufficient?

A fourth factor has been the impact of the Charismatic movement, and a concern for a better understanding of the role of the Holy Spirit in baptism and in the Church. This has also implications for adult baptism and 'conversion' and the role of personal testimony in the ritual.

A fifth factor, which is only slowly emerging, is the apparent move from the period of modernity to postmodernity, though some would prefer to call this 'late modernity'.[6] These terms are tossed around in recent literature, and are difficult to pin down. They appear to mean different things when applied to art and architecture than when applied to historiography and textual interpretation. At times postmodernity seems to be a catch-all term for modern high-tech global culture. However, despite this uncertainty in precise definition of these terms, there has been in the last two or three decades a shift away from absolute faith in the rational method of argument, of the 'progress' of science, and of trust in the expert, as well as the assumption of the superiority of Euro-North American culture. What is significant is that some rites considered here – notably the Roman Catholic rites, the Episcopal Church in the United States of

---

[3] A.M. Rouget, *Christ Acts Through Sacraments*, Liturgical Press, Collegeville, MN, 1954, p. 62.

[4] A.G. Martimort, *The Signs of the New Covenant*, English translation Liturgical Press, Collegeville, MN, 1963, pp. 135–6.

[5] See Chapter 6 for this and the role of T.F. Torrance.

[6] See Fredric Jameson, *Postmodernism or, The Cultural Logic of Late Capitalism*, Duke University Press, Durham, NC, 1991; Glenn Ward, *Postmodernism*, Hodder Headline Ltd, London, 1997.

America's *Book of Common Prayer* (1979), and the *Lutheran Book of Worship* (1978), were compiled at the end of modernity; other rites, such as *A Prayer Book for New Zealand*, belong to the era many identify as postmodern. It is against this background that we now consider some of the many rites of baptism which have been compiled in recent decades.

The Roman Catholic Rites

The Roman Catholic Church issued a rite for Infant Baptism in 1969, followed by the rite for Confirmation in 1971, and in 1972, the Rites of Christian Initiation of Adults (RCIA).[7] The latter is regarded as the norm, and has been influential in other Western churches.

The rite for infant baptism represented a new departure – as we have noted, the rite used prior to this was a telescoped version of the older rites of initiation which presupposed adults as the main candidates. This was the first rite of baptism which the Catholic Church compiled specifically for infant baptism. The structure of the rite is as follows:

- Question to the parents regarding name and if baptism is desired
- Brief address to the parents
- Brief address to godparents
- Signing with the cross
- [Processional psalm]
- Scripture readings and homily
- Intercessions
- Prayer of Exorcism and Pre-baptismal anointing
- [Psalm]
- Blessing of the Baptismal water
- Renunciation and Profession of Faith
- Three-fold pouring/immersion with triune formula
- Post-Baptismal anointing with chrism
- Clothing with white garment
- Giving of the lighted candle
- [Effeta – optional]
- Lord's Prayer
- Blessing.

After the parental request for the child's baptism, the priest addresses the parents and asks them if they will do everything possible to bring the child up in the faith. Here

---

[7] *The Rites of the Catholic Church as Revised by the Second Vatican Council*, 2 vols, Pueblo Press, New York, 1976, 1980.

there is a pastoral recognition – found in nearly all modern rites – that, whatever the role of godparents or sponsors, in a world of the nuclear family and a highly mobile population, it is the parents who will play the greatest role in the child's faith. The godparents are addressed after the parents, recognizing their historic, but now lesser nurturing role.

The soteriological themes are conveyed in the exorcisms, the first of which mentions original sin, and in the renunciations, which are addressed to parents and godparents. Two forms of the latter are given, the traditional form, and a new one:

> Do you reject sin, so as to live in the freedom of God's children? (I do.)
> Do you reject the glamour of evil, and refuse to be mastered by sin?
> Do you reject Satan, father of sin and prince of darkness?

The rite recognizes that the infant has no personal sin. Original sin is still there (in one exorcism) but it is removed by God, not renounced by the infant.

Of some interest is the blessing of the water. The emphasis in this revised prayer is entirely paschal – the Red Sea, and dying and rising. The older prayer blended paschal themes with new birth imagery. Thus the imagery in the new prayer has a narrower focus. It does say: '... cleanse him/her from sin in a new birth to innocence by water and the Spirit', but this is lost in an overwhelmingly paschal narrative.[8] The congregation are given a role in the assent to the Creed, indicating that the baptizand is baptized into the community of the faith of the Creed.

The rite of Confirmation was published in 1971, and in the bull *Divinium consortium naturae*, Pope Paul VI asserted that this rite was the completion of initiation and endowed the candidate with the Holy Spirit. However, it has been RCIA, published in 1972, that has been of most interest to, and a major influence on other churches. RCIA is a series of staged rites. It addresses a two-fold problem. First, in parts of secularized Europe, converts to Catholicism often have no former church affiliation; and secondly, in the so-called mission fields, particularly in South America and Africa, a form of adult baptism is required. The rites have been patterned on the sequence found in the so-called *Apostolic Tradition*, and on the rites outlined in the fourth-century catecheses of Ambrose, Cyril of Jerusalem, and St John Chrysostom. They provide for a catechumenate with instruction over a period of time, initiation being completed at the Paschal liturgy at the Easter Vigil, with first eucharist at Easter.

The full document includes rites such as Reception into the Roman Catholic Church for those validly baptized in other churches. Our concern will be with the main rites of adult initiation, which cover paragraphs 4 through 224. These divide into three sections:

1   Explanation of the catechumenal stages of initiation, paras 4–67

---

[8] Dominic E. Serra, *The Blessing of Baptismal Water at the Paschal Vigil (Ge 444–448): Its Origins, Evolution, and Reform*, Thesis ad Lauream n.136, Pontificium Athenaeum S. Anselmi De Urbe Pontiicium Institutum Liturgicum, Rome, 1989.

2   The Catechumenate, paras 68–207
3   Baptism, confirmation and eucharist, paras 208–24.

Paragraph 4 explains:

> The initiation of catechumens is a gradual process that takes place within the
> community of the faithful. Together with the catechumens, the faithful reflect
> upon the value of the paschal mystery, renew their own conversion, and by their
> example lead the catechumens to obey the Holy Spirit more generously.

Thus catechesis is not something which takes place in a classroom, but in a community
actively living out its Christian faith. Furthermore, there are stages in the process
which can be ritualized: the initial conversion when someone decides they want to
belong to the Church, and welcoming the person into the community. It is called a
period of evangelization, and enables the candidate to reinterpret his or her life story
in the light of the Gospel.

A second stage is the beginning of instruction and officially entering the
catechumenate. Assembling publicly before the local church for the first time, the
candidates make their intention known to the Church. The rite consists of the
preparation of the candidates, a Liturgy of the Word, and dismissal of the catechumens.
Where it is deemed appropriate, a rite of exorcism and a renunciation of non-Christian
worship may be included. There was considerable debate over the exorcism, since it
might suggest that the candidates were in some sense possessed by demons. However,
some converts in African countries have worshipped spirits, and in such a context it
was considered a legitimate option.[9] The rite has a dismissal which serves as a
reminder that the catechumen is not at this stage a full member of the Church.

According to para.19, the catechumenate is an extended period during which the
candidates are given pastoral formation and are trained by suitable discipline. During
this time candidates are instructed in all aspects of Christian life, initiated into the
mysteries of salvation and into the practice of a gospel way of life, and enriched by
the liturgical rites. RCIA includes liturgies of the Word for celebration from time to
time with the catechumens. Minor exorcisms are provided which are more in the
nature of prayers for assistance.

No time frame is set for this process, since each person has different needs. However,
in practice, where RCIA has been implemented, a timescale emerges for practical
reasons. When the baptism itself is in sight, the catechumens become 'the elect', and
a time of purification and enlightenment begins. The rite of election or enrolment of
the names is generally celebrated on the First Sunday of Lent. It is recommended that
the bishop preside at this, and to make this practical, often this service takes place at
a cathedral with people from the whole diocese attending. During the Sundays of Lent,

---

[9] See Balthasar Fischer, 'Baptismal Exorcism in the Catholic Baptismal Rites after Vatican II', *Studia
Liturgica* 10 (1974), 48–55; J.D. Crichton, *Christian Celebration*, Geoffrey Chapman, London, 1981, Part
2, 'Sacraments', p. 47.

for the third, fourth and fifth Sundays, Cycle A of the Roman Lectionary is to be used, with Gospel readings from St John – the Samaritan woman at the well, the cure of the man born blind, and the raising of Lazarus, giving the sequence Water, Light and Life. Rites for prayers of the elect and laying-on of hands are provided. The Creed and Lord's Prayer are also formally handed over to the candidates.

The baptism takes place during the Easter Vigil on Holy Saturday. The Vigil readings which follow the blessing of the Paschal candle cover the themes of creation, Exodus, and the passage through the waters of the Red Sea. The celebration of baptism is introduced with the Litany of Saints. Candidates gather at the font visible to the assembled faithful. The blessing of the water follows, with renunciation, pre-baptismal anointing, Creed, and the three-fold immersion, or pouring, with the classical formula.

Then comes what some have perceived to be a confusion regarding post-baptismal anointing. In the ancient Roman rite there were two post-baptismal anointings: one by a presbyter, and then one by the bishop with laying-on of hands. It was the latter which became detached from the rite, and became 'Confirmation', reserved for the bishop. In the new rites, confirmation may be delegated to presbyters, and thus in theory, even in the absence of a bishop, adult initiation includes both baptism and confirmation. Para. 34 stipulates:

> According to the ancient practice preserved in the Roman liturgy, adults are not to be baptized without receiving confirmation immediately afterward unless serious reasons prevent this. This combination signifies the unity of the paschal mystery, the link between the mission of the Son and the outpouring of the Holy Spirit, and the connection between the two sacraments through which the Son and the Spirit come with the Father to those baptized.

However, in the rite, provision is made for the possibility that confirmation, either episcopal or presbyteral, will not follow immediately. In that event, there is a presbyteral anointing with a particular formula; if confirmation follows, this formula is omitted, and the confirmation formula is used. Aidan Kavanagh writes:

> Since two chrismations so closely conjoined appear cumbersome, the document omits the postbaptismal chrismation when confirmation is to follow directly [para. 224]. This clarification of structure is not, however, accompanied by an enlargement of language such a change seems to require. By this is meant that the prayer to be said at the postbaptismal chrismation speaks of the meaning of the act in terms of the neophyte's being anointed 'As Christ was anointed Priest, Prophet, and King,' so that he or she may always live as a member of his Body, the Church [224]. The prayer said for the chrismation at confirmation speaks, instead, of the neophyte's being given the Holy Spirit and his sevenfold gifts [230]. Thus when confirmation is celebrated *apart from* baptism, the chrismation after baptism is christic and messianic in character: when it is celebrated *with* baptism, the chrismation is pneumatic and charismatic. It could be argued that in this particular case a structural peculiarity in the Roman Rite has been exchanged for a verbal anomaly.[10]

---

[10] Aidan Kavanagh, *The Shape of Baptism*, Pueblo Press, New York, 1978, p. 140.

After the possible presbyteral anointing comes the clothing with a white garment and the presentation of the lighted candle. The intention of the rite is to unite 'confirmation' as part of the one adult initiation rite. In this part of the rite, the Roman Catholic Church has kept the laying-on of hands and prayer for the sevenfold gifts of the Spirit, but has adopted the Eastern Orthodox formula for anointing, '*N*, be sealed with the Gift of the Holy Spirit.' Maxwell Johnson has aptly commented:

> ... this new formula was consciously adopted and adapted in 1971 from the single, post-baptismal chrismation inseparably connected to baptism of the Byzantine liturgical tradition. Never before had the Roman confirmation anointing been this explicitly pneumatic in language and orientation and, with the omission of the traditional Roman postbaptismal anointing in the RCIA in favor of this confirmation anointing alone, an interesting new parallel between Roman confirmation and Byzantine postbaptismal chrismation has been decidedly established.[11]

Following the pattern of fourth-century baptismal practice, there is a post-baptismal period of instruction, which is explained thus:

> The key to this period is meditation, reflective thinking in the context of the community. Mystery of its nature can never be fully comprehended. Through imagination, association and meditation, triggered by sound liturgical preaching, the newly baptized come to a deeper understanding of the meaning of God's word and assimilate it in their lives. Through the experience of the liturgical action of the breaking of the bread, they offer thanks to God for his action in their lives and take on a new sense of faith and celebration. Where the rite of dismissal has been used during the previous stages, there is a newness or a sense of freshness after prolonged absence that allows the neophytes to experience the celebration of Eucharist in a new way. They have a new appreciation of the richness of the symbolic action, through which Christ is present among his people to nourish and sustain them, to bond them into communion as the covenanted People of God. Through postbaptismal catechesis and shared reflection on Word and sacrament in and with the Christian community, they perceive reality in a new way. Life, Church, and Word, are envisioned in light of the paschal mystery.[12]

In summary we may note that RCIA is, at least in theory, the normative baptismal rite, from which infant baptism is derived. It offers staged rites, giving liturgical expression to the idea that coming to faith is a journey. The rites are designed to be public celebrations, reinforcing the belief that initiation is into a community – it is ecclesiological. The rite is less concerned with the individual escaping from original sin through baptism, as with the individual, through baptism, entering a community freed from sin. This can be described as a shift from an Augustinian soteriological rite to a Cyprianic ecclesiological rite.

In infant baptism, the concern with parents reflects a pastoral reality, but historically it represents a move to the position established by the Reformed tradition. The commentary cited also uses the covenant concept so dear to the Reformed tradition.

---

[11] Johnson, *The Rites of Christian Initiation*, p. 316.

[12] Roman Catholic Church, *Study Text 10 CIA: Commentary*, Washington, DC, 1985, p. 73.

The influence of modernity in these rites is seen in that, that although pastoral issues were important, the liturgical basis for revision was trust in documents regarded as authoritative by 'experts' in liturgy.

RCIA has been implemented more quickly in some Roman Catholic countries than others. However, its staged rites and presentation of adult initiation as the normative rite have been influential on other churches.

Anglican Rites

The 1662 Rites of Baptism became the foundational liturgy for all parts of the Anglican Communion, and although some provinces in the early twentieth century made their own distinctive revisions of those rites, on the whole the rites were still close to that liturgical headwater. As they did in the Roman Catholic Church, a number of concerns surfaced in the twentieth century, particularly about private baptism and the baptism of infants of parents who were only nominal members of the church. Some felt that the stress on original sin in the rite suggested that sexual intercourse and procreation were sinful. However, the major concern was with the relation of confirmation to baptism.

Since the nineteenth century, there had been considerable debate amongst Anglicans as to whether confirmation was a sacramental rite which conferred gifts of the Spirit not given in baptism, or whether it was merely the conscious confession of faith for those who were baptized in infancy. The former case was advanced by A.J. Mason in the nineteenth century, and by Gregory Dix in the twentieth century; it became known as the Mason-Dix view. The latter was argued strongly by G.W. Lampe in 1951 in *The Seal of the Spirit*. In this work Professor Lampe of Cambridge argued that in the early Church only one rite of initiation was known, and it was baptism in water. The Holy Spirit was believed to be imparted in the water rite.

Official Church of England reports from 1948 to 1971 swung as a pendulum from one view to another. The Ely Report of 1971 (Professor Lampe being in the diocese of Ely), *Christian Initiation: Birth and Growth in the Christian Society*, declared that baptism should be recognized as the full and complete rite of Christian initiation. Confirmation would continue, administered by a bishop or priest, and would be a service of commitment and commissioning. The Knaresnorough Report, *Communion Before Confirmation?* (1985), suggested that baptized children should be admitted to communion before confirmation. In the meantime, since 1959 the Liturgical Commission of the Church of England attempted to reunite baptism and confirmation in a single adult rite of initiation, put forward as normative, with infant baptism as a derived rite. This view was continued in the 'Series 2' experimental rites of 1967.

These concerns in the Church of England were echoed in other Anglican provinces, and some of the Reports were also influential. In the Episcopal Church of the United States of America, *Prayer Book Studies* 1 promoted the Mason-Dix view that there were two distinct parts in initiation: water baptism and laying of hands for the Spirit.[13] One of the guiding figures in the early process was Professor Massey Shepherd, Jr. Shepherd progressed from advocating public baptism, to reuniting baptism and confirmation in a single rite for adults, to a position in which, in 1964, he was convinced that initiation was complete in baptism, and that whatever confirmation was, it should be contained in the baptismal service. All the baptized – and hence infants – should be admitted to communion.[14] *Prayer Book Studies* 18 would propose such a rite to the Church.

Two other key persons who influenced the revision process of the baptismal rite in the Episcopal Church were Leonel Mitchell and Marion Hatchett. Urban Holmes wrote:

> 1970 was an important year. Probably the bravest and most consistent with scholarship of all of the *Prayer Book Studies* was 18: On Baptism and Confirmation. It was written by a subcomittee of the SLC [Standing Liturgical Commission] with E.C. Whitaker's *Documents of the Baptismal Liturgy* (London: SPCK, 1960) in one hand and Marion Hatchett's STM thesis, *Thomas Cranmer and the Rites of Christian Initiation*, in the other. Spencer was the chairman of that remarkable committee, which I had the privilege to join only in its later days. Margaret Mead and Lee Mitchell were some of the other leading lights. Its recommendations were more than the bishops of the Episcopal Church could fathom. They had been out of seminary too long and were too threatened; so it never came to be. Here was an educational failure.[15]

Holmes here condenses a whole number of factors. First, the STM thesis of Hatchett, as has been noted in a previous chapter, was concerned to show that Cranmer had incorporated the formula from confirmation into the baptismal rite, and so had subsumed confirmation into baptism. Thus, he felt, the original Anglican rite had initiation complete in baptism. Secondly, Mitchell's book on anointing pointed out that in most rites other than the Roman tradition, the post-baptismal anointing and formula was the 'sealing' of the Spirit, leaving open whether this was given in the water or the subsequent anointing. Third, the proposals in *Prayer Book Studies* 18 were for a service of baptism and laying-on of hands. There was no subsequent rite of confirmation, and the service would be presided over by priests as well as by the bishops. The bishops rejected this abolition of confirmation, and in subsequent proposals confirmation remained an episcopal rite, but was not required for admission to communion.[16]

---

[13] For full discussion of the process, see Ruth A. Meyers, *Continuing the Reformation. Re-Visioning Baptism in the Episcopal Church*, Church Publishing Incorporated, New York, 1997.

[14] See ibid.

[15] Urban T. Holmes, 'Education for Liturgy: An Unfinished Symphony in Four Movements', in Malcolm C. Burson (ed.), *Worship Points the Way. Celebration of the Life and Work of Massey H. Shepherd, Jr.*, Seabury Press, New York, 1981, pp. 116–41, p. 133.

[16] See Meyers, *Continuing the Reformation*, pp. 136–47; Leonel L. Mitchell, 'Mitchell on Hatchett on Cranmer', in J. Neil Alexander (ed.), *With Ever Joyful Hearts. Essays on Liturgy and Music Honoring Marion J. Hatchett*, Church Publishing Incorporated, New York, 1999, pp. 103–38.

The final forms of baptism in the Episcopal Church were published in draft in 1973, for provisional adoption in 1976, and final ratification in *The Book of Common Prayer* in 1979. Thus although the definitive rites were published in 1979, they were based on work done in the 1960s and early 1970s – the period of modernity. The same holds true for the rites contained in the Church of England *Alternative Service Book* of 1980.

The Episcopalian rite is entitled 'Holy Baptism', and is a complete eucharistic service in which there is provision for baptism of infants and adults. The notes beforehand assert:

> Holy Baptism is full initiation by water and the Holy Spirit into Christ's Body the Church. The bond which God establishes in Baptism is indissoluble.

After the Liturgy of the Word comes the Presentation and Examination of the Candidates, with different provisions for adults and older children on the one hand, and infants and young children on the other. This section includes the renunciations. The Creed is contained in a following section which is headed, 'The Baptismal Covenant'. This section contains the Creed, and various other questions such as

> Will you continue in the apostles' teaching and fellowship, in the breaking of the bread, and in the prayers?

And,

> Will you strive for justice and peace among all people, and respect the dignity of every human being?

To all the questions the response is 'I will, with God's help.'

Brief versicle-response type intercessions for the candidates follow. Then comes the Thanksgiving over the water, which was mainly the work of Leonel Mitchell. After the baptism comes the following prayer and formula:

> Heavenly Father, we thank you that by water and the Holy Spirit you have bestowed upon *these* your *servants* the forgiveness of sins, and have raised *them* to the new life of grace. Sustain *them*, O Lord, in your Holy Spirit. Give *them* an inquiring and discerning heart, the courage to will and to persevere, a spirit to know and to love you, and the gift of joy and wonder in all your works. *Amen.*
>
> *Then the Bishop or Priest places a hand on the person's head, marking on the forehead the sign of the cross [using Chrism if desired] and saying to each one:*
>
> *N.*, you are sealed by the Holy Spirit in Baptism and marked as Christ's own for ever. *Amen.*

Confirmation can follow the baptismal rite, but it is for those renewing their commitment, and not seen as a special imparting of the Spirit. It is not a prerequisite for communion. The rite copies the Eastern rites in making the signing (optional use of Chrism) the final act of complete initiation, but follows the Reformation understanding of Confirmation as a mature confession of faith. Those who wanted to argue that the Spirit is imparted in Confirmation would have to interpret the sealing and optional anointing as Confirmation on analogy with the Eastern rites.

A baptismal candle is frequently given, but no formula is provided. The rite itself concludes with a congregational declaration receiving the person into the Church, and the Peace. The eucharist then follows as usual.

Perhaps the greatest surprise and innovation is the section entitled 'The Baptismal Covenant'. In somewhat of an understatement, Daniel Stevick noted, 'The term "covenant" has not been familiar in the liturgy or the theological discourse of Anglicanism.'[17] In fact, as we have observed, whereas covenant was the term used by Zwingli and Calvin and others in the Reformed tradition, initially to defend infant baptism, and then as part of a wider soteriology, it was not a term used by Cranmer other than in passing, and does not occur in his baptismal rite. Furthermore, the liturgical structure in the Cranmerian rite is baptism followed by exhortation to the godparents on their duties. In other words, the sequence is grace received followed by a response.

The Baptismal Covenant seems to reverse this order, and thus the questions suggest a contract or human promise upon which baptism rests. The liturgical sequence becomes promises and then baptism, or contract/undertakings and then grace – the very reversal of Cranmer. Stevick is incorrect to suggest that the terminology of covenant for baptism is not Anglican – the post-Reformation divines took it over as normal theological jargon, but it was never given liturgical expression. Here the Episcopal Church seems to have adopted the Reformed terminology and, when applied to infant baptism, Reformed parental obligations first found in William Farel's rite of Neuchâtel in 1533. It is certainly asking for things beyond the Creed, and could be regarded as semi-Pelagian. In this it has been followed by the Anglican Church of Canada's *The Book of Alternative Services* (1985), though there the Baptismal Covenant follows rather than precedes the blessing over the water.[18]

There was debate in ECUSA over the restoration of the catechumenate, and services were compiled and then shelved. However, at a later date it was decided to provide a catechumenate for adults. These forms would be placed in a separate compilation, *The Book of Occasional Services*. There is a special rite for admission of the candidates, which takes place in the main Sunday service, after the sermon. The candidate has sponsors who will be involved in the instruction and welcoming into the community. The candidates are marked with the sign of the cross. Prayers are provided with the laying-on of hands during the process. There is a rite of enrolment, with baptism ideally taking place at the Easter Vigil. It is not hard to see the influence of RCIA here, and beyond that an appeal to the classical rites of the fourth century.

Meanwhile, in the Church of England experimentation with the forms issued as *Series 2* gave place to a modern English version, *Series 3* in 1977. Its authorized form

---

[17] Daniel B. Stevick, *Baptismal Moments; Baptismal Meanings*, The Church Hymnal Corporation, New York, 1987, p. 156.

[18] The Canadian Doctrine and Worship Committee worked closely with the American Commission on baptismal policy. See Meyers, *Continuing the Reformation*, p. 252.

of 1979 would find its place in the *ASB* 1980. Under 'Christian Initiation', in addition to baptism, were such rites as thanksgiving for the birth of a child, thanksgiving after adoption, prayers after the death of a newborn or stillborn child, and renewal of baptismal vows.

The ideal service was set out as Baptism, Confirmation and Holy Communion, with separate adaptations for the baptism of children, and separate confirmation. However, given that the Church of England is an established church, the norm in many parishes was to have the Baptism of Children as a separate (semi-private) service rather than at the main Sunday service. Where the rite was administered in Holy Communion, it began after the homily and concluded with the exchange of peace.

The rite for the Baptism of Children began after the sermon with a brief exhortation stressing that children are baptized on the understanding that they will be brought up in the family of the Church. It concluded:

> Parents and godparents, the *children* whom you have brought for baptism *depend* chiefly on you for the help and encouragement *they* need. Are you willing to give it to *them* by your prayers, by your example, and by your teaching?

If the rite was not in the context of a main service, a brief exordium was provided, giving a summary of the New Testament meaning of baptism. Next came the Decision, which was in fact a threefold renunciation. However its form was:

> Do you turn to Christ?
> *I turn to Christ.*
> Do you repent of your sins?
> *I repent of my sins.*
> Do you renounce evil?
> *I renounce evil.*

Specific mention of the devil, or Satan, had been exorcised from the rite. The signing with the cross followed here, or after the actual baptism, and although oil could be used, its permissibility was noted in a rubric at the beginning of the service, and no special formula was provided for it, either here or elsewhere. This is because originally E.C. Whitaker argued that the symbolism of oil, abolished at the Reformation for baptism, and only used by a few Anglo-Catholics, would be lost on a modern North Atlantic people. However, at the last moment it was allowed as an option, but provision was by an introductory note rather than liturgical text.

The blessing of the water followed. This was a brief prayer, picking up on imagery from the Old Testament and Romans 6:3, asking God to bless the water, and to send the Spirit upon the candidates. Then came the confession of faith, which was a brief credal form:

> Do you believe and trust in God the Father, who made the world?
> Do you believe and trust in his Son Jesus Christ, who redeemed mankind?
> Do you believe and trust in his Holy Spirit, who gives life to the people of God?

This was a compromise attempt to retrieve the baptismal formula from the so-called *Apostolic Tradition*, supplemented with phrases from the Catechism.[19] It was also defended by some clergy on pastoral grounds that it was less difficult to understand for those families who were not regular church-goers! This trinitarian confession was followed by the priest and congregation saying:

> This is the faith of the Church.
> *This is our faith.*
> *We believe and trust in one God,*
> *Father, Son, and Holy Spirit.*

The baptism with the traditional formula followed, and then a lighted candle could be given to a parent or godparent for the child:

> Receive this light.
> This is to show that you have passed from darkness to light.
> *All:*   *Shine as a light in the world*
> *To the glory of God the Father.*

This was followed by a congregational welcome into the Body of Christ.

Although this rite did not contain something called 'The Baptismal Covenant', it did, like the American rite, place obligations and promises (though not the traditional Apostles' Creed!) on parents and godparents prior to the baptism. In practice, some clergy introduced policies that, unless the parents lived up to the promises and were regular members of the congregation, baptism would be postponed until they complied. Gordon Kuhrt, who championed the concept of covenant as agreement/ contract, wrote:

> It is therefore clear that both the [Canon] law and the liturgy of the Church of England require parents bringing a child to be baptized to be confessing, practising Christians themselves.[20]

Such clergy were accused of having a closed, discriminatory baptismal policy, and they in turn accused their critics of having an open, indiscriminate policy. However, since parental undertakings were required prior to the act of baptism, even for practising members, the rite suggested that one person's baptism depended on someone else's ecclesiastical commitment rather than on God's grace.

The 1980 *ASB* rite, like the Roman rite and the 1979 ECUSA rite, was composed with the classical patterns in mind, and reflects the liturgical thinking of the 1960s and 1970s. In 2000 the 1980 ASB rite was replaced by *Common Worship 2000*.[21] The

---

[19] See R.C.D. Jasper and Paul F. Bradshaw, *A Companion to the Alternative Service Book*, SPCK, London, 1986, pp. 356–7.

[20] Kuhrt, *Believing in Baptism*, p. 146.

[21] James Leachman, 'The New Family of Common Worship Liturgical Books of the Church of England (2): An Introduction to the Initiation Services and their Theology', *Ecclesia Orans* 21 (2004), 67–97 gives an overview, though he seems unaware of some of the wider unofficial but formative theological discussions which are recorded below.

new initiation rites reflect debates over a number of issues: the implications of the *ASB* rite for infant baptism and open or restrictive infant baptism, communion of those baptized, and a possible catechumenate. These were given some articulation in the report, *Christian Initiation – A Policy for the Church of England* (1991).[22] This report drew attention to different patterns of initiation:

a   The 'traditional' Church of England sequence of infant baptism, confirmation on profession of faith (at puberty or shortly afterwards), followed by communion
b   The Eastern pattern of baptism, chrismation and communion of infants
c   Confirmation at a much earlier age
d   Communion before confirmation

There were five appendices, two of which argued for a covenant concept of baptism and called for infant baptism to be restricted to infants of believing parents. In the fifth appendix this author was critical, not of parental promises *per se*, but of their positioning as a pre-baptismal contract, arguing strongly that the pattern should be grace-response, or baptism-promises/obligations:

> As the Church of Scotland reports put it, we are unable to believe, and ask the Lord to help our unbelief, for we are constantly (however theologically articulate and cult-committed) proved faithless; baptism tells us that all the promises of God are completely fulfilled in Christ, and on the ground of his faith and faithfulness we are baptised. He stands surety for us. He acts in baptism to us as he did in his ministry on earth – sometimes requiring some prior belief, sometimes acting through the belief of a parent or master, and sometimes without any prior belief at all. All the Church can do is to confess, or proclaim the mighty acts of God in Christ. Anything else is to reduce baptism to an ecclesiastical ceremony expressing someone's psychological feelings.
>
> If this Christocentric approach is helpful in rescuing baptism from being simply an ecclesiastical ceremony, it remains true that every baptism is an opportunity for preaching and teaching. At a pastoral level it is an opportunity to renew or deepen our understanding of God's act in Christ, whether the candidate is an adult, or the infant of fully paid up Christians, or of fringers or of strangers. It is a time for preaching the Gospel and discussing some of its problems and difficulties. And it is difficult to see how in present society pastoral preparation can do anything else than involve the parents of infant candidates. There should also be a place for such involvement to be expressed liturgically, yet without falling into the dangers of the bilateral covenant of the *ASB*. Perhaps we can again learn from the Church of Scotland. In its 1986 Order for Holy Baptism, the parents or sponsors profess their desire to present the infant for baptism into the Church, and

---

[22] See *Christian Initiation – A Policy for the Church of England. A Discussion Paper by Canon Martin Reardon*, Church House Publishing, London, 1991. See also *Communion Before Confirmation?*, Church Information Office Publishing, London, 1985; Mark Dalby, *Open Baptism*, SPCK, London, 1989; Colin Buchanan, *Infant Baptism and the Gospel. The Church of England's Dilemma*, Darton, Longman and Todd, London, 1993.

acknowledge belief in the Trinity. Only after the baptism are the parents asked to make promises. Theoretically at least the parents could decline, but it would not affect the baptism. The sacrament as a free gift of God has no hidden penalty clauses! Perhaps this might suggest a liturgical structure for the Church of England, and would safeguard the sacrament as prevenient grace, but still take seriously the pastoral obligations expected of parents.[23]

Although the Church of England theologian, John Macquarrie, in 1997 published *A Guide to the Sacraments*, his two sections on baptism offered nothing new, and he preferred to take the 1662 rite as the liturgical model on which to offer comment, suggesting that Anglican systematics had little to offer those engaged in liturgical revision.[24] A more important catalyst was the collection of essays entitled *Growing in Newness of Life*, which had been given at the Fourth International Anglican Liturgical Consultation held in Toronto in 1991.[25] However, many of these essays were representative of the American Episcopal and Canadian churches and argued for initiation being complete in baptism and infant communion, with the assumption that what was right for the Anglican Church in North America was right for the whole Communion.

Some hints of what the revision might entail were given in a brief paper, *Christian Initiation and its Relation to Some Pastoral Offices*, issued in 1991. It noted the problems in Anglicanism over the role of confirmation, and the widening role of the bishop in initiation rites. More importantly, it drew attention to the fact that faith is a journey, and that people come to faith and practice by at least three routes. The first is by infant baptism, leading to confirmation and communion. The second, for those who are old enough to answer for themselves, and set out as the norm in the *ASB*, is baptism, confirmation and eucharist as an integral whole. The third, which recognizes the growth into mature faith, may require staged rites. The paper stated:

> Under this pattern, three groups of people emerge, requiring an adapted form of Christian initiation, not for the sake of proliferation, but in order to ritualise reality. These may be summarised as follows:
>
> a Those who have been baptised, and may even have been confirmed and received Holy Communion regularly; but who – perhaps after a period of lapse, but usually after a special experience of renewal of some sort – want to renew their faith in an impressive public rite which the Church is anxious not to confuse with Baptism.
>
> b Those who have been members of another Church but who now – perhaps even after a period as regular communicants – wish to 'join the Church of England as full members.'

---

[23] Bryan Spinks, 'Reflections based on a study of Church of Scotland reports', in *Christian Initiation – A Policy for the Church of England*, pp. 63–4. Cf. Spinks, 'Luther's Timely Theology', p. 42.

[24] John Macquarrie, *A Guide to the Sacraments*, Continuum, New York, 1997. He took up Stephen Sykes's discussion of the 1552/1662 rite.

[25] David R. Holeton (ed.), *Growing in Newness of Life. Christian Initiation in Anglicanism Today*, The Anglican Book Centre, Toronto, 1993.

Either or both these rites should be able to be combined easily and coherently with the normal episcopal confirmation.

To these may be added the following group:

c Those who come to public services of healing, or who already 'go to confession,' but whose deepest need is a public rite of reconciliation, a solemn assurance of their spiritual wholeness in the sight of God.[26]

The paper drew attention to the possible revival of a catechumenate, which was given further impetus in *On the Way: Towards an Integrated Approach to Christian Initiation* (1995).[27] It also singled out two particular criticisms of the existing *ASB* rite: its omission of the Apostles' Creed as the form of confession of faith, and its emphasis on death/resurrection imagery to the virtual exclusion of rebirth imagery.[28]

The *Common Worship Initiation Services* were published for use in 1998, though a note warned that the texts might be further revised in a definitive text of 2000. The main, or normative, rite is Holy Baptism in the context of the main Sunday Eucharist. The rite begins with a greeting (the Grace) and introduction which has seasonal forms, the *Gloria in excelsis*, collect, Liturgy of the Word consisting of readings and sermon. After the sermon the Liturgy of Baptism has the following structure:

- Presentation of candidates
- Decision [renunciation]
- Signing with the Cross
- Prayer over the Water [Seasonal options]
- Profession of Faith
- Baptism
- [Clothing]
- Signing with formula [if not signed after Decision]
- Commission
- Prayers of Intercession
- Welcome and Peace
- [After Communion]
- Sending out with blessing and giving of candle with formula.

A number of formulae and prayers indicate the areas of revision and rethinking on the *ASB* rite. First, indicating a postmodern interest in symbolism, there is open encouragement to use oil, a baptismal robe/christening gown, and the giving of the

---

[26] General Synod of the Church of England, *Christian Initiation and its Relation to Some Pastoral Offices*, GS Misc 366, London, 1991, p. 7.

[27] *On the Way: Towards an Integrated Approach to Christian Initiation*, Church House Publishing, London, 1995. Mainly written by the late Michael Vasey of the Church of England Liturgical Commission.

[28] *Christian Initiation and its Relation to Some Pastoral Offices*, p. 9.

lighted candle. Secondly, at the Presentation there is provision for a personal testimony, reflecting the fact that there is no such thing as generic baptism, but only the baptism of particular people with particular stories. The congregation at this point are also asked to support the candidates, and parents and godparents are asked to pray for them, set an example, and walk with them in the way of Christ, and to care for and help them to take their place within the life and worship of Christ's Church. These requests are far less severe and contractual than in the *ASB* rite.

The Decision reintroduces reference to the devil, reacting against the 1960s and 1970s view this was too mythological, and aware that in the culture of cinema and TV, the devil and evil are alive and well in the postmodern world:

> Do you reject the devil and all rebellion against God?
> *I reject them.*
> Do you renounce the deceit and corruption of evil?
> *I renounce them.*
> Do you repent of the sins that separate us from God and neighbour?
> *I repent of them.*

The rite expresses recognition of the fact that there are a number of powerful images for baptism by having alternative blessings of water according to season, to supplement the one for 'General' use. The Easter/Pentecost blessing focuses on Paschal imagery and dying and rising; that for Epiphany and Trinity is more concerned with creation/new creation/new birth; and that for All Saints celebrates the new covenant in the blood of Jesus, the covenant of grace, and sharing the divine nature.

The profession of faith is an interrogatory form of the Apostles' Creed, professed by the whole congregation. The *ASB* forms are provided in an Appendix and may be used where there are 'strong pastoral reasons'. The baptismal formula is the classical trinitarian form, the Commission having felt that the alternatives proposed by some feminists were inadequate, and that inclusivity should be sought by other means. The formula provided to accompany the optional clothing with a white garment is:

> You have been clothed with Christ.
> As many as are baptized into Christ have put on Christ.

The post-baptismal signing formula does allude to anointing, thus at least anchoring the use of oil in the formula, if oil is used:

> May God who had received you by baptism into his Church,
> pour upon you the riches of his grace,
> that within the company of Christ's pilgrim people
> you may daily be renewed by his anointing Spirit,
> and come to the inheritance of the saints in glory.

This is followed by the Commission, which spells out the duties of parents and godparents and the congregation, or questions and responses to those who can answer for themselves. In placing this *after* the baptism, the structure reverts to the older traditional Prayer Book pattern, and addresses the theological issue raised by the present writer. Simon Jones and Phillip Tovey comment:

> Whereas the *ASB* required parents and godparents to give their assent to certain duties explained by the priest at the beginning of the liturgy, *CW* replaces this section with the Presentation of the Candidates, while the Duties of Parents and Godparents have become a post-baptismal Commission. This is no innovation. The Prayer Books of 1549, 1552 and 1662 all contained an exhortation to godparents at the end of the rite. That said, this marks an important shift from the theological stance of the *ASB* and clearly states that divine grace is not dependent upon human initiative, but that the grace of God in baptism invites human response and responsibility.[29]

The repositioning is a shift from the *ASB*, as well as a break from the ECUSA 1979 pattern.

The inclusion of intercessions, which begin 'As a royal priesthood, let us pray to the Father …', anchors baptism in mission, since prayer for the world is part of the mission of the baptized. Placing the giving of a lighted candle at the conclusion of the rite also symbolizes the dismissal of all the baptized into the world as bearers of the light of Christ. Using the symbols of water, oil, robe and light, as well as giving place for testimony, the rite envisions baptism as a journey, a story and a pilgrim way.[30]

A number of other Anglican Provinces have published new Prayer Books. Of these, *A Prayer Book for Australia* (1995); *The Book of Common Prayer* of the Church of The Province of the West Indies (1995); *Our Modern Services*, Anglican Church of Kenya (2002); and *The Book of Common Prayer*, Church of Ireland (2004), though not using the term 'Baptismal Covenant', have all followed the ECUSA 1979 and Church of England *ASB* pattern of having parental promises and undertaking before the baptism. Anticipating the Church of England *Common Worship*, and with an even greater structural stress on baptism as grace without pre-condition is the rite in *A New Zealand Prayer Book* (1989). The rite commences with God's Call:

> Dear friends in Christ, God is love, God gives us life.
> We love because God first loves us.
> In baptism God declares that love;
> in Christ God calls us to respond.

This Call sums up the rite – baptism as God's free grace. The candidate is presented, and a short exordium explaining the meaning of baptism is given, followed by the question, 'How do you respond to this promise?' The response is 'I/we hear God's call and ask for baptism.'

This is followed by the renunciations, the blessing over the water, and the baptism. All recite a formula welcoming the person into the family of God, and a signing follows (with oil optional). A lighted candle may be given to the candidate. Confirmation by the bishop may follow, but if not Confirmation, the Affirmation (a

---

[29] Paul Bradshaw (ed.), *Companion to Common Worship*, Vol. 1, Alcuin Club Collection 78, SPCK, London, 2001, pp. 171–2.

[30] Gilly Myers, *Using Common Worship: Initiation*, Church House Publishing, London, 2000, pp. 27–32.

series of blessings of God) comes next, and then a short credal formula. The parents and godparents of infants are simply asked 'How then will you care for this child?', and the congregation are briefly addressed on their role as the community of faith. The Apostles' Creed in interrogatory form comes next, and the service continues with the Peace. In this rite baptism is presented as God first loving us, which then evokes its own response. However, neither the candidate, nor the parents of infants give an explicit expression of commitment to Christian life.

Anglican rites thus fall into two patterns: the North American-*ASB* pattern, of promises/baptism, and the *CW*-New Zealand and older Prayer Book pattern of baptism/response. However, behind all the rites can be seen a concern to make baptism part of public worship, emphasizing that it is entrance into the Body of Christ, the Church. There is a desire to stress that infant baptism is not simply an insurance against original sin and, as a move against indiscriminate baptisms, the liturgy stresses the role and responsibility of parents, godparents and the congregation.

Lutheran Rites

Amidst the many modern Lutheran baptismal rites, our consideration will be limited to three which have emerged from the American Lutheran Churches, and the rite of the Church of Sweden.

In 1978 the *Lutheran Book of Worship (LBW)* was published for use by various Lutheran churches in America which had worked together through the Inter-Lutheran Commission on Worship (ILCW) to produce a common liturgy.[31] These were the American Lutheran Church (ALC), the Evangelical Lutheran Church of Canada (ELCC), the Lutheran Church in America (LCA), and the Lutheran Church-Missouri Synod (LCMS). These entities in turn were the result of a number of amalgamations of separate linguistic synods. The LCMS is a Lutheran Confessional Church, not in communion with the other churches, and although it participated in the compilation of the *LBW*, and some of its congregations use *LBW*, it withdrew from the joint venture in 1978 and subsequently published its own book, *Lutheran Worship*, 1982.[32] In 1988 the ALC and LCA, together with breakaway congregations from the LCMS called the Association of Evangelical Lutheran Churches, joined together to form the Evangelical Lutheran Church of America (ELCA). Another confessional Lutheran synod, the Wisconsin Evangelical Lutheran Synod, published *Christian Worship. A Lutheran Hymnal* in 1993.

The work of the ILCW on baptism was influenced strongly by Eugene Brand of the ALC, who had studied with the German Lutheran theologian and ecumenist, Peter

---

[31] For a full discussion of the making of this book, Ralph W. Quere, *In the Context of Unity. A History of the Development of Lutheran Book of Worship*, Lutheran University Press, Minneapolis, MN, 2003.

[32] In addition to Quere, ibid., see Timothy C.J. Quill, *The Impact of the Liturgical Movement on American Lutheranism*, Scarecrow Press, Inc., Lanham, MD, 1997.

Brunner, and Hans C. Boehringer of the LCMS, who had studied liturgy with the Roman Catholic scholar, Aidan Kavanagh.[33] Boehringer had listed sixteen specific suggestions for the theology and liturgy of baptism:

1   Christian initiation should be considered as a series of events – baptism, laying-on of hands, first communion.
2   There should be a period of preparation [that is, catechesis] before and after the rite.
3   The baptismal rite should be a combination of myth and ritual, words and actions.
4   The baptismal rite should be adaptable for infants alone, adults alone, or both.
5   The baptismal rite should include the laying-on of hands.
6   The baptismal rite should take place in the setting of the Eucharist, but should also be usable outside the eucharistic liturgy.
7   The baptismal rite should involve the entire congregation.
8   If sponsors are present, they should be agents of the congregation.
9   There should be provision for movement by the congregation.
10 Baptism should be celebrated on few occasions:

    a   for the sake of the rite itself
    b   for historical reasons.

11 The rite should include a ritual wherein the catechumen [candidate] expresses a desire for membership and the congregation assumes responsibility for the neophyte.
        Christian Initiation should also include:
12 Congregational prayers for the catechumens
13 A rite to commune those already baptized
14 A rite for acknowledgment of emergency baptism
15 A service of confession and reconciliation
16 A rite for confirmation.[34]

After several drafts, a provisional service was published, *Contemporary Worship 7: Holy Baptism*. A number of issues provoked debate and comment, including the idea of baptismal seasons rather than baptism on demand, the lack of emphasis on original sin, the petition for consecration in the thanksgiving over the water, and the signing, garment and candle formulas. *Prayer Book Studies* 26 of the Episcopal Church was influential in one or two places. The relation of baptism to confirmation, and the meaning of confirmation were also contested issues, particularly whether the term

---

[33] Jeffrey A. Truscott, *The Reform of Baptism and Confirmation in American Lutheranism*, Scarecrow Press, Inc, Lanham, MD, 2003. The background information to *LBW* in this chapter is indebted to Truscott's work.
[34] Ibid., p. 24.

'covenant' should be used for baptism and the intention in *Contemporary Worship* 8, which was subtitled *Affirmation of the Baptismal Covenant.*[35]

The Introduction in the 1978 *LBW* usefully summarizes the intention of the baptismal and other rites:

> … to restore to Holy Baptism the liturgical rank and dignity implied by Lutheran theology, and to draw out the baptismal motifs in such acts as the confession of sin and burial of the dead; to continue to move into the larger ecumenical heritage of liturgy while, at the same time, enhancing Lutheran convictions about the Gospel; to involve lay persons as assisting ministers who share the leadership of corporate worship; to bring the language of prayer and praise into conformity with the best current usage.

The rite of 1978, which can be used for infants and adults, begins with a baptismal hymn and the gathering at the font, and a short address by the minister to the effect that baptism liberates us from sin and death by joining us to the death and resurrection of Christ; though fallen humanity, we are reborn as children of God and inheritors of eternal life; by water and the Holy Spirit we are made members of the Church which is the body of Christ. Sponsors present the candidates, and those who can answer for themselves request baptism. The minister then addresses the sponsors and parents about the duties of teaching children, concluding with the words 'that, living in the covenant of *their* baptism and in communion with the Church, *they* may lead *godly lives* until the day of Jesus Christ'. The parents are then asked if they will fulfil these obligations. Although this is not named 'Baptismal Covenant', it suggests that baptism is a covenant, which drew objections during the revision process. The response of the ILCW was that the covenant was a unilateral one, though, as with the ECUSA and *ASB* Anglican rites, its position prior to baptism suggests otherwise.[36]

Intercessions may follow at this point if the rite takes place within a eucharistic service. The Thanksgiving over the Water comes next, with its themes of creation, the flood (echoing Luther), the baptism of Jesus, death and resurrection, and freedom from sin. Rebirth is mentioned, but this is not developed. The prayer petitions:

> Pour out your Holy Spirit, so that those who are here baptized may be given new life. Wash away the sin of all those who are cleansed by this water and bring them forth as inheritors of your glorious kingdom.

Earlier drafts asked for the Spirit to bless or come upon the water, but this was criticized, and the final form is ambiguous. The *Commentary*, however, suggests that the minister might spread his/her hands over the font at the words 'Pour out your Holy Spirit', which, at least in gesture, suggests that the Spirit is being asked to come upon the water.[37]

---

[35] Ibid. for full discussion of these issues.

[36] Ibid., pp. 207–08 argues that my explanation of Osiander's omission of an admonition is patient of another interpretation. He does not, however, deal with Luther's theology and whether the term 'baptismal covenant' is really appropriate in a Lutheran order.

[37] For the problems over the earlier drafts, ibid., pp. 59–64.

This is followed by a short renunciation and the Creed in interrogatory style. Two baptismal formulas are given, the traditional Western, and the Eastern passive form. The baptismal party then move to stand before the altar. There follows a laying-on of hands with a prayer which is based in part on the traditional Roman Confirmation prayer – and certainly Boehringer regarded this as full and complete initiation. The candidate is sealed and for this oil may be used. The robing which was found in earlier drafts did not survive into the final text. There is an optional giving of the candle, and a congregational welcome.

The *Commentary* reinforces that certain Sundays should be set apart for the celebration of the rite, and these are to be seen as 'baptismal festivals'. The service is congregational and private baptisms should be discouraged. The paschal candle should be placed by the font to recall paschal associations. If the water is not circulating, it should be in an ewer, ready to be poured into the font at the thanksgiving.[38]

In the *Occasional Offices* there is a rite for the Enrolment of Candidates. The book explains:

> This service is new to Lutherans, as well as to those of other traditions, and does not reflect the general practice of the present. This recovery of the ancient progressive entrance into the Christian community is designed to teach and to lead congregations towards a more responsible and useful baptismal practice.[39]

It envisages an Inquirer's Class, Enrolment of Candidates for baptism, Instruction, Holy Baptism and Incorporation. The *Commentary on the Occasional Services* gives a chart comparing the Lutheran structure with RCIA and the ECUSA, indicating the sources of inspiration for staged rites.

The *LW* 1982 rite was in some respects a reaction against the proposals in *LBW*, often on the grounds that too many ideas from the Roman Catholic Liturgical Movement which were not compatible with the Lutheran Confessions had infiltrated *LBW*. In comparison with *LBW*, the *LW* rite represents an interesting mixture of simplification and enrichment. The rite begins with the invocation of the Trinity, which is customary in *LBW*. An opening statement gives the rationale for baptism from Matthew 28 and from the Acts of the Apostles. The candidate is signed with the cross, and a brief Gospel reading follows, from Mark 10 for children, and for adults, John 3. An address to the sponsors of infants follows, listing their duties. The term 'covenant' is not used, though the word 'obligations' occurs in the Short Order in *Lutheran Worship: Agenda* (1984). Such a word is odd in this context in a Confessional Lutheran rite.

Next, the minister lays hands on each candidate, and the congregation prays the Lord's Prayer, as in Luther's rite. The baptismal party gather at the font, and make the renunciations and an interrogatory creed. Baptism follows, and then a laying-on of hands and prayer, and an optional bestowal of a white garment and giving of a lighted

---

[38] For such fonts, see the Chapel at Valparaiso University, Indiana.

[39] *Occasional Offices*, p. 20.

candle. A prayer is said before the altar, and then a congregational welcome. One of the most obvious omissions is Luther's *sindflutgebet*, or any other thanksgiving over the water. The theology at work here seems to be a very strict interpretation of Luther that, providing the Word is spoken (a short Gospel reading), and water used with the trinitarian formula, nothing else is required.[40]

In *Christian Worship. A Lutheran Hymnal*, the Wisconsin Synod provided a meagre rite for baptism. The preamble explained that it had combined the sacrament of baptism with the confession of sins. The rite seems to take place within normal Sunday worship. After a baptismal hymn the minister says the Grace, which is followed by a brief explication on baptism, with a call for repentance, followed by a confession and ministerial absolution. A short statement on baptism is read at infant baptism, whereas adults respond to brief credal questions. The sign of the cross follows, and baptism with the classical formula. The minister says:

> The Almighty God – Father, Son, and Holy Spirit – has forgiven all your sins. By your baptism, you are born again and made a dear child of your father in heaven. May God strengthen you to live in your baptismal grace all the days of your life. Peace be with you.

The rite concludes with an exhortation to parents and godparents, and a prayer. This rite, in contrast to both *LBW* and *LW*, shows few signs, if any, of drawing on a tradition wider than nineteenth-century German Lutheran rites.

The ELCA proposes a new series of services entitled *Renewing Worship* after 2005. The proposed services are available in draft form for experimental use and evaluation.[41] They offer a proposed shape, consisting of Presentation, Profession, Baptism and Welcome. The Presentation provides an introductory statement and presentation of candidates, with questions to them and to sponsors. The Profession consists of alternative renunciations and either a short credal profession or the Apostles' Creed in interrogatory form. A number of alternative Thanksgivings over the water are provided, each with different key themes or baptismal emphases. The notes explain:

> While the thanksgiving prayer in the rite may be used on any occasion of baptism, the alternate forms of thanksgiving provided in the supplemental texts may be particularly appropriate for baptismal festivals (alternate B, C, D, or E for the Easter Vigil; alternate B,C, or F for the Baptism of Our Lord; alternate C or G for the Day of Pentecost; and alternate D or H for All Saints Day).

Thanksgiving F, for example, reads:

> Blessed are you, holy God.
> You are the creator of the waters of the earth.
> You are the river of life.
> You led your people through the Red Sea
> and called them to life in covenant.

---

[40] For theological commentary, Nagel, 'Holy Baptism', pp. 262–87.

[41] These were available from the ELCA website until the end of 2005. The final draft was made in January 2006, and will appear in *Evangelical Lutheran Worship*, October 2006.

> Your Son was baptized in the river Jordan
> to begin his mission among us.
> Come also into this water
> and into those who are here baptized.
> Create us all anew
> that we may serve this needy world;
> for we trust in the name of Jesus, your Son,
> one God, now and forever.
> *Amen.*

Baptism is by threefold pouring or immersion with the triune formula, followed by a congregational acclamation. The laying-on of hands with prayer for sustaining with the gifts of the Spirit follows and the signing of the cross, with permissible use of oil. The giving of a baptismal garment with formula is also permissible, as is the welcome with the giving of a candle and congregational formula.

The baptismal rite of the Church of Sweden, though currently under review, dates from 1986, and the English translation from 1988. This rite begins with a hymn, and a brief introduction, which leads to a prayer of thanksgiving. The Gospel narrative is read, Mark 10:13–16. After the child's name is asked, a prayer of deliverance follows:

> God, you alone can save us from all evil. Deliver *NN* from the power of darkness,
> write *his* name in the Book of Life and keep *him* in your light now and always.

An optional signing on forehead, mouth and heart may follow, and after this a Scripture reading, from either Matthew 28:18–20, Acts 2:38, or 19:5, or Romans 6:4–5, Galatians 3:27–8, or Titus 3:4–5. An optional homily and hymn come next, and then a very brief baptismal prayer and the Creed. The baptism follows, and after the triune formula the priest says, 'God of life, fill *NN* with your Spirit and help *him* day to day to live as your child.' Then comes a welcome, and a lighted candle may be given, with a formula x provided. Intercessions follow, Lord's Prayer, Blessing, Hymn and Dismissal. The rite is quite terse, and provides no blessing of the water.

Reformed Rites

Two English-speaking Presbyterian churches produced new books of public worship within the space of a year: the Presbyterian Church USA its *Book of Common Worship (BCW)* in 1993, and the Church of Scotland's *Common Order (CO)* in 1994. The former can trace many of its origins to the latter. However, their situations are vastly different. PCUSA is a large Church, but consists of 'gathered' congregations. In contrast, the Church of Scotland, though small, is a national Church, and its role is analogous to that of the Church of England in England. This has an interesting impact on the ecclesiology assumed by the baptismal rites in the two books.

BCW was a replacement for an earlier book, *Worshipbook* (1970), which in turn had replaced the *Book of Common Order* (1946). The Committee had the experience and lessons from the 1970 book, but was also in a position to consider other rites which had appeared – such as the ECUSA *Book of Common Prayer* (1979), and the Lutheran *LBW* (1978), as well as liturgies from other churches and countries which had appeared after 1970. It could also draw on the implications of *BEM*.[42] Harold Daniels notes:

> Four members of the committee responsible for overseeing the final preparation of the manuscript, and submitting it for approval, had liturgical training in an ecumenical setting, having earned either a doctorate or a master's degree in the liturgical studies program at the University of Notre Dame. The chairperson of the committees subsequently served for several years as COCU's executive secretary.[43]

The committees were able therefore to learn from their own mistakes of 1970, and other churches' strengths and weaknesses. There was certainly a conscious ecumenical element to the revision. The purpose is expressed by Daniels thus:

> Our baptismal practice gives little clue to the rigors of Christian discipleship. Its impact on life following Baptism is negligible. Marginalized, Baptism has become trivialized.
>
> Baptism in the *Book of Common Worship* is clearly portrayed as Baptism with water and the Spirit, signifying cleansing from sin, new birth, death and resurrection with Christ, and incorporation into the body of Christ. These aspects of Baptism are of the very essence of the Christian life. Baptism not only marks the beginning but continues to be the pivotal reference point shaping our discipleship each day of our lives.[44]

The BCW has in fact two rites of baptism. One is revised from an 1985 supplemental liturgical resource; the other is from the 1990 Consultation on Common Texts, an ecumenical liturgical group. Here we shall consider the one compiled for *BCW* from the 1985 rite.

It begins with words of scriptural warrant, starting with Matthew 28:18–20 and then a selection of other scriptural quotes. After the candidates are presented, with questions to parents, sponsors and the congregation, the renunciations and profession of faith in the Creed follow. Then comes the Thanksgiving over the Water. Two texts are provided, and an outline for those who prefer to use their own words. The baptism with the traditional formula comes next, and then the laying-on of hands. A permissible use of oil for signing with one of two formulas follows:

> *N*, Child of the covenant,
> you have been sealed by the Holy Spirit in baptism,
> and marked as Christ's own forever.
> Amen

---

[42] Harold M. Daniels, *To God Alone Be Glory. The Story and Sources of the Book of Common Worship*, Geneva Press, Louisville, KY, 2003, p. 80.

[43] Ibid., p. 81. Notre Dame is a Roman Catholic University which has a lively liturgy program; COCU is Commission of the Consultation on Church Union.

[44] Ibid., p. 108.

N, Child of God,
you have been sealed by the Holy Spirit in baptism,
and grafted into Christ forever.
Amen.

After a welcome by the minister and congregational response, comes the Peace.

In a comparison with the rite in *CO*, James Kay believed that, whereas the former had stressed an anti-Pelagian emphasis on the priority of grace, this stress was muted in *BCW* because it had chosen to 'gather the harvest of the post-Vatican II ecumenical liturgical renewal'.[45] Though the articulation of the traditional Reformed concept of covenant was toned down in both, it was weaker in *BCW*. Moreover, 'the Americans also remove the synoptic proof-texts inferentially warranting infant baptism and, in restoring renunciations, may directly undercut the covenantal basis for this practice'.[46]

CO retains separate baptisms for child and adult candidates. The rite for a child begins with scriptural warrants, as does the *BCW* rite, but a different selection, which includes some Old Testament sentences. A Statement follows, the final paragraph of which stresses the love of God in baptism. The parents are asked if they receive the teaching of the Church, and the Apostles' Creed is recited. The prayer over the water follows – it places in brackets the rehearsal of the mighty deeds of God in the flood, Noah, and Moses, and the baptism of Jesus; these may be omitted. However, when the minister pours water into the font he asks God to:

Send your Holy Spirit
upon us and upon this water,
that *N* ..., being buried with Christ in baptism,
may rise with him to newness of life;
and being born anew of water and the Holy Spirit
may remain for ever in the number of your faithful children;
through ... .[47]

Then the minister reads a Declaration which was taken from the rite of the French Reformed Church, and which stresses the grace of baptism:

N ...,
For you Jesus Christ came into the world:
for you he lived and showed God's love;
for you he suffered the darkness of Calvary
and cried at the last, 'It is accomplished';
for you he triumphed over death
and rose in newness of life;

---

[45] James F. Kay, 'The New Rites of Baptism: A Dogmatic Assessment', in Bryan D. Spinks and Iain R. Torrance (eds), *To Glorify God. Essays on Modern Reformed Liturgy*, T & T Clark, Edinburgh, 1999, pp. 201–12, p. 212.

[46] Ibid., p. 212.

[47] The original draft omitted the concept of rebirth, and the reference was added after the intervention of the present writer.

for you he ascended to reign at God's right hand.
All this he did for you, N ...,
Though you do not know it yet.
And so the word of Scripture is fulfilled:
'We love because God loved us first.'

Baptism follows, and a blessing, and then the promises of the parents and their duties. Like the Church of England *Common Worship* rites, this one has the sequence grace/response, though with the liturgical Declaration from the French Reformed Church, the emphasis on sheer grace is more forcefully expressed in the Scottish rite. The Commitment of the congregation follows, and then the prayers. For adult baptism, the rite is very similar, except that after the baptism, in place of parental promises, the candidate makes his/her own promise. There is a short form if confirmation is not taking place; otherwise the candidate makes the confirmation promises.

James Kay was critical of the *BCW* restoration of renunciations, noting that they are superfluous in the context of infant baptism. Furthermore he found the wording of the renunciations in *BCW* Pelagian. Iain Torrance, too, suggested that the *BCW* was contractual rather than covenantal, and that 'God's sacrament of grace is turned into something we do anxiously.'[48] However, there were different factors in these two revisions. As Kay noted, *BCW* was prepared to recapture the Vatican II ecumenical liturgical pattern. *CO*, in contrast, was still working out liturgically the implications of its reports on baptism overseen by T.F. Torrance. In many ways *CO* is an expression of T.F. Torrance's theology.[49]

The United Church of Christ in the USA, a union of Congregationalist, Evangelical and Reformed churches, produced its *Book of Worship* in 1986. Not only did this book attempt to provide for the various strands within the United Church, but also had as its overriding mandate the use of inclusive language – for God and for humans. While other churches have responded to the challenge of inclusive language by adopting expansive language (male and female imagery), *BW* simply tried to avoid engendered language, and the result is a collection of liturgies with little linguistic beauty.[50]

The rite of baptism provides an outline, and then alternative texts in parallel columns. Provisions are made for both adult and infant baptism. After a Welcome, the pastor addresses those gathered, using one of the options provided, or other words based on Scripture. Promises follow, and then a congregational assent. A very brief trinitarian confession of faith is provided, and 'Prayer of Baptism', which is a blessing over the water. Concerns for inclusivity have led to the inclusion of a reference to 'nurtured in the water of Mary's womb', and to the woman at the Samaritan well. The active and Eastern passive formulae for baptism are given, and after the baptism there is a laying-on of hands. The rite ends with an act of praise, prayer for the baptized,

---

[48] Iain R. Torrance, 'Fear of Being Left Out', in *To Glorify God*, pp. 159–72.

[49] See Spinks, '"Freely by His Grace"', pp. 218–42.

[50] For a review of the book, John W. Riggs, 'Traditions, Tradition, and Liturgical Norms: The United Church of Christ Book of Worship', *Worship* 62 (1988), 58–72.

and a blessing. One of these prayers addresses God as 'O Holy One, mother and father of all the faithful'. However, this, like the language in the 'Prayer of Baptism', is about inclusive language policy, and adds nothing of particular theological note to the understanding of baptism.

The British United Reformed Church published *Worship* in 2003, replacing its earlier *Service Book* of 1989. The URC had originated as an amalgamation of Congregationalists and Presbyterians, but in 1981 the Reformed Association of Churches of Christ in Great Britain and Ireland became part of the URC. The latter, like the Disciples of Christ, practised believer's baptism. In comparison with 1989, a shift in structure has taken place; whereas in the 1989 rite the promises come before baptism, in 2003 – as in *CO* – they come after it. The rite opens with versicles and responses, and then scriptural warrants, including Old Testament passages, as in *CO*. The paschal candle may then be lit, and the Apostles' Creed may be said.

Affirmations are made by candidates for believer's baptism, and a testimony may be given. In the case of infants, parents are asked if they believe in the one God, Father, Son and Holy Spirit, maker of heaven and earth, giver of life, redeemer of the world. A prayer over the water, beginning in the fashion of a *berakah* (Jewish blessing formula), follows, and then the baptism and signing with the sign of the cross. A declaration of reception into the one, holy, catholic and apostolic church is made, followed by the Aaronic blessing. Promises then follow, with provision for confirmation – presumably for believer's baptism candidates. Then comes a welcome, the right hand of fellowship may be given, and a lighted candle presented to the candidate.

Lastly under the heading of Reformed, we may mention the rite of the Evangelical Reformed Church of the Canton of Zurich (1969), which witnesses to the continuation of the short order in the mode of Zwingli in the sixteenth century, with a reading from Mark 10:13–16, an address to the parents, a baptismal question, the baptism, blessing and prayers.

Two Methodist Rites

The United Methodist Church of the USA published a new *Book of Worship* in 1992.[51] The compilers decided to call the variety of initiation rites 'Services of the Baptismal Covenant'. Each of the services is numbered by Roman numerals. The Baptismal Covenant I is concerned with baptism, confirmation, reaffirmation of faith, reception into the United Methodist Church and reception into a local congregation; II, baptism for those unable to answer for themselves, but with alternative rites II-A and II-B, the latter being of the rite of the former Methodist and former Evangelical United Brethren Churches; III is the latter churches' version of I, and IV is a service of reaffirmation

---

[51] For fuller background of American Methodist worship, Karen B. Westerfield Tucker, *American Methodist Worship*, Oxford University Press, New York, 2001.

of the baptismal covenant. Thus there is provision for different candidates, and different traditions within the United Methodist Church. In so far as 'The Baptismal Covenant I' is presented first as a type of normative rite, it is that service we will comment on here.

A brief introduction by the minister states in summary the purpose of baptism:

> Brothers and Sisters in Christ:
> Through the sacrament of Baptism
> we are initiated into Christ's holy Church.
> We are incorporated into God's mighty acts of salvation
> and given new birth through water and the Spirit.
> All this is God's gift, offered without price.

If there is a confirmation, a further paragraph is added, referring to renewing 'the covenant declared in baptism' – which is odd, since the first introduction makes no mention of the term 'covenant'. The service presents what we might by now term 'the ecumenical classical' structure, with presentation, renunciation and confession of faith, thanksgiving over the water, and baptism with laying-on of hands. This provision is for infants also, since it is also found in 'The Baptismal Covenant II'. Hence initiation is complete in baptism. Karen Westerfield Tucker has commented:

> Following the design of earliest Christian praxis and the continuing custom of the Orthodox, the intention was to complete Christian initiation for children and adults at one event. Yet the rites reflecting the normative practice of adult initiation in the early church proved insufficient for the pedobaptist and personal-profession-requiring United Methodists: laying on of hands (designated 'confirmation') might accompany baptism, but there was still the expectation that a person baptized in childhood would later make public profession, at which time denominational loyalty would also be vowed. While the rite implies that a child at baptism becomes a member of Christ's church universal and local, the denomination was more reticent to establish legislation to that effect.[52]

Provision is made for signing and the use of oil, clothing with new clothing with formula, and the giving of a lighted candle.

A contrast is found in *The Methodist Worship Book* (1999), of the Methodist Church in Great Britain. The 'normative' rite is entitled 'The Baptism of Those who are able to answer for themselves, and of Young Children, with Confirmation and reception into Membership'. The British Methodist rite makes no mention of covenant either in its title or in the rite, and presents baptism as grace/response, with the promises coming after the baptism. The compilers seem to have been influenced by the Scottish *CO*, drawing on the statement (called 'Declaration' in *CO*) which comes from the French Reformed rite. Its own opening Declaration says:

> Sisters and brothers,
> Baptism is a gift of God.
> It declares to each of us the love and grace of God.

---

52 Ibid., p. 115.

In this sacrament we celebrate
the life of Christ laid down for us,
the Holy Spirit poured out on us,
and the living water offered to us.
God claims and cleanses us,
rescues us from sin,
and raises us to new life.

He plants us into the Church of Christ
and sustains and strengthens us with the power of the Spirit.
Although we do not deserve these gifts of grace,
or fully understand them,
God offers them to all,
and, through Christ, invites us to respond.

This is much more detailed than the American opening statement, and the objective work of God is given much more expression. Scriptural warrants follow, and then a brief presentation of the candidates. The Thanksgiving over the Water is shorter and not so rich as in the American rite, and unlike the American rite, does not ask that the water may be blessed – 'Pour out your Holy Spirit that those baptized in this water may die to sin … .' The Affirmation of Faith begins with a brief turning from evil, unlike the more comprehensive renunciations of the American rite. The Creed follows, and then the adaptation from the French Reformed rite which *CO* had used:

N and N,
for you Jesus Christ came into the world;
for you he lived and showed God's love;
for you he suffered death on the Cross;
for you he triumphed over death,
rising to newness of life;
for you he prays at God's right hand:
all this for you,
before you could know anything of it.
In your Baptism,
the word of Scripture is fulfilled:
'We love, because God first loved us.'

Provision is made for signing with the cross, and the giving of a lighted candle. The Aaronic blessing follows, and then parental promises. Confirmation comes next, but only for newly baptized *candidates* and any other candidates who have previously been baptized. Unlike the American rite, the rite for infant baptism in *The Methodist Worship Book* has no hand-laying for infants, and thus liturgically suggests that confirmation is necessary for full membership of the Methodist Church. A congregational welcome is included.

Baptist Traditions

Although the Baptist churches grew out of the radical Reformation and groups which rejected set forms of prayer, by the twentieth century some Baptist churches published manuals for ministers' optional use. Here we may briefly review the rites of believer's baptism in two of these books. The first is in *Orders and Prayers for Church Worship: A Manual for Ministers*, by two British Baptists, Ernest A. Payne and Stephen F. Winward, published in 1960, and adapted for use in the Southern Baptist Church in the USA in 1969. The rite is to be administered in the presence of the congregation during public worship, and it is desirable that the Lord's Supper follows the baptism. After a baptismal hymn the minister reads a selection of Scripture sentences relating to baptism, possibly concluding with Matthew 28:18–20. The minister then reads an exhortation, which is a summary of baptismal benefits: union with Christ, washing of sin, the gift of the Spirit and membership in the Church. It concludes with the assertion that baptism is:

> An act of obedience to the command of our Lord Jesus Christ:
> A following of the example of our Lord Jesus Christ who was baptized in the river Jordan, that he might fulfil all righteousness:
> A public confession of personal faith in Jesus Christ as Saviour and Lord:
> A vow or pledge of allegiance to Jesus Christ, an engagement to be his for ever.

The minister asks two questions about faith in Jesus Christ, to which the candidates reply 'I do.' A prayer follows, and then baptism with the formula:

> On thy profession of repentance toward God and faith in our Lord Jesus Christ, I baptize thee in the name of the Father and of the Son and of the Holy Spirit. Amen.

The Aaronic blessing follows, together with intercessions for the candidates, a hymn and a final blessing.

A Manual of Worship was produced by some ministers of the American Baptist Church, and published in 1993 by the Judson Press, Valley Forge. The opening rubrics are very similar to the 1960 rite, though they suggest that the baptism might take place at the offertory. Several passages of Scripture are read, and an exhortation explains the meaning of baptism. Those being baptized are asked to affirm their faith in Christ as Lord and Saviour. A prayer invoking the Spirit follows, and then the baptism with triune formula. A subsequent prayer asks the Spirit to 'baptize us afresh', and allows the congregation to renew their baptismal vows. Immediately after the baptismal rite, coming just prior to the Lord's Supper, is a rite for Commissioning those who have been baptized. In this rite, the ministers and lay people lay hands on the newly baptized.

The Baptist Union of Great Britain produced a new worship book for ministers in 1991, *Patterns and Prayers for Christian Worship*. That book is to be replaced by a new one in 2005.[53] The 1991 book set out two patterns, one within the Lord's Supper,

---

[53] My thanks to Dr Chris Ellis for supplying me with these drafts.

and one simply entitled 'Baptismal Service'. The textual provision included suitable sentences of Scripture, an opening statement, prayers, declaration of faith, the baptism with formulae, laying-on of hands, and reception into membership. In the drafts for the proposed 2005 book, the 'Welcoming in the Community of Disciples' begins with a discussion on the meaning of baptism, and suggests that instead of disputing whether it is a sacrament or not, three related questions should be asked: What does the new Christian do in the act of baptism? What does the Church do in the act of baptism? What does God do in the act of baptism?

These three questions pinpoint much of the recent discussion in British Baptist circles on the meaning of baptism. The document says:

> The rich meaning of baptism will be expressed through symbol, explanation and words or faith and prayer. But these layers of meaning will shape, as well as express, the faith and expectations of the congregation. Baptism has a significance beyond the service itself, and it addresses the faith of the congregation as well as the faith of those being baptized. Here may be embodied convictions about salvation, the nature of the Christian Church and the cost and glory of discipleship.[54]

The liturgical provisions include some Scripture readings, and an introduction. A prayer follows, which may be extempore, or use the form provided. It is similar to a Thanksgiving over the Water, and asks for the sending of the Spirit, 'that this baptism may be for your servant(s) a union with Christ in his death and resurrection, so that, as Christ was raised from death through the glory of the Father, *they* also might be raised to newness of life'. The petition is for the candidate(s), not for the element of water. The Declaration of Faith combines trinitarian belief with renunciation, and then the candidates are invited to give, in their own words, 'the story of God's call upon their lives'. As each candidate enters the baptismal pool, the minister greets him by name, and reads aloud a Scripture verse chosen for him. Two forms for the baptismal formula are given:

> … we have heard of your repentance and faith.
> I now baptize you, my *sister/brother*,
> in the name of God, the Father, the Son and the Holy Spirit. Amen.

Or:

Minister:	Christ is risen!
All:	He is risen indeed.
Candidate:	Jesus is Lord!
All:	Hallelujah!
Minister:	… you are called to be a disciple of Jesus Christ.
	I now baptize you in the name of God the Father,
	God the Son, and God the Holy Spirit.

After the baptized have dried themselves, the laying-on of hands and reception into the Church takes place. The congregation may say together a Covenant promise, and the baptizand is welcomed into the Church.

---

54 *Welcoming in the Community of Disciples*, Draft 1, courtesy Chris Ellis.

British Baptists have generally been divided on whether to admit people from other churches who had been baptized as infants and subsequently been confirmed. Some have accepted infant baptism as imperfect but valid, and others have regarded it as invalid. However, there has been a growing recognition that faith is a journey and entails growth, and so, although they do not baptize infants, provision is made for 'An Act of Presentation and Blessing with the Dedication of Parents'. The introduction notes:

> As we read scripture we are reminded that the emphasis of the gospels is not so much on what we can do, or promise to do, for children, as on what they can do for all of us. Jesus tells us that they are, for the church, a sign of the kingdom of God: a reminder that those who would seek to enter that kingdom must do so as little children. They are a gospel sign in the Christian community and their presentation before God provides an opportunity for this to be expressed and celebrated.

Here is a recognition that prevenient grace and human need for celebration of birth need some ritual expression, even if baptism is not the appropriate one.

From the Mennonite tradition in America came the publication in 1995, *Welcoming New Christians. A Guide for the Christian Initiation of Adults.*[55] This is a pastoral and practical guide rather than a liturgical book, though it contains sample rites. It has been influenced by the RCIA, and more directly by a presentation in June 1992 by Robert Webber on the second-century catechumenate. It presents four stages for an adult Christian initiation cycle: Stage One, invitation, which concludes with a service of welcome; Stage Two, inquiry and exploration, ending with a service of decision; Stage Three, preparation for baptism, concluding with the service of baptism, and Stage Four, post-baptism, which includes study and discussion, which might include a service of anointing and/or renewal of baptismal vows. It suggests that these be linked to the liturgical calendar, beginning with the welcome between Pentecost and Advent, and concluding after an Easter baptism with Stage Four in Pentecost. Three sample services of baptism are given. Sample Service 2 suggests an outline as follows.[56]

First, the use of visual arts might be encouraged – in this case, a grouping of white candles with different heights and thicknesses on the table in front of the worship space. The candidate is introduced to the congregation, and then there is a Scripture reading and some 'Special Music'. A congregational hymn follows, and the candidate's testimony, baptismal vows and baptism with the triune formula. The pastor prays for the anointing of the Spirit and lays hands on the candidate's head and prays. The candidate is greeted by the community, some of whom come to the table, take a candle, and form a semi-circle behind the candidate. This forms the ritual setting for a welcome and covenant into the community. The pastor may present the candidate with

---

[55] Jane Hoober Peifer and John Stahl-Wert, *Welcoming New Christians. A Guide for the Christian Initiation of Adults*, Faith and Life Press, Kansas and Mennonite Publishing House, Scottdale, PA, 1995.

[56] Ibid., pp. 77–8.

a ceramic oil lamp, symbolizing the eternal light of Jesus. In this collection of staged rites we find a church of the Radical Reformation appropriating elements from contemporary Roman Catholicism, from their understanding of early church practice, and using symbolism to enhance their ritual.

An Australian Ecumenical Rite

One fruit of the Faith and Order Movement and the ecumenical movement has been the amalgamation of certain churches. The Uniting Church in Australia was formed in June 1977, and was a union of Congregational, Methodist and Presbyterian Churches. *Uniting in Worship* was published in 1988, and an amended edition in 1997.[57] The rite of 'Baptism and the Reaffirmation of Baptism Called Confirmation' follows the Preaching of the Word. After the brief presentation and scriptural warrants, the minister reads a brief explanation of the meaning of baptism and confirmation. This is followed by the renunciations and creed. Two Thanksgivings over the Water are provided, both of which ask for blessing on the water. The baptism follows, with the minister signing the candidate with the sign of the cross, and declaring that the person is now received into the holy catholic church. The laying-on of hands with 'Responses' follow, the latter being promises of commitment. In the rite for infant baptism, prior to the baptism, a version of the French Reformed address to children is used (as in *CO* and the British Methodist rite, but it is in the 1988 version and so prior to both of these):

> Little child,
> for you Jesus Christ has come,
> has lived, has suffered;
> for you, he has endured the agony of Gethsemane
> and the darkness of Calvary;
> for you, he has uttered the cry, 'It is accomplished!'
>
> For you, he has triumphed over death;
> for you, he prays at God's right hand;
> all for you, little child,
> even though you do not know it.
> In baptism,
> the word of the apostle is fulfilled:
> 'We love, because God first loved us'.

Parental promises follow the baptism. Geraldine Wheeler explains:

> The shape and movement of the baptismal service, whether that of the adult or the child, express a Reformed emphasis more explicitly than the inherited

---

[57] For the background, see Geraldine Wheeler, 'Traditions and Principles of Reformed Worship in the Uniting Church in Australia', in Lukas Vischer (ed.), *Christian Worship in Reformed Churches Past and Present*, Eerdmans, Grand Rapids, MI, 2003, pp. 261–79.

Presbyterian and Congregational services. This is achieved by placing the words of repentance and confession of faith (individual and credal) before the baptism (or before the confirmation prayer with laying on of hands) but having the vows or promises following in order to show that baptism is not conditional upon these. Rather, they are a response to the love of God. The service of the baptism of a child includes a translation of the declaration from the French Reformed liturgy, 'Little child, for you Jesus Christ has come ...' a brilliant expression of God's grace preceding human response.[58]

Concluding Remarks

From this selection of more recent baptismal rites, a number of observations emerge. First, that the Roman Catholic Church's Vatican II revisions have been a catalyst amongst a good many churches, in recapturing the classical pattern of the fourth and fifth centuries, to give what James Kay has described as the harvest of the post-Vatican II ecumenical liturgical renewal movement pattern. This includes the reintroduction of a renunciation prior to the confession of faith. It is interesting that, just as at the Reformation when the Western Catholic baptismal rite was the parent rite of the Reformation Churches, so also in the twentieth century the new Roman rite has exerted a profound influence on many of the Reformation Churches.

Second, the Vatican II RCIA have also encouraged some other churches to reintroduce a catechumenate, or at least, staged rites of some sort; Christian Initiation is again seen as a process. Third, in paedobaptism churches there is a move to make the normative rite that of adult baptism, with infant baptism being a derivation from that norm. Fourth, in infant baptism, the involvement and commitment of the parents has been given new emphasis. However, this has resulted in two structures.

On the one hand, many churches have placed both parental and individual promises prior to the act of baptism, often calling this a baptismal covenant, yielding the pattern of contract/grace. Others have insisted that any promises or response should come after the baptism, and thus have the pattern grace/response. British Baptists have taken seriously the need to provide some liturgical rite for infants, even if it is not baptism. Fifth, baptism is seen as a congregational concern. It should take place within normal Sunday worship, and involve congregational commitments and welcome. Sixth, there is a shift from seeing baptism as merely salvation from something, to it being also salvation to something, namely being within the community of faith. Last, amongst Protestant Churches there is less anxiety about using older ceremonials such as oil, the sign of the cross, robing and giving of a lighted candle; symbols jettisoned at the Reformation have made a reappearance.

---

[58] Ibid., p. 273.

CHAPTER 8

Some Reflections on the Waters

This study began with the self-conscious and deliberate theological revisions of the Reformation, considered some contributions from Pietistic and Restorationist movements, and looked at modern twentieth-century self-conscious retrieval of older traditions and ceremonial. In *Early and Medieval Rituals and Theologies of Baptism*, I stated that both historically and theologically all baptismal rituals look back to the baptism of Jesus in the Jordan. In so far as that event, recorded in kerygmatic genre, crystallizes the whole salvific work of God in Christ both for, and in place of, humanity, it is foundational, and all liturgical rituals need to be grounded in that one baptism. Older rites seem to be a ritual unpacking of this event, with dipping (Christological), naming (trinitarian), and gestures to symbolize the descent of the Spirit (pneumatological) and adoption into an eschatological community (ecclesiological). Other rituals were added to express sin and repentance, coming to faith, being a new creation, or a resurrected being. Post-Reformation Protestant rites have tended to take up some of these themes – sin, forgiveness, new birth – but have concentrated them all into the ritual action in water, and relied on explication and paraphrase, the printed or spoken word, to 'fill out' the rest. This reliance on the read or spoken word has not been a great success. The New Testament gives a vast number of images and metaphors about baptism, and an attempt to cram all of these verbally into every baptismal rite is aurally overwhelming and unhelpful, and can lead to a liturgy that is visually and sensorily impoverished. While twentieth-century baptismal rites have not been a mere replication of fourth-century models, those models were certainly the tradition upon which many of them drew and from which they found their inspiration.

Drawing on older traditions is one way in which liturgical rites grow and mutate. At a recent symposium on sacramentality, Anne Loades said:

> Tradition should be seen as of its essence creative and innovative, mustering every grace of intelligence and skill in enabling us to learn from the past, generate critical dissonance with the present, open up new vistas and walkways, generate new insights, negotiate dead ends, endure experiences of profound alienation, and live with criteria which themselves may change, or if they remain more or less constant, will change in their application.[1]

Yet the anthropologist Roy Rappaport noted:

---

[1] Anne Loades, 'Finding new sense in the "Sacramental"', in Geoffrey Rowell and Christine Hall (eds), *The Gestures of God. Explorations in Sacramentality*, Continuum, New York, 2004, pp. 161–72, p. 164. These papers were originally given at a symposium on 'Sacraments and Sacramentality' held at St George's Chapel, Windsor, September 2003.

It may first be noted that the role of deliberate and calculated invention in the establishment of rituals, particularly religious rituals with which we will be almost exclusively concerned, is problematic and probably effectively limited. Conscious attempts are sometimes made to cut new rituals from whole cloth, but they are likely to strike those witnessing them to be forced or even false. Those present may fail to become performers or participants because they may not know what is expected of them, because the expectations of the inventors may not be in accord with the impulses of the potential performers or because they may be reluctant to undertake formal, stereotyped, solemn or, possibly, grotesque public behavior unless it is sanctioned by time and custom, that is to say, by previous performances. A ritual which has never been performed before may seem to those present not so much a ritual as a charade. Rituals composed entirely of new elements are, thus, likely to fail to become established (the test of establishment being that they be performed again on categorically similar occasions). Rituals composed entirely of new elements are, however, seldom if ever attempted. 'New' rituals are likely to be composed of elements taken from older rituals.[2]

Thus, in developing rituals, it is always a question of balance between the inherited ritual patterns and new developments. In the historical development of rites, the different place of anointing in the Eastern rites might be explained by different bathing etiquettes in the Mediterranean areas. In other words, rite was impacted by culture. As baptismal rites continue to develop and 'mutate', culture might well figure in such developments. By way of conclusion, I would like to offer reflections on three 'cultural' expressions.

Feminist Critique

In one sense feminist critique is cultural, and where it relates to a discussion on gender and language in the English-speaking world it becomes a parochial concern – often a North American parochial concern. The gender-neutral rite of the American UCC results in a bland, uninteresting rite. The rite authored by Rosemary Radford Ruether, 'Naming Celebration for a New Child; signing with the Promise of Baptism', uses candles, salt and oil, and the signing of a book as well as water. The texts however, are 'all about us' and the ritual seems to fall within Rappaport's strictures. Most alarming, however, is the fact that there is no indication that the presence of God is needed or even expected.[3]

Two rites of baptism are included in Ruth Duck's *Bread of Life*. The first, compiled by Mitzi Eilts, centres on the parents and congregation making covenants. It is devoid of Christological narrative, and uses Creator, Sustainer and Redeemer in place of the Matthean formula. The closing 'Benediction', 'Come with me, with us, into the soul

---

[2] Roy A. Rappaport, *Ritual and Religion in the Making of Humanity*, Cambridge University Press, Cambridge, 1999, p. 32.

[3] Rosemary Radford Ruether, *Women-Church. Theology and Practice of Feminist Liturgical Communities*, Harper and Row, San Francisco, CA, 1985, pp. 183–6.

of creation. The waters have opened and flow even now. New Life is ahead!' again sums up a service which is all about the community and a generic 'God' without history. The second rite, authored by two UCC ministers, is equally human centred, with thin prose and devoid of symbol.[4]

Ruth Duck and Patricia Wilson-Kastner provide a richer service in *Praising God. The Trinity in Christian Worship*. This rite includes use of water, candle and oil.[5] However, in common with the previous feminist rites mentioned, the whole interest is in avoiding 'patriarchal' words for God. None of these rites actually add anything of significance to baptism as sacramental event or foundational ritual, and are ultimately disappointing, muting baptism rather than attempting creatively to mutate and enrich the tradition. Susan Ross has argued for the need for a feminist perspective on sacraments and sacramental worship.[6] Her hope for extravagant affections is likely to be found, not in gender-neutral and emasculated language, but in the deep well of the traditions. Why not develop the rich womb/rebirth imagery of the Eastern rites which would so enrich Western rites, or the extravagant language of Zinzendorf with the Trinity as family? Tradition has much to inspire the imagination in more fruitful rituals that those which so far have emerged from feminist culture.

Non-Western Global Culture

Perhaps the most seminal thinking on cultural adaptation will come not from North Atlantic agendas at all, but from other cultures and ethnic groups. The Lutheran World Federation Chicago Statement on Worship and Culture said:

> The traditional 'explanatory symbols' of Baptism may need to be replaced, by the means of dynamic equivalence, or reinforced, by the means of creative assimilation, so that the power of the water-bath may be more clearly perceived in local context. Each local church will need to ask: what local symbols may express the gift of the Spirit, the adoption of a new identity, baptismal dignity and vocation, death and resurrection, and the unity of the community, and do so without obscuring the central importance of the water and the Word? The 'explanatory symbols' should never overshadow the water-bath itself.[7]

Elisha Mbonigaba of Uganda noted that across Africa there are various rituals and ceremonies in connection with pregnancy, childbirth, naming, weaning and initiation, all of which intend to incorporate and integrate the child and the young adult into the

---

4 Ruth Duck (ed.), *Bread for the Journey. Resources for Worship*, The Pilgrim Press, New York, 1981, pp. 6–8.

5 Ruth Duck and Patricia Wilson-Kastner, *Praising God. The Trinity in Christian Worship*, Westminster John Knox Press, Louisville, KY, 1999, pp. 148–53.

6 Susan Ross, *Extravagant Affections. A Feminist Sacramental Theology,* Continuum, New York, 1998.

7 S. Anita Stauffer (ed.), *Baptism, Rites of Passage, and Culture*, Lutheran World Federation Studies, Geneva, 1998, p. 18.

community – a series of staged rites, in fact.[8] He urged that some of these might be adapted and incorporated into the rite of baptism, particularly the important giving of a name. F. Kabasele Lumbala describes a rite of adult baptism in Zaire, where the renunciation entails the baptizand lying down on a mat and being covered with banana leaves while a song of penitence or mourning is struck up. During the baptism, incense is wafted around. An elaborate conferring of the name takes place, and the godfather may give an instrument of trade. The candidate is anointed with oil, and then kaolin. In the rite of infant baptism Lumbala explains:

> It should be noted that this white kaolin rite has replaced the lit candle and the white garment. This colour is most meaningful in our Bantu traditions. Here it evokes the crossing of a vital threshold, a personal maturity, as well as assuming a role in society. That is why it is given to the newly initiated, the newborn children during the rites of restoring harmony. It is also given to chiefs who make an official sortie to exercise their duties. All these meanings totally cover the symbolism of the lit candle and the white garment of the official ritual.[9]

Francis Wickremesinghe has described an experiment of the Christian Workers' fellowship in Sri Lanka, where Muslims and Buddhists, who make up the majority religions, are given a part in the rite symbolizing Jesus's identification with the majority of common people.[10] The rite includes a pre-baptismal ceremony of striking each candidate with an ekel (cane) and breathing on their faces. A prayer says:

> … all blessings from the Ultimate Reality who said 'I am who I am' be with you. May Jesus Christ, the Anointed One who liberates us, protect you from every kind of evil, keep you free from every blind fantasy of mind and will, and bring you from darkness into light. And may the Holy Spirit who sanctifies us dwell in your body and give you good health and the power to avoid all sin, that you may be well and happy. Just as the rivers swollen with rain flow into the sea and fill it, may you be filled with the plentiful grace of the Holy Trinity.[11]

The signing of the cross on the forehead may be made with a paste of sandalwood and salt, and the infant might be given a ginger (palm) oil bath. The blessing of the water alludes to the national 'water-cutting ceremony', giving it a Christian interpretation, 'the water cutting for cleansing and rain'. Threefold immersion or pouring of water is used, and a lock of hair is cut from the crown of the head – a traditional custom at the first visit of an infant to a religious place. A white garment and lighted earthenware lamp are given to the newly baptized.

---

[8] Elisha Mbonigaba, 'Indigenization of the Liturgy,' in Thomas J. Talley (ed.), *A Kingdom of Priests: Liturgical Formation of the People of God*, Alcuin/GROW Liturgical Study 5, Grove Books, Nottingham, 1988, pp. 39–47, p. 44.

[9] F. Kabasele Lumbala, 'Black Africa and Baptismal Rites', in Thomas F. Best and Dagmar Heller (eds), *Becoming a Christian. The Ecumenical Implications of our Common Baptism*, WCC Publications, Geneva, 1999, pp. 36–40.

[10] Francis Wickremesinghe, 'An Asian Inculturation of the Baptismal Liturgy', in David R. Holeton (ed.), *Growing in Newness of Life*, Anglican Book Centre, Toronto, 1993, pp. 213–17.

[11] Ibid., p. 214.

The ELCA 1999 *This Far by Faith* liturgy for African–American congregations includes provision at baptism for the giving of salt, a garment of naturally coloured fabric or a band of kente, and a bangle to be placed on the wrist. Thus it may be that non-Western cultures may lead the way in weaving some of their deep cultural symbols and customs to the ritual of baptism.

Postmodern Culture

We have already encountered this slippery term in the previous chapter. It is typified by global corporations, reality TV, digital special effects, the internet and virtual reality, simulacra and simulations, with an increased emphasis on individual self-fulfilment, and a free market represented by the shopping mall. According to David Lyon, the Disney Corporation theme parks portray much of postmodernity:

> The Magic Kingdom is all about fantasy, illusion, slippery surfaces, revised realities, multiple meanings. It is also centered on play and the pleasure principle … In the pastiche style that unblushingly mixes disparate images and experiences, Disneyland epitomizes the postmodern. The simulated nations of the world – Canadian Mounties, British Beefeaters, Japanese *samurai* – meet in one place. Like zapping with the remote, to visit Disneyland is to walk through a TV set. Different epochs and cultures jostle together, mocking the old distinctions of time and space.[12]

Indeed, in Disneyworld there are castles and houses which are not castles or houses, and a steam locomotive which emits steam, but has no fire. Reality is simulated. It provides fun and entertainment, but is not real. In this context the BBC report of the 'christening' arranged by the soccer star David Beckham and his wife Victoria (formerly of the Spice Girls pop group) for their two children seems to suggest an event straight from this culture of virtual reality:

> David and Victoria Beckham have hosted a star-studded christening for sons Romeo and Brooklyn, with Elton John heading the guest list. A private chapel was constructed for the occasion in the grounds of the family's Hertfordshire mansion. Former Spice Girls Emma Bunton, Geri Halliwell and Melanie Chisholm were all seen entering the estate. It was rumoured the bash would see a reunion of all five group members, but 'Scary Spice' Mel B did not attend. The Beckhams were believed to have chosen Sir Elton John and his partner, David Furnish, as godparents to Brooklyn, five, and two-year-old Romeo. Sir Elton arrived for the black-tie affair in a silver Rolls Royce. Other guests at the lavish ceremony included Liz Hurley and her boyfriend Arun Nayar, as well as Greg and Lucy Rusedski and David's former Manchester United team-mate Gary Neville. Stars to receive invitations included Hollywood actor Tom Cruise, Wayne Rooney and Coleen McLoughlin, along with Sven Goran Eriksson and Nancy Dell'Olio. The rest of the guest list consisted of close friends and family, including

---

12 David Lyon, *Jesus in Disneyland. Religion in Postmodern Times*, Polity Press, Cambridge, 2000, p. 11.

the Beckhams' parents and siblings. Earlier on Thursday afternoon David Beckham's mother Sandra drove to the couple's home near Sawbridgeworth, closely followed by Victoria's parents, Tony and Jackie, and then her sister, Louise. Victoria, who is expecting her third child in March, is understood to have planned the ceremony. Although Brooklyn and Romeo were to have a traditional Christian ceremony, the chapel appears to have two Buddhist shrines at its entrance. The couple have flirted with different religions and earlier this year Victoria was spotted wearing a red Kabbalah bracelet. After Brooklyn's birth, David remarked: 'I definitely want Brooklyn to be christened, but I don't know into what religion yet.'[13]

According to a Reuters report, to the suggestion that a six-meal course was to be served at a cost of £2,500 per person, Beckham replied, 'It will be much more than that.'[14] There was also mystery over the rite. According to the *Mail on Sunday*, the Rt Reverend Paul Colton, Bishop of Cork, who had presided at the wedding of the couple, officiated – a report the bishop quickly denied.[15] The Vicar of Sawbridgeworth noted that the chapel was not consecrated, had no baptismal register, and that no local clergy had been invited to officiate. No minister has so far owned up to officiating at the christening, and thus it remains unclear what this 'christening' was. The setting in a specially constructed chapel with Buddhist shrines, which has no congregation or regular worship, and a collection of famous guests but no obvious Christian congregation, together with the ambiguity of the rite actually performed, and by whom, suggest a simulacrum; the event would not have been out of place in the Magic Kingdom of Disney or any other make-believe theme park. The lavish economic context of this 'christening' places it mockingly (even if with the best of uninformed intentions) as far away as is humanly possible from the meaning of Christian baptism.

If there are problems for the Christian faith in a postmodern culture where spiritualities compete as stores in a shopping mall, and where do-it-yourself religion is in vogue, there are also aspects of the culture which seem to benefit Christian faith and its rituals. Carol Wade identifies the implications:

> Beginning roughly with people born in the late 1940s and continuing with every subsequent generation in ever increasing speed, print as the metaphor of choice is being supplanted by visual image, story and symbol as our chief means to receive and process information, to experience and construct meaning, to convey emotion and communicate.[16]

As George Lakoff and Mark Johnson have pointed out in their book, *Philosophy in the Flesh:The Embodied Mind and Its Challenge to Western Thought,* reason is not completely conscious, but mostly unconscious; it is not purely literal, but largely

---

[13] <http://news.bbc.co.uk/l/hi/uk/4120477.stm>

[14] <http://dailytelegraph.news.com.au>

[15] *The Mail on Sunday*, 26 December 2004, p. 3. 'Beckham christening is invalid, says their vicar' – though that is not what the vicar actually said.

[16] Carol L. Wade, 'Stories of Resurrection: Traces of God in New Community', STM Thesis. Yale Institute of Sacred Music and Yale Divinity School, 2004.

metaphorical and imaginative; it is not dispassionate, but emotionally engaged.[17] Thus image, symbol and imagination are once more becoming crucial in how we express ourselves, and words and reasoned argument become less important.

Stanley Hauerwas suggested that in sacraments – and in baptism in particular – we are taken up into Christ's story; or, to use T.F. Torrance's terms, we are baptized into the one vicarious baptism of Christ. This does not mean that our stories are unimportant. We join our journey of faith to the objective faith of the Church in the recitation of the Creed, which is found in most rites. But there should be room for a more personal story because in the context of baptism, personal testimony or personal story is important. Richard Bowers, who has Down's Syndrome, was baptized at the Central Baptist Church in Bloomsbury, London in March 1990. He later gave this account:

> Bloomsbury Central Baptist Church is a very nice place. I was baptized there four years ago, when I became like a Christian. My family all came to the worship of the church. Howard Williams and Barbara and Maurice Johns were there. I wore special clothes – white shirt and cream trousers and just feet. Maurice Johns led Barbara into the water – it was open. Then he took me to the baptismal water. I go down the steps. Barbara was preaching. My hands together on my tummy. Barbara said: 'Father, Son and Holy Spirit take me' and I was baptized. Barbara tip me over under water. My brother came in the water and helped me, wrapped me up to keep me warm. I changed my clothes. Afterwards all my family in the porch in the front of the church – my father took photographs. Then we come back downstairs and everyone helped celebrate me – with nice cards and presents. I am a member of the church. I like the communion service. I wear a little cross to show I am a Christian.[18]

In an Anglican context, but in a swimming pool in South America, Caroline Goodman tells her story (see also Fig. 8.1):

> I have believed in God all my life, but it was not until December 1999, a few years after making a decision to follow Him, that I decided to formalise my commitment by getting baptised. At the time, I was on my third year abroad as part of my University course in Brazil.
>
> I had joined the Anglican church in Rio de Janeiro and felt that it was as good a time as any (not to mention a fantastic location!) to make public my commitment of faith. I wanted to make a declaration that really demonstrated that I was taking my decision to follow Jesus seriously.
>
> It has always seemed to me that as an adult baptism is such a symbolic act: to have one's sins washed away and to be washed clean, born a new creation by God's grace. So I wanted to make sure that it was a memorable occasion. Originally I had wanted to get baptised in the sea at Copacobana beach, but was advised against it as there were too many dangerous items floating in the waters! So instead myself and another girl, Ana, went to a swimming pool, in a church

---

[17] George Lakoff and Mark Johnson, *Philosophy in the Flesh: The Embodied Mind and Its Challenge to Western Thought,* Basic Books, New York, 1999, p. 4.

[18] Cited by Roger Hayden, 'Believers Baptized: An Anthology', in Fiddes, *Reflections on the Water. Understanding God and the World through the Baptism of Believers,* pp. 9–21, p. 17.

Figure 8.1   Baptism of Caroline Goodman in Niteroi, Brazil, 2 January 2000

member's garden. Ana's mother had recently been to Israel and brought back some water from the River Jordan, so after the official dunking we were sprinkled with that as well! It was rather amusing to see the vicar swim across the pool, fully robed! After the prayers and service we sang some hymns and worship songs.

I was pleased that I'd decided to get baptised where I did, although many of the people who have encouraged me in my faith were not there (most are from the UK). This was possibly the only missing ingredient in the whole ceremony. However, ultimately my baptism was a declaration between myself, God and His people, the church. God's family exists all over the world, which is one of the most wonderful things about it. We belong, wherever we are, amongst fellow-believers and being baptised was a public demonstration of my commitment to this family.[19]

Those recent rites which, following the tradition in Believer's Baptism churches, allow a place for a testimony or personal story are to be commended.

Adults are able to articulate something of their narrative, tying it to the central narrative of God in Christ, even if not always in the context of the ritual performance itself. At present, however, most baptisms are still of infants. What of their story? Though infants who are baptized may have no such personal narrative themselves, those who bring them for baptism do have their own stories. In his book *Only Connect*,

---

[19] Email to the writer, 5 September 2004.

Robin Green gives this scenario between a single parent, Diane, and Mary, a Methodist minister:

Diane: I've come to see if you'll do my baby.

Mary: Do your baby, Diane? Tell me more.

Diane: Well, you see, I took him to this Church of England vicar up the road. He wanted to know if I believed in Jesus as my Saviour and who the godparents were to be … oh. He called them something like sponsors … and what did they believe and did they go to church regular … Christ, the kid ain't got a father let alone sponsors!

Mary: It sounds as if you're under a lot of pressure, Diane.

Diane: You can say that again. You see, my mum insists that I get 'im done. Well, that's fine. I agree he ought to be done, but that vicar said we'd have to go at 9.30 in the morning … oh, I bet they're a really snotty crowd up there. I don't want to go and be looked down on.

Mary: Are you feeling a bit guilty about … what's his name?

Diane: Oh, it's Jimmy … at least it will be when you've given 'im a name.

Mary: You say you agree with your mum that Jimmy should be baptised.

Diane: Well, I think so. It's a sort of feeling right down inside me … (*She bursts into tears*). Oh, God, it's all too much … I don't know how I'm going to cope … please, please. I just want 'im done. I don't want all this trouble. Please do 'im … please.

(*Silence as Diane continues to cry.*)

Mary: It feels to me as though there is a great big struggle going on inside you. The struggle seems to overwhelm you.

Diane: (*still crying*): Oh, I don't know what it is. The other night …

Mary: Uhm?

Diane: The other night I just shook 'im … and shook 'im … then I thought I was looking into this dark hole …

Mary: That must have been really terrifying.[20]

This is not the story of articulate theological discourse or spiritual reflection, but a *cri de coeur* that this ritual washing might bring some good in what otherwise appears to be a desperate narrative. Even this is an expression of faith of some sort, and in Hoffman's terms, an important ingredient of the meaning of baptism. We should ask whether such a place should be provided (but not mandated) for parents to tell some of their story. It is not that parents should be made to feel embarrassed, but perhaps they should be given an opportunity within the service to say what their hopes are for their child in baptism. 'Diane' might not want to blurt out her difficult story in public, but with 'Mary's' help, she might want to say something, however brief, about her hopes for her child.

This story/testimony, however, needs to be separated from questions about promises and undertakings. We have noted how, in modern twentieth-century liturgies, those rites which have tried to adapt the older renunciations to a modern setting of infant baptism, have developed a series of questions and undertakings for parents to answer,

---

[20] Robin Green, *Only Connect. Worship and Liturgy from the Perspective of Pastoral Care*, Darton, Longman and Todd, London, 1987, pp. 51–2.

even calling this a, or 'the' Baptismal Covenant, and placing it prior to the baptism. The pastoral intentions are good, but, it has been suggested, this smacks too much of a contractual arrangement, with a liturgical sequence of conditions/grace. Other churches have seen the Pelagian danger here, and have either toned these down, or placed such questions after the baptism, to give a liturgical sequence of grace/response. Theologically the second is preferable. Some churches have used the formula from the French Reformed 1940 rite to express that we – whoever we are – love God because he *first* loved us before we knew it. Yet churches which baptize infants need to avoid the idea that baptism is simply some informal religious birth rite. Joseph D. Small writes:

> In typical baptismal services, everything focuses on celebrating the incorporation of an infant into the life of the congregation. While the words of Scripture and prayers may describe a broader, deeper reality, the action itself narrows the sacrament to only one aspect of its significance. The folksy demeanor of the pastor, introductions of the family and friends, a hasty recital of brief readings and prayers, the minimal sight and sound of water, reminders of church programs, and the leisurely stroll through the congregation all combine to collapse meaning into the reception of a singular child into a particular congregation.
>
> Baptism is the sacrament of welcome into the community of believers, of course. But it is not only that … baptism is a sign of the fullness of God's gracious love and effectual calling that, in one moment, is poured over a single human being. The moment is not isolated, however, as a point in time that recedes into distant memory. Baptism is the sure promise of God's continuing faithfulness, inaugurating new life within God's Way … How can our baptismal *practice* begin to open us to the flood of significance for our very being as humans together before God? … How can an unabridged sacramental theology, expressed in rich liturgical texts, be incorporated in faithful sacramental practice?[21]

Perhaps the implications are that, when words are used (and they cannot be avoided), more attention is needed to words which *resonate* rather than words which summarize doctrine, and to including suitable hymns and music, which so often are an afterthought in services of baptism. Movement from one space to another within the rite may also help to symbolize that this is part of an ongoing journey in faith. In this context, Carol Wade has explored a post-baptismal catechesis or mystagogy, using story, drama, dance and art – inspired from medieval liturgical drama.[22] Personal story is enmeshed with image and symbol.

We have noted that many Churches of the Reformation tradition are reappropriating some of the secondary symbolism which gives expression to the fullness of baptism beyond mere words. Churches reluctant to compromise their Protestant suspicion of additional ceremonies (*adiaphora*) may well find themselves both culturally adrift and with impoverished rites. The permissible use of oil and candles, and the

---

[21] Joseph D. Small, 'A Church of the Word and Sacrament', in Lukas Vischer (ed.), *Christian Worship in Reformed Churches Past and Present*, Eerdmans, Grand Rapids, MI, 2003, pp. 311–23, pp. 318–19.

[22] Wade, 'Stories of resurrection'. It was presented at the Yale Institute of Sacred Music, and subsequently at a seminar on liturgy and postmodernism at Calvin College, Grand Rapids.

reintroduction of a white robe or putting-on clothing at the baptism can all be useful. It is true that, with the fourth-century compiler of the *Apostolic Constitutions*, we can agree that all that is needed in baptism is water, but that minimum does not prevent churches from unpacking the meaning of baptism by retrieving and extending secondary symbolism.

However, one important challenge is for churches to maximize the primary symbol of baptism, namely the water. The Northern European climate in ages before central heating resulted in dipping to avoid risk of cold to infants. This later became an excuse to argue about the minimal amount of water for validity. In those churches which have fonts for infant baptism, the font is often so small as to preclude dipping an infant in the water. Often the baptistery area is dull and without ornamentation, or tucked with pews, or so small as to be unnoticeable. It is little wonder that baptism has been undervalued if its symbolism and place of celebration is muted.

Congregations can raise huge amounts for the decoration of the sanctuary, and to provide stained-glass windows, but seem to show less enthusiasm for a baptistery.

Figure 8.2   The Revd Dr Bryan Spinks baptizing Alexander Irving at St Mary's Church, Eaton Socon, Cambridgeshire, 20 June 1993

Perhaps it is because the baptistery will always be for others, 'outsiders', and never themselves. But if baptism is an important ritual, then the place where the ritual is carried out needs to be seen as important. There is no excuse for not stripping and dipping babies (bathing them in warmed water, not submerging them). See Figure 8.2.

Churches which practice Believer's baptism are also often negligent. The sunken font/tank is covered over, or out of sight. There may be a safety element, but there should be some indication of the presence of the font/tank, for even when it is not in use it speaks volumes about the importance of the rite. The placing of banners or candles around the place of baptism at least marks it out as a focal point of ecclesial activity. All the exotic liturgies in the world, and all the fine words of theologians are useless if churches do not physically proclaim through their worship space and practice the importance of this ritual.

The New Testament gives a vast number of images and metaphors about baptism, and an attempt to cram all these into every baptismal ritual is likely to be overwhelming and unhelpful. *Common Worship 2000* of the Church of England and the proposed ELCA rites may suggest one way of handling this – to have special propers and prayers over the water for different seasons of the year, in order to bring home and reinforce the multi-layered significance of baptism. Thus at Epiphany new birth/womb imagery, and at Easter paschal imagery, but other emphases at other times of the liturgical year. These can be reinforced with different banners, icons, paintings or projected images on baptistery walls for the appropriate season.

Concluding Remarks

Lars Hartmann commented that baptism is the door into a new community.[23] But this community is on a journey to a promised land. The ritual of baptism expresses some dimensions of the journey – rebirth, and from death to life. It is a journey with the risen Lord Jesus Christ, which he begun in the incarnation, but publicly launched at his baptism in the Jordan and concluded in the *baptisma* on the Cross, and beyond in eternity. In the ritual of baptism we are called to follow over the Jordan and beyond; in the words of the American folk-hymn:

> I'm just a poor wayfaring stranger
> Travelling through this world of woe
> But there's no sickness, toil or danger
> In that bright land to which I go.

> Well I'm going there to meet my mother
> Said she'd meet me when I come
> I'm only going over Jordan
> I'm only going over home.

---

[23] Hartmann, *Into the Name of the Lord Jesus*, p. 46.

I know dark clouds will gather 'round me
I know my way will be rough and steep
But beautiful fields lie just before me
Where God's redeemed their vigils keep.

Well I'm going there to meet my loved ones
Gone on before me, one by one
I'm only going over Jordan
I'm only going over home.

I'll soon be free of earthly trials
My body rest in the old church yard
I'll drop this cross of self-denial
And I'll go singing home to God.

Well I'm going there to meet my Saviour
Dwell with Him and never roam
I'm only going over Jordan
I'm only going over home.

The ritual of baptism is always a step in 'going over Jordan', and the beginning of a journey home.

The Liturgy or Manner of Celebrating Divine Service in the Church of Geneva, 1743

THE LITURGY OF BAPTISM

May our help be in the name of GOD, who made Heaven and Earth. Amen.

The Minister, addressing the Father and Godfather, says to them:
Do you present this Child to be baptised?

Answer: Yes.

Our LORD teaches us that we must be born anew if we wish to enter the Kingdom of GOD. This means that there must be a great change within us when we enter into Communion with our Saviour and become members of His Church. We must renounce all that is impure and vice-ridden within us, and consecrate ourselves to GOD by sincere and constant application to all pious, temperate, and righteous duties. If by this process we do not become new men, then we shall not know how to partake of Christianity's advantages, in particular, the glory of GOD's Kingdom. This change is represented to us in a tangible manner through the ceremony of Baptism. Just as water cleanses the impurities from our bodies, so do we find in our Saviour's Communion everything necessary to cleanse our souls of their stains. We also learn that, as GOD bestows upon us His Grace (by pardoning our sins) and Spirit's aid (by receiving us into his Covenant), so also must we, for our part, purify ourselves from all blemishes of body and spirit and perfect our holiness in the fear of GOD.

In days gone by, baptism was performed by plunging the entire body in water and then pulling it out soon afterward. On this practice, Saint Paul draws our attention to the fine symbol of our Lord's Death and Resurrection. Similarly, we must die to sin by renouncing it entirely and live a new life that is totally pure, holy, and conforming to the spirit of JESUS CHRIST and to the Laws of His Gospel.

Such are the great and sacred agreements into which we enter through Baptism. We make these promises on behalf of our Children, as best we can, when we consecrate them to GOD through this holy ceremony and present them to Him in His Church. And when they themselves come to the age of Reason, they will be obliged to fulfill these promises if they wish to partake in the blessings of GOD's Covenant, which is destined only to true Believers.

For his part, GOD – who extends His blessings to both Children and Fathers, and who had in bygone days wished that Children be dedicated to Him through Circumcision – can only look with a favorable eye upon those offered to Him through

Baptism. Nor is our Saviour (who so willingly received little Children presented to Him, laying hands upon them and recommending them to God, His Father) any less disposed to receive and bless those presented to Him in His Church.

And so, MY BROTHERS, let us all join together to consecrate this Child to GOD and commend him to His grace by our Prayer.

LORD GOD, Eternal Father, since it has pleased you, in your infinite goodness, to promise us that you will be our GOD and the GOD of our Children, we beseech you to fulfill this promise in the child here present, born of a Father and a Mother whom you have received into your Church. We offer him to you, we consecrate him to you, O our GOD. Grant him your protection and receive him into your holy Convenant. And since all the Descendants of Adam are in a state of corruption and adversity, may it please you to proclaim yourself the GOD and Saviour of this Child and sanctify him by your Spirit, so that, when it reaches the age of Reason, he will adore you as his only GOD. Being in fellowship with your Son, may he receive all of the graces that you have promised us in your Gospel. May he be cleansed of his sins, may he become a new Creature formed in your image, in holiness and righteousness, and may he partake of the heavenly heritage that you destine for your Children. Grant us, Father of mercy. We ask you in the Name of your Son, JESUS-CHRIST, our Lord, Amen.

After this Prayer, the Minister thus addresses those presenting the Child:

By presenting this Child to be received into the Church of GOD you are promising to undertake, as he grows, his instruction in the Christian Doctrine that GOD has revealed to us in the Sacred Books of the Old and New Testaments, and which we have summarised in the Confession of Faith, which begins thusly: I believe in God, etc. You are also committing him to live according to the rule that the LORD has given in his Law, which refers to these two general duties: to love GOD with all our heart and to love our neighbor as ourselves. In so doing, may this Child renounce himself and his evil desires to consecrate himself entirely to GOD, and by strengthening the Church, may he advance his own salvation, through our Saviour, JESUS-CHRIST.

Is this not what you are promising?
The Father and Godfather reply: Yes:

The Minister says:
May GOD grant you the grace to fulfill your promise.

Then the Minister comes down from the Pulpit, pours water upon the Child, and pronouncing his name, says:

N.N. I baptise you in the Name of the Father, of the Son, and of the Holy Spirit. Amen.

Liturgic Hymns of the United Brethren, Revised and Enlarged, 1770; Translated From the German, London, 1793

LITURGIES AT BAPTISM

A. OF CHILDREN

(After the singing of some suitable verses and short discourse.)

T.539.a.

L. Christ thou Lamb of God, which takest away
    the sin of the world,
C. Leave thy peace with us, Amen.

L. With thy holy Sacraments,
A. Bless us, gracious Lord and God!

T.96.

C. An infant, Lord, we bring to thee,
    As thy redeemed property,
    And thee especially intreat,
    Thyself this child to consecrate
    By baptism, and it's soul to bless
    Out of the fullness of thy grace.

L. What is baptism?
Children. The answer of a good conscience towards God, the washing of
    regeneration and renewing of the Holy Ghost, which is shed on us
    abundantly thro' Jesus Christ our Savior.

T.201.

C. The eye sees water, nothing more,
    How it is poured out by men;
    But faith alone conceives the pow'r
    Of Jesu's blood, to make us clean;
    Faith sees it as a cleansing flood,
    Replete with Jesu's blood and grace,

Which heals each wound, and makes all good,
What Adam brought on us, his race,
And all, that we ourselves have done.

L.   May children also be made partakers of this grace?

Children.   Yes

L.   What is the ground of this hope?

Children.   The words of Christ: Suffer little children to come unto me,
            and forbid them not, for of such is the kingdom of Heaven.

[*Then the child which is to be baptized, is brought in, and the minister offers up a prayer in it's behalf; instead of which, also a suitable verse may be sung; for instance*:]

T.14.a.

L.   Be present with us, Lord our God,
      This water can't make us clean,
      But whilst we pour it, cleanse by blood
      This infant from all sin.

Question: Ye, who are baptized into Christ Jesus, how were ye baptized?

Answer: Into his death.

L.   Into the death of Jesus I baptize thee N.N. in the name of the Father, and of the
      Son, and of the Holy Ghost.

[*During the imposition of hands the minister continues*:]

Thus art thou now buried with him by baptism into his death,

A.   In the name of Jesus, Amen.

Sung.   His death and passion ever,
         Till soul and body sever,
         Shall in thy heart engrav'd remain.

L.   Now therefore live, yet not thou, but Christ live in thee. And the life, which
      thou now livest in the flesh, live by the faith of the Son of God, who loved
      thee and gave himself for thee.

T.132.a.2d p.

Sung.   This grant according to thy word,
         Thro' Jesus Christ, our only Lord,
         God, Father, Son and Spirit.

L.   The Lord bless thee and keep thee!
      The Lord make his face to shine upon thee, and be gracious unto thee!
      The Lord lift up his countenance upon thee, and give thee peace!

A.   Amen.

The Liturgy of the New Church, Signified by the New Jerusalem in the Revelation: Third Edition, Printed by R. Hindmarsh, 1790

The FORM of the Administration of Baptism to Infants in the New Church.

A Bason of pure Water being placed on the Table, and the Child to be baptized being present, the Minister is to begin with the Lord's Prayer.

Our Father who art in the Heavens; Hallowed be thy Name. Thy Kingdom come. Thy Will be done, as in Heaven, so also upon Earth. Give us this Day our daily Bread. And forgive us our Debts, as we also forgive our Debtors. And lead us not into Temptation, but deliver us from Evil: For thine is the Kingdom, and the Power, and the Glory, for Ages. Amen.

Then the Minister is to read as follows.

Forasmuch as the Order, wherein Man was originally created, has been perverted and destroyed by the Abuse of his Free-Will, and in Consequence thereof we are all born in the Love of Self and of the World; and since no one can enter into the Kingdom of God, except he be regenerate, and born again of Water and of the Spirit, that is, by the Truths of Faith, and a Life in Conformity to them; therefore Baptism was instituted by the Lord as a Sign and Memorial that Man may be purified from his Evils and Falses, and thereby become regenerate. Thus the Lord was pleased to suffer himself to be baptized by John, in Token that his HUMANITY was to be GLORIFIED, for hereby was all righteousness fulfilled in his own Divine Person.

By the Waters of Baptism are also signified Temptations, or spiritual Conflicts against Evils and Falses; for Purification and Regeneration can only be effected by Means of Temptations. And inasmuch as Baptism is for a Sign and Memorial of such Things, therefore it may lawfully be administered to Infants, or if neglected at that Age, to Adults.

The first Use of Baptism is Introduction into the Christian Church, and Insertion at the same Time amongst Christians in the Spiritual World. Baptism itself, however, is only a Sign of Introduction into the Church, as is evident from the Baptizing of Infants, before they come to the use of Reason, and consequently before they are capable of receiving any Thing relating to Faith. Yet this Sign is perceived in the

Christian Heaven, and thereupon Guardian-Angels are appointed over them by the Lord to take Care of them; wherefore as soon as Infants are baptized, they are placed under the Care of Guardian-Angels, by whom they are kept in a State of receiving Faith in the Lord; and as they grow up, and become capable of thinking and acting for themselves, they draw into Association with them such Spirits as make one with their Life and Faith. Hence it is evident, that Baptism is an Insertion amongst Christians, even in the Spiritual World; and that the Person baptized afterwards becomes associated with the Spirits of this or that Society, according to the Quality of his Life and Faith.

The second Use of Baptism is, that the Person baptized may know and acknowledge the Lord and Saviour Jesus Christ, and follow him. This Acknowledgement consists in a firm Belief that He is the Only God of Heaven and Earth, the Creator, Redeemer, and Regenerator; that in Him there is a Divine Trinity, consisting of Father, Son, and Holy Spirit, like Soul, Body, and Operation in Man; and also in a Life of Obedience to his Commandments.

The third and final Use of Baptism is, that Man may be regenerated; in which Case he is baptized with the Holy Spirit or with Fire; that is, he is admitted into Association either with the Angels of the Lord's spiritual Kingdom, or with those of his celestial Kingdom; and after Death he himself becometh either a spiritual or a celestial Angel.

Now, whereas these three Uses follow each other in Order, and join with each other in the ultimate or last Use, and consequently in the Idea of Angels cohere together as one, therefore whensoever Baptism is performed, or read in the Word, or named, the Angels who are present do not understand Baptism, but Regeneration. Wherefore by these Words of the Lord, 'Whosoever believeth, and is baptized, shall be saved,' is understood by the Angels in Heaven, that whosoever acknowledgeth the Lord, and is regenerated, will be saved. Be it known therefore to every Christian, that whosoever doth not believe on the Lord, and keep his Commandments, cannot be regenerated, notwithstanding his having been baptized; and that being baptized, without Faith in the Lord, is of no Avail; for Baptism itself neither giveth Faith, nor Salvation, but is a Testimony to such as are baptized, that they may be saved, if they are regenerate.

After which the Minister is to say,

Let us pray.
Almighty and everlasting Lord, our heavenly Father, who dost invite little Children to be brought unto thee, that they may receive thy Blessing, and be made Partakers of thy eternal Kingdom, we beseech thee favourably to receive *this Infant* now presented before thee; admit *him* into the Fellowship and Communion of thy New Church, embrace *him* with the Arms of thy Divine Mercy, and give thy Holy Spirit unto *him*; that being enrolled by Baptism among the Number of those who acknowledge the DIVINITY of thy HUMANITY, and who rejoice in the Glory of thy Second Advent; *he* may hereafter deny *himself,* and take up *his* Cross by resisting the Loves of Self and of the World, and finally through thy Assistance overcome all the Powers of Darkness. Amen.

Then the Minister shall say to the Parents or Friends of the Child,

Ye have brought *this Child* here to be baptized in the Faith of the New Heaven and New Church.

Let me ask therefore,
Dost thou believe, that God is One both in Essence and in Person, in whom is a Divine Trinity, consisting of Father, Son, and Holy Spirit; and that the Lord and Saviour Jesus Christ is He?

Answer.   I do.
Minister.   Dost thou believe, that in Order to Salvation Man must live a Life according to the Ten Commandments, by shunning Evils as Sins against God?
Answer.   I do.
Minister.   Art thou desirous to have *this Child* baptized in this Faith?
Answer.   I am.

Then the Minister is to pray as follows.

O MERCIFUL Lord Jesus, who didst give Commandment to thy Disciples that they should go and teach all Nations, baptizing them in the Name of the Father, and of the Son, and of the Holy Spirit; and didst also promise to be with them until the Consummation of the Age; thereby instructing us, that thyself art Father, Son, and Holy Spirit, and that on the Destruction of the former Christian Church, thou wouldest depart from it, and take up thy Abode in thy New Church; we beseech thee to be present in this Assembly, and to sanctify this Water to the Use which thou hast ordained in thy Word, that *this Child* now to be baptized may hereafter be cleansed from all *his* Impurities, and by a living Faith in thy DIVINE HUMANITY be prepared to dwell with thee in thy eternal Kingdom. Amen.

Then the Minister, after taking the Child into his Arms, shall say to the Parents or Friends of this Child,

Name this Child.

And then naming it after them, he shall sprinkle the Water on the Child's Forehead, saying,

I Baptize thee in the Name of the Lord Jesus Christ, who is at once the Father, Son, and Holy Spirit. Amen.

Then the Minister shall say,

WE receive *this Child* into the Congregation of the New Church, that *he* may hereafter be initiated into the Ackowledgment and true Worship of the Lord, agreeable to the Heavenly Doctrines of the New Jerusalem. And as there is Joy in Heaven over one Sinner that repents, so let us rejoice on Earth, that it has pleased the Lord to add to the Number of those, who by the Baptism of Repentance and Regeneration may finally inherit the Crown of everlasting Life.

Then the Minister returning the Child, gives the following
Exhortation to the Parents or Friends of the Child.

I Earnestly exhort you, who have the Care of *this Child*, to take Charge of *his* Education, and as far as lies in your Power, to see that *he* be properly instructed in the Principles of true Religion. Let *him* be well acquainted with the Holy Word, and with the Heavenly Doctrines of the New Jerusalem, as revealed in the Writings of his Servant Emanuel Swedenborg; but particularly see that *he* learn by Heart the Lord's Prayer, the Ten Commandments, and the Creed of the New Church. Teach *him* the Necessity of shunning continually all Evils as Sins against God, and by renouncing the Loves of Self and the World, of loving the Lord above all Things, and *his* Neighbour as *himself*. So will you be preparing for *his* Happiness in this Life, and for *his* eternal Salvation in the World to come.

Then the Minister is to repeat the following Thanksgiving and Prayer.

We give thee most humble and hearty Thanks, O heavenly Father, that thou hast been graciously pleased to accept our Service at this Time, and to receive this child into the Congregation of thy New Church upon Earth. As he grows in Stature, may he grow in the Knowledge and Love of Thee and thy Kingdom. Support him in the future Hour of Temptation, give him Power over all his spiritual Enemies; and, having followed thy Footsteps in the Regeneration, may he finally be received into thy New Angelic Heaven, to glorify and praise thee, World without End. Amen.

Then the Lord's Prayer is to be repeated by all.

Our Father who art in the Heavens; Hallowed be thy Name, Thy Kingdom come. Thy Will be done, as in Heaven, so also upon Earth. Give us this Day our daily Bread. And forgive us our Debts, as we also forgive our Debtors. And lead us not into Temptation, but deliver us from Evil: For thine is the Kingdom, and the Power, and the Glory, for Ages. Amen.

And lastly the Minister concludes with the following Benediction.

The Grace of our Lord Jesus Christ be with you all. Amen. *Rev*.xxii.21.

Bibliography

'Beckhams host glitzy christening.' *BBC News*, UK edition. 23 December 2004. <http://news.bbc.co.uk/l/hi/uk/4120477.stm>.

'Israel Trip Report.' *Amcan Travel,* March, 2001, pp. 149–80 <http://www.goamcan.com/travelogues/IsraelTrip.html>.

Aelfric, Abbot of Eynsham. *Aelfric's Catholic Homilies: The Second Series.* Edited by Malcolm Godden. London and New York: Oxford University Press, 1979.

Agende für die Evangelische kirche in den königlich Preußischen Landen, Berlin, 1829.

Akeley, T.C. *Christian Initiation in Spain c.300–1100.* London: Darton, Longman and Todd, 1967.

Aland, Kurt. *Did the Early Church Baptize Infants?* Translated by G.R. Beasley-Murray. Philadelphia, PA: Westminster Press, 1963.

Alla, Waheed Hassab. *Le Baptême des Enfants dans la Tradition de l'Église copte d'Alexandrie.* Fribourg: Éditions Universitaires Fribourg Suisse, 1985.

Ames, William. *The Marrow of Theology.* Edited and translated by John Dykstra Eusden. Grand Rapids, MI: Baker Books, 1997.

Amish Country News. Edited by Brad Igou. 2005. <http://www.amishnews.com/amisharticles/religioustraditions.htm>.

Aquinas, Saint Thomas. *Summa Theologiae.* Vol. 56, edited by David Brooks, 1974; Vol. 57, edited by James J. Cunningham, 1975. London: Blackfriars and Eyre and Spottiswood.

Arensen, Sherl. 'The Rite Stuff.' *Today's Christian* 38 (2), March/April 2000, p. 63. <http://www.christianitytoday.com/tc/2000/002.7.63.html>.

Armour, Rollin Stely. *Anabaptist Baptism.* Eugene, OR: Wipf and Stock, 1998, 59–62.

Armstrong, O.K. and Marjorie Armstrong. *The Baptists in America.* New York: Doubleday, 1979.

Arndt, Johann. *Paradislustgard.* Stockholm: F. and G. Bekjers Forlag, 1975, 117–18.

———. *True Christianity.* Translated by Peter Erb. New York: Paulist Press, 1979.

Arranz, M. ' Les Sacrements de l'ancien Euchologe constantinopolitain.' *Orientalia Christiana Periodica* 52 (1986), 145–78.

Attridge, Harold W. 'The Original Language of the *Acts of Thomas*.' In *Of Scribes and Scrolls. Studies on the Hebrew Bible, Intertestamental Judaism, and Christian Origins presented to John Strugnell on the Occasion of his Sixtieth Birthday.* Edited by Harold W. Attridge, John J. Collins and Thomas H. Tobin. Lanham, MD: University of America Press, 1990, 241–50.

Augustine, Saint. *De Peccatorum Meritis et Remissione et de Baptismo Parvulorum.* <http://www.newadvent.org/fathers>.

————. *Sermons on the Liturgical Seasons.* Translated by Mary Sarah Muldowney. New York: The Fathers of the Church, 1959.

Aytoun, K.A. 'The Mysteries of Baptism by Moses bar Kepha Compared with the Odes of Solomon.' In *The Syrian Churches Series 6,* edited by J. Vellian. Kottayam, Kerala, India: CMS Press, 1973, 1–15.

Baker, J.Wayne. *Heinrich Bullinger and the Covenant: The Other Reformed Tradition.* Athens, OH: Ohio State University Press, 1980.

Balke, Willem. *Calvin and the Anabaptists.* Translated by William J. Heynen. Grand Rapids, MI: Eerdmans, 1981.

Baptism, Confirmation and the Eucharist in the Church of the East. Syriac Commission Study Seminar, Holy Apostolic Catholic Assyrian Church of the East Commission on Inter-Church Relations and Education Development. February–March 2000 <http://www.cired.org/east/0402_initiation_rites.pdf>.

Baptism, Eucharist and Ministry. Faith and Order Paper No. 111. Geneva: World Council of Churches, 1982.

Baptism, Rites of Passage, and Culture. Edited by S. Anita Stauffer. Geneva: Lutheran World Federation, 1999.

Barber, E. *A Small Treatise of Baptisme or Dipping.* London, 1642.

Bardy, Gustave and Maurice Lefévre. 'Hippolyte: Commentaire sur Daniel.' *Sources Chrétiennes* 14 (1947).

Barrett, Ivan J. *Joseph Smith and the Restoration.* Provo, UT: Brigham Young University Press, 1973.

Barth, Karl, *Church Dogmatics*, I Part 1–IV Part 4 Fragment. Edinburgh: T & T Clark, 1936–69.

————. *The Teaching of the Church Regarding Baptism.* Translated by Ernest Payne. London: SCM Press, 1948.

Barth, Markus. 'Baptism.' In *The Interpreter's Dictionary of the Bible*, Supplementary Volume. Edited by Keith Crim. Nashville, TN: Abingdon, 1972, 85–9.

————. *Die Taufe – Ein Sakrament?* Zollikon-Zurich: Evangelischer Verlag, 1951.

Basil, Saint. 'Concerning Baptism.' In *Ascetical Works.* Translated by Sister M. Monica Wagner. New York: Fathers of the Church, 1950, 339–430.

Battles, Ford Lewis. *Institutes of the Christian Religion*, 1536 edition. Grand Rapids, MI: Eerdmans, 1975.

Baun, Jane. 'The Fate of Babies Dying Before Baptism in Byzantium.' In *The Church and Childhood, Studies in Church History 31.* Edited by Diana Wood. Oxford: Blackwell, 1994, 113–125.

Baxter, Richard. *The Practical Works of Richard Baxter.* 23 volumes. Edited by William Orme. London: J. Duncan, 1830.

Beardslee III, John W. *Reformed Dogmatics: J. Wollebius, G. Voetius [and] F. Turretun.* Edited and translated by John W. Beardslee III. New York: Oxford University Press, 1965.

Beasley-Murray, G.R. *Baptism in the New Testament.* London: Macmillan, 1963.

Bede, the Venerable. 'Chapter 2.' Bede, *Historia Ecclesiastica* 2.2. <http://www.ccel. org/ccel/bede/history.v.ii.ii.html>.

————. *Homilies on the Gospels*. Translated by Lawrence T. Martin and David Hurst. Kalamazoo, MI: Cistercian Publications, 1991.

Bedingfield, M. Bradford. *The Dramatic Liturgy of Anglo-Saxon England*. Woodbridge: The Boydell Press, 2002, 171–90.

Bellarmine, Robert. *Christian Doctrine*, English edition, 1676.

(Bender, Harold S.?) 'An Amish Church Discipline of 1781.' *The Mennonite Quarterly* 4 (1930), 140–48.

Bernard, J.H. *The Odes of Solomon*. Cambridge: Cambridge University Press, 1912.

Bettenson, Henry. *Documents of the Christian Church*. Oxford: Oxford University Press, 1979.

Betz, Hans Dieter. 'Transferring a Ritual: Paul's Interpretation of Baptism in Romans 6.' In *Paul in His Hellenistic Context*. Edited by Troels Engberg-Pederson. Edinburgh: T & T Clark, 1994.

Biel, Gabriel. 'Whether the Sacraments of the New Covenant are effective causes of grace.' Edited and translated by Alfred J. Freddoso <http://www.nd.edu/~afreddos/ translat/biel.htm>.

Bierma, Lyle D. *German Calvinism in the Confessional Age. The Covenant Theology of Caspar Olevianus*. Grand Rapids, MI: Baker Books, 1996.

Bomberger, J.H.A. 'The Old Palatinate Liturgy of 1563.' *Mercersburg Review* 2 (1850), 277–83.

Bonaventure, Saint. *Commentaries on Lombard's Sentences*. English translation in <http://www.franciscan-archive.org/bonaventure/opera>.

Bonner, G. *St. Augustine of Hippo. Life and Controversies*. Philadelphia, PA: Westminster Press, 1963.

The Book of Concord. Edited by T.G. Tappert. Philadelphia, PA: Westminster, 1959.

The Book of Marganitha on the Truth of Christianity. Translated by His Holiness Nar Eshai Shimun XXIII. Ernakuluam, Kerala, India: Mar Themotheus Memorial Printing House, 1965.

Borgen, Ole E. *John Wesley on the Sacraments*. Grand Rapids, MI: Francis Asbury Press, 1972, 1985.

Bornert, René. *Le Reforme Protestante du Culte à Strasbourg au XVI siècle (1523–1598)*. Leiden: E.J. Brill, 1981.

Botte, Bernard. 'L'Eucologe de Serapion est-il authentique?' *Oriens Christianus* 48 (1964), 50–57.

————. *From Silence to Participation*. Washington, DC: Pastoral Press, 1988.

Bouhot, Jean-Paul. *La confirmation, sacrement de la communion ecclésiale*. Lyons: du Chalet, 1968.

Bradshaw, Paul F. 'Baptismal Practice in the Alexandrian Tradition: Eastern or Western.' In *Essays in Early Christianity*. Edited by Paul Bradshaw. Bramcote: Alcuin/GROW Liturgical Study, Grove Books, 1988, 5–17. Reprinted in *Living Water, Sealing Spirit*. Edited by Maxwell Johnson. Collegeville, MN: Pueblo Liturgical Press, 1995, 82–100.

———— (ed.). *Companion to Common Worship*, Vol. 1. London: SPCK, 2001, 171–2.

————. 'Redating the *Apostolic Tradition*: Some Preliminary Steps.' In *Rule of Prayer, Rule of Faith*. Edited by Nathan Mitchell and John Baldovin. Collegeville, MN: Pueblo Liturgical Press, 1996, 3–17.

————. *The Search for the Origins of Christian Worship*. New York: Oxford University Press, 2002.

————, Maxwell E. Johnson and L. Edward Phillips. *The Apostolic Tradition*. Minneapolis, MN: Augsburg Fortress Press, 2002.

Braniste, Ene. 'Le déroulement de l'Office de l'Initiation dans les Églises de Rite Byzantin et son Interprétation.' *Ostkirchliche Studien* 20 (1971), 115–29.

Bremmer, Jan N. 'The *Acts of Thomas*: Place, Date and Women.' In *The Apocryphal Acts of Thomas*. Edited by Jan N. Bremmer. Louvain: Peeters, 2001, 74–90.

Brent, Allen. *Hippolytus and the Roman Church in the Third Century: Communities in Tension before the Emergence of a Monarch-Bishop*. Leiden: E.J. Brill, 1995.

Brock, Sebastian. 'The Baptismal Anointings According to the Anonymous Expositio Officiorum', *Journal of Syriac Studies* 1 (1998), 1–9.

————. 'Baptismal Themes in the Writings of Jacob of Serugh.' *Symposium Syriacum 1976*, Rome: Pontificial Oriental Institute, 1978, 325–47.

————. 'The Consecration of the Water in the Oldest Manuscripts of the Syrian Orthodox Baptismal Liturgy.' *Orientalia Christiana Periodica* 37 (1971), 317–31.

————. *The Luminous Eye*. Rome: Placid Lectures, CIIS, 1985.

————. 'A New Syriac Baptismal *Ordo* attributed to Timothy of Alexandria.' *Le Muséon* 83 (1970), 367–431.

————. 'A Remarkable Syriac Baptismal Ordo.' *Parole de l'Orient* 2 (1971), 365–78.

————. 'Severos' letter to John the Soldier.' In *Erkenntnisse und Meinungen II*. Edited by G.Wiessner. Wiesbaden: Otto Harrassowitz, 1978, 53–75.

————. 'Some Early Syriac Baptismal Commentaries.' *Orientalia Christiana Periodica* 46 (1980), 20–61.

————. 'Studies in the Early History of the Syrian Baptismal Liturgy.' *Journal of Theological Studies* 23 (1972), 16–64.

————. 'The Transition to a Post-baptial Anointing in the Antiochene Rite.' In *The Sacrifice of Praise. Studies on the themes of thanksgiving and redemption in the central prayers of the Eucharistic and baptismal liturgies*. Edited by Bryan D. Spinks. Rome: Edizioni Liturgiche, 1981, 214–25.

Brooks, E. *Letters*. London: Text and Translation Society, 1903.

Brown, R.E. *The Gospel According to John*, 2 volumes. Garden City, NJ: Doubleday, 1966/70.

Buchanan, Colin. *Infant Baptism and the Gospel. The Church of England's Dilemma.* London: Darton, Longman and Todd, 1993.

Buerger, David John. *The Mysteries of Godliness: A History of Mormon Temple Worship.* San Francisco, CA: Smith Research Associates, 1994.

Bullinger, Heinrich. *Decades*, Volume 5. Cambridge: Parker Society edition, Cambridge University Press, Cambridge, 1850, pp. 367–8.

Bultmann, Rudolph. *The Gospel of John.* Philadelphia, PA: E.T. Westminster Press, 1971.

Bunyan, John. *The Miscellaneous Works of John Bunyan*, Volume 4. Edited by Roger Sharrock. Oxford: Clarendon Press, 1976–94.

Burges, Cornelius. *Baptismall regeneration of Elect Infants, Professed by the Church of England, according to the Scriptures, the Primitive Church, the present reformed Churches, and many particular Divines apart.* London, 1629.

Burrage, Champlin. *The Early English Dissenters,* 2 volumes. Cambridge: Cambridge University Press, 1912.

Burreson, Kent. 'The Saving Flood: The Medieval Origins, Historical Development, and Theological Import of the Sixteenth Century Lutheran Baptismal Rites.' Ph.D. Dissertation, University of Notre Dame, 2002.

Cabasilas, Nicholas. *The Life in Christ.* Translated by Carmino J. de Catanzaro. Crestwood, NY: St.Vladimir's Seminary Press, 1974.

Calvin, Jean. *Institutes of the Christian Religion, 1536 Edition*, translated by Ford Lewis Battles. Grand Rapids, MI: Eerdmans, 1975; 1559 edition, translated by Henry Beveridge, 2 volumes. London: James Clarke & Co. Ltd, 1962.

———. *Tracts and Treatises on the Doctrine and Worship of the Church. Volume 2.* Translated by H. Beveridge, edited by T.F. Torrance. Revised edition, Edinburgh and London: Oliver and Boyd, 1958, 85–9.

Campbell, Alexander. *Christian Baptism: with its Antecedents and Consequents.* Bethany, VA: Alexander Campbell, 1851.

———. *The Christian System.* Cincinnati, OH: Standard Publishing Company, 1901.

The Canons and Decrees of the Sacred and Oecumenical Council of Trent. Edited and translated by J. Waterworth. London: Dolman, 1848.

Capelle, B. 'L'Anahore de Serapion: Essai d'exégèse.' *Le Muséon* 59 (1964), 425–43.

Cardale, John. *Readings in the Liturgy and Divine Offices of the Church*, 2 volumes. London: Thomas Bosworth, 1874–75.

Catholic Church. *Catechism of the Catholic Church.* Città del Vaticano: Liberia Editrice Vaticana, 2000.

———. *Catechism of the Council of Trent for Parish Priests. Issued by Order of Pope Pius V.* Translated by John A. McHugh and Charles J. Callan. New York: Joseph F. Wagner, 1923.

————. *Le Pontifical Romano-Germanique Du Dixième Siècle.* Edited by Cyrille Vogel in collaboration with Reinhard Elze. Vatican City: Biblioteca Apostolica Vaticana, 1963–72.

————. *The Rites of the Catholic Church as Revised by the Second Vatican Council,* 2 volumes. New York: Pueblo Press, 1976, 1980.

————. *The Winchcombe Sacramentary.* Edited by Anselme Davril. London: Henry Bradshaw Society, 1995.

————. Diocese of St. Maron. *Mysteries of Initiation. Baptism, Confirmation, Communion According to the Maronite Antiochene Church.* Washington, DC: Diocesan Office of Liturgy, 1987.

Chalfoun, P. Khalil. 'Baptême et Eucharistie chez 'Ammar Al-Basri.' *Parole de l'Orient* 27 (2002), 321–34.

Charlesworth, J.H. 'The Odes of Solomon – not Gnostic.' In *The Catholic Biblical Quarterly* 31 (1969), 357–69.

————. *The Old Testament Pseudepigrapha,* Volume 1. Garden City, NJ: Doubleday, 1983.

————. *The Pseudepigrapha and Modern Research.* Chico, CA: Scholars Press, 1981.

Chemnitz, Martin. *Ministry, Word, and Sacraments. An Enchiridion.* Edited, translated and briefly annotated by Luther Poellot. St. Louis, MO: Concordia, 1981.

Church Book: St. Andrews' Street Baptist Church, Cambridge, 1720–1832. Edited by K. A. Parons. London: Baptist Historical Society, 1991, 41–42.

Church of England. *Christian Initiation – A Policy for the Church of England. A Discussion Paper by Canon Martin Reardon.* London: Church House Publishing, London, 1991.

————. *Communion Before Confirmation?: The Report of the General Synod Board of Education Working Party on Christian Initiation and Participation in the Eucharist.* London: Church Information Office Publishing, 1985.

————, Liturgical Commission. *On the Way: Towards an Integrated Approach to Christian Initiation.* London: Church House Publishing, 1995.

Church of Scotland, Special Commission on Baptism. *The Biblical Doctrine of Baptism.* Edinburgh: Saint Andrew Press, 1958.

Colish, Marica L. *Peter Lombard,* Volume 2. Leiden: E.J. Brill, 1994.

Collins, A. Jefferies. *Manuale ad usum Percelebris Ecclesie Sarisburiensis.* Chichester: Henry Bradshaw Society, 1960.

Collins, Adela Yarbro. 'The Origin of Christian Baptism.' In *Living Water, Sealing Spirit.* Edited by Maxwell E. Johnson. Collegeville, MN: Pueblo, 1995, 35–57.

Connell, Martin F. *Church Worship in Fifth-Century Rome: The Letter of Innocent I to Decentius of Gubio.* Cambridge: Grove Books, 2002.

Connolly, R.H. *Anonymi Auctoris Expositio Officiorum Ecclesiae Georgio Arbelensi vulgo adscripta. Accedit Abrahae Bar Lipheh Interpretatio Officiorum,* 4 volumes, 2nd edn. Louvain: Corpus Scriptorum Christianorum Orientalium, 1953–61.

————. *The Liturgical Homilies of Narsai, with an Appendix by Edmund Bishop.* Cambridge: Cambridge University Press, 1909.

———— and H.W. Codrington. *Two Commentaries on the Jacobite Liturgy.* London: Williams and Norgate, 1913.

Conybeare, F.C. 'The Character of the Heresy of the Early British Church.' *Transactions of the Society of Cymmrodorion*, 1897–98, 84–117.

Coptic Church. *Coptic Offices.* Translated by R.M.Woolley. London: SPCK, 1930.

Coster, Will. *Baptism and Spiritual Kinship in Early Modern England.* Aldershot: Ashgate, 2002.

Cottrell, Jack Warren. 'Covenant and Baptism in the Theology of Huldreich Zwingli.' Th.D. Dissertation, Princeton Theological Seminary, 1971.

Couratin, A.H. 'Justin Martyr and Confirmation – A Note.' *Theology* 55 (1953), 458–60.

Cranfield, Charles. *The Epistle to the Romans* 1. Edinburgh: ICC T&T Clark, 1975, 300.

Cranmer, Thomas. *A Catechism set forth by Thomas Cranmer.* Edited by D.G. Selwyn. Appleford: Sutton Courtenay Press, 1978.

Cressy, David. *Birth, Marriage and Death. Ritual, Religion, and the Life-Cycle in Tudor and Stuart England.* Oxford: Oxford University Press, 1997.

Crichton, J.D. *Christian Celebration.* London: Geoffrey Chapman, 1981.

Cross, Anthony R. *Baptism and the Baptists. Theology and Practice in Twentieth-century Britain.* Carlisle: Paternoster Press, 2000.

Cross, Richard. *Duns Scotus.* New York: Oxford University Press, 1999.

Cullman, Oscar. *Baptism in the New Testament.* Translated by J.K.S. Reid. London: SCM Press, 1950.

Cuming, G.J. *A History of Anglican Liturgy.* London: Macmillan and Co., 1969.

————. 'John Knox and the Book of Common Prayer: a short note.' *Liturgical Review* 10 (1980), 80–81.

————. 'The Post-baptismal Prayer in the *Apostolic Tradition*: Further Considerations.' *Journal of Theological Studies* 39 (1988), 117–19.

————. 'Thmuis Revisited: Another Look at the Prayers of Bishop Serapion. *Theological Studies* 41 (1980), 568–75.

Cummings, Owen F. 'Is Mormon Baptism Valid?' *Worship* 71 (1997), 146–53.

Curtis, Mark H. 'Hampton Court Conference and its Aftermath.' *History* 46 (1961), 1–16.

Cyprian, Saint. *To Donatus.* In *Born to New Life.* Edited by Oliver Davies and translated by Tim Withrow. Brooklyn, NY: New City Press, 1992, 21–2.

Cyril, Saint. *St Cyril of Jerusalem's Lectures on the Christian Sacraments.* Edited by F.L. Cross. London: SPCK, 1966.

Cyrus of Edessa. S*ix Explanations of the Liturgical Feasts.* Translated and edited by William F. Macomber. Louvain: Corpus SCP, 1974.

Dalby, Mark. *Open Baptism.* London: SPCK, 1989.

Danielou, Jean. 'Chrismation Prebaptismale et Divinité de l'Esprit chez Gregoire de Nysse.' *Recherches de Science Religieuse* 56 (1968), 177–98.

Daniels, Harold M. *To God Alone Be Glory. The Story and Sources of the Book of Common Worship.* Louisville, KY: Geneva Press, 2003.

Dankbaar, W.F. and Marten Micron. *De Christlicke Ordinancien der Nederlantscher Ghemeinten Te Londen (1554)*, s-Gravenhage: Martinus Nijhoff, 1956, 73–9.

Davies, Douglas J. *An Introduction to Mormonism.* Cambridge: Cambridge University Press, 2003.

Davril, Anselme. *The Winchcombe Sacramentary.* London: Henry Bradshaw Society, 1995.

Day, Juliette. 'The Mystagogic Catecheses of Jerusalem and their Relationship to the Eastern Baptismal Liturgies of the Fourth and Early Fifth Centuries.' Ph.D. dissertation, University of London, 2003.

De Simone, Russell J. 'Modern Research on the Sources of Saint Augustine's Doctrine of Original Sin.' *Augustinian Studies* 11 (1980), 205–27.

De Vinck, Jose. *The Works of Bonaventure,* Volume 2. Paterson, NJ: St Anthony Guild Press, 1963.

Defence 3.2. In *Writings and Disputations of Thomas Cranmer relative to the sacrament of the Lord's Supper.* Edited by J.E. Cox. Cambridge: Parker Society, 1844, 89 (cited as PS I).

Deferrari, Roy J. *Hugh of Saint Victor on the Sacraments of the Christian Faith.* Cambridge, MA: Mediaeval Academy of America, 1951.

Devotional Services for Public Worship. Glasgow: Maclehouse, 1892.

De Vries, W. 'Die Erklärung aller Göttlichen Geheimnisse des Nestorianers Johannan Bar Zo'bi (13 Jahrh.).' *Orientalia Christiana Periodica* 96 (1943), 191–203.

————. 'Zur Liturgie der Erwachsenentaufe bei den Nestorianern.' *Orientalia Christiana Periodica* 96 (1943), 460–73.

Dionysius, the Areopagite, Saint. *Dionysius the Pseudo-Areopagite.* Translated by Thomas L. Campbell. Lanham, MD: University of America Press, 1981.

'Discourse d'adieux aux ministres', 28 April 1564, in *Corpus Reformatorum* ix, 894.

Dixon, Philip. *Nice and Hot Disputes. The Doctrine of the Trinity in the Seventeenth Century.* New York: Continuum, 2003.

Dodd, C.H. *Interpretation of the Fourth Gospel.* Cambridge: Cambridge University Press, 1951.

Dolan, John Patrick. *The Influence of Erasmus, Witzel, and Cassander in the Church Ordinances and Reform Proposals of the United Duchy of Cleve During the Middle Decades of the Sixteenth Century.* Münster: Aschendorff, 1957.

Dold, P. Alban. *Die Konstanzer Ritualientexte in ihrer Entwicklung von 1482–1721.* Münster in Westfalia: Ascendorff, 1923.

Doval, Alexis. *Cyril of Jerusalem, Mystagogue: The Authorship of the Mystagogic Catecheses.* Washington, DC: Catholic University of America Press, 2001.

Draper, Jonathan A. (ed.). *The Didache in Modern Research.* Leiden: E.J. Brill, 1996.

————. 'Ritual Process and Ritual Symbol in Didache 7–10.' *Vigiliae Christianae* 54 (2000), 121–58.

Duck, Ruth (ed.). *Bread for the Journey. Resources for Worship.* New York: The Pilgrim Press, 1981, 6–8.

————. *Gender and the Name of God. The Trinitarian Baptismal Formula.* Cleveland, OH: Pilgrim Press, 1991.

———— and Patricia Wilson-Kastner. *Praising God. The Trinity in Christian Worship.* Louisville, KY: Westminster John Knox Press, 1999, 148–53.

Duckworth, Dennis. *A Branching Tree. A Narrative History of the General Conference of the New Church.* London: The General Conference of the New Church, 1998.

Duffy, Eamon. *The Stripping of the Altars.* New Haven, CT and London: Yale University Press, 1992.

Duncan, Edward J. 'The Administration of Baptism in the Demonstrations of Aphraates.' In *Studies in Syrian Baptismal Rites,* Volume 6 (Syrian Church Series). Edited by Jacob Vellian. Kottayam, Kerala, India: CMS, 1973.

Dunn, James D.G. '"Baptized" as Metaphor.' In *Baptism in the New Testament and the Church. Historical and Contemporary Studies in Honour of R.E.O. White.* Edited by Stanley E. Porter and Anthony R. Cross. Sheffield: Sheffield Academic Press, 1999, 294–310.

Edgeworth, Roger. *Sermons very fruitfully, godly and learned, preched and sette forth by Maister Roger Edgeworth, doctoure of diuinitie.* London, 1557.

Edwall, P., E. Hayman and W.D. Maxwell (eds). *Ways of Worship.* London: SCM Press, 1951.

Ellis, Christopher. 'Baptism and Sacramental Freedom.' In *Reflections on the Water. Understanding God and the World through the Baptism of Believers.* Edited by Paul S. Fiddes. Oxford: Regent's Park College, 1996, 23–45.

————. *Gathering. A Theology and Spirituality of Worship in Free Church Tradition.* London: SCM Press, 2004.

Elwood, Christopher. *The Body Broken. The Calvinist Doctrine of the Eucharist and the Symbolism of Power in Sixteenth-Century France.* Oxford: Oxford University Press, 1999.

Emerton, J. 'Some Problems of Text and Language in the Odes of Solomon.' *Journal of Theological Studies* 18 (1967), 372–406.

Engberding, H. *Das eucharistische Hochgebet der Basileiosliturgie. Textgeschichtliche Untersuchengen und kritische Ausgabe* (Inaugural Dissertation), Münster: no publisher, 1931.

Euchologion, 2nd edition. Edinburgh: Blackwood and Sons, 1869.

Evans, Earnest. 'Introduction.' *Tertullian's Homily on Baptism.* London: SPCK, 1964 <http://www.tertullian.org/articles/evans_bapt/evans_bapt_text_trans.htm>.

Fagan, Garrett G. *Bathing in Public in the Roman World.* Ann Arbor: University of Michigan Press, 1999.

Fawcett, Timothy. *The Liturgy of Comprehension 1689.* Southend on Sea: Mayhew-McCrimmon, 1973.

Felton, Gayle Carlton. *This Gift of Water. The Practice and Theology of Baptism Among Methodists in America.* Nashville, TN: Abingdon Press, 1992.

Fenwick, John. *The Free Church of England. Introduction to an Anglican Tradition.* London: T & T Clark, 2004.

———— and Bryan Spinks. *Worship in Transition. The Liturgical Movement in the Twentieth Century.* New York: Continuum, 1995.

Fiddes, Paul. 'Baptism and Creation.' In *Reflections on the Water. Understanding God and the World through the Baptism of Believers.* Edited by Paul S. Fiddes. Oxford: Regent's Park College, 1996.

Finn, Thomas M. 'The Ritual Process and Survival in Second-Century Rome.' *Journal of Ritual Studies* 3 (1989), 69–89.

————. *Early Christian Baptism and the Catechumenate – Volume 2: Italy, North Africa, and Egypt.* Collegeville, MN: Liturgical Press, 1992.

————. *Early Christian Baptism and the Catechumenate – Volume 1: West and East Syria.* Collegeville, MN: Liturgical Press, 1992.

Fischer, Balthasar. 'Baptismal Exorcism in the Catholic Baptismal Rites after Vatican II.' *Studia Liturgica* 10 (1974), 48–55.

Fisher, J.D.C. *Christian Initiation. Baptism in the Medieval West.* London: SPCK, 1965.

————. *Christian Initiation. The Reformation Period.* London: SPCK, 1970.

————. *Confirmation Then and Now.* London: SPCK/Alcuin Club, 1978, 128–9.

Fitzer, Joseph. 'The Augustinian Roots of Calvin's Eucharistic Thought.' *Augustinian Studies* 7 (1976), 69–98.

Flegg, Columba. *Gathered Under Apostles. A Study of the Catholic Apostolic Church.* Oxford: Clarendon Press, 1992.

Fowler, Stanley K. *More Than a Symbol. The British Baptist Recovery of Baptismal Sacramentalism.* Carlisle: Paternoster Press, 2002.

Fox, George. *The Journal of George Fox.* Edited by John L. Nickalls. London: Religious Society of Friends, 1975, 4, 11–12.

Freeman, Arthur J. *An Ecumenical Theology of the Heart: The Theology of Count Nicholas Ludwig von Zinzendorf.* Bethlehem, PA: The Moravian Church in America, 1998.

Fugel, Adolf. *Tauflehre und Taufliturgie bei Huldrych Zwingli.* Berne: Peter Lang, 1989.

Fulton, Gayle, and Karen Westerfield-Tucker. *American Methodist Worship.* Oxford and New York: University Press, 2001.

Garite, Gerard. *Documents pour l'étude du livre d'Agathange.* Vatican City, 1946, 98–100.

Garrigan, Siobhán. *Beyond Ritual.* Aldershot: Ashgate Publishing, 2004.

Gelston, Anthony. 'A Note on the Text of the *Apostolic Tradition* of Hippolytus.' *Journal of Theological Studies* 39 (1988), 112–17.

General Synod of the Church of England. *Christian Initiation and its Relation to Some Pastoral Offices*, GS Misc. 366, London, 1991.

George, Timothy. 'The Presuppositions of Zwingli's Baptismal Theology.' In *Prophet, Pastor, Protestant*. Edited by E.J. Furcha and H. Wayne Pipkin. Allison Park, PA: Pickwick Publications, 1984, 71–87.

Germanus, Saint. *Expositio Antiquae Liturgiae Gallicanae*. Edited by E.C. Ratcliff. London: Henry Bradshaw Society, 1971.

Gerrish, Brian. 'The Lord's Supper in the Reformed Confessions.' In *Major Themes in the Reformed Tradition*. Edited by Donald K. McKim. Grand Rapids, MI: Eerdmans, 1992, 245–58.

Gilbert, H.S. 'The Liturgical History of Baptism.' In *Memoirs of the Lutheran Liturgical Association*, Philadelphia, PA: 1906–07, 113–23.

Goode, William. *The Doctrine of the Church of England as to the Effects of Baptism in the Case of Infants*. New York: Stanford and Swords, 1849.

Grebaut, Selvain. 'Ordre du Baptême et de la confirmation dans l'Église Éthiopienne.' *Revue de l'Orient Chrétien* 6 (1927–28), 105–89.

Green, Robin. *Only Connect. Worship and Liturgy from the Perspective of Pastoral Care*. London: Darton, Longman and Todd, 1987, 51–2.

Gregory of Nazianus. *Oration on Holy Baptism*. Nicene and Post-Nicene Fathers series <http://www.ccel.org/fathers2/NPNF2-07/Npnf2-07-52.htm TopOfPage>.

Gregory of Nyssa. *On the Holy Spirit*. Nicene and Post-Nicene Fathers series <http://www.ccel.org/fathers2/NPNF2-05/Npnf2-05-26.htm P2435 1676104>.

Gregory of Tours, Saint. *The History of the Franks*, Volume 2. Translated by O.M. Dalton. Oxford: Clarendon Press, 1927, 69–70.

Grell, Ole Peter. *The Scandinavian Reformation*. Cambridge: Cambridge University Press, 1995.

Grenz, Stanley J. and John R. Francke. *Beyond Foundationalism. Shaping Theology in a Postmodern Context*. Louisville, KY: Westminster John Knox Press, 2001.

Grimes, Ronald L. *Deeply into the Bone: Re-inventing Rites of Passage*. Berkeley, CA: University of California Press, 2000.

Grönvik, Lorenz. *Die Taufe in der Theologie Martin Luthers*. Åbo: Åbo Akademi, 1967.

Grundtvig, Nicolaj F.S. 'Elementary Christian Teachings.' *A Grundtvig Anthology*. Edited by N.L. Jensen. Cambridge: James Clarke & Co., 1984.

Hanssens, J.M. *La Liturgie d'Hippolyte*. Rome: Pontifical Oriental Institute, 1959.

Hapgood, Isabel. *Service Book of the Holy Orthodox-Catholic Apostolic Church*. New York: Association Press, 1922, 271–83.

Harding, Vincent G. 'Menno and the Role of Baptism.' *Mennonite Quarterly Review* 33 (1959), 323–34.

Harmless, William. *Augustine and the Catechumenate*. Collegeville, MN: Pueblo Liturgical Press, 1995.

Harrison, Robert and Robert Browne. *The Writings of Robert Harrison and Robert Browne*. Edited by Albert Peel and Leland H. Carlson. London: Allen and Unwin, 1953.

Hartman, Lars. *Into the Name of the Lord Jesus. Baptism in the Early Church*. Edinburgh: T & T Clark, 1997.

Hatchett, Marion. *The Making of the First American Book of Common Prayer*. New York: Seabury Press, 1982, 124–5.

————. 'Prayer Books.' In *The Study of Anglicanism*. Edited by S. Sykes and J. Booty. London: SPCK, 1988.

Hauerwas, Stanley. *The Peaceable Kingdom*. Notre Dame, IN: University of Notre Dame Press, 1983, 107–108.

Hayden, Roger. 'Believers Baptized: An Anthology.' In *Reflections on the Water. Understanding God and the World through the Baptism of Believers*. Edited by Paul S. Fiddes. Oxford: Regent's Park College, 1996.

Hayek, Michel. *Ammar Al-Basri, Apologie et Controverses*. Beirut, 1977.

Haykin, Michael A.G. *Kiffin, Knollys and Keach – Rediscovering our English Baptist Heritage*. Leeds: Reformation Today Trust, 1996.

Henderson, W.G. *Manuale et Processionale ad usum Insignis Ecclesiae Eboracensis*. London: Surtess Society, 1875.

Hill, C.L. *The Loci Communes of Philip Melanchthon*. Boston, MA: Meador Publishing House, 1944.

Hindmarsh, Robert. *The Rise and Progress of the New Jerusalem Church*. London: Hodson & Son, 1861.

Hoffman, L.A. *Beyond the Text: A Holistic Approach to Liturgy*. Indianapolis: Indiana University Press, 1987.

Hohler, Christopher. 'The Red Book of Darley.' In *Nordiskt Kollokvium II. 1. Latinsk Liturgiforskning*. Stockholm: Stockholm University, 1972, 39–47.

Holeton, David R. *Growing in Newness of Life. Christian Initiation in Anglicanism Today*. Toronto: The Anglican Book Centre, 1993.

Holifield, E. Brooks. *The Covenant Sealed. The Development of Puritan Sacramental Theology in Old and New England, 1570–1720*. New Haven, CT and London: Yale University Press, 1979.

Holland, Bernard G. *Baptism in Early Methodism*. London: Epworth Press, 1970.

————. 'The Doctine of Infant Baptism in Non-Wesleyan Methodism.' Wesley Historical Society Occasional Paper 1 (cyclostyled), n.p., 1970, 1–5.

Holmes, Urban T. 'Education for Liturgy: An Unfinished Symphony in Four Movements.' In *Worship Points the Way. Celebration of the Life and Work of Massey H. Shepherd, Jr*. Edited by Malcolm C. Burson. New York: Seabury Press, 1981, 116–41.

The Homilies of the Anglo-Saxon Church, 2 volumes. Edited by B.Thorpe. London: The Aelfric Society, London, 1844–46.

Honders, A.C. *Valerandus Pollanus. Liturgica Sacra (1551–1555)*. Leiden: E.J. Brill, 1970.

Hope, Nicholas. *German and Scandinavian Protestantism 1700–1918.* Oxford: Clarendon Press, 1995.

Horsch, John. 'Did Menno Simons Practice Baptism by Immersion?' *Mennonite Quarterly Review* 1 (1927), 54–6.

Hough, James. *The History of Christianity in India*, Volume 2. London: Nisbet, 1845, 645–50 <http://www.nd.edu/~afreddos/translat/biel.htm>.

Huber, Raphael M. 'The Doctrine of Ven. John Duns Scotus. Concerning the Causality of the Sacraments.' *Franciscan Studies* 4 (1926), 9–38.

Hubert, F. *Die Strassburger Liturgischen Ordnungen in Zeitalter der Reformation.* Göttingen: Vandenhoek und Ruprecht, 1900.

Hunsinger, George. 'The Dimension of Depth: Thomas F. Torrance on the Sacraments of Baptism and the Lord's Supper.' *Scottish Journal of Theology* 54 (2001), 155–76.

————. *How to Read Karl Barth.* New York: Oxford University Press, 1991.

Hunt, Arnold. 'Laurance Chaderton and the Hampton Court Conference.' In *Belief and Practice in Reformation England.* Edited by Susan Wabuda and Caroline Litzenberger. Aldershot: Ashgate, 1998, 207–28.

Hürlimann, Gebhard. *Das Rheinauer Rituale.* Freiburg: Universitätsverlag Freiburg Schweiz, 1959.

Hut, Hans. *True Baptism* <http://www.anabaptistchurch.org/Baptism.htm>.

Irving, Edward. *The Day of Pentecost, or the Baptism with the Holy Ghost.* Edinburgh: John Lindsay, 1831.

————. *Homilies on the Sacraments – Volume 1: Baptism.* London: Andrew Panton, 1828.

Isaac, J. (ed.). 'Emmanuel Bar Shahhare, Memra on the Explanation of Baptism.' *Bayn al-Nahrayn* 11 (1983), 26–66.

Jackson, Ralph. 'Spas, waters, and Hydrotherapy in the Roman World.' In *Roman Baths and Bathing.* Edited by J. DeLaine and D.E. Johnston. Portsmouth, RI: *Journal of Roman Archaeology*, 1999, 107–116.

Jacob of Serugh. *Homiliae Selectae Mar-Jacobi Sarugensis,* Volume 3. Edited by Paulus Bedjan. Paris: Harrassowitz, 1905–10.

Jacobs, Elfriede. *Die Sakramentslehre Wilhelm Farels.* Zurich: Theologischer Verlag, 1978.

Jagger, Peter J. *Clouded Witness.* Allison Park, PA: Pickwick Publications, 1982.

James,E. *The Articles of Faith.* 11th edition. Salt Lake City, UT: The Deseret News, 1919.

Jameson, Fredric. *Postmodernism or, The Cultural Logic of Late Capitalism.* Durham, NC: Duke University Press, 1991.

Jasper, R.C.D. and Paul F. Bradshaw. *A Companion to the Alternative Service Book.* London: SPCK, 1986, 356–7.

Jeanes, Gordon. *The Day has Come. Easter and Baptism in Zeno of Verona.* Collegeville, MN: The Liturgical Press, 1995.

————. 'A Reformation Treatise on the Sacraments.' *Journal of Theological Studies* 46 (1995), 149–90.

————. 'Signs of God's Promise: Thomas Cranmer's Sacramental Theology and Baptismal Liturgy.' Ph.D. dissertation, University of Wales, Lampeter, 1998.

Jeffers, James S. *Conflict at Rome: Social Order and Hierarchy in Early Christianity.* Minneapolis, MN: Fortress Press, 1991.

Jefford, Clayton N. (ed.). *The Didache in Context.* Leiden: E.J. Brill, 1995.

Jeremias, Joachim. *Infant Baptism in the First Four Centuries.* Translated by D. Cairns. Philadelphia, PA: Westminster Press, 1963.

Jetter, Werner. *Die Taufe beim jungen Luther.* Tübingen: Mohr, 1954.

Johnson, Caroline. 'Ritual Epiclesis in the Greek *Acts of Thomas*.' In *The Apocryphal Acts of the Apostles.* Edited by F. Bovan, A.G. Brock and C.R. Matthews. Harvard Divinity School Studies, Cambridge, MA: Harvard University Press, 1999, 171–204.

Johnson, Maxwell E. 'The Postchrismational Structure of Apostolic Tradition 21, the Witness of Ambrose of Milan, and a Tentative Hypothesis Regarding the Current Reform of Confirmation in the Roman Rite.' *Worship* 70 (1996), 16–34.

————. *The Prayers of Serapion of Thmuis: A Literary, Liturgical, and Theological Analysis. Orientalia Christiana Analecta* 249, Rome: Pontifical Oriental Institute, 1995.

————. 'Reconciling Cyril and Egeria on the Catechetical Process in Fourth Century Jerusalem.' In *Essays in Early Christian Initiation.* Edited by Paul Bradshaw. Bramcote: Grove Books, 1988, 18–30.

————. *The Rites of Christian Initiation.* Collegeville, MN: Liturgical Press, 1999, 66–7.

Jones, Simon. 'Womb of the Spirit. The Liturgical Implications of the Doctrine of the Spirit for the Syrian Baptismal Tradition.' Ph.D. Thesis, University of Cambridge, 1999.

Kadicheeni, Paul B. (ed.). *The Mystery of Baptism: the text and translation of the chapter 'On Holy Baptism' from the causes of the seven mysteries of the Church of Timothy II, Nestorian patriarch (1318–1332).* Bangalore: Dharmaram Publications, 1980.

Kalb, Friedrich. *Theology of Worship in 17th Century Lutheranism.* Translated by Henry P.A. Hamann. St Louis, MO: Concordia Publishing House, 1965.

Kavanagh, Aidan. *Confirmation: Origins and Reform.* Collegeville, MN: Pueblo Liturgical Press, 1988.

————. *The Shape of Baptism.* New York: Pueblo Press, 1978.

Kawerau, Gustav. 'Liturgische Studien zu Luthers Taufbüchlein von 1523.' *Zeitschrift für kirchliche Wissenschaft und kirchliches Leben* 10 (1898), 407–31, 466–77, 519–47, 578–99, 625–43.

Kay, James F. 'The New Rites of Baptism: A Dogmatic Assessment.' In *To Glorify God. Essays on Modern Reformed Liturgy.* Edited by Bryan D. Spinks and Iain R. Torrance. Edinburgh: T & T Clark, 1999, 201–12.

Keefe, Susan Ann. 'The Claim of Authorship in Carolingian Baptismal Expositions: The Case of Odilbert of Milan.' In *Fälschungen im Mittelalter: Internationaler Kongress der Monuementa Germaniae Historica, München, 16–19 September 1986.* Hannover: Hahnsche Buchhandlung, 1988, 385–401.

————. *Water and the Word. Baptism and Education of the Clergy in the Carolingian Empire*, 2 volumes. Notre Dame, IN: University of Notre Dame Press, 2002.

Keefer, Sarah Larratt. 'Manuals.' In *The Liturgical Books of Anglo-Saxon England.* Edited by Richard W. Pfaff. Kalamazoo, MI: Medical Institute Publications, Western Michigan University, 1995, 99–109.

Kelly, Henry Ansgar. *The Devil at Baptism. Ritual, Theology, and Drama.* Ithaca, NY and London: Cornell University Press, 1985.

Khs-Burmester, O.H.E. 'The Baptismal Rite of the Coptic Church. A Critical Study.' *Bulletin de la Société d'Archéologie Copte* 11 (1945), 27–86.

————. *The Egyptian or Coptic Church. A Detailed Description of Her Liturgical Services and the Rites and Ceremonies Observed in the Administration of her Sacraments.* Cairo: Publications de la Société d'Archéologie Copte, 1965.

Klijn, A.F.J. *The Acts of Thomas.* Leiden: E.J. Brill, 1962.

Knox, John. 'Answers to some Questions concerning Baptism.' In *Works.* Edited by David Laing, Volume IV. Edinburgh, 1855, 199–22.

Kohlberg, A. *Die älteste Agende in der Diozese Ermland und den Deutschordensstaate Preussen nach dem ersten Druckausgaben von 1512 und 1529.* Braunsberg: Rudlowski, 1903.

Kreitzer, Larry J. 'On Board the Eschatological Ark of God: Noah-Deucalion and the 'Phrygian Connection' in 1 Peter 3.19–22.' In *Baptism in the New Testament and the Church. Historical and Contemporary Studies in Honour of R.E.O. White.* Edited by Stanley E. Porter and Anthony R. Cross. Sheffield: Sheffield Academic Press, 1999, 228–72.

Kretschmar, G. 'Die Geschichte des Taufgottesdienstes in der alten Kirche.' In *Leiturgia, Handbuch des evangelischen Gottesdienstes.* Edited by Karl Ferdinand Muller and Walter Blakenburg. Kassel-Wilhennshohe: J. Stauda-Verlag, 1970.

Kuhrt, Gordon. *Believing in Baptism.* London: Mowbray, 1987.

Kuyper, A. *Joannis a Lasco Opera*, 2 volumes. Amsterdam: F. Muller, 1866, 107–14.

La Piana, George. 'The Roman Church at the End of the Second Century.' *Harvard Theological Review* 18 (1925), 214–77.

Lages, Mario. 'The Hierosolymitian Origin of the Catechetical Rites in the Armenian Liturgy.' *Didaskalia* 1 (1971), 233–50.

Lakoff, George and Mark Johnson. *Philosophy in the Flesh: The Embodied Mind and Its Challenge to Western Thought.* New York: Basic Books, 1999.

Lara, Jaime. '"Precious Green Jade Water": A Sixteenth-Century Adult Catechumenate in the New World.' *Worship* 71 (1997), 415–28.

Lausten, Martin Schwarz. *A Church History of Denmark.* Aldershot: Ashgate, 2002.

Leachman, James. 'The New Family of Common Worship Liturgical Books of the Church of England (2): An Introduction to the Initiation Services and their Theology.' *Ecclesia Orans* 21 (2004), 67–97.

Ledwich, William. 'Baptism, Sacrament of the Cross: Looking behind St. Ambrose.' In *The Sacrifice of Praise. Studies on the themes of thanksgiving and redemption in the central prayers of the Eucharistic and baptismal liturgies. In honour of Arthur Hubert Couratin*. Edited by Bryan D. Spinks. Rome: CLV, 1981.

Lee, Daniel B. *Old Order Mennonites. Rituals, Beliefs, and Community*. Chicago, IL: Burnham Inc., 2000.

Leenhardt, F.-J. *Le Baptême chrétien, son origine, sa signification*. Neuchâtel: Delachaux & Niestlé, 1946.

Leeper, Elizabeth A. 'From Alexandria to Rome: The Valentinian Connection to the Incorporation of Exorcism as a Prebaptismal Rite.' *Vigiliae Christianae* 44 (1990), 6–24.

Lentz, Harold H. *Reformation Crossroads*. Minneapolis, MN: Augsburg Publishing House, 1958.

Lester, Hiram J. 'Alexander Campbell's Millennial Program.' *Discipliana* 48 (1988), 35–9.

Lewis, A.J. *Zinzendorf the Ecumenical Pioneer*. London: SCM Press, 1962.

Linyard, Fred and Phillip Tovey. *Moravian Worship*. Bramcote: Grove Books, 1994.

Liturgic Hymns of the United Brethren, Revised and Enlarged: Translated from the German. London, 1793.

Liturgie à l'usage des Réformées. Paris, 1874.

The Liturgy of the Frankfurt Exiles 1555. Edited by Robin A. Leaver. Bramcote: Grove Books, 1984, 9–11.

The Liturgy of the Holy Apostles Addai and Mari, and the Order of Baptism. London: SPCK, 1893. Reprinted Piscataway, NJ: Georgias Press, 2002.

A Liturgy: or, Order of Christian Worship. Philadelphia, PA, 1865.

Loades, Anne. 'Finding New Sense in the "Sacramental."' In *The Gestures of God. Explorations in Sacramentality*. Edited by Geoffrey Rowell and Christine Hall. New York: Continuum, 2004, 161–72.

Logan, Alastair H. *Gnostic Truth and Christian Heresy*. Edinburgh: T & T Clark, 1996.

———. 'The Mystery of the Five Seals: Gnostic Initiation Reconsidered.' *Vigiliae Christianae* 51 (1997), 188–206.

Lombard, Peter. 'Sacrum signans et sacrum signatum.' In *Sententiae in IV Libris Distinctae*, 2 volumes. Grottaferrata: Collegii S. Bonaventurae ad Claras Aquas, 1981 <http://franciscan-archive.org/lombardus/index.html#writings>.

Lukken, G.M. *Original Sin in the Roman Liturgy*. Leiden: E.J. Brill, 1973.

Lumbala, F. Kabasele. 'Black Africa and Baptismal Rites.' In *Becoming a Christian. The Ecumenical Implications of our Common Baptism*. Edited by Thomas F. Best and Dagmar Heller. Geneva: WCC Publications, 1999, 36–40.

Lumpkin, William L. *Baptist Confessions of Faith.* Valley Forge, PA: Judson Press, 1969.

Luther, Martin. *Luther's Works, American Edition*, 55 volumes. Edited by Jaroslav Pelikan and Helmut T. Lehman. St Louis, MO: Concordia Publishing House and Philadelphia: Fortress Press, 1955–86.

———. *Luthers Werke, Kritische Gesamtausgabe*, 57 volumes. Edited by J.F.K. Knaake et al. Weimer: Bühlau, 1883–2003.

Lutheran Liturgical Association. 'The Liturgical Deterioration of the Seventeenth and Eighteenth Centuries.' *Memoirs of the Lutheran Liturgical Association IV.* Philadelphia, PA: 1906–07, 67–78.

———. 'The Liturgy in Denmark.' *Memoirs of the Lutheran Liturgical Association II.* Philadelphia, PA: 1906–07, 63–73.

Lynch, Joseph H. *Christianizing Kinship. Ritual Sponsorship in Anglo-Saxon England.* Ithaca, NY and London: Cornell University Press, 1998.

———. *Godparents and Kinship in Early Medieval Europe.* Princeton, NJ: Princeton University Press, 1986.

Lyon, David. *Jesus in Disneyland. Religion in Postmodern Times.* Cambridge: Polity Press, 2000.

MacCulloch, Diarmaid. *Thomas Cranmer.* New Haven, CT and London: Yale University Press, 1996.

Mackenzie, Ross. *The Epistles of Paul the Apostle to the Romans and to the Thessalonians.* Edinburgh: Oliver and Boyd, 1961.

Macomber, W.F. (ed.). *Six Explanations of the Liturgical Feasts* (CSCO 356). Louvain: Corpus Scriptorum Christianorum Orientalium, 1974.

———. 'The Theological Synthesis of Cyrus of Edessa, an East Syrian Theologian of the Mid Sixth Century.' *Orientalia Christiana Periodica,* 1964, 1–38, 150, 363–84.

Macquarrie, John. *A Guide to the Sacraments.* New York: Continuum, 1997.

The Mail on Sunday, 26 December 2004, p. 3.

Maring, Norman H. and Winthrop S. Hudson. *A Baptist Manual of Polity and Practice.* Valley Forge, PA: Judson Press, 1963, 129–36.

Martimort, A.G. (ed.). *The Church at Prayer. Volume III: The Sacraments.* London: Geoffrey Chapman, 1988.

———. *The Signs of the New Covenant.* Collegeville, MN: ET Liturgical Press, 1963, 135–6.

Mateos, Juan. 'Théologie du Baptême dans le formulaire de Severe D'Antioche.' *Symposium Syriacum 1972.* Rome: Pontifical Oriental Institute, 1974, 135–61.

Matheson, Peter. *The Collected Works of Thomas Müntzer.* Edinburgh: T & T Clark, 1988.

Maurice, F.D. *The Faith of the Liturgy and the Doctrines of the Thirty-Nine Articles, Two Sermons.* Cambridge, 1869, 19–20.

Mbonigaba, Elisha. 'Indigenization of the Liturgy.' In *A Kingdom of Priests: Liturgical Formation of the People of God*. Edited by Thomas J. Talley. Nottingham: Alcuin/ GROW Liturgical Study 5, 1988, 39–47.

McAllister, Lester G. and William E. Tucker. *Journey in Faith*. St Louis, MO: Bethany Press, 1975, 61–2, 73.

McClendon, James William Jr. *Systematic Theology: Doctrine*. Nashville, TN: Abingdon Press, 1994.

McGrath, Alister E. *Iustitia Dei. A History of the Christian Doctrine of Justification. Volume 2: From 1500 to the Present Day*. Cambridge: Cambridge University Press, 1986, 10–20.

McHugh, John A. and Charles J. Callan (trans). *Catechism of the Council of Trent for Parish Priests. Issued by Order of Pope Pius V*. New York: Joseph F. Wagner, 1923.

McKillop, Sybil. 'A Romano-British Baptismal Liturgy?' In *The Early Church in Western Britain and Ireland*. Edited by Susan M. Pearce, BAR British Series 102 (1982), 35–48.

Mcleod, Frederick G. 'The Christological Ramifications of Theodore of Mopsuestia's Understanding of Baptism and the Eucharist.' *Journal of Early Christian Studies* 10 (2002), 37–75.

Meeter, Daniel James. *'Bless the Lord, O my Soul'. The New-York Liturgy of the Dutch Reformed Church, 1767*. Lanham, MD: Scarecrow Press, 1998.

Melanchthon, Philip. *Commentary on Romans*. Translated by Fred Kramer. St. Louis, MO: Concordia Publishing House, 1992.

Methuen, Charlotte. 'Widows, Bishops and the Struggle for Authority in the *Didascalia Apostolorum*.' *Journal of Ecclesiastical History* 46 (1995), 197–213.

Meyers, Ruth A. *Continuing the Reformation. Re-Visioning Baptism in the Episcopal Church*. New York: Church Publishing Incorporated, 1997.

Mingana, Alphonse. *Woodbrooke Studies*, Volume 6. Cambridge: Heffers, 1933.

Mirk, John. *Instructions for Parish Priests*. Edited by Edward Peacock. London: Kegan Paul, Trench, Trübner, 1902.

———. *Mirk's Festial: A Collection of Homilies*. London: Kegan Paul, Trench and Trübner (for the Early English Text Society), 1905.

———. *Quatuor Sermones*. Edited by R. Pynson. London, 1502.

Mitchell, Leonel L. 'Mitchell on Hatchett on Cranmer.' In *With Ever Joyful Hearts. Essays on Liturgy and Music Honoring Marion J. Hatchett*. Edited by J. Neil Alexander. New York: Church Publishing Incorporated, 1999, 103–38.

Mitchell, Nathan. 'Baptism in the Didache.' In *The Didache in Context*. Edited by Clayton N. Jefford. Leiden: E.J. Brill, 1995, 226–55.

Moltmann, Jürgen. *The Church in the Power of the Spirit. A Contribution to Messianic Ecclesiology*. London: ET SCM Press, 1977.

Moravian Church. *The Liturgy and Canticles authorized for use in the Moravian Church in Great Britain and Ireland*. London: Moravian Publication Office, 1914.

Morris, Richard. *Old English Homilies and Homiletic Treatises.* New York: Greenwood Press, 1968.

Mouhanna, Augustin. *Les Rites de l'initiation dans l'Église Maronite.* Rome: Orientalia Periodica Analecta, 1980.

Muller, Richard. *Post-Reformation Dogmatics. Volume 1: Prolegomena to Theology.* Grand Rapids, MI: Baker Book House, 1987, 13–52.

Myers, Gilly. *Using Common Worship: Initiation.* London: Church House Publishing, 2000, 27–32.

Mysteries of Initiation. Baptism, Confirmation, Communion According to the Maronite Antiochene Church. Washington, DC: Diocesan Office of Liturgy, 1987.

Myers, Susan. 'Initiation by Anointing in Early Syriac-Speaking Christianity.' *Studia Liturgica* 31 (2001), 150–70.

Nagel, Norman E. 'Holy Baptism.' In *Lutheran Worship. History and Practice.* Edited by Fred L. Precht. St Louis, MO: Concordia Publishing House, 1993.

Nevin, John W. 'The Mystical Presence: A Vindication of the Reformed or Calvinistic Doctrine of the Holy Eucharist.' In *The Mystical Presence and Other Writings on the Eucharist.* Edited by Bard Thompson and George H. Bicker. Philadelphia, PA: United Church Press, 1966.

Niederwimmer, Kurt. *Didache.* Minneapolis, MN: ET Augsburg Fortress Press, 1998.

Nischan, Bodo. 'The Exorcism Controversy and Baptism in the Late Reformation.' *The Sixteenth Century Journal* 18 (1987), 31–50.

———. *Prince, People and Confession. The Second Reformation in Brandenburg.* Philadelphia: University of Pennsylvania Press, 1994.

Noll, Mark A. *The Rise of Evangelicalism. The Age of Edwards, Whitefield and the Wesleys.* Downers Grove, IL: Intervarsity Press, 2003.

Null, Ashley. *Thomas Cranmer's Doctrine of Repentance.* Oxford: Oxford University Press, 2000.

Nümann, F.K. 'Zur Entstehung des lutherischen Taufbüchleins von Jahre 1523.' *Monatschrift für Gottesdienst und kirchliche Kunst* 33 (1928), 214–19.

Oberman, Heiko. *The Harvest of Medieval Theology.* Cambridge, MA: Harvard University Press, 1963.

Old, H.O. *The Shaping of the Reformed Baptismal Rite in the Sixteenth Century.* Grand Rapids, MI: Eerdmans, 1992.

The Old Testament Pseudepigrapha, Volume 1. Edited by J.H. Charlesworth. Garden City, NJ: Doubleday, 1983.

The Order of Baptism according to the Rite of the Armenian Apostolic Orthodox Church. Evanston, IL: n.p., 1964.

Ostervald, J.F. *A Compendium of Christian Theology.* Translated by John McMains. Hartford, CT: Nathaniel Patten, 1788.

Page, R.I. 'Old English Liturgical Rubrics in Corpus Christi College, Cambridge, MS 422.' In *Anglia. Zeitschrift für Englische Philologie* 96 (1978), 149–58.

Pahl, P.D. 'Baptism in Luther's Lectures on Genesis.' *Lutheran Theological Journal 1* (1967), 26–35.

Pannenberg, Wolfhart. *Systematic Theology*, Volume 3. Translated by Geoffrey W. Bromiley. Grand Rapids, MI: Eerdmans, 1998.

Parenti, Stefano and Elena Velkovska. *L'Eucologio Barberini gr. 336.* Rome: Centro Liturgico Vincenziano, 1995.

Parker, Kenneth L. and Eric J. Carlson. *'Practical Divinity'. The Works and Life of Revd. Richard Greenham.* Aldershot: Ashgate, 1998.

Parons, K.A. (ed.). *Church Book: St Andrews' Street Baptist Church, Cambridge, 1720–1832.* London: Baptist Historical Society, 1991, 41–2.

Pater, C.A. *Karlstadt as the Father of the Baptist Movement: The Emergence of Lay Protestantism.* Toronto: University of Toronto Press, 1984, 92–114.

Payne, John B. 'Nevin on Baptism.' In *Reformed Confessionalism in Nineteenth-century America. Essays on the Thought of John Williamson Nevin.* Edited by Sam Hamstra and Arie J. Griffion. Lanham, MD: Scarecrow Press, 1995, 125–51.

Pearson, Brook W.R. 'Baptism and Initiation in the Cult of Isis and Sarapis.' In *Baptism in the New Testament and the Church. Historical and Contemporary Studies in Honour of R.E.O. White.* Edited by Stanley E. Porter and Anthony R. Cross. Sheffield: Sheffield Academic Press, 1999, 42–62.

Peaston, A.E. *The Prayer Book Tradition in the Free Churches.* London: James Clarke, 1964.

Peifer, Jane Hoober and John Stahl-Wert. *Welcoming New Christians. A Guide for the Christian Initiation of Adults.* Scottdale, PA: Faith and Life Press, Kansas and Mennonite Publishing House, 1995.

Pepperdene, Margaret. 'Baptism in the early British and Irish Churches.' *Irish Theological Quarterly* 22 (1955), 110–23.

Perkins, William. *Works*, 3 volumes. Cambridge: J. Legatt and C. Legge, 1616–18.

Peter Lombard <http://franciscan-archive.org/lombardus/index.html#writings>.

Pettigree, Andrew. *Foreign Protestant Communities in Sixteenth-Century London.* Oxford: Clarendon Press, 1986.

Pierce, Mark. 'Themes in the "Odes of Solomon" and other early Christian Writings and their Baptismal Character.' *Ephemerides Liturgicae* 98 (1984), 35–59.

Podmore, Colin. *The Moravian Church in England, 1728–1760.* Oxford: Clarendon Press, 1998.

Porter, H. Boone. 'Hispanic Influences on Worship in the English Tongue.' In *Time and Community. In Honor of Thomas Julian Talley.* Edited by J. Neil Alexander. Washington, DC: Pastoral Press, 1990, 171–84.

———. *Jeremy Taylor, Liturgist.* London: Alcuin Club/SPCK, 1979.

———. 'Maxentius of Aquileia and the North Italian Baptismal Rites.' *Ephemerides Liturgicae* 69 (1955), 3–8.

Porter, Stanley E. and Anthony R. Cross. *Baptism in the New Testament and the Church. Historical and Contemporary Studies in Honour of R.E.O. White.* Sheffield: Sheffield Academic Press, 1999.

Primus, John H. *Richard Greenham. The Portrait of an Elizabethan Pastor.* Macon, GA: Mercer University Press, 1998.

Probert, J.C.C. *The Worship and Devotion of Cornish Methodism* (cyclostyled), n.p., 1978 (copy in the Bodleian Library, Oxford).

Psalmodia Christiana. Translated by Arthur Anderson. Salt Lake City: University of Utah Press, 1993.

Pusey, Edward. *Tracts for the Times*, 3 volumes. New York: Charles Henry, 1839–40.

Quenstedt, J. *Theologica Didactio-Polemica sive Systema Theologicum*, 1685.

Quere, Ralph W. *In the Context of Unity. A History of the Development of Lutheran Book of Worship.* Minneapolis, MN: Lutheran University Press, 2003.

Quill, Timothy C.J. *The Impact of the Liturgical Movement on American Lutheranism.* Lanham, MD: Scarecrow Press, 1997.

Randall, Max Ward. *The Great Awakenings and the Restoration Movement.* Joplin, MO: College Press Publishing Company, 1983.

Rappaport, Roy A. *Ritual and Religion in the Making of Humanity.* Cambridge: Cambridge University Press, 1999.

Ratcliff, E.C. (ed.). *Expositio Antiquae Liturgiae Gallicanae.* London: Henry Bradshaw Society, 1971.

————. 'Justin Martyr and Confirmation.' *Theology* 51 (1948), 133–9.

————. 'The Old Syrian Baptismal Tradition and its Resettlement under the Influence of Jerusalem in the Fourth Century.' In *Liturgical Studies.* Edited by A.H. Couratin and D.H. Tripp. London: SPCK, 1976, 135–54, 142–3.

Reed, Jonathan. 'The Hebrew Epic and the *Didache*.' In *The Didache in Context.* Edited by Clayton N. Jefford. Leiden: E.J. Brill, 1995, 213–25.

Reid, Alcuin. *The Organic Development of the Liturgy.* Farnborough: Saint Michael's Abbey Press, 2004.

Renoux, Charles. *Initiation chrétienne. 1. Rituels arméniens du baptême.* Paris: Les Éditions du Cerf, 1997, 5ff.

Reports to the General Assembly. Edinburgh, 1955.

Rex, Richard. *The Lollards.* New York: Palgrave, 2002.

Rican, Rudolf. *The History of the Unity of Brethren.* Bethlehem, PA: The Moravian Church in America, 1992.

Richardson, Robert. *Memoirs of Alexander Campbell,* Volume 1. Cincinnati, OH: Standard Publishing Company, 1913, 396–8.

Richter, A.L. *Die evangelischen Kirchenordnungen des sechzehnten Jahrhunderts*, Volume 1. Nieuwkoop: B. Degraaf, 1967.

Ridgley, Thomas. *A Body of Divinity*, Volume 2. Edited by John M. Wilson. New York: Robert Carter and Brothers, 1855.

Riggs, John W. *Baptism in the Reformed Tradition.* Louisville, KY: Westminster John Knox Press, 2002.

————. 'Traditions, Tradition, and Liturgical Norms: The United Church of Christ Book of Worship.' *Worship* 62 (1988), 58–72.

Riley, Hugh M. *Christian Initiation.* Washington, DC: Catholic University of America, 1974.

Rittgers, Ronald. *The Reformation of the Keys. Confession, Conscience, and Authority in Sixteenth-Century Germany.* Cambridge, MA: Harvard University Press, 2004.

Roberts, Paul J. 'The Pattern of Initiation: Sacrament and Experience in the Catholic Apostolic Church and its implications for modern liturgical and theological debate.' Ph.D. thesis, University of Manchester, 1990.

Robinson, H. Wheeler. *Baptist Principles.* London: Kingsgate Press, 1938.

Robinson, J.A.T. 'The Baptism of John and the Qumran Community.' In *Twelve New Testament Studies.* London: SCM, 1962, 11–17.

Rodgers, Dirk W. *John à Lasco in England.* New York: Peter Lang, 1994.

Roman Catholic Church. *Study Text 10 CIA: Commentary.* Washington, DC, 1985.

Rordorf, Willi. 'Baptism according to the Didache.' In *The Didache in Modern Research.* Edited by Jonathan A. Draper. Leiden: E.J. Brill, 1996, 212–22.

Rorem, Paul. *Calvin and Bullinger on the Lord's Supper.* Bramcote: Alcuin/GROW Liturgical Study 12, Grove Books, 1989.

Ross, Susan. *Extravagant Affections. A Feminist Sacramental Theology.* New York: Continuum, 1998.

Ross, Woodburn O. *Middle English Sermons.* London: Oxford University Press, 1940.

Rouget, A.M. *Christ Acts Through Sacraments.* Collegeville, MN: The Liturgical Press, 1954.

Ruether, Rosemary Radford. W*omen-Church. Theology and Practice of Feminist Liturgical Communities.* San Francisco, CA: Harper and Row, 1985, 183–6.

St. Thomas Aquinas, Summa Theologiae, ST 3a.60.1, 56. Edited by David Bourke. London: Blackfriars and Eyre and Spottiswoode, 1974, 5.

Samuel, Metropolitan Mar Athanasius Yeshue. *The Sacrament of Holy Baptsim according to the Ancient Rite of the Syrian Orthodox Church of Antioch.* Hackensack, NJ, 1974.

Sanders, E.P. *Paul.* Oxford: Oxford University Press, 1991.

———. *Paul and Palestinian Judaism: A Comparison of Patterns of Religion.* London: SCM Press, 1977.

Scaer, David P. *Baptism. Confessional Lutheran Dogmatics*, Volume XI. St Louis, MO: The Luther Academy, 1999.

Schaff, Philip. *The Creeds of Christendom.* Grand Rapids, MI: Baker Books, 1998.

Scharen, Christian. *Public Worship and Public Work. Character and Commitment in Local Congregational Life.* Collegeville, MN: Pueblo Liturgical Press, 2004.

Schleiermacher, F. *The Christian Faith*, Edinburgh: ET T & T Clark, 1989.

Schmid, Heinrich. *The Doctrinal Theology of the Evangelical Lutheran Church.* Translated by Charles A. Hay and Henry E. Jacobs. Philadelphia, PA: Lutheran Bookstore, 1876, 553–70.

Scirughi, Thomas J. *An Examination of the Problems of Inclusive Language in the Trinitarian Formula of Baptism.* Lewiston, NY: Edwin Mellon Press, 2000.

The Scriptures, Internet Edition. The Church of Jesus Christ of Latter-Day Saints <http://scriptures.lds.org>.

The Second Helvetic Confession <http://www.ccel.org/creeds/helvetic.htm>.

Segelberg, E. 'The Baptismal Rite according to some of the Coptic-Gnostic Texts of Nag Hammadi.' *Studia Patristica* 5, Part Three (1962), 117–28.

Serra, Dominic E. *The Blessing of Baptismal Water at the Paschal Vigil (Gr. 444–448): Its Origins, Evolution, and Reform.* Diss. Pontifical Institute of Liturgy, St Anselmo, Rome, 1989.

Severus of Antioch. *The sixth book of the select letters of Severus, patriarch of Antioch, in the Syriac version of Athanasius of Nisbis.* Edited and translated by E.W. Brooks. London: Williams and Norgate, 1903.

Shaw, P.E. *The Catholic Apostolic Church.* New York: Kings Crown Press, 1946.

Shriver, Fred. 'Hampton Court Re-Visited: James I and the Puritans.' *Journal of Ecclesiastical History* 33 (1982), 48–71.

Small, Joseph D. 'A Church of the Word and Sacrament.' In *Christian Worship in Reformed Churches Past and Present.* Edited by Lukas Vischer. Grand Rapids, MI: Eerdmans, 2003, 311–23, 318–19.

Smith, Joseph Jr. *History of the Church of Jesus Christ of Latter-day Saints*, Volume 4. Salt Lake City, UT: Deseret Book Co., 1976.

Soskice, Janet Martin. *Metaphor and Religious Language.* Oxford: Clarendon Press, 1985.

Spencer, Mark. 'Dating the Baptism of Clovis, 1886–1993.' *Early Medieval Europe* 3 (1994), 97–116.

Spener, Philip. *Pia Desideria.* Edited and translated by Theodore G. Tappert. Philadelphia, PA: Fortress Press, 1964.

Spinks, Bryan D. 'The Anaphora attributed to Severus of Antioch: a note on its character and theology.' In Θυσία αινέσες. *Mélanges liturgiques offerts à la mémoire de l'archevêque George Wagner.* Edited by J. Getcha and A. Lossky. Paris: Presses Saint-Serge, 2005, 345–51.

———. 'Calvin's Baptismal Theology and the Making of the Strasbourg and Genevan Baptismal Liturgies 1540 and 1542.' *Scottish Journal of Theology* 48 (1995), 55–78.

———. 'Cranmer, Baptism, and Christian Nurture; or, Toronto Revisited.' *Studia Liturgica* 32 (2002), 98–110.

———. '"Freely by His Grace": Baptismal doctrine and the reform of the baptismal liturgy in the Church of Scotland, 1953–1994.' In *Rule of Prayer, Rule of Faith: Essays in Honor of Aidan Kavanagh, OSB.* Edited by Nathan Mitchell and John F. Baldovin. Collegeville, MN: Liturgical Press, 1996, 218–42.

———. *From the Lord and 'The Best Reformed Churches.'* Rome: CLV, 1984.

———, 'Johannes Grabe's Response to William Whiston.' In *Lord Jesus Christ, Will You Not Stay. Essays in Honor of Ronald Feuerhahn on the Occasion of His Sixty-Fifth Birthday.* Edited by Bart Day et al. St Louis, MO: Concordia Publishing House, 2002, 91–104.

————. 'Karl Barth's Teaching on Baptism: Its Development, Antecedents and the "Liturgical Factor."' *Ecclesia Orans* 14 (1997), 261–88.

————. 'Luther's Timely Theology of Unilateral Baptism.' *Lutheran Quarterly* 9 (1995), 23–45.

————. 'Reflections based on a study of Church of Scotland Reports.' In *Christian Initiation – A Policy for the Church of England.* A discussion paper by Canon Martin Reardon. London: Church House Publishing, London, 1991.

————. *Two Faces of Elizabethan Anglican Theology. Sacraments and Salvation in the Theology of William Perkins and Richard Hooker.* Lanham, MD: Scarecrow Press, 1999, 35–7.

————. 'Two Seventeenth Century Examples of *Lex Credendi, Lex Orandi*: The Baptismal and Eucharistic Liturgies of Jeremy Taylor and Richard Baxter.' *Studia Liturgica* 21 (1991), 165–89.

————. *Sacraments, Ceremonies, and the Stuart Divines. Sacramental Theology and Liturgy in England and Scotland 1603–1662.* Aldershot: Ashgate, 2001, 126–7.

————. 'Treasures Old and New: A Look at Some of Thomas Cranmer's Methods of Liturgical Compilation.' In *Thomas Cranmer: Churchman and Scholar.* Edited by Paul Ayris and David Selwyn. Woodbridge: The Boydell Press, 1993, 175–88.

Sprengler-Ruppenthal, A. *Mysterium und Riten nach der Londoner Kirchordnung der Niederländer.* Köln: Böhlau Verlag, 1967.

Sprott, G.W. *Scottish Liturgies of the Reign of James VI.* Edinburgh: William Blackwood, 1901.

Starck (Stark), Johann F. *Tägliches Hand-Buch in guten und bösen Tagen.* Milwaukee, WI: Verlag von Georg Brumder, n.d.

Stauffer, S. Anita (ed.). *Baptism, Rites of Passage, and Culture.* Geneva: Lutheran World Federation Studies, 1998.

Stephens, Peter. *The Holy Spirit in the Theology of Martin Bucer.* Cambridge: Cambridge University Press, 1970.

————. *The Theology of Huldrych Zwingli.* Oxford: Clarendon Press, 1986.

————. 'Zwingli's Sacramental Views.' In *Prophet, Pastor, Protestant.* Edited by E.J. Furcha and H. Wayne Pipkin. Allison Park, PA: Pickwick Publications, 1984, 155–69.

Steuart, Walter. *Collections and Observations Methodiz'd Concerning the Worship, Discipline, and Government of the Church of Scotland in Four Books.* Edinburgh, 1709.

Steven, James H.S. *Worship in the Spirit. Charismatic Worship in the Church of England.* Carlisle: Paternoster Press, 2002.

Stevenson, K.W. 'The Byzantine Liturgy of Baptism.' *Studia Liturgica* 17 (1987), 176–90.

Stevick, Daniel B. *Baptismal Moments; Baptismal Meanings.* New York: The Church Hymnal Corporation, 1987.

Stewart-Sykes, Alistair. 'Manumission and Baptism in Tertullian's Africa: A Search for the Origin of Confirmation.' *Studia Liturgica* 31 (2001), 129–49.

Strabo, Walafrid. *'Libellus de exordiis et incrementis quarundam in observationibis ecclesiae.'* In *Christianizing Kinship. Ritual Sponsorship in Anglo-Saxon England.* By Joseph H. Lynch. Ithaca, NY and London: Cornell University Press, 1998.

Sutcliffe, E.F. 'Baptism and Baptismal Rites at Qumran.' *Heythrop Journal* 1 (1960), 69–101.

Swedenborg, Emanuel. *The True Christian Religion*, Volume 2. London: Swedenborg Society, 1988.

Sykes, Stephen. 'Baptisme doth represente unto us oure profession.' In *Thomas Cranmer, Essays in Commemoration of the 500th Anniversary of his Birth.* Edited by Margot Johnson. Durham: Turnstone Ventures, 1990.

Syrian Orthodox Church. 'The Baptism of the Lord Jesus.' *The Patriarchal Journal* 32 (1994), No. 131–2, 2–7 <http://syrianorthodoxchurch.org/library/sermons.baptism.htm>.

Talmage, James E. *The Articles of Faith* [1890], *The Deseret News* edition, Salt Lake City, UT: 1919.

Tanner, Sandra. 'Baptism for the Dead and the Twelve Oxen Under the Baptismal Font.' <http://www.utlm.org/onlineresources/twelveoxenbaptismalfont.htm>.

Taylor, Jeremy. *Works*, Heber-Eden edition, Volume 7. London, 1847–52.

Thodberg, Christian. 'The Importance of Baptism in Grundtvig's View of Christianity.' In *Heritage and Prophecy. Grundtvig and the English-Speaking World.* Edited by A.M. Allchin et al., Aarhus: Aarhus University Press, 1993, 133–52.

Thomas, John Christopher. *Footwashing in John 13 and the Johannine Community.* Sheffield: Sheffield Academic Press, 1991.

Thomson, Robert. *Agathangelos History of the Armenians.* Albany, NY: SUNY, 1976.

Thomson, Robert W. *The Teaching of Saint Gregory*, 2nd edition. New Rochelle, NY: St. Nersess Armenian Seminary, 2001, 120ff.

Toews, Abraham P. *American Mennonite Worship.* New York: Exposition Press, 1960.

Toon, Peter. *Evangelical Theology 1833–1856. A Response to Tractarianism.* Atlanta, GA: John Knox Press, 1979.

Torrance, Iain R. 'Fear of Being Left Out.' In *To Glorify God. Essays on Modern Reformed Liturgy.* Edited by Bryan D. Spinks and Iain R. Torrance. Edinburgh: T & T Clark, 1999, 159–72.

Torrance, T.F. 'The One Baptism Common to Christ and His Church.' In *Theology in Reconciliation.* Edited by Thomas Torrance. London: Geoffrey Chapman, 1975.

———. 'Report of the Special Commission on Baptism 1955.' In *Reports to the General Assembly*, Church of Scotland, Edinburgh, 1955, 623.

Tovey, Philip. *Essays in West Syrian Liturgy.* Kottayam, Kerala, India: Oriental Institute of Religious Studies, 1998.

Tranvik, Mark David. 'The Other Sacrament: the doctrine of baptism in the late Lutheran Reformation.' Th.D. Thesis, Luther North Western Seminary, 1992.

Trigg, Jonathan. *Baptism in the Theology of Martin Luther.* Leiden: E.J. Brill, 1994.

Trobridge, G. *Swedenborg. Life and Teaching.* London: Swedenborg Society, 1935.

Truscott, Jeffrey A. *The Reform of Baptism and Confirmation in American Lutheranism.* Lanham, MD: Scarecrow Press, Inc., 2003.

Tucker, Karen B. Westerfield. *American Methodist Worship.* New York: Oxford University Press, 2001.

Turner, Paul. 'The Origins of Confirmation: An Analysis of Aidan Kavanagh's Hypothesis.' In *Living Water, Sealing Spirit.* Edited by Maxwell E. Johnson. Collegeville, MN: Pueblo, 1995, 238–58.

Turrettin, Francis. *Institutes of Elenctic Theology*, Volume 3. Translated by George Giger; edited by. James T. Dennison. Phillipsburg, NJ: Presbyterian and Reformed Publishing Company, 1997, 341–2.

Umble, John. 'An Amish Minister's Manual.' In *The Mennonite Quarterly* 15 (1941), 95–117, 106–7.

Underwood, Grant. *The Millenarian World of Early Mormonism.* Urbana and Chicago: University of Illinois, 1993.

Underwood, T.L. *Primitivism, Radicalism, and the Lamb's War. The Baptist–Quaker Conflict in Seventeenth-Century England.* Oxford: Oxford University Press, 1997.

Van de Sandt, Huub and David Flusser. *The Didache.* Minneapolis, MN: Fortress Press, 2002.

Van Gennep, Arnold. *The Rites of Passage.* Chicago, IL: University of Chicago Press, 1960.

Van Slyke, Daniel. 'Augustine and Catechumenal "Exsufflatio": An Integral Element of Christian Initiation.' *Ephemerides Liturgicae* 118 (2004), 175–208.

The Vercelli Book Homilies. Edited by Lewis E. Nicholson. Lanham, MD and London: University Press of America, 1991.

Vial, Theodore M. *Liturgy Wars. Ritual Theory and Protestant Reform in Nineteenth-Century Zurich.* New York: Routledge, 2004.

Vogel, Cyrille. *Le Pontifical Romano-Germanique Du Dixième Siècle*, 3 volumes. Vatican City: Biblioteca Apostolica Vaticana, 1963–72.

—————. *Medieval Liturgy. An Introduction to the Sources*, Washington, DC: Pastoral Press, 1986.

Vokes, F.E. *The Riddle of the Didache: Fact or Fiction, Heresy or Catholicism?* London: SPCK, 1938.

Von Rad, Gerhard. *Old Testament Theology*, Volume 2. Edinburgh: Oliver and Boyd, 1965.

Wade, Carol. *Stories of Resurrection: Traces of God in New Community*, STM Thesis. Yale Institute of Sacred Music and Yale Divinity School, 2004.

Walker, Joan Hazelden. 'A pre-Marcan Dating for the Didache: Further Thoughts of a Liturgist.' *Studia Biblica* 1978, 403–411.

Ward, Glenn. *Postmodernism.* London: Hodder Headline Ltd, 1997.

Watson, Richard. *The Works of the Rev. Richard Watson*, 12 volumes, Volume XII. London, 1834–38.

Ways of Worship: the report of a theological commission of faith and order. Edited by P. Edwall, E. Hayman and W.D. Maxwell. London: SCM Press, 1951.

Webb, D. 'The Mimra on the Interpretation of the Mysteries by Rabban Johannam Bar Zo'bi and its symbolism.' *Le Muséon* 88 (1975), 297–326.

Webster, John. *Barth's Ethics of Reconciliation.* Cambridge: Cambridge University Press, 1995.

Wedderburn, A.J.M. *Baptism and Resurrection. Studies in Pauline Theology Against its Graeco-Roman Background.* Tübingen: J.C.B. Mohr, 1987.

Weir, D.A. *The Origins of the Federal Theology in Sixteenth-Century Reformation Thought.* Oxford: Clarendon Press, 1990.

'Welcoming in the Community of Disciples.' Unpublished Draft 1, Baptist Church of Great Britain, 2004.

Wenger, John C. *The Complete Writings of Menno Simons.* Scottdale, PA: Herald Press, 1956.

Wesley, Charles. *The Journal of the Rev. Charles Wesley*, Volume 1. London: John Mason and Grand Rapids, MI: Baker Book Reprint [1849], 1980.

Wesley, John. *The Journal of the Rev. John Wesley*, Volume 2. Edited by Nehemiah Curnock. London: Epworth Press, 1938.

———. *The Works of the Rev. John Wesley*, Volume 6. London: John Mason, 1856, 73–4.

West, Charles C. 'Baptism in the Reformed Tradition.' In *Baptism, Peace and the State in the Reformed and Mennonite Traditions.* Edited by Ross T. Bender and Alan P.F. Sell. Waterloo, IA: Wilfrid Laurier Press, 1991, 13–36.

Westminster Assembly. *The Westminster Directory.* Edited by Ian Breward. Bramcote: Grove Books, 1980.

Wettach, Theodor. *Kirche bei Zinzendorf.* Wuppertal: Theologischer Verlag Rolf Brockhaus, 1971.

Wheeler, Geraldine. 'Traditions and Principles of Reformed Worship in the Uniting Church in Australia.' In *Christian Worship in Reformed Churches Past and Present.* Edited by Lukas Vischer. Grand Rapids, MI: Eerdmans, 2003, 261–79.

Whitaker, E.C. *Documents of the Baptismal Liturgy.* Revised and expanded by Maxwell E. Johnson, 3rd edition. Collegeville, MN: Liturgical Press, 2003, 18–19.

White, B.R. *The English Baptists of the Seventeenth Century.* Didcot: Baptist Historical Society, 1996.

Wickremesinghe, Francis. 'An Asian Inculturation of the Baptismal Liturgy.' In *Growing in Newness of Life.* Edited by David R. Holeton. Toronto: Anglican Book Centre, 1993, 213–17.

Wiles, Maurice. 'Triple and Single Immersion: Baptism in the Arian Controversy.' *Studia Patristica* 30, Peeters, Leuven, 1997, 337–49.

Williams, Rowan. 'Baptism and the Arian Controversy.' In *Arianism After Arius*. Edited by Michael R. Barnes and Daniel H. Williams. Edinburgh: T & T Clark, 1993, 149–80.

Williard, G.W. *The Commentary of Dr. Zacherias Ursinus on the Heidelberg Catechism*. Grand Rapids, MI: Eerdmans, 1954.

Winkler, Gabriele. 'Confirmation or Chrismation? A Study in Comparative Liturgy.' In *Living Water, Sealing Spirit*. Edited by Maxwell E. Johnson. Collegeville, MD: Pueblo, 1995.

————. *Das Armenische Initiationsrituale. Orientalia Christiana Analecta* 217. Rome: Pontifical Oriental Institute, 1982.

————. 'Nochmals zu den Anfängen der Epiklese und des Sanctus im Eucharistischen Hochgebet.' *Theologische Quartalschrift* 174 (1994), 214–31.

————. 'The Original Meaning of the Pre-baptismal Anointing and Its Implication.' *Worship* 52 (1978), 24–45.

Wolf, William J. 'Frederick Denison Maurice.' In *The Spirit of Anglicanism*. Edited by William J. Wolf, John E. Booty and Owen C. Thomas. Edinburgh: T & T Clarke, 1979.

Wolfgramm, Luke. 'An Examination of the Pietistic Content of Johann Friedrich Stark's *Tägliches Hand-Buch, in guten und bösen Tagen*, Stark's *Gebet-Buch*, 10 February 1995 <hhtp://www.wls.wels.net/library/Essays/Authors/w/WolfgrammPietistic/WolfgrammPietistic.pdf>.

Woolley, R.M. *Coptic Offices*. London: SPCK, 1930.

Wright, David. 'Infant Baptism and the Christian Community in Bucer.' In *Martin Bucer. Reforming Church and Community*. Edited by David Wright. Cambridge: Cambridge University Press, 1994.

Wulfstan, Archbishop of York. 'Sermo de Baptismate.' In *The Homilies of Wulfstan*. Edited by Dorothy Bethurum. Oxford: Clarendon Press, 1957, 175–84.

Yarnold, Edward. *The Awe Inspiring Rites of Initiation*. Slough: St Paul Publications, 1971.

Yarnold, E.J. 'The Authorship of the Mystagogic Catecheses Attributed to Cyril of Jerusalem.' *Heythrop Journal* 19 (1978), 143–61.

Yegül, Fikret. *Baths and Bathing in Classical Antiquity*. Cambridge, MA: MIT Press, 1992, 354–5.

Yelverton, Eric E. *The Swedish Rite, a translation of 'Handbok for svenska kyrkan.'* London: SPCK, 1921, 88–91.

Zakka, Patriarch Ignatius. 'The Baptism of the Lord Jesus.' *The Patriarchal Journal* 32 (131–2) (1994), 2–7, translated 1996 <http://www.syrianorthodoxchurch.org/library/sermons/baptism.htm>.

Zinzendorf, Nikolaus Ludwig Graf von. *Maxims, Theological Ideas And Sentences out of the Present Ordinary of the Brethren's Churches: His Dissertations and Discourses From the Year 1738 till 1747*. Extracted by J. Gambold, London, 1751.

Index

Abraham 38, 43, 111, 151–2
Aland, Kurt 139
Alternative Service Book (*ASB*) 153, 174–82
Ambrose, St 168
American Baptist Convention 155
Ames, William 50–51
Amish community 91–3
Amling, Wolfgang 22
Amman, Jacob 91
Anabaptists 31–2, 41, 84, 87–91, 99
Anglican rites of baptism 65, 172–83
anointing 14, 36, 112, 161, 170
Anwald, Hermann 86
Apostolic Constitutions, the 78, 210
Apostolic Tradition, the 159, 164, 168, 177
Aquinas, Thomas 7
Aristotelianism 50
Arminianism 76, 109, 111
Armour, Rollin Stely 88–9
Arndt, Johann 22–3
atonement, the 132
Augsburg Confession 15, 102, 104
August, elector of Saxony 22
Augustine, St 7, 13, 66, 138
Aurifaber, John 22
Australia, liturgy in 198–9

Baptism, Eucharist and Ministry (*BEM*)
    160–62
baptisma and *baptismos* 11, 148–50
Baptist churches 154–8, 195–8
baptistries 210–12
Barber, Edward 96
Barlow, William 72–3
Barrett, Ivan 129
Barrow, Henry 95
Barth, Karl 63, 137–46, 149–50, 154, 161,
    165
Barth, Markus 139–42
Barthianism 145
Basel, baptismal rite at 38
Baxter, Richard 59, 74–7
Baxter, Robert 120
Beckham, David and Victoria 204–5
Bedell, William 73
Bedford, Thomas 73
Believer's Baptism 207, 211

Berne, baptismal rite at 39–40, 43
Bersier, Eugène 62
Bertelsen, Iver 26–7
Beza, Theodore 50
Blake, Willem 41
Blarer, Ambrosius 19
Blunt, Richard 96–7
Boehringer, Hans C. 184, 186
Book of Common Prayer 44–5, 53, 61,
    65–82, 108–12, 118, 123, 174
Book of Common Worship (*BCW*) 188–91
Borgen, Ole 108
Bornert, René 37
Bourne, Hugh 113
Bowers, Richard 206
Brand, Eugene 183–4
Brandenburg, baptismal rite at 17, 19
Brenz, Johannes 14, 17–19
Brevint, Daniel 107
Brown, Robert 95
Brunner, Peter 183–4
Bucer, Martin 20, 34–8, 41–2, 69
Buchholzer, George 17
Bucke, Daniel 95
Bugenhagen, Johannes 14, 26
Bullinger, Heinrich 33–4, 63, 99
Bunyan, John 98
Burges, Cornelius 73, 77
Burreson, Kent 10, 15–18
Burrough, Edward 98
Bushnell, Horace 61

Calvin, John 31–4, 40–43, 46, 50, 56, 63,
    74, 138, 150, 175
Calvinism 22, 31, 111, 155
Campbell, Alexander 125–30 *passim*
Campbell, Mary 120
Campbell, Thomas 125–6
Capito, Wolfgang 35–6
Cardale, John 120–24
Catechism of the Catholic Church 162–3
catechumenate process 169, 175, 180, 199
Catholic Apostolic Church 120–21, 128–31
Chaderton, Laurance 73
Chalcedon, Council of 57
Charismatic movement 166
Charles I of England 74

Charles XII of Sweden 114
Chemnitz, Martin 20–22
chrism 29, 124, 174
Christian, elector of Saxony 22
Christian IV of Denmark 27
Christology 57, 99, 120, 144, 147–51, 154,
   161–2, 200–201
circumcision 33–4, 41, 46–7, 115
Clarke, Samuel 78
Clowes, John 116
Cole, William 44
Colton, Paul 205
Common Worship 2000 177, 211
confirmation, rites of 70, 147, 166–74
   passim, 179, 182, 184, 191
Costen, Will 63
'covenant', theological concept of 6–7, 63,
   82, 91, 112, 151–2, 175
Cowdery, Oliver 129
Cowper, William 73–4
Cranmer, Thomas x, 20, 65–71, 82, 173, 175
Cruciger, Caspar 15
Cullman, Oscar 139
Cuming, Geoffrey 66
Cyril of Jerusalem 168

Daniels, Harold 189
Datheen, Petrus 49
Deane, Henry 95
Denmark, liturgy in 26
Dix, Gregory 172
Dordt, Synod of 49, 76
Douglas, John 45
Downame, John 73
Dresden Liturgical Commission 25
Drummond, Henry 120–25
Duck, Ruth 159, 201–2
Dutch reformed liturgy 48–50
Dybvad, Jørgen 27

Eaton, Samuel 96
ecclesiology 125, 128, 153, 161, 165–6, 200
ecumenism 164
Edward VI 65, 71
Eilts, Mitzi 201
election, doctrine of 96
Elijah 88
Elizabeth I 72
Ellis, Christopher x, 155–8
Elwood, Christopher 41–2
Ely Report (1971) 172

An Enchiridion 20–21
Enlightenment, the 24
Erasmus 84
Ernst, Joachim 22
eschatological baptism 86
eschatology 143–4, 161–2
evangelization, period of 169
exorcism 11–14, 22, 26–31, 36, 63, 168

faith 5–8, 19, 24, 146, 154
Farel, Guillaume (William) 39–43, 46, 175
Felton, Gayle 107
feminist theology 158–9, 181, 201–2
Fiddes, Paul 162
Finsler, Georg 62
Fisher, John 66
Formula of Concord 20
Fox, George 98
Foxe, John 44, 99
Frederik, Duke of Schleswig and Holstein
   26
Fuller, Andrew 158

Galloway, Patrick 72–3
Gardiner, Stephen 67, 70
Garrigan, Siobhan ix
General Baptists 95
Geneva Catechism 42, 46
Geneva Form of Prayers 44–5
Geneva liturgy (1743) 213–14
Gerhard, Johann 22
Gerrish, Brian 35
Gilby, Anthony 44
Gill, John 158
God-consciousness 57–8, 81
godparents, role of 17, 20, 26, 33, 45, 56,
   63, 72, 76–7, 83, 85, 110, 168, 173,
   177
Goode, William 80
Goodman, Caroline 206–7
Gorham, George 79
grace 7, 15, 21, 24, 46, 55, 66, 75–6, 79, 99,
   111, 138–40, 143, 157, 161, 175, 191
Grantham, Thomas 95
Green, Robin 207–8
Greenham, Richard 73
Greenwood, John 95
Grönvik, Lorenz 7
Grundtvig, Nicolaj F.S. 27–9

Habermas, Jürgen ix

Hafenreffer, Mattheus 22
Harding, Vincent G. 89–90
Harrison, Robert 95
Hartmann, Lars 211
Hatchett, Marion 70, 173
Hauerwas, Stanley 206
Hemmingsen, Niels 26
Henry VIII 65
Hildersham, Arthur 73
Hindmarsh, James 116
Hindmarsh, Robert 116–17
Hippolytus 164
Hirzel, Heinrich 62
Hodge, Charles 60
Hoffman, Larry ix
Hoffman, Melchior 87–8
Holland, Bernard 108–9
Holmes, Urban 173
Hooker, Richard 72–3, 77–8, 121
Horsch, John 90
Hubmaier, Balthasar 32, 84–6
Hunsinger, George 150
Hunt, Arnold 73
Hunter, John 69
Hut, Hans 86–7

infant baptism 7, 15, 19, 21, 24, 29, 32–4,
    41–7 *passim*, 50–51, 55–8, 61–4, 68,
    75–9, 82–9, 95–100, 104, 109, 112–13,
    126, 129–30, 133, 138–9, 142–8, 153,
    156–8, 161–2, 165, 167, 171–2, 178–9,
    183, 199, 207–9
Irving, Edward 120–25

Jacobs, Elfriede 39
Jagger, Peter 79–80
James VI of Scotland 72–3
Jeanes, Gordon 67–70
Jeremias, Joachim 139
Jessey, Henry 96–7
Jesus Christ
    baptism of x, 12, 15, 69, 89, 141, 147,
        150, 152, 185, 200
    death and resurrection of 43, 102, 107,
        127, 138–9, 144–5, 153–4, 160
    disciplines of 125–8, 133
    eschatology of 144
    expected return of 120
Jetter, Werner 3–4
John, St 8–9, 12
John XXIII, Pope 164

John the Baptist 15, 115, 129, 139–44
    passim
John Chrysostom, St 168
John Sigismund, elector of Brandenburg 22
Johnson, Mark 205
Johnson, Maxwell 171
Jonas, Justus 14–17
Jones, Simon 181–2
Jordan, River x, 3, 12, 31, 69, 77, 115, 141,
    200
Jud, Leo 18, 31
justification 4–7, 11–13, 30, 75, 99, 145

Karlstadt, Andreas 7, 9, 83
Kavanagh, Aidan 170, 184
Kawerau, Gustav 10
Kay, James 159, 190–91, 199
Kentucky, Synod of 126
Kiffin, William 96
The King's Book 66–8
Knaresborough Report (1985) 172
Knox, John 44–5, 73
Konig, Johann 22
Krage, Nicolaus 16
Kuhrt, Gordon 151–3, 161, 177

Lakoff, George 205
Lampe, G.W. 172
Laski, Jan 48–9
Lee, Daniel B. 94
Lee, Robert 59
Leenhardt, F.-J. 139
Lentz, Harold 14
Lima Statement (1982) 160
Lindsey, Theophilius 78
Liston, W. 59
Liturgical Commission of the Church of
    England (1959) 172
Liturgical Movement, Catholic 164, 186
Loades, Anne 200
Lombard, Peter 15
Lumbala, F. Kabasele 203
Luther, Martin x, 3–31, 35–6, 40–41, 50,
    61, 68, 83–4, 116, 138, 146, 154, 161,
    187
    baptismal rites of 9–17, 25–6, 29, 183–8
Lutheranism 14, 20–26, 38, 48, 82, 102,
    107, 115, 141, 145, 154
Lyon, David 204

McClendon, James 155–7

Macquarrie, John 179
Magdeburg Agenda x, 10
Marbach, Johann 38
Mark, St, Gospel of 144
Marpeck, Pilgram 88–9
Martmort, A.G. 166
Mary, Queen of England 71–2
Mason, A.J. 172
Mason-Dix view 172–3
Matthew, St, Gospel of 12, 144
Maurice, F.D. 81–2
Mbonigaba, Elisha 202–3
Megander, Kasper 38
Melanchthon, Philip 14–17, 20–22
Menius, Justus 21–2
Mennonite church 91–4
Mercerburg theology 60–62
Merula, George 21–2
Methodism 107, 110–13, 132
   rites of baptism 192–4
Meyrick, Frederick 80
Micron, Marten 48–9
Minden, baptismal rite at 16
Mitchell, Leonel 173–4
Moltmann, Jürgen 142–6, 165
Moravian church 101–8, 132
Mormonism 128–33, 154
Moses 151–2
Mozley, J.B. 80
Muller, Richard 50, 54
Müntzer, Thomas 9, 83–6

Native Americans 106–7
Nelson, Robert 107
Neoplatonism 32
Nevin, John 60–61
New Church, liturgy of (1790) 217–20
New Zealand, liturgy in 182–3
Newton, Isaac 78
Neyman, Jane 131
Nischan, Bodo 21
Nowell, Alexander 73
Null, Ashley 65–6
Nümann, F.K. 10
Nürnberg 16–19

Oecolampadius 18, 38, 86
Okely, Francis 102
Old, H.O. 35
Olevianus, Caspar 46
opus operatum theology 7

original sin 15, 32–3, 56, 61, 63, 67, 74, 76,
   84, 121, 153, 168, 172, 183
Osiander, Andreas 14–17, 23
Ostervald, Jean Frederick 55–6
Overall, John 73

Pahl, P.D. 7
Palladius, Peder 26
Pannenberg, Wolfhart 145–7, 161
Particular Baptists 95, 97, 155
Pater, C.A. 7
patriarchy 158–60, 202
Paul, St 39, 45, 132, 144, 156
Paul VI, Pope 168
Payne, Ernest A. 195
Payne, John 61
Peaston, A.E. 104
penitence 146
Penn, William 99
Penry, John 95
Pepys, Samuel 77
Perkins, William 72, 77–8
Petri, Olavus 29
Phillpotts, Henry 79
Pietism 22–4, 30, 101–2, 107, 132, 161–2,
   200
pneumatology 57, 99, 125, 128
postmodernity 166–7, 180, 204–5
Poullain, Valerand 48–9
Prussian baptismal rite 25
Pusey, Edward 79

Quaker baptism 98–100
Quenstedt, Johann 22–3

Rappaport, Roy 200–201
rationalism 24, 30
Reformation, the 3
Reformed rites of baptism 188–92
regeneration 109–13, 122, 145, 155
remission of sins 43, 63, 66, 82, 86, 90, 121,
   127–30, 133, 155
Resen, Hans Poulsen 27
Reublin, Wilhelm 84
Ridgley, Thomas 50, 54–5
Rigdon, Sidney 127, 129
Riggs, John 57
Rites of Christian Initiation of Adults
   (RCIA) 167–72, 199
Riverside Church, New York 159
Roberts, Paul 122–4

Robertson, Harry 58
Roman Catholic baptismal rites 167–72, 199
Ross, Susan 202
Rouget, A.M. 165–6
Row, John 45
Ruether, Rosemary Radford 201

sacraments 5–6, 32, 51–2, 57, 73, 100, 139, 143
Sarum rite x, 67–70, 82
Scaer, David 153–4, 161
Schaff, Philip 60–61
Scharen, Christian ix
Schleiermacher, Friedrich Daniel 57–8, 81, 138
Schmid, Heinrich 26
Schnedf, Erhard 19
scholasticism 50
Schwartz, Diobald 35
Schweizer, Alexander 62
Scotland, liturgy in 58–60, 188, 191
Scotus, Duns 66
Second Vatican Council 164, 191, 199
Separatism 95–6
'Series 2' rites 172, 175
'Series 3' rites 175
Shepherd, Massey Jr 173
Sherlock, William 77
Sibly, Manoah 118
Simeon, Charles 80
Simon Magus 39
Simons, Menno 89–91
Small, Joseph D. 209
Smith, Joseph 128–32
Smith, Samuel 116
Smyth, John 95–6
Society of Friends 98–9
soteriology 150–51, 154, 161–2, 168, 171, 175
Spener, Philipp Jacob 23
Spilsbury, John 96
Spottiswoode, John 45
Sri Lanka, liturgy in 203
Stark, Johann Friedrich 24
Stephens, Peter 37
Steven, James ix
Stevick, Daniel 175
Stone, Barton W. 125–7
Stratner, Jacob 17
Strauss, David Friedrich 52
Swedberg, Jesper 114

Sweden, liturgy in 29, 188
Swedenborg, Emmanuel 101, 107, 114–20, 130–33
Sykes, Stephen 71, 82

Talmage, James E. 130–33
Tausen, Hans 26
Taylor, Jeremy 74–7
Temple, Frederick 80
Tertullian 112
Theosophical Society 116
Thodberg, Christian 28
Thompson, J. 122
Tombes, John 75–6, 96
Torrance, Iain 191
Torrance, T.F. 147–54 *passim*, 161, 191, 206
Tovey, Phillip 181–2
Tractarian movement 80–81
Trigg, Jonathan 7
Tucker, Karen Westerfield 193
Turretin, Francis 52–3

Underwood, T.L. 98
United Brethren, liturgy of (1770) 215–16
United States, liturgy in 60–62
Ursinus, Zacharias 46–8, 63

Vasa, Gustav 26
Vermigli, Peter Martyr 69
Vial, Theodore 52

Wade, Carol 205, 209
Wall, William 107–8
Ward, Samuel 73, 77
Watson, Richard 111–12
Weaverland Mennonites 94
Webber, Robert 197
Webster, John 141–2
Weid, Hermann von 20
Wesley, Charles 109, 111
Wesley, John 101, 107–13, 116, 132
Wesley, Samuel 108–9
Westminster Confession, the 53, 74, 97, 126
Westminster Directory, the 74, 76, 78, 128
Wheeler, Geraldine 198–9
Whiston, William 78
Whitaker, E.C. 176
Whitefield, George 111
Whittingham, William 44
Wickremesinghe, Francis 203
Wied, Hermann von 67

Willock, John 45
Wilson-Kastner, Patricia 202
Winram, John 45
Winward, Stephen F. 195
Wisconsin Synod 187
Witzel, George 17
Wolf, William J. 81
Wolfensberger, Rudolph 62
Wolfgramm, Luke 24
Wollebius, Johannes 51–2
World Council of Churches 160, 162, 164

Wright, David 37
Wright, Joseph 95
Württemberg rite 19

Zaire, liturgy in 203
Zell, Martin 35
Zimmermann, George Rudolf 62
Zinzendorf, Nikolaus Ludwig von 101–4,
    107, 132, 202
Zwingli, Ulrich 7, 18, 31–3, 38–40, 46, 63,
    84–5, 99–100, 138, 142, 155, 175, 192